中国式资本市场、公司治理与企业发展

Capital Market with Chinese Characteristics,
Corporate Governance, and Corporate Development

夏立军 等◎著

上海交通大学出版社
SHANGHAI JIAO TONG UNIVERSITY PRESS

内容提要

中国资本市场从无到有、从小到大,目前已经成为全球第二大资本市场。中国资本市场三十年的发展历史,既是可歌可泣、波澜壮阔的伟大历史,同时也是摸着石头过河、跌跌撞撞的艰难历史。如何真正地实现"三十而立""四十不惑",是中国资本市场面临的重要挑战,关系到中国经济未来能否持续、高质量地发展。本书作者长期探索和研究中国国情下资本市场、公司治理与企业发展的机制、机理及其制度条件,将十多年来的主要思考和研究成果凝集成书。希望此书的出版,能够有助于各方对中国资本市场上政府、企业与市场关系的理解,并促进中国资本市场制度体系的转型升级。

图书在版编目(CIP)数据

中国式资本市场、公司治理与企业发展 / 夏立军等著. —上海:
上海交通大学出版社,2019

ISBN 978 - 7 - 313 - 22547 - 4

Ⅰ.①中… Ⅱ.①夏… Ⅲ.①资本市场-研究-中国②公司-企业管理-研究-中国③企业发展-研究-中国 Ⅳ.①F832.5②F279.2

中国版本图书馆 CIP 数据核字(2019)第 263485 号

中国式资本市场、公司治理与企业发展
ZHONGGUOSHI ZIBEN SHICHANG、GONGSI ZHILI YU QIYE FAZHAN

著　　者：夏立军 等
出版发行：上海交通大学出版社　　　　地　　址：上海市番禺路 951 号
邮政编码：200030　　　　　　　　　　电　　话：021 - 64071208
印　　刷：上海万卷印刷股份有限公司　经　　销：全国新华书店
开　　本：710mm×1000mm　1/16　　印　　张：25
字　　数：447 千字
版　　次：2019 年 12 月第 1 版　　　　印　　次：2019 年 12 月第 1 次印刷
书　　号：ISBN 978 - 7 - 313 - 22547 - 4
定　　价：98.00 元

献给中国资本市场设立三十周年

致敬中国资本市场的建设者和研究者

前　言

本书是过去十多年中我和合作者一起从事中国资本市场研究的主要成果汇集。自从踏上学术道路,我的研究方向基本上可以概括为探索和研究中国国情下资本市场、公司治理与企业发展的机制、机理及其制度条件。而走上学术道路,确立这个研究方向,源自我的求学和工作经历,尤其是在上海财经大学的求学经历。

1993年至1997年期间,我在杭州电子科技大学(原杭州电子工业学院)读本科。这所学校不是"985",也不是"211",校园占地只有百余亩,不过倒是出了不少名人。比如,当时郑钧刚刚离开这所学校,出了他的第一张摇滚专辑《赤裸裸》;马云当时正在校园里教英语,不久后离职创立了阿里巴巴;现任中国证券监督管理委员会主席易会满也曾在这所学校求学。本科毕业后,我在苏州市的一家会计师事务所工作了近三年时间,从事独立审计、资产评估等工作。在此期间,我接触了当地的大量民营和外资企业,经历了当地乡镇企业和国有企业的改制历程,同时也经历了会计师事务所自身的改制过程。2000年,我考取了向往已久的上海财经大学会计学硕士研究生,开始接触实证会计研究,之后又于2003年考取了上海财经大学会计学博士研究生。

当时的上海财经大学,已是中国实证会计研究的一面旗帜。无论是1995年发起设立中国会计教授会,吸引海外学者来访授课、开展学术交流和合作,还是改革博士生培养体系,倡导和实践实证会计研究,在国内外顶级期刊发表研究成果,都是领全国风气之先,为中国会计学界注入了科学研究的范式和方法,同时也注入了立足中国制度背景开展中国本土问题研究的基因。一大批海外学者如李志文(Jevons Lee)、陈建文(Kevin Chen)、范博宏(Joseph Fan)、黄德尊(T. J. Wong)、陈杰平(Charles J. Chen)、陈世敏(Shimin Chen)、苏锡嘉(Xijia Su)、张国昌(Guochang Zhang)、Mary Barth、Mark DeFond、Charles M. C. Lee、Katherine Schipper、Ross Watts等,一批谙熟中国国情和中国资本市场制度背景的名师如汤云为、张为国、孙铮、陈信元等,与一批优秀的博士生如李东平、赵宇龙、李树华、原红旗、王跃堂、陈冬华、李增泉、张田余等,在大量的课堂、讲座、研讨和研究中,共同绘就了实证会计研究在上海财经大学兴起的画卷,孕育了一批具有持续影响的中国会计与资本市场问题研究成果。陈信元教授长期担任上海财经大学会计学院院长,克服了种种困难,勤力改革,为博士生和年轻教师开展高水平学术研究营造了优良的学术环境。我身处其中,耳濡目染,深受影响。

攻读博士期间,我更是有幸师从陈信元教授和黄德尊教授两位名师,也由此注定了中国问题与国际视野相结合的研究方向。2006年博士毕业后,我应黄德尊教授邀请赴香港中文大学做博士后研究。在那里,我与黄德尊教授更加深入地讨论与合作,继续修改完善博士论文的主体内容,最终共同完成了发表于国际顶级会计期刊之一 *Journal of Accounting and Economics*、日后产生较大影响的成果。犹记得,在香港中文大学美丽的"天人合一"山水风景中,与黄德尊教授一起思考、讨论中西交融时代背景下中国资本市场会计与公司治理问题的日子。收入本书的多项研究成果得益于两位老师的指导、启发或合作,同时也受益于诸多海内外学者的影响。在此,我要向两位老师以及其他开拓中国实证会计研究和中国资本市场研究之路的学者们致以深深的敬意和感谢。

本书的内容分为上下两个部分。

第一部分是"产权类型、地区市场化进程与公司治理"。这部分立足于探讨中国上市公司的政府与企业关系,为理解中国上市公司的公司治理与企业发展提供了"产权＋地区"的基本分析框架(如图1所示)。这部分收录的研究成果,连同学界同行开展的大量后续研究表明,这一框架解释了中国上市公司在公司治理结构、投资行为、融资行为、会计审计、信息披露与企业发展等方面的诸多差异。

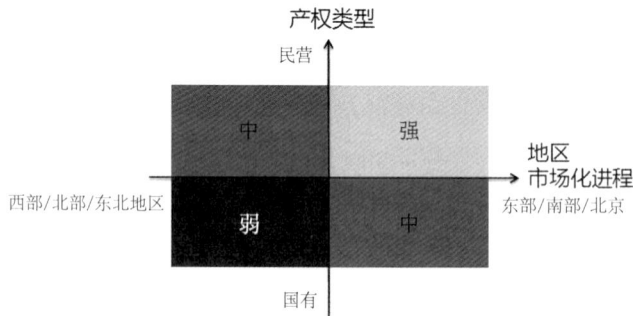

图1　产权、地区与公司治理

一个基本的发现是,就平均意义上而言,国有上市公司的治理效率低于民营上市公司。前者面临的主要问题是股东与经理之间代理问题引起的价值创造激励不足,而后者面临的主要问题是大小股东之间代理问题引起的价值分配激励不足。此外,无论是国有上市公司还是民营上市公司,随着公司所处地区的市场化进程提高,公司治理效率也显著提高。这一基本发现支持了国有企业改革的"抓大放小"和"战略调整"改革方向,同时也揭示了地区市场化进程在公司治理与企业发展中的重要性。

时至今日,观察中国资本市场的上市公司群体,依然可以发现在民营控股的产权类型中以及在市场化程度高的地区,更可能出现优秀的、有竞争力的、具有长期成长性的上市公司,而经过"抓大放小"和"战略调整"的国有上市公司也展现出了相对以往更强的竞争力。考察中国上市公司的治理问题,国有与民营以及地区间制度差异已经成为上市公司的基本分类维度。然而,产权类型、地区市场化进程的背后又是什么?是历史、地理、气候,还是改革开放的先后顺序和路径依赖,或是官员的选拔、激励和考核机制?产权、地区与公司治理的未来演进方向、逻辑及后果又将如何?这些问题仍有待于进一步思考和研究。

第二部分是"资本市场制度(会计/监管/司法)与市场效率"。这部分立足于探讨中国资本市场的政府与市场关系,重在考察和分析中国资本市场制度体系的有效性。收录其中的研究成果显示,中国资本市场缺乏自发地对高质量会计、审计和公司治理的需求和供给。其背后的原因可能是资本市场制度体系上长期对上市公司实际控制人、内部决策者以及中介机构等市场参与者缺乏立法、执法和司法的强约束,同时市场理性不足,由此造成资本市场自身机能不良,资源配置效率缺失。尤其是长期以来,司法系统未能有效地参与资本市场的治理,资本市场法治基础不牢,法治的理念、结构、内容和质量都有待深化改革。

随着中国资本市场规模日益扩大,并成为全球第二大资本市场,资本市场的法治需求显著增加。当法治供给严重地滞后于法治需求,就可能造成资本市场乱象频频,产生系统性风险,阻碍资本市场服务实体经济发展的效率(如图2所示)。无论在"油门"(市场化)层面,还是在"刹车"(法治化)层面,中国资本市场的制度体系还存着大量改革空间。2018年上海金融法院的设立,2019年上海证券交易所设立科创板并试点注册制,2019年中国证券监督管理委员会提出的资本市场全面深化改革总体方案,以及目前正在修订中的《证券法》,是对这些基础性问题的重要回应。在中国资本市场设立近三十周年之际,这一系列的重大改革将有望从根本上促进中国资本市场三十而立、走向成熟。

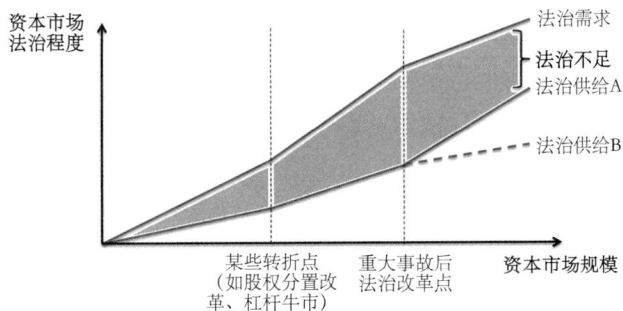

图 2　资本市场规模、法治需求与法治供给

本书收录的中英文成果大多曾经发表于国内外期刊,如《经济研究》《管理世界》《经济学(季刊)》及 *Journal of Accounting and Economics* 等,其中多项成果

是与合作者一起完成的。(为保持原状,本书所选 3 篇英文文章,不做翻译处理;部分成果根据出版规范做了相关修改。)这些合作者除了包括我的两位老师陈信元教授和黄德尊教授以外,还包括陆铭、芮萌、Mark DeFond、Oliver Zhen Li、Qian Wang、周勤业、朱红军、高新梓、方轶强、李莫愁、杨海斌、郭建展、余为政、林志伟,感谢他们的合作研究。近年来,在安泰经济与管理学院的经济与管理、理论与实践相融合的新环境中,我对过去的研究有了更多思考。尤其是在分别参与安泰的两个智库中国发展研究院和中国企业发展研究院的研究项目——中国城市资本活力指数报告、中国上市公司竞争力百强榜单的研究过程中,对中国资本市场和上市公司有了更深入的理解。感谢上海交通大学和安泰经济与管理学院提供的研究平台。此外,要感谢国家自然科学基金、教育部新世纪优秀人才计划、财政部"会计名家培养工程"等项目提供的研究资助。在长期的研究生涯中,学术成绩或许无足挂齿,但要感谢的人太多,恕我无法一一列举。

　　回顾十多年来的研究历程,最重要的一个感受是,要理解处于中国现代化进程中的资本市场,殊非易事。其原因是中国资本市场不仅具有全球资本市场的共性,它还受到其所处的中国政治、经济环境及其演变的深刻塑造。这样的资本市场,可以称作"中国式"的,这种"中国式"由全球资本市场的共性与中国资本市场的特性所构成。无论是当初的诞生过程,还是后来的发展演变,中国资本市场都可以说是特性时空中所发生的"中国式"现象。它不是全球资本市场共性与中国资本市场特性的简单叠加,而是两者错综复杂的交融。其结果是中国资本市场一路走来,高速成长与顽疾难解长期并存。

　　这种"中国式",并非意味着中国资本市场是杂乱无章、不可知的,而意味着要理解中国资本市场,既需吸收借鉴成熟资本市场的一般性知识,同时还需要付出更大的心力去认识它所处的政治、经济环境及其与资本市场的交互关系。如果说中国资本市场设立三十年来存在一个基本演变逻辑的话,那可能就是其初始的诞生条件,服务中国经济发展的目标,及其改革开放的基本战略,共同塑造了其总体上朝着市场化、法治化和国际化方向演变的制度体系,进而决定了其螺旋式上升的演变路径。随着资本市场在中国经济持续、高质量发展中"牵一发而动全身"的重要性日益凸显,以及资本市场制度体系的转型升级,相信中国终会在不远的未来拥有一个强大而高效的资本市场。

　　本书所汇集的成果,与其说是形成了关于中国资本市场的科学研究结论,不如说代表了我和合作者对中国资本市场的观察、思考和理解的渐进过程。这个过程难免错误、疏漏或不足,希望读者明辨,批评指正。本书的出版,是这个过程的一个记录,也是未来研究的一个新起点。

夏立军

2019 年 12 月

目　录

上　篇

产权类型、地区市场化进程与公司治理

（政府与企业关系）

政府控制、治理环境与公司价值
——来自中国证券市场的经验证据[*]

内容提要：本文承袭刘芍佳、孙霈、刘乃全（2003）一文所使用的"终极产权论"，根据上市公司披露的终极控制人数据，首次将上市公司细分为非政府控制（即民营、乡镇或外资资本控制）、县级政府控制、市级政府控制、省级政府控制以及中央政府控制这五种类型。同时，我们利用樊纲、王小鲁（2003）编制的中国各地区市场化进程数据及其子数据构建各地区公司治理环境指数，具体包括市场化进程指数、政府干预指数以及法治水平指数。在此基础上，我们以 2001 年至 2003 年期间的上市公司为样本，对政府控制、治理环境与公司价值的关系进行了实证分析。研究发现，政府控制尤其是县级和市级政府控制对公司价值产生了负面影响，但公司所处治理环境的改善有助于减轻这种负面影响。其政策含义是，解决中国上市公司的公司治理问题，不仅需要继续"抓大放小"，还需要从根本上改善公司治理环境。对研究者来说，需要把目光转移到影响公司治理的根本因素上来，加强对公司治理环境的分析。

关键词：政府控制；政府层级；公司治理；治理环境；公司价值

---

* 本文选自：夏立军、方轶强：政府控制、治理环境与公司价值——来自中国证券市场的经验证据，《经济研究》，2005 年第 5 期，第 40－51 页。本文被《上海证券报》2005 年 6 月 10 日第 8 版"声音"栏目介绍；获中国社科院经济学部"2009 中国青年经济学者优秀论文奖"、上海财经大学第十二届中振科研基金优秀论文奖。在 CSSCI 系统数据库中，本文被引 500 余次，是截至目前《经济研究》历年发表的论文中前十高被引论文。

一、问题的提出

中国证券市场是一个新兴市场,同时中国证券市场又根植于中国转型经济中。新兴加转轨的双重特征导致在中国证券市场上政府行为对资源配置具有重要影响,上市公司主要由政府控制,以及投资者法律保护水平低下。因此,中国上市公司的公司治理问题可能与西方国家大大不同,考察中国上市公司的公司治理问题必须对中国上市公司所处的特殊环境进行分析。然而,以往关于中国上市公司的公司治理问题的研究过多地关注股权结构对公司治理的影响,而忽视了对上市公司背后的政府行为以及公司所处治理环境的分析。

我们认为,公司治理环境至少包括产权保护、政府治理、法治水平、市场竞争、信用体系、契约文化等方面。显然,这些组成公司治理环境的要素会影响到契约的顺利签订和履行,进而影响到公司治理的效率。更重要的是,公司治理环境是相对股权结构安排、独立董事制度、信息披露制度、独立审计制度、经理人市场机制、接管和购并市场机制等公司治理机制更为基础性的层面。没有良好的治理环境,这些公司治理的内部和外部机制便很难发挥作用。

本文承袭刘芍佳、孙霈、刘乃全(2003)一文所使用的"终极产权论",根据上市公司披露的终极控制人数据,首次将上市公司细分为非政府控制(即民营、乡镇或外资企业控制)、县级政府控制、市级政府控制、省级政府控制以及中央政府控制这五种类型。同时,我们利用樊纲、王小鲁(2003)编制的中国各地区市场化进程数据及其子数据构建各地区公司治理环境指数,具体包括市场化进程指数、政府干预指数以及法治水平指数。在此基础上,我们以 2001 年至 2003 年期间的上市公司为样本,对政府控制、治理环境与公司价值的关系进行实证分析。研究发现,政府控制尤其是县级和市级政府控制对公司价值产生了负面影响,但公司所处治理环境的改善有助于减轻这种负面影响。

二、文献述评

与国外公司治理研究进程类似,关于中国上市公司治理问题的研究也是从股权结构与公司业绩的关系开始。这些研究主要涉及以下两大方面。

(1) 国有股比例、法人股比例、流通股比例与公司业绩的关系。例如,Xu and Wang(1999)发现,国家股比例与公司业绩负相关,而法人股比例与公司业绩正相关。陈晓、江东(2000)发现,在竞争性较强的行业,国有股比例与公司业绩负相关,法人股和流通股比例与公司业绩正相关,而在竞争性较弱的行业则没有发现这些结果。Tian(2001)发现,民营资本控制的上市公司业绩明显优于混合股份公司,并且国有股比例与公司价值之间呈正"U"形关系。朱武祥、宋勇(2001)以竞争性较激烈的家电行业上市公司为样本,研究发现国家股比例、法人股比例和流通股比例与公司价值没有显著关系。陈小悦、徐晓东(2001)发现,国有股比例和法人股比例与企业业绩之间没有显著的负相关关系,但流通股比例与公司业绩显著负相关。Sun and Tong(2003)则发现,在公司上市后,国家股对公司业绩存在负面影响,法人股对公司业绩存在正面影响,但外资股对公司业绩没有显著的正面影响。

(2)股权集中度与公司业绩的关系。Xu and Wang(1999)以前十大股东持股比例之和以及赫芬戴尔指数衡量股权集中度,考察了股权集中度与公司业绩的关系,结果发现,股权集中度与公司业绩具有显著的正相关关系。孙永祥、黄祖辉(1999)发现,第一大股东持股比例与公司 Tobin Q 值呈倒"U"形关系,并且有一定集中度、有相对控制股东并且有其他大股东存在的股权结构在总体上有利于经营激励、收购兼并、代理权竞争、监督机制作用的发挥,因此具有该种股权结构的公司价值最高。Bai et al.(2004)、白重恩等(2005)则发现,第一大股东持股比例对公司价值存在负面影响并且这种影响呈正"U"形关系,同时,政府机构作为第一大股东对公司价值有负面影响,而非控股股东持股比例对公司价值有正面影响。

从现有文献看,国内关于上市公司股权结构与公司业绩关系的实证研究虽然丰富,但未能取得一致成果。究其原因,可能有三:第一,研究者所采用的业绩衡量指标不尽一致,很多研究直接采用会计指标,如净资产收益率衡量公司业绩,而会计指标难以反映公司的长期业绩,同时容易受到人为操纵;第二,现有的关于股权结构与公司业绩关系的研究往往视股权结构为外生变量,但正如陈信元、陈冬华、朱凯(2004)所指出,以及冯根福、韩冰、闫冰(2002)、李涛(2002)的研究所显示,股权结构可能是内生的,因此不先回答股权结构的形成原因则难以认清股权结构与公司业绩的关系;第三,如刘芍佳、孙霈、刘乃全(2003)所指出,由于法人股最终可能是政府控制也可能是非政府控制,因此官方统计报告中对股权类型所做的国家股和法人股之分类,不可避免地使先前从事股权结构对公司业绩影响的研究误入歧途。

更进一步,我们认为股权只是法律规定的股东权利,但如果法律对股东权利的保障不力或者政府力量对股权的实现产生重大影响,股权或者股权结构是否还具有其在成熟市场经济中的含义便值得怀疑。从这个角度讲,股权结构可能只是形式上的问题。探寻中国上市公司的公司治理问题,可能应该从更为实质、更为根本的因素出发,而这离不开对上市公司背后的政府行为以及公司所处治理环境的考察。相应的问题则是,在中国的制度背景下,各级政府的动机和行为对其控制的上市公司产生了什么影响? 上市公司所处的治理环境如市场化进程、政府干预程度、法治水平对其产生了什么影响? 遗憾的是,现有研究几乎未能涉及这些方面。本文试图对此进行探索。

三、理论分析与假说发展

(一)政府控制、政府层级与公司价值

如前所述,中国证券市场脱胎于中国转型经济中,其设立初衷是为国企改革和解困服务。因此,可以看到,在中国证券市场上,上市公司大部分由国有企业改制而来。同时,为保持国家对上市公司的控制力,国有股权在上市公司中占据了很大比例,并且这些国有股权不能上市流通。鉴于大部分上市公司依然被各级政府控制,政府的动机和行为对上市公司可能会产生重要影响。已有研究发现,转型经济中国有企业的一个主要问题是其承担了政府的多重目标,如经济发展战略、就业、税收、社会稳定等,并由此造成了国有企业的政策性负担(Lin,Cai,and Li,1998)。虽然国有企业通过改制上市,其治理结构和监管环境发生了很大变化,但由于政府依然控制这些改制而来的上市公司,政府依然有能力将其自身目标内部化到这些公司中。

另一方面,在我国从计划经济走向市场经济的过程中,在政府权力配置上,经历了从集权到分权的过程,地方政府在此过程中获得了财政自主权、经济管理权等权力。分权的结果是地方政府发展地方经济的积极性被调动起来,同时地方政府竞争资源的动机也随之产生(Cao,Qian,and Weingast,1999;Poncet,2004)。正如吸引外资一样,从证券市场获得资源同样有利于发展地方经济,解决就业问题,改善当地形象,并最终给当地带来利益。在我国证券市场投资者法律保护不力的情况下,从证券市场获取资源的使用成本非常低。在某种程度上,证券市场资源甚至类似于一种"免费午餐"。因此,个另政府有动机利用上市公司来"圈钱",以实现其自身的目标。

由此可见,各级政府既有动机又有能力将其自身的社会性目标内部化到其控

股的上市公司中。而上市公司承担政府的社会性职能必然会使公司活动偏离公司价值最大化这一目标,并进而损害公司的价值。① 李增泉、余谦、王晓坤(2005)发现,某些控股股东或地方政府具有支持或掏空上市公司的动机,支持是为了获得配股资格,而掏空则是赤裸裸的利益侵占行为。实际上,在现有的制度环境下,支持的最终目的很可能还是为了掏空,即所谓的"放长线钓大鱼"。支持的方式有财政补贴(陈晓、李静,2001)、资产重组(陈信元、叶鹏飞、陈冬华,2003)、关联交易(Ming and Wong,2003)等,而掏空的手段则有资产评估(周勤业、夏立军、李莫愁,2003)、关联交易(Ming and Wong,2003)、资金占用(李增泉、孙铮、王志伟,2004)等。虽然对于非政府控制的上市公司来说,其控制人同样具有侵害中小股东的动机和能力,但与某些政府相比,其侵害能力相对较小,原因是监管力量和法律约束更难以限制政府权力。因此,相对于非政府控制的上市公司来说,政府控制的上市公司其公司价值可能更低。

以上分析没有考虑各级政府动机和行为的差异。在中国现有的行政架构下,政府层级从上到下可细分为中央政府、省级政府、市级政府和县级政府。② 由于各级政府权力和职能不同,各级政府在资本市场的动机和行为可能不同。由于行政分权,中央政府的角色更像是一个委托人,而地方政府的角色更类似于一个代理人。实际上,在中国经济发展过程中,地方政府具体承担了各地区经济发展的职能,并且地方政府官员的政绩由上级政府考核。因此,在从证券市场竞争资源方面,地方政府比中央政府具有更强的动机。另一方面,由于在各级地方政府中,上下级政府之间同样存在着类似的委托代理关系,因此相对下级政府来说,上级政府更可能约束自身的行为,注意自身的形象。这样,在侵害中小股东的行为上,下级政府可能更为严重。根据上述分析,我们提出研究假说1,即H1。

H1:相对于非政府控制的上市公司来说,政府控制的上市公司其公司价值更低,并且这主要是由于低层级政府控制的上市公司价值更低所引起。

① 诚然,政府对其控制的上市公司也可能会扮演"帮助之手"的角色,例如陈晓、李静(2001)发现地方政府对其控制的上市公司进行了大面积的税收优惠和财政补贴,然而,政府的这种行为更多的是为了帮助上市公司获得配股资格,以便从证券市场获得更多的资源。由于大股东"掏空"动机强烈,因此中小股东并不能真正分享到政府支持的利益,却可能会付出更多的代价。

② 此处县级政府是指县、县级市或其他县级政府机构,市级政府是指地级市、自治州以及其他地区级机构,省级政府是指省、自治区或直辖市政府的政府机构。某些城市如南京、宁波等的政府具有副省级行政权力,但由于在省级政府和市级政府之间,它们更接近于市级政府,因此我们将这类城市的政府机构划分为市级政府。

(二)政府控制、治理环境与公司价值

近年来,La Porta et al.(1998)的一系列研究发现,一国的法律体系对其公司治理具有重要影响。具体来说,他们发现,普通法系国家的投资者法律保护程度最高,德国和斯堪的纳维亚大陆法系国家的投资者法律保护程度次之,而法国大陆法系国家的投资者法律保护程度最低。并且,他们还发现,一国的投资者法律保护程度与其上市公司的股权集中度负相关(La Porta et al.,1999),与其上市公司的股利支付比率正相关(La Porta et al.,2000a),与其上市公司的公司价值正相关(La Porta et al.,2000b),与其资本市场的发达程度正相关(La Porta et al.,1997)。这些研究表明,一国法律体系在很大程度上决定了其公司治理结构和水平,良好的公司治理必定要以有效的投资者法律保护为基础。可以说,拉波特(La Porta)等人的这一系列研究从根本上改变了以往对公司治理的看法,促使人们把目光转移到影响公司治理的根本因素上来,而这些根本因素则构成公司治理环境。

在我国证券市场上,公司欺诈、舞弊以及大股东对中小股东的肆意侵害行为屡屡发生。其中一个很重要的原因就是投资者法律保护不力。虽然证券市场于1990年早就设立,但《中华人民共和国证券法》(以下简称《证券法》)直到1998年年底才颁布。然而,即使在《证券法》颁布实施之后,投资者依然难以得到实质性的法律保护。一个典型的表现是,虽然备受投资者期待,但证券民事赔偿制度至今未能得到有效施行。究其原因,固然与执法力量和执法水平有关,但更重要的原因可能是上市公司大部分由各级政府所控制,而法律约束难以限制政府权力,同时,股票市场设立的初衷本就是为国企改革和解困服务,而有效的投资者法律保护与这样的目标很可能是矛盾的。因此,政府和法律的因素交织在一起,构成了中国上市公司所处治理环境的主要特征。然而,对于不同地区的上市公司来说,虽然其所处的国家大环境是一样的,但其所处地区的市场化进程、政府干预程度、法治水平却相差甚大,很不平衡(樊纲、王小鲁,2003)。因此,将拉波特等人的跨国比较框架应用到中国各地区的比较中,我们便可以在经验上验证治理环境对公司治理的影响。

可以预期,在一个政府干预程度较低的地区,政府将会更少地将其社会性负担转嫁到其控制的上市公司中,也可能会更约束自身的行为,减少对上市公司中小股东的利益侵害。并且,由于诉讼管辖通常采用"原告从被告"的原则,在一个法治水平较高的地区,上市公司内部人或大股东对中小股东的利益侵害行为可能

会更受到约束。同样,由于较高的市场化程度与较少的政府干预以及较高的法治水平联系在一起,可以预期,在一个市场化进程较快的地区,上市公司中小股东受到的利益侵害程度也会相对更轻。因此,上市公司所处地区的市场化进程越快、政府干预程度越低、法治水平越高,那么其公司价值可能越高。进一步,由于政府控制的上市公司受到的政府干预相对更为严重,并且,在政府控制的上市公司中,其控制人侵害中小股东的能力相对更强。因此,在政府控制的上市公司中,治理环境对公司治理的影响可能更为明显。由此,我们提出研究假说2。

H2:上市公司所处地区的市场化进程越快、政府干预越少、法治水平越高,则公司价值越高,并且这种关系在政府控制的上市公司中更为明显。

四、研究设计

(一)样本选择

由于上市公司自2001年度报告起才开始披露终极控制人资料,我们以2001至2003年度所有上市公司作为初选样本,然后对其执行如下筛选程序:①剔除含B股或H股的上市公司。这些公司面临境内外双重监管环境,与其他上市公司不同,为了集中于本文所要研究的问题,以及计算公司价值的方便,我们剔除这些公司。②剔除终极控制人不详的上市公司。由于本文研究非政府控制以及各级政府控制对公司价值的影响,因此只要根据上市公司披露的终极控制人资料无法确定是政府控制还是非政府控制,或者无法确定是哪一级的政府控制,我们就认定其终极控制人不详。③剔除年末股票价格数据缺失的上市公司。本文计算公司价值时需要用到上市公司年末股票价格数据,但部分公司由于重大事件公告停牌或其他原因没有股票价格数据,因此剔除这些公司。④剔除注册地在西藏的上市公司。本文使用的公司治理环境指数建立在樊纲、王小鲁(2003)编制的各地区市场化进程数据及其子数据的基础上,但他们未编制西藏地区的相应数据,因此我们剔除这些公司。经过上述程序,我们最后获得2 543家样本公司,其中2001年、2002年和2003年的样本公司分别为788家、851家和904家。表1列出了样本筛选过程。

表 1   样本筛选过程

样本来源	2001 年至 2003 年	2001 年	2002 年	2003 年
各年末上市公司总数	3671	1160	1224	1287
减:含 B 股或 H 股的公司数	414	135	139	140
终极控制人不详的公司数	647	200	214	233
无年末股票价格的公司数	49	31	14	4
注册地在西藏的公司数	18	6	6	6
最终样本公司数	2543	788	851	904

(二)数据来源

上市公司终极控制人类型数据由我们根据上市公司年度报告中"股本变动及股东情况"进行逐一整理,上市公司年度报告来自中国证监会指定信息披露网站——巨潮资讯网。若公司终极控制人可确定为自然人、职工持股会、民营企业、村办集体企业、街道集体企业、乡镇一级的政府部门、乡镇集体企业或外资企业,则认定其为非政府控制。① 若终极控制人为县级或县级以上各级政府的有关政府机构,则认定其为相应级别的政府控制。对于部属院校控制的上市公司和地方政府教育部门所属院校控制的上市公司,分别认定其为中央政府控制和相应级别的地方政府控制。② 表 2 给出了样本公司终极控制人的特征。从表 2 可见,在样本公司中,79% 的公司被各级政府控制,其中县级政府、市级政府、省级政府以及中央政府控制的上市公司分别占 8%、25%、23% 和 23%。

表 2   样本公司的终极控制人特征

终极控制人类型	2001 年至 2003 年		2001 年		2002 年		2003 年	
	数量	比例	数量	比例	数量	比例	数量	比例
非政府(民营、乡镇、外资)	540	21%	150	19%	173	20%	217	24%
政府	2003	79%	638	81%	678	80%	687	76%

---

① 由于乡镇一级的政府部门控制的上市公司实为乡镇集体企业性质,其所受政府干预较少,更类似于民营企业,而不是国有企业,因此将这些上市公司也归入"非政府控制"类型。我们对样本中所有集体企业控制的上市公司进行了单独分析,发现在公司价值上,它们与民营资本控制的上市公司类似(限于篇幅,未报告结果)。

② 在本文的研究样本中,部属院校和地方司之后的样本进行政府教育部门所属院校控制的上市公司分别有 27 家(涉及 73 个观测值)和 4 家(涉及 8 个观测值)。我们对剔除这些做了敏感性分析,研究结论不变。

（续表）

终极控制人类型	2001 年至 2003 年		2001 年		2002 年		2003 年	
	数量	比例	数量	比例	数量	比例	数量	比例
地方政府	1426	56%	460	58%	484	57%	482	53%
县级政府	204	8%	66	8%	67	8%	71	8%
市级政府	625	25%	214	27%	211	25%	200	22%
省级政府	597	23%	180	23%	206	24%	211	23%
中央政府	577	23%	178	23%	194	23%	205	23%
合　计	2543	100%	788	100%	851	100%	904	100%

　　治理环境数据根据樊纲、王小鲁(2003)编制的各地区市场化进程数据及其子数据构建而成。樊纲、王小鲁(2003)根据大量的统计和调查资料,采用"主因素分析法",编制出中国各地区 1999 年和 2000 年市场化相对进程指标。这一指标涉及五个方面,分别是政府与市场的关系、非国有经济的发展、产品市场的发育程度、要素市场的发育程度以及市场中介发育和法律制度环境。其中,第一个方面和第五个方面与本文所要研究的治理环境有关,分别代表了各地区的政府干预程度以及法治水平。因此,我们将樊纲、王小鲁(2003)提供的各地区市场化相对进程得分、政府与市场的关系得分以及市场中介发育和法律制度环境得分,分别作为本文中各地区的市场化指数、政府干预指数以及法治水平指数,从而获得各地区治理环境数据。由于各地区市场化进程、政府干预程度以及法治水平在不同年度间相对稳定,我们采用了樊纲、王小鲁(2003)报告的 2000 年度数据。

　　表 3 是各地区治理环境数据。在表中,市场化指数越大代表市场化进程越快,政府干越指数越大代表政府干预越少,法治水平指数越大代表法治水平越高。从表 3 可见,市场化进程最快和最慢的分别是广东和新疆,政府干预程度最强和最弱的分别是青海和浙江,法治水平最高和最低的分别是北京和湖南。并且,广东的市场化进程得分 8.41,是新疆得分 3.15 的两倍多;浙江的政府干预得分 8.37,是青海得分 3.04 的两倍多;北京的法治水平得分 7.97,是湖南得分 2.62 的三倍多。这说明各地区公司治理环境差异明显。

　　另外,文中使用的其他数据如公司年末股票价格、股权结构、总资产以及行业类型等数据来自 CSMAR 中国股票市场研究数据库(China Stock Market and Marketing Accounting Research)。

表 3　各地区公司治理环境指数

地区	市场化指数	政府干预指数	法治水平指数	地区	市场化指数	政府干预指数	法治水平指数	地区	市场化指数	政府干预指数	法治水平指数
安徽	6.40	7.43	5.32	黑龙江	5.16	3.60	5.34	山东	7.15	7.38	5.63
北京	5.74	6.40	7.97	湖北	5.61	5.11	5.05	山西	4.53	4.54	5.53
福建	8.10	7.12	6.32	湖南	5.48	5.73	2.62	陕西	4.15	5.30	3.21
甘肃	4.86	5.94	3.98	吉林	5.51	5.70	5.81	上海	7.04	7.49	6.98
广东	8.41	7.99	7.29	江苏	7.90	8.12	6.29	四川	5.70	7.43	4.69
广西	5.95	7.89	4.92	江西	5.46	6.15	4.78	天津	6.89	6.05	6.96
贵州	4.62	5.43	4.36	辽宁	6.40	6.14	5.53	新疆	3.15	3.16	4.10
海南	6.41	6.02	6.33	内蒙古	4.76	3.27	4.93	云南	4.89	6.56	3.87
河北	6.39	7.13	5.15	宁夏	4.02	3.79	5.16	浙江	8.32	8.37	6.24
河南	5.64	5.54	4.93	青海	3.40	3.04	4.69	重庆	6.33	7.61	3.83

（三）检验模型

根据上文分析,我们构建如下检验模型并使用普通最小二乘法(OLS)回归分析方法检验本文的两个研究假说。

$$Tobin\ Q = \beta_0 + \beta_1 * Control + \beta_2 * Index + \beta_3 * Top1Cen +$$
$$\beta_4 * Top1CenSq + \beta_5 * Top2To5 + \beta_6 * Top6To10 +$$
$$\beta_7 * ComSize + \beta_8 * Year02 + \beta_9 * Year03 +$$
$$\sum_{i=1}^{20} \beta_{9+1} * Industry_i + \varepsilon$$

其中,β_0 为截距,$\beta_1 \sim \beta_9$ 为系数,ε 为残差。模型中各变量的含义如下:

1. 因变量

Tobin Q 是因变量,代表年末公司价值。这个变量反映的是公司市场价值与公司重置成本的比值。由于重置成本难以获取,采用年末总资产代替。市场价值为公司债务资本的市场价值与权益资本的市场价值之和。债务资本的市场价值采用账面的短期负债和长期负债的合计数来计算。另外,由于我国上市公司存在流通股和非流通股,权益资本的总市值则等于流通市值加上非流通股份的价值。而非流通股份的价值,由于没有完全市场化的数据,并且非流通股的转让价格通常是以净资产为基准,因此采用非流通股份数与每股净资产之积计算。这样,公司价值的计算公式为:Tobin Q = 市场价值/重置成本＝(每股价格×流通股份数＋每股净资产×非流通股份数＋负债账面价值)/总资产。公式中所有数据均为当年年末数。由于样本公司中没有含 B 股或 H 股的公司,因此公式中每股价格和流通股份数分别为 A 股价格和 A 股股数。上述公司价值计算方法与苏启林、朱文(2003)以及汪辉(2003)的计算方法一致。

2. 测试变量

Control 是公司终极控制人类型的统称。根据不同研究目的,我们以非政府控制的公司为参照系,在实际检验中使用 Gov,LocalGov,CenGov,County,City,Province 这些哑变量中的一个或几个来替代模型中的 Control 变量。如果公司被政府控制,那么 Gov 取值为 1,否则取值为 0;如果公司被地方政府控制,那么 LocalGov 取值为 1,否则取值为 0;如果公司被中央政府控制,那么 CenGov 取值为 1,否则取值为 0;如果公司被县级政府控制,那么 County 取值为 1,否则取值为 0;如果公司被市级政府控制,那么 City 取值为 1,否则取值为 0;如果公司被省级政府控制,那么 Province 取值为 1,否则取值为 0。虽然本文使用这些变量来刻画各级政府的影响很难说完美,但和以往研究相比,这是一个很大的改进,并且可以更好地减轻可能的内生性问题。

Index 是公司治理环境指数的统称。根据不同研究目的,我们在实际检验中分别纳入 IndexMar,IndexGov 和 IndexLeg 这三个变量来代替 Index。IndexMar,IndexGov 和 IndexLeg 分别代表公司注册地所在省、自治区或直辖市的市场化指数、政府干预指数以及法治水平指数。根据本文的研究假说,这些变量应与 Tobin Q 正相关。

3. 控制变量

Top1Cen 和 Top1CenSq 分别是经过中心化处理后的第一大股东持股比例及其平方值,用以控制第一大股东持股比例对公司价值的影响。由于在检验模型中直接纳入第一大股东持股比例及其平方项会引起共线性问题,我们对第一大股东持股比例进行中心化处理。具体来说,根据我们的统计,在所有样本公司中,第一大股东持股比例的平均值为 43.45%,因此 Top1Cen 为各样本公司第一大股东持股比例与 43.45% 的差额。Top1CenSq 为 Top1Cen 的平方。

Top2To5 和 Top6To10 分别是公司第二大股东至第五大股东持股比例之和以及第六大股东至第十大股东持股比例之和,用以控制公司其他大股东持股比例对公司价值的影响。从对中小股东的侵害角度来看,公司第一大股东以外的其他大股东可能会对第一大股东形成制约,从而提高公司价值。但另一方面,这些大股东也可能与第一大股东合谋以侵害中小股东利益。因此,Top2To5 和

Top6To10 对公司价值可能产生正面影响,也可能产生负面影响。

ComSize 为公司年末总资产的自然对数值,用以控制规模因素对公司价值的影响。为了控制公司价值的年度间差异,我们以 2001 年度为参照系,在模型中设置 Year02 和 Year03 这两个哑变量。对于 2002 年度的样本公司,Year02 取值为 1,其他情况下 Year02 取值为 0。对于 2003 年度的样本公司,Year03 取值为 1,其他情况下 Year03 取值为 0。

Industry$_i$ 为行业类型哑变量,用以控制行业因素对公司价值的影响。根据中国证监会 2001 年颁布的《上市公司行业分类指引》,我们将样本公司的行业类型分为 21 类(制造业由于公司数量特别多,取两位代码分类,其他行业取一位代码分类),并以农业类上市公司为参照系,设置 20 个行业控制变量,即 Industry$_1$ ~ Industry$_{20}$。由于篇幅关系,我们在检验结果中未报告这些行业控制变量的回归系数及显著性。

我们对检验模型中所有变量进行了描述性统计(限于篇幅,未报告)。发现样本公司 Tobin Q 的平均值为 1.528,标准差为 0.715,中位数为 1.371,最小值为 0.827,而 75% 分位数和最大值分别为 1.652 和 16.982,说明样本公司的 Tobin Q 可能存在异常值。为此,在下文的分析中,我们剔除 Tobin Q 距其平均值 5 倍标准差以外的异常值样本,即剔除 Tobin Q 处于(1.528 - 0.715 * 5, 1.528 + 0.715 * 5)以外的观测值。这样,共有 6 个观测值被剔除,最终样本数为 2 537。

五、实证检验结果及分析

(一)对全体样本公司的多元回归分析

表 4 是对全体样本公司的多元回归分析结果。其中,模型(1)至(3)是不纳入治理环境变量时的结果,模型(4)至(6)是在检验模型中分别纳入市场化进程、政府干预程度以及法治水平这三个变量时的结果。

表 4　对全体样本公司的多元回归分析(因变量为 Tobin Q)

自变量	预测符号	(1)	(2)	(3)	(4)	(5)	(6)
截距	?	8.409 *** (43.71)	8.431 *** (44.07)	8.494 *** (44.28)	8.442 *** (43.68)	8.402 *** (43.13)	8.442 *** (44.07)

（续表）

自变量	预测 符号	（1）	（2）	（3）	（4）	（5）	（6）
County	−			−0.112 ***	−0.112 ***	−0.112 ***	−0.112 ***
				（−3.59）	（−3.57）	（−3.59）	（−3.59）
City	−			−0.101 ***	−0.100 ***	−0.100 ***	−0.097 ***
				（−4.38）	（−4.33）	（−4.33）	（−4.19）
Province	−			−0.034	−0.026	−0.029	−0.028
				（−1.45）	（−1.08）	（−1.22）	（−1.18）
LocalGov	−		−0.076 ***				
			（−3.76）				
CenGov	−		0.030	0.033	0.039 *	0.037	0.030
			（1.29）	（1.43）	（1.65）	（1.59）	（1.27）
Gov	−	−0.043 **					
		（−2.22）					
IndexMar	＋				0.012 **		
					（2.12）		
IndexGov	＋					0.015 ***	
						（2.63）	
IndexLeg	＋						0.025 ***
							（4.19）
Top1Cen	−	−0.468 ***	−0.496 ***	−0.519 ***	−0.522 ***	−0.525 ***	−0.540 ***
		（−7.19）	（−7.64）	（−7.96）	（−8.01）	（−8.05）	（−8.28）
Top1CenSq	＋	1.298 ***	1.232 ***	1.224 ***	1.206 ***	1.202 ***	1.191 ***
		（5.29）	（5.05）	（5.02）	（4.95）	（4.94）	（4.90）
Top2To5	？	−0.574 ***	−0.613 ***	−0.629 ***	−0.628 ***	−0.625 ***	−0.643 ***
		（−7.01）	（−7.51）	（−7.68）	（−7.68）	（−7.64）	（−7.87）
Top6To10	？	0.325	0.300	0.285	0.261	0.244	0.275
		（1.03）	（0.96）	（0.91）	（0.83）	（0.78）	（0.88）
ComSize	−	−0.312 ***		−0.316 ***	−0.318 ***	−0.316 ***	−0.321 ***
		（−34.45）		（−34.97）	（−35.05）	（−35.06）	（−35.34）
Year02	−	−0.208 ***		−0.209 ***	−0.209 ***	−0.209 ***	−0.209 ***
		（−11.33）		（−11.50）	（−11.50）	（−11.52）	（−11.54）

自变量	预测符号	（1）	（2）	（3）	（4）	（5）	（6）
Year03	—	−0.341 ***	−0.313 ***	−0.343 ***	−0.343 ***	−0.343 ***	−0.342 ***
		（−18.75）	（−34.74）	（−19.01）	（−19.00）	（−19.04）	（−19.03）
Industry		控制	控制	控制	控制	控制	控制
样本数		2 537	2 537	2 537	2 537	2 537	2 537
模型 F 值		70.66 ***	70.07 ***	66.19 ***	64.35 ***	64.49 ***	65.09 ***
Adj-R^2		0.435	0.441	0.444	0.444	0.445	0.447

注：括号内数字为 T 值。 *** 、** 和 * 分别表示在 0.01、0.05 和 0.10 水平以下统计显著（双尾检验）。

　　从模型（1）可见，Tobin Q 与 Gov 显著负相关，这说明相对非政府控制的公司来说，政府控制的公司其公司价值更低。从模型（2）可见，Tobin Q 与 LocalGov 显著负相关，而 Tobin Q 与 CenGov 正相关，但不显著。这说明地方政府控制的公司其公司价值比非政府控制的公司更低，而中央政府控制的公司则不然。从模型（3）至（6）可见，Tobin Q 与 County 和 City 都显著负相关，与 Province 负相关但不显著，与 CenGov 正相关，但仅在模型（4）中在 0.10 水平以下显著。这说明县级政府和市级政府控制的公司其公司价值比非政府控制的公司更低，而省级政府和中央政府控制的公司其公司价值与非政府控制的公司没有显著区别。因此，上述结果表明，与非政府控制的上市公司相比，政府控制的上市公司其公司价值更低，并且这主要是由于县级政府和市级政府控制的公司其价值更低所引起。这印证了研究假说 1。

　　进一步，从模型（4）至（6）可见，Tobin Q 与 IndexMar、IndexGov 和 IndexLeg 分别在 0.05、0.01 和 0.01 以下水平显著正相关，这说明公司治理环境的改善对公司价值具有正面影响，初步印证了研究假说 2。此外，IndexLeg 的回归系数大于 IndexMar 和 IndexGov 的回归系数，说明法治水平对公司价值的影响较之市场化进程和政府干预程度的影响更为明显。考察 Tobin Q 与控制变量的关系可以发现，在模型（1）至（6）中，Tobin Q 与 Top1Cen 都显著负相关，与 Top1CenSq 都显著正相关。这表明公司价值与第一大股东持股比例之间存在着正"U"型关系①。这一结果与 Bai et al.（2004）、白重恩等（2005）的发现一致。

① 这种正"U"型关系可能源自：在第一大股东持股比例比较小的区域，第一大股东持股比例增加引起的"侵害效应"的增加超过"利益一致效应"的增加，而在第一大股东持股比例较大的区域，第一大股东持股比例增加引起的"利益一致效应"的增加超过"侵害效应"的增加。

Tobin Q 与 Top2To5 显著负相关,与 Top6To10 正相关但不显著,说明第二大股东至第五股东对第一大股东的"合谋"效应超过了"制约"效应,而第六大股东至第十大股东对第一大股东的"合谋"效应与"制约"效应没有显著区别。[①] Tobin Q 与 ComSize 都显著负相关,说明公司规模越大,其公司价值就越低。这可能是因为大规模公司的成长潜力更小,并且小规模公司由于规模效应导致股票价格更高。Tobin Q 与 $Year$02 和 $Year$03 都显著负相关,并且 $Year$03 的回归系数小于 $Year$02,这体现了 2001 年到 2003 年期间股票价格的整体下跌走势。

(二)对政府控制和非政府控制的公司的单独分析

为进一步检验本文的研究假说,我们对政府控制的上市公司和非政府控制的上市公司再进行单独分析。表 5 给出了检验结果,其中模型(1)至(3)是对政府控制的公司进行单独分析的结果,模型(4)至(6)是对非政府控制的公司进行单独分析的结果。从模型(1)至(3)可见,Tobin Q 与 City 都正相关但不显著,与 Province 和 CenGov 都显著正相关。这说明市级政府控制的公司其公司价值与县级政府控制的公司没有显著区别,但省级政府和中央政府控制的公司比县级政府控制的公司的价值更高。这进一步验证了研究假说 1,即低层级政府控制的公司其公司价值更低。

表 5　对政府控制和非政府控制的公司的单独分析(因变量为 Tobin Q)

自变量	预测符号	政府控制的上市公司			非政府控制的上市公司		
		(1)	(2)	(3)	(4)	(5)	(6)
截距	?	8.064 ***	7.981 ***	8.092 ***	9.764 ***	9.827 ***	9.542 ***
		(39.87)	(39.08)	(40.25)	(18.00)	(18.21)	(17.75)
City	—	0.011	0.012	0.014			
		(0.40)	(0.41)	(0.51)			
Province	—	0.080 ***	0.079 ***	0.077 ***			
		(2.79)	(2.76)	(2.70)			

---

① Bai et al.(2004)、白重恩等(2005)发现,第二大股东至第十大股东的持股集中度与公司价值正相关,这与本文的研究发现不一致。我们猜测,本文与 Bai et al.(2004)、白重恩等(2005)的不一致可能是因为他们在模型中直接纳入第一大股东持股比例及其平方项但未能考虑共线性问题,或者是因为 Tobin Q 的计算方法不同。

（续表）

自变量	预测符号	政府控制的上市公司			非政府控制的上市公司		
		（1）	（2）	（3）	（4）	（5）	（6）
CenGov	−	0.146 ***	0.146 ***	0.139 ***			
		(4.99)	(4.99)	(4.73)			
IndexMar	+	0.013 **			0.003		
		(2.15)			(0.22)		
IndexGov	+		0.020 ***			−0.005	
			(3.42)			(−0.32)	
IndexLeg	+			0.019 ***			0.039 **
				(3.18)			(2.18)
Top1Cen	−	−0.489 ***	−0.498 ***	−0.499 ***	−0.773 ***	−0.768 ***	−0.811 ***
		(−7.03)	(−7.16)	(−7.18)	(−3.81)	(−3.79)	(−4.01)
Top1CenSq	+	1.058 ***	1.057 ***	1.061 ***	1.249	1.276	1.159
		(4.22)	(4.23)	(4.24)	(1.41)	(1.43)	(1.31)
Top2To5	?	−0.671 ***	−0.670 ***	−0.678 ***	−0.670 ***	−0.674 ***	−0.705 ***
		(−7.71)	(−7.72)	(−7.80)	(−3.06)	(−3.08)	(−3.23)
Top6To10	?	0.409	0.367	0.427	0.387	0.387	0.472
		(1.18)	(1.06)	(1.23)	(0.53)	(0.53)	(0.65)
ComSize	−	−0.305 ***	−0.303 ***	−0.307 ***	−0.377 ***	−0.377 ***	−0.377 ***
		(−31.98)	(−32.07)	(−32.09)	(−15.21)	(−15.23)	(−15.29)
Year02	−	−0.195 ***	−0.195 ***	−0.195 ***	−0.268 ***	−0.268 ***	−0.267 ***
		(−10.56)	(−10.60)	(−10.59)	(−5.12)	(−5.12)	(−5.12)
Year03	−	−0.310 ***	−0.310 ***	−0.310 ***	−0.468 ***	−0.468 ***	−0.463 ***
		(−16.73)	(−16.79)	(−16.77)	(−9.33)	(−9.33)	(−9.27)
Industry		控制	控制	控制	控制	控制	控制
样本数		2 002	2 002	2 002	535	535	535
模型 F 值		55.58 ***	56.00 ***	55.91 ***	14.86 ***	14.86 ***	15.17 ***
Adj-R^2		0.458	0.460	0.460	0.412	0.412	0.417

注:括号内数字为 T 值。 *** , ** 和 * 分别表示在 0.01,0.05 和 0.10 水平以下统计显著(双尾检验)。

模型(1)至(3)还显示,Tobin Q 与 IndexMar 在 0.05 水平以下显著正相关、与 IndexGov 和 IndexLeg 在 0.01 水平以下显著正相关。这说明在政府控制的公司中,治理环境变量对公司价值具有显著影响。具体来说,公司所处地区的市场化进程越快、政府干预越少、法治水平越高,其公司价值则越高。从模型(4)至(6)可见,Tobin Q 与 IndexMar 正相关但不显著,与 IndexGov 负相关但不显著,与 IndexLeg 在 0.05 水平以下显著正相关,并且 IndexMar 和 IndexGov 的回归系数接近于 0。这表明在非政府控制的公司中,市场化程度以及政府干预程度对公司价值没有显著影响,但法治水平对公司价值有显著影响。其原因可能是,在投资者尤其是中小投资者看来,对于非政府控制的公司,由于所受政府干预较少,影响其公司治理的环境因素可能主要是法治水平,而不是其所处地区的市场化进程或者政府干预程度。从总体上看,治理环境的变量对公司价值的影响在政府控制的公司中更为明显,进一步印证了研究假说 2。

(三)研究结果可靠性分析

从表 4 和表 5 可见,各模型的 F 值都在 0.01 以下水平显著,Adj-R^2 都在 0.40 以上,说明检验模型的拟合效果较好。我们还考察了各模型中自变量的 VIF 值,发现所有自变量的 VIF 值都小于 2,表明模型没有共线性问题。另外,我们对上述研究结果进行了如下敏感性分析,以考察其可靠性:①将 Tobin Q 的计算公式中非流通股每股价值按照 A 股股票价格计算;②剔除中心化后的第一大股东持股比例的二次项 Top1CenSq;③剔除 Tobin Q 值三倍标准差以外的异常值样本公司;④分年度对检验模型进行多元回归分析;⑤剔除部属院校以及地方政府教育部门所属院校控制的样本公司。敏感性分析结果表明,表 4 和表 5 的主要研究结论没有实质性改变。

六、研究结论和启示

本文以 2001 年至 2003 年的上市公司为样本,考察了政府控制、治理环境与公司价值的关系。由于政府更可能将其社会性负担转嫁给其控制的上市公司,而监管力量和法律约束更难以限制政府权力,从而使得政府对其控制的上市公司具有更强的侵害能力,并且由于层级较高的政府可能更注意自身的形象,约束自身的行为,从而政府控制对公司价值的负面影响将主要来自低层级政府。因此,本文预期相对非政府控制的上市公司来说,政府控制的上市公司的价值更低,并且这主要是由低层级政府控制的公司价值更低引起。进一步,由于上市公司所处地区的市场化进程越快、政府干预越少、法治水平越高,其受到的政府干预程度将会越低,其中小股东可能较少会受到侵害,并且由于政府控制的公司受到的政府干预更多、法律约束更难对其发挥作用,从而在政府控制的公司中治理环境对公司价值的影响更为明显。因此,我们预期公司所处地区的市场化进程越快、政府干预越少、法治水平越高,其公司价值越高,并且这种关系在政府控制的公司中更为明显。

　　本文的实证分析结果支持上面的两个研究假说。研究发现,政府控制尤其是县级和市级政府控制对公司价值产生了负面影响,但公司治理环境的改善有助于减轻这种负面影响。研究结果的政策含义是,解决中国上市公司的治理问题,不仅需要进一步"抓大放小",继续推进对县级政府和市级政府控制的上市公司的产权改革步伐,还需要从根本上减少政府对上市公司的干预,加强中小投资者法律保护,以从根本上改善公司治理环境。对于研究者来说,需要把目光转移到影响公司治理的根本因素上来,加强对公司治理环境的分析。未来尚待研究的重要问题:中国的公司治理环境是怎样的? 它是怎样形成的,又是如何影响公司治理的内部和外部机制,并进而影响公司及其利益相关者行为的?

参考文献

　　白重恩,刘俏,陆洲,等.中国上市公司治理结构的实证研究[J].经济研究,2005(02):81-91.

　　陈晓,江东.股权多元化、公司业绩与行业竞争性[J].经济研究,2000(08):28-35.

　　陈晓,李静.地方政府财政行为在提升上市公司业绩中的作用探析[J].会计研究,2001(12):20-28.

　　陈小悦,徐晓东.股权结构、企业绩效与投资者利益保护[J].经济研究,2001(11):3-11.

　　陈信元,陈冬华,朱凯.股权结构与公司业绩:文献回顾与未来研究方向[J].中国会计与财务研究,2004(4):1-47.

　　陈信元,叶鹏飞,陈冬华.机会主义资产重组与刚性管制[J].经济研究,2003(05):13-22+91.

　　樊纲,王小鲁.中国市场化指数——各地区市场化相对进程报告(2001年)[M].北京:经济科学出版社,2003.

　　冯根福,韩冰,闫冰.中国上市公司股权集中度变动的实证分析[J].经济研究,2002(08):12-18.

李涛.混合所有制公司中的国有股权:论国有股减持的理论基础[J].经济研究,2002(08):19－27＋92.

李增泉,孙铮,王志伟."掏空"与所有权安排——来自我国上市公司大股东资金占用的经验证据[J].会计研究,2004(12):2－12＋96.

李增泉,余谦,王晓坤.掏空,支持与并购重组——来自我国上市公司的经验证据[J].经济研究,2005(01):95－105.

刘芍佳,孙霈,刘乃全.终极产权论、股权结构及公司绩效[J].经济研究,2003(04):51－62＋93.

苏启林,朱文.上市公司家族控制与企业价值[J].经济研究,2003(08):36－45＋91.

孙永祥,黄祖辉.上市公司的股权结构与绩效[J].经济研究,1999(12):24－31＋40.

汪辉.上市公司债务融资、公司治理与市场价值[J].经济研究,2003(08):28－35＋91.

周勤业,夏立军,李莫愁.大股东侵害与上市公司资产评估偏差[J].统计研究,2003,20(10):39－44.

朱武祥,宋勇.股权结构与企业价值——对家电行业上市公司的实证分析[J].经济研究,2001(12):66－72＋92.

Cao Y Z，Qian Y Y，Weingast B R. From federalism，Chinese style to privatization，Chinese style[J]. Economics of transition，1999，7(1)：103－131.

La Porta R，Lopez-de-Silanes F，Shleifer A. Corporate ownership around the world[J]. The journal of finance，1999，54(2)：471－517.

La Porta R，Lopez-de-Silane F，Shleifer A，et al. Legal determinants of external finance[R]. NBER working papers，1997，52(3)：1131－1150.

La Porta R，Lopez-de-Silanes F，Shleifer A，et al. Law and finance[J]. Journal of political economy，1998，106(6)：1113－1155.

La Porta R，Lopez-de-Silanes F，Shleifer A，et al. Agency problems and dividend policies around the world[J]. The journal of finance，2000，55(1)：1－33.

La Porta R，Lopez-De-Silanes F，Shleifer，et al. Investor protection and corporate valuation[J]. Journal of finance，2002，57(3)：1147－1170.

Lin Y F，Cai F，Li Z. Competition，policy burdens，and state-owned enterprise reform[J]. American economic review，1998，88(2)：422－427.

Ming J J，Wong T J. Earnings management and tunneling through related party transactions：evidence from Chinese corporate groups[J/OL]. SSRN electronic journal，2003[2019－06－07]. http://papers.ssrn.com/sol3/papers.cfm?abstract_id=424888.

Poncet S. A fragmented China：measure and determinants of Chinese domestic market disintegration[J]. Review of international economic，2005，13(3)：409－430.

Sun Q，Tong W H. China share issue privatization：the extent of its success[J]. Journal of financial economics，2003，70(2)：183 - 222.

　　Tian L H. Government shareholding and the value of China's modern firms［R］. University of Michigan Business School working paper，2001.

　　Xu X N，Wang Y. Ownership structure and corporate governance in Chinese stock companies［J］. China economic review，1999，10(1)：75 - 98.

　　▶作者感谢香港中文大学制度与治理研究中心 T. J. Wong 教授以及 Joseph Fan 教授在上海财经大学会计学院所授课程"经济制度与财务会计信息""公司组织与治理"以及日常交流中的启发，同时感谢匿名审稿人的宝贵意见。夏立军特别感谢导师陈信元教授的悉心指导。作者文责自负。

市场化进程、国企改革策略与公司治理结构的内生决定[*]

内容提要：本文以 2001 至 2003 年期间中国地方政府控制的上市公司为对象，考察了各地区市场化进程差异以及中央政府基于公司规模和行业特征采取的"抓大放小"和"战略调整"的国企改革策略对公司最终控制人政府级别、政府持股比例以及政府持股方式的影响。研究发现：在市场化进程越快的地区，上市公司更可能由低级别地方政府控制、政府持有股权比例更低；并且大规模公司、管制性行业公司更可能由高级别地方政府控制、政府持有股权比例更高。但在政府持股方式上，市场化进程的影响并不稳定，而大规模公司由政府直接持股的可能性更小，并且管制性行业与非管制性行业公司无显著区别。这些结果表明，地区市场化进程以及中央政府采取的国企改革策略对公司治理结构的形成具有重要影响（主要体现在政府级别和持股比例上）——地区市场化进程减轻了地方政府控制公司的经济动机，而国企改革策略使得地方政府具有控制大规模公司和管制性行业公司的政治动机。上述结论在剔除深圳和上海地区公司以减轻样本特殊性问题、采用工具变量法以减轻内生性问题以及一系列稳健性检验后仍成立。

关 键 词：治理结构；内生决定；市场化进程；国企改革策略

---

* 本文选自：夏立军、陈信元：市场化进程、国企改革策略与公司治理结构的内生决定，《经济研究》，2007 年第 7 期，第 82 - 95 页。本文获教育部第五届高等学校科学研究优秀成果奖（人文社会科学）二等奖、上海市哲学社会科学优秀成果奖三等奖、上海财经大学第十四届中振科研基金优秀论文奖；被《中国改革年鉴》（2007—2008）卷"观点荟萃"栏目收录和介绍。

一、引言

传统上,公司治理研究主要关注治理结构与公司绩效之间的关系。虽然取得了很多成果,但这一研究思路忽略了治理结构背后的更重要、更基本的因素,即公司所处的制度环境。由于公司总是处于特定的制度环境中,并且其行为倾向于趋利避害,适应所处环境,因此公司治理结构在很大程度上内生于公司所处的制度环境。了解制度环境如何影响治理结构,应当是公司治理研究的基础(Williamson,2000;陈信元、陈冬华、朱凯,2004;夏立军、方轶强,2005)。近年来,随着研究积累及认识加深,公司治理研究已逐渐推进到分析制度环境与治理结构之间关系的层面。例如,La Porta et al.(1998,1999)的一系列研究发现,一国法律体系对其治理结构具有重要影响。他们发现,普通法系国家的投资者法律保护程度最高,德国和斯堪的纳维亚大陆法系国家的投资者法律保护程度次之,法国大陆法系国家的投资者法律保护程度最低,并且一国投资者法律保护程度与其上市公司股权集中度负相关。Roe(2000)则认为,社会民主主义是造成欧洲上市公司股权高度集中的一个重要因素,其原因是社会民主主义加剧了公司经理与股东的利益冲突,因而股东需要集中股权以监督经理。Faccio(2006)考察了47个国家中上市公司的政治联系情况,研究发现,在腐败程度越高、限制对外投资越严重以及官员行为越不受制约的国家中,具有政治联系的公司更为普遍。Leuz and Oberholzer-Gee(2006)以印尼上市公司为例,考察了公司政治联系与其融资策略及长期绩效的关系,结果发现,具有政治联系的公司进行国外融资的可能性更小,并且当这些公司的政治保护人失去权力时,那些未能顺利地与新政府建立政治联系的公司,业绩将会下滑,并由此导致其转而增加国外融资。

在以中国为背景的研究中,Fan,Wong,and Zhang(2007a)以中国上市公司为对象,考察了公司总经理的政府任职背景对治理结构和企业价值的影响,他们发现总经理的政府任职背景对董事会职业化程度及企业价值具有显著负面影响。Chen,Li,and Su(2005)对中国私人控制的上市公司建立政治联系的原因和后果进行了研究。他们发现财政赤字和政府任意行为越严重的地区,公司越倾向于建立政治联系,而具有政治联系的公司往往拥有集权式的股权结构和董事会结构。Fan,Rui,and Zhao(2006)基于中国23起省部级高官腐败案件,考察了上市公司管理层与腐败官员的密切联系对公司融资结构的影响。研究发现,在腐败官员被逮捕之后,相对于和腐败官员无联系的公司来说,和腐败官员有联系的公司负债融资程度明显下降。Fan，Wong，and Zhang(2007b)考察了中国地方政府控制的上市公司建立金字塔式组织结构的原因和后果。他们发现在财政赤字越少、失业率越低、政府更具有长期目标以及市场化进程越快、法治水平越高的地区，地方政府控制的公司与其最终控制人之间的层级越多。他们认为这主要源自法律对国有股权转让的限制，而层级数的增加是国有股权转让受到限制时的一种替代性分权方式。

　　从现有文献来看，关于制度环境如何影响治理结构的研究已经取得不少进展，这些研究对于理解不同制度环境中公司治理结构的形成原因和后果具有重要意义。然而，这一领域的研究尚属起步阶段，相关的很多重要问题尚待深入研究(Roe，2008)，尤其是关于一国内部以及转型经济和新兴市场中的制度环境因素如何影响其治理结构的研究还很缺乏。从以中国为背景的研究来看，虽然近年来研究者已经开始关注公司治理结构的形成原因，但少有研究能够回答中国上市公司治理结构的主要方面是怎样形成的。[①] Fan，Wong，and Zhang(2007b)主要关注上市公司与最终控制人之间的层级数是如何决定的(层级数为1相当于政府直接持股，层级数大于1意味着政府间接持股)，本文则进一步考察了上市公司最终控制人政府级别以及政府持股比例的内生决定，而这两者可能是相对层级数来说更为重要的治理结构特征。在考察治理结构的形成原因时，我们不仅考虑了地方政府控制公司的经济动机，还考虑了其政治动机，从而使得中国上市公司治理结构内生决定的理论更加完整。此外，在分析政府持股方式的内生决定时，我们还考虑了政府级别、政府持股比例、公司改制上市期间、样本特殊性等因素对政府持股方式的可能影响，这也是对上市公司与最终控制人之间的层级数内生决定的进一步检验。具体而言，本文以中国地方政府控制的上市公司为研究对象，考察各地区市场化进程差异以及中央政府基于公司规模和行业特征采取的"抓大放小"和"战略调整"的国企改革策略对公司最终控制人政府级别、政府持股比例以及政府持股方式的影响。[②] 这三方面均与公司股权相关，代表了公司治理结构中最重要的内容。我们认为地区市场化进程以及中央政府采取的国企改革策略将

[①]　李涛(2002)考察了公司改制上市前业绩对上市时政府持股比例的影响，冯根福、韩冰、闫冰(2002)研究了上市公司绩效、公司规模、持股主体与行业分布等因素与上市公司股权集中度变动的关系，郑国坚、魏明海(2006)考察了控股股东与上市公司IPO前的业务关联性、组织形式和产权性质等特征形成的内部资本市场，对上市公司IPO股权结构的影响。但这些研究仍是从企业层面因素出发考察股权结构的形成原因，未能分析更为基础性的制度环境因素对治理结构的影响，研究结果也难以避免内生性问题的困扰。

[②]　选择地方政府控制的上市公司作为研究对象，主要是因为绝大部分上市公司最终被各级地方政府控制，并且这些公司与地区制度环境关系密切，便于从经验上考察不同地区制度环境对治理结构的影响。

分别影响地方政府控制企业的经济和政治动机,从而影响公司治理结构安排。本文的实证检验结果支持这一理论,研究结果有助于进一步了解中国上市公司治理结构的形成原因,增进关于一国内部以及转型经济和新兴市场中的制度环境因素如何影响其治理结构的研究积累。

后文安排如下:第二部分对地区市场化进程、国企改革策略与公司治理结构的关系进行理论分析,并提出待检验的研究假说;第三部分给出本文的实证检验方法;第四部分是实证检验结果及分析;最后一部分给出研究结论和启示。

二、理论分析和研究假说

本部分内容结合中国的有关制度背景,对市场化进程、国企改革策略与公司治理结构之间的关系进行理论分析,在此基础上提出待检验的研究假说。大体上,市场化进程与公司治理结构的关系可以由经济收益理论来解释,而国企改革策略与公司治理结构的关系可以由政治成本理论来解释。

(一)经济收益理论:市场化进程与公司治理结构

中国传统的计划经济体制的主要弊端在于缺乏竞争和价格机制,无法解决资源配置中的信息和激励问题。为解决这一问题,中国自 1978 年以来的市场化改革主要沿着分权化的方向进行,这种分权式改革既包括中央政府向地方政府的经济分权(尤其是财政分权),也包括各级政府向下属企业的经济分权(主要是扩大企业自主权)。政府间的经济分权调动了各级地方政府发展地方经济的积极性,而政治上的集权及以 GDP 为基准的政绩考核方式进一步提高了这种积极性(Blanchard and Shleifer,2001;周黎安,2004;Jin,Qian,and Weingast,2005;Li and Zhou,2005;王永钦等,2007)。随着市场化改革的推进,地方政府过多地控制下属企业对企业效率和地方经济的不利影响逐渐显露出来。为了发展地方经济,地方政府有动机放松对下属企业的控制。放松控制的方式,不仅体现为在生产经营计划、产品销售、产品价格、投融资等方面扩大企业的自主权,还体现为企业治理结构的改变,如将企业的控制权下放到下级政府、鼓励当地的低级别或限制当地的高级别政府投资兴办企业、减少企业控制权的上收、降低企业中的国有股权比例、将政府直接持股改为间接持股，等等。[①] 地方政府控制企业的动机既可能影响到公司上市前的治理结构安排，也可能影响上市当时和之后的治理结构调整。例如，据上市公司年报的披露，"芜湖港"于 2003 年上市，在上市之前的 2002 年，安徽省政府将"芜湖港"的控股股东芜湖港务管理局正式下放给芜湖市政府管理，从而使得"芜湖港"的最终控制人由安徽省政府变更为芜湖市政府；"大同水泥"于 1997 年上市，在上市之后的 2001 年，山西省政府将"大同水泥"的控股股东山西云冈水泥集团有限公司下放到大同市政府管理，从而使得"大同水泥"的最终控制人由山西省政府变更为大同市政府。[②] 可见，地方政府控制下的上市公司，其治理结构的决定，内生于地方政府控制企业的动机。而这一动机与当地的市场化进程密切相关。

由于政策、地理、交通、历史等因素的影响，中国各地区的市场化进程差异明显。根据樊纲、王小鲁（2003）的研究，市场化进程可以分为五个方面，分别是政府与市场的关系、非国有经济的发展、产品市场的发育程度、要素市场的发育程度以及市场中介发育和法律制度环境。总体上，在这五个方面，逐渐形成了东部优于中部、中部优于西部的不平衡格局。那么，这五个方面如何影响政府控制企业的动机呢？首先，在政府干预市场越少的地区，政府由"干预型"向"服务型"的功能转型可能越快，因而越倾向于和企业保持适当的距离，并且政府官员从企业中获得不当私利的机会也会越少。其次，在非国有经济发展程度越高的地区，非国有经济提供的就业机会也越多，从而地方政府通过控制国有企业实现就业目标的动机也越弱。第三，在非国有经济发展程度越高、产品和要素市场越发达的地区，国有企业面临的竞争越强，因而经营和维持国有企业所需的专门知识也越多，成本也越大，而这将减轻地方政府控制国有企业的动机（Jensen and Meckling，1992；

---

① 从放松控制的程度来看，提高当地国有企业中低级别政府所属企业的比例以及减少企业中的国有股权比重应当高于将政府直接持股改为间接持股，因为前两种方式均涉及法定控制权的调整，而后一种方式仅仅是持股方式的调整，政府仍然拥有同样的法定控制权。从国有股权比例的调整来看，虽然上市公司国有股权的转让需要层层审批，但国有股权并非完全不能转让，并且政府可以选择在新设立的上市公司中保留较少的股权比例。极端的情况是，政府干脆放弃其对企业的控制权，即民营化。

② 在中国市场化改革过程中，国有企业控制权在上下级政府间的下放，是一个非常普遍的现象。上市公司年报中披露的例子还有：山东黄金（股票代码 600547）的控股股东山东黄金集团有限公司的前身——山东省黄金公司成立于 1975 年，隶属于山东冶金厅，1979 年改为由冶金部、山东省双重领导，1988 年冶金部将山东省黄金公司下放给山东省管理；东方钽业（股票代码 000962）的控股股东宁夏有色金属冶炼厂原隶属于国家有色金属工业局和中国稀有稀土金属集团公司，2000 年，国务院将宁夏有色金属冶炼厂正式下放宁夏回族自治区管理；2001 年，财政部将国家有色金属工业局持有的中金岭南（股票代码 000060）股权全部划转给广东省政府的资产经营公司——广东省广晟资产经营有限公司持有。此外，根据 2003 年 12 月 16 日《甘肃日报》的报道，2003 年，甘肃省政府将其控制的 70 户国有工业企业，下放给省内的 12 个市州地，实行属地化管理（尚德琪、牛彦君，2003）。

张维迎、栗树和,1998);同时,由于国有企业面临的竞争越强,可以用来监督国有企业经理的市场信息也越充分,这使得政府对企业放松控制后的监督变得更容易(林毅夫、蔡昉、李周,2014)。此外,在中介机构发育和法律执行越好的地区,政府官员从企业中获得不当私利受到的约束可能越强,地方政府对企业放松控制后也可以更有效地利用中介和法律系统对国有企业经理实施监督。① 以上分析意味着,在市场化进程越快的地区,地方政府越愿意、越需要、也越能够放松其对企业的控制,即地方政府控制企业的动机更弱。从本文所要考察的治理结构来看,放松控制的方式包括政府级别、政府持股比例以及政府持股方式三个方面,因此,我们提出研究假说1,即 H1。

H1:在地方政府控制的上市公司中,公司所处地区的市场化进程越快,其越可能被低级别政府控制、政府持有的股权比例更低、政府直接持股的可能性更小。

(二)政治成本理论:国企改革策略与公司治理结构

在地区市场化进程以外,中央政府的国企改革策略也会对地方政府在公司治理结构安排上的动机和行为产生不可忽视的影响。在国有企业改革的过程中,一直面临着两难:一方面,国有企业低效率是客观事实;另一方面,公有制的主体地位不容动摇。为解决这一两难问题,1995 年后,中央政府采取了"抓大放小"和"战略调整"的国企改革策略。② "抓大放小",是指要重点抓好一批大型企业和企业集团,充分发挥它们在国民经济中的骨干作用,同时区别不同情况,采取改组、联合、兼并、股份合作制、租赁、承包经营和出售等形式,加快国有小企业改革改组步伐。"战略调整",是指国有经济需要在涉及国家安全的行业、自然垄断的行业、提供重要公共产品和服务的行业以及支柱产业和高新技术产业(本文称之为"管制性行业")中的重要骨干企业中保持控制地位,而在其他行业和领域(本文称之为"非管制性行业"),可以通过资产重组和结构调整,集中力量,加强重点,提高国有经济的整体素质。换言之,在国有企业改革上,中央政府根据公司规模和行业特征采取了不同策略,即鼓励对小规模、非管制性行业的国有企业放松控制,而限

---

① 这与夏立军、方轶强(2005)的发现也是一致的,他们发现市场化进程等公司治理环境的改善有助于减轻低级别政府控制对公司价值的负面影响。这意味着在市场化进程越快的地区,低级别政府控制的负面影响更小。

② 1995 年,十四届五中全会提出,要着眼于搞好整个国有经济,对国有企业实施战略性改组,搞好大的,放活小的。1999 年,十五届四中全会提出,国有经济应该战略调整,有所为有所不为;应该积极探索公有制的多种有效实现形式,大力发展股份制和混合所有制经济。2003 年,十六届三中全会强调,要大力发展国有资本、集体资本和非公有资本等参股的混合所有制经济,实现投资主体多元化,使股份制成为公有制的主要实现形式。

制对大规模或管制性行业的国有企业放松控制。这些国企改革策略作为中央全会的政治决定,自然会对地方政府的国企改革动机和行为产生影响。

由于中央政府采取这些国企改革策略,地方政府对大规模公司或管制性行业的公司放松控制的政治成本,将会高于其对小规模公司或非管制性行业的公司放松控制的政治成本,因此地方政府将会保留对大规模或管制性行业的公司更高程度的控制。当然,在政治成本以外,地方政府也会考虑其放松企业控制权的经济收益。在公司规模上,大规模公司因管理复杂性相对较高,对经营管理的专门知识具有更高的需求,这将使得地方政府对大规模公司放松控制的经济收益较高,从而放松控制的动机较强。在行业管制性特征上,由于上述管制性行业的公司面临的竞争相对较弱,经营管制性行业的公司所需的专门知识较少,这使得地方政府对管制性行业的公司放松控制的经济收益较低,从而放松控制的动机较弱。但是,鉴于"抓大放小"和"战略调整"的国企改革策略是中央政府的政治决定,政治动机将是地方政府对大规模公司或管制性行业公司放松控制的主要考虑因素。因此,我们预期,地方政府对大规模公司或管制性行业的公司放松控制的程度更低。放松控制的方式,同样可以表现在政府级别、持股比例或持股方式上。因此,我们提出研究假说 2,即 H2。

H2:在地方政府控制的上市公司中,大规模公司(相对小规模公司)、管制性行业的公司(相对非管制性行业的公司)更可能被高级别政府控制、政府持有的股权比例更高、政府直接持股的可能性更大。

三、实证检验方法

(一)样本选择和数据来源

由于中国上市公司自 2001 年年报起开始披露最终控制人资料,而本文需要利用这一信息,因此我们以 2001 年至 2003 年年末所有上市公司作为初选样本。然后对其依次执行如下筛选程序:①剔除最终控制人不详的公司。最终控制人是指对上市公司拥有最大股权比例的最终股东。本文需判断上市公司是否最终由政府控制以及由哪一级政府控制,因此只要根据上市公司披露的最终控制人资料无法确定是政府控制还是非政府控制,或者无法确定是哪一级的政府控制,我们就认定其最终控制人不详。②剔除中央政府控制的公司。这类公司不便考察各地区市场化进程对治理结构的影响,根据研究目标,剔除这类公司。③剔除非政府控制的公司。本文考察公有产权情况下的治理结构决定,非政府控制的上市公司与本文研究目标不符。④剔除注册地在西藏的公司。本文使用的各地区市场化进程指数来自樊纲、王小鲁(2003),但他们未编制西藏地区相应数据,因此剔除这些公司。经过上述程序,最后获得 1 674 家样本公司,这些公司最终被各级地方政府控制,其中 2001 年、2002 年和 2003 年的公司数分别为 556 家、561 家和557 家。表 1 是样本筛选过程。

表 1　样本筛选过程

最终控制人类型	三年合计		2001 年		2002 年		2003 年	
	数量	比例	数量	比例	数量	比例	数量	比例
各年末上市公司总数	3671	100%	1160	100%	1224	100%	1287	100%
减:最终控制人不详公司数	706	19.23%	216	18.62%	237	19.36%	253	19.66%
中央政府控制的公司数	682	18.58%	217	18.71%	228	18.63%	237	18.41%
非政府控制的公司数	596	16.24%	166	14.31%	193	15.77%	237	18.41%
注册地在西藏的公司数	13	0.35%	5	0.43%	5	0.41%	3	0.23%
最终样本公司数(地方政府控制)	1674	45.60%	556	47.93%	561	45.83%	557	43.28%

上市公司最终控制人类型数据根据上市公司年度报告中"股本变动及股东情况"逐一整理而得,年度报告则来自中国证监会指定信息披露网站——巨潮资讯网。若公司最终控制人可确定为自然人、职工持股会、民营企业、村办企业、街道企业、乡镇一级的政府部门、乡镇集体企业或外资企业,则认定其为非政府控制。① 若最终控制人为县级或县级以上各级政府的有关政府机构,则认定其为相应级别的政府控制。这些做法与夏立军、方轶强(2005)一致。在政府持股比例上,本文将其(第一大股东持股比例)分为不低于 30%(代表政府持股比例高)和低于 30%(代表政府持股比例低)两种情况。② 这样界定的理由是,在持股比例低于 30%时,作为第一大股东的地方政府通常难以单独、有效地控制公司。在持股方式上,若公司第一大股东为政府部门或类似机构,如国有资产管理局、财政局、

---

① 由于乡镇一级的政府部门控制的上市公司实为乡镇集体企业性质,其所受政府干预较少,更类似于民营企业,而不是国有企业,与夏立军、方轶强(2005)一致,我们将这些公司归入"非政府控制"类型。

② 根据 Fan,Wong, and Zhang(2007b)的研究,在地方政府控制的上市公司中,地方政府与上市公司之间的中间层公司,通常是国有独资的集团公司或资产经营公司。换言之,政府对上市公司的控制权主要取决于上市公司母公司拥有的上市公司股权比例。我们对采用 20%、25%、35%、40%、45%、50%为界以及对政府直接持股和间接持股的公司单独检验的情况进行了稳健性分析,结论不变。

国有资产管理委员会,那么界定为政府直接持股,否则界定为政府间接持股。上市公司第一大股东名称和持股比例数据来自 CSMAR 中国股票市场研究数据库。

表 2 是样本公司的治理结构情况。从中可见,省级、市级和县级政府控制的公司比例分别为 42.89%、43.49% 和 13.62%,政府持股比例高和低的公司比例分别为 75.87% 和 24.13%,政府直接持股和间接持股的公司比例分别为 13.44% 和 86.56%。这说明大部分地方政府控制的上市公司最终被省级和市级政府控制、政府持股比例高并且由政府间接持股。从表 2 还可以看出,公司最终控制人的政府级别越高,政府持股比例高的可能性越大,并且省级政府控制的公司中政府直接持股的可能性最小。从表 2 中各年度间的变化来看,政府直接持股的比例逐年降低,到 2003 年年末仅有 10.23% 的样本公司为政府直接持股。

表 2　样本公司的治理结构特征

治理结构	2001 年至 2003 年		2001 年		2002 年		2003 年	
	数量	比例	数量	比例	数量	比例	数量	比例
省级政府控制	718	42.89%	229	41.19%	243	43.32%	246	44.17%
政府持股比例高	590	35.24%	190	34.17%	204	36.36%	196	35.19%
政府持股比例低	128	7.65%	39	7.01%	39	6.95%	50	8.98%
政府直接持股	35	2.09%	16	2.88%	12	2.14%	7	1.26%
政府间接持股	683	40.80%	213	38.31%	231	41.18%	239	42.91%
市级政府控制	728	43.49%	252	45.32%	243	43.32%	233	41.83%
政府持股比例高	522	31.18%	180	32.37%	173	30.84%	169	30.34%
政府持股比例低	206	12.31%	72	12.95%	70	12.48%	64	11.49%
政府直接持股	146	8.72%	60	10.79%	50	8.91%	36	6.46%
政府间接持股	582	34.77%	192	34.53%	193	34.40%	197	35.37%
县级政府控制	228	13.62%	75	13.49%	75	13.37%	78	14.00%
政府持股比例高	158	9.44%	53	9.53%	51	9.09%	54	9.69%
政府持股比例低	70	4.18%	22	3.96%	24	4.28%	24	4.31%
政府直接持股	44	2.63%	15	2.70%	15	2.67%	14	2.51%
政府间接持股	184	10.99%	60	10.79%	60	10.70%	64	11.49%
地方政府控制	1 674	100.00%	556	100.00%	561	100.00%	557	100.00%
政府持股比例高	1 270	75.87%	423	76.08%	428	76.29%	419	75.22%
政府持股比例低	404	24.13%	133	23.92%	133	23.71%	138	24.78%

（续表）

治理结构	2001 年至 2003 年		2001 年		2002 年		2003 年	
	数量	比例	数量	比例	数量	比例	数量	比例
政府直接持股	225	13.44%	91	16.37%	77	13.73%	57	10.23%
政府间接持股	1449	86.56%	465	83.63%	484	86.27%	500	89.77%

樊纲、王小鲁（2003）根据大量的统计和调查资料，采用"主因素分析法"，编制出中国各地区 1999 年和 2000 年市场化相对进程指标。这一指标涉及五个方面，分别是政府与市场的关系、非国有经济的发展、产品市场的发育程度、要素市场的发育程度以及市场中介发育和法律制度环境。[①] 由于各地区市场化相对进程在不同年度间相对稳定，本文采用他们报告的 2000 年度数据，指数越大代表地区市场化进程越快。从图 1 可见，市场化进程各分指标与市场化进程指标呈正相关关系，但不完全一致。市场化进程最快和最慢的分别是广东和新疆，且广东的市场化进程指数是新疆的两倍多，这也说明各地区市场化进程差异明显。另外，其他数据如公司注册地址、行业类型、总资产以及上市时间等数据来自 CSMAR 中国股票市场研究数据库，我们对数据进行了抽样核对。本文数据处理使用 Stata 8.0 计量分析软件进行。

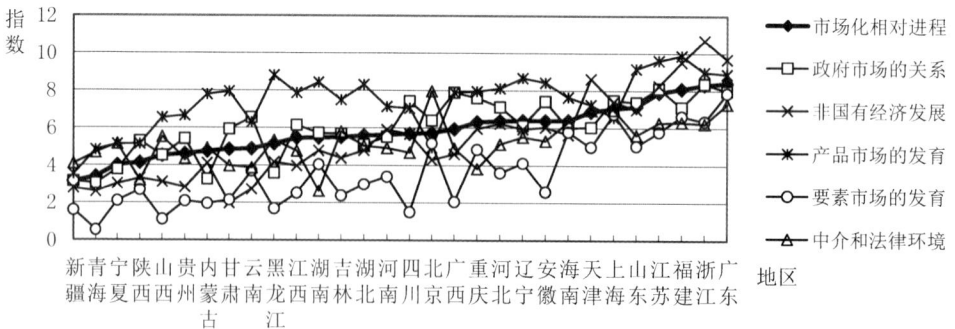

图 1　各地区（省、自治区、直辖市）市场化相对进程指数

（二）检验模型和变量设定

根据上文分析，我们构建下面三个多元回归模型以检验本文的两个研究

[①]　樊纲、王小鲁（2003）编制的各地区市场化相对进程指标及其分指标已被广泛地用于研究中国各地区的制度环境，并显示出较好的解释力，如夏立军、方轶强（2005），孙铮、刘凤委、李增泉（2005），Fan，Wong, and Zhang（2007b），方军雄（2006），等等。

假说。

模型（1）：Descend $= \beta_0 + \beta_1 * \mathrm{IndexMrk} + \beta_2 * \mathrm{ReguSize} + \beta_3 * \mathrm{ReguInd} +$
$\qquad \beta_4 * \mathrm{Develop} + \beta_5 * \mathrm{HaveBH} + \beta_6 * \mathrm{List97\_00} +$
$\qquad \beta_7 * \mathrm{List01\_03} + \beta_8 * \mathrm{Year02} + \beta_9 * \mathrm{Year03} + \varepsilon$

模型（2）：Disperse $= \beta_0 + \beta_1 * \mathrm{IndexMrk} + \beta_2 * \mathrm{ReguSize} + \beta_3 * \mathrm{ReguInd} +$
$\qquad \beta_4 * \mathrm{City} + \beta_5 * \mathrm{Province} + \beta_6 * \mathrm{Develop} +$
$\qquad \beta_7 * \mathrm{HaveBH} + \beta_8 * \mathrm{List97\_00} + \beta_9 * \mathrm{List01\_03} +$
$\qquad \beta_{10} * \mathrm{Year02} + \beta_{11} * \mathrm{Year03} + \varepsilon$

模型（3）：Indirect $= \beta_0 + \beta_1 * \mathrm{IndexMrk} + \beta_2 * \mathrm{ReguSize} + \beta_3 * \mathit{ReguInd}$
$\qquad + \beta_4 * \mathrm{City} + \beta_5 * \mathrm{Province} + \beta_6 * \mathrm{Disperse} +$
$\qquad \beta_7 * \mathrm{Develop} + \beta_8 * \mathrm{HaveBH} + \beta_9 * \mathrm{List97\_00} +$
$\qquad \beta_{10} * \mathrm{List01\_03} + \beta_{11} * \mathrm{Year02} + \beta_{12} * \mathrm{Year03} + \varepsilon$

其中，β_0 为截距，$\beta_1 \sim \beta_{12}$ 为系数，ε 为残差。模型中各变量的含义如下：

1. 因变量

Descend 为序数变量，代表公司最终控制人的政府级别，当公司最终被省级、市级和县级政府控制时，该变量分别取值为 1、2 和 3；Disperse 为哑变量，代表政府持股比例，若公司第一大股东持股比例低于 30%，该变量取值为 1，否则为 0；Indirect 为哑变量，代表持股方式，若公司第一大股东为政府部门或类似机构，如国有资产管理局、财政局、国有资产管理委员会，即政府直接持股，则该变量取值为 0，否则为 1。由于 Descend 是序数变量，而 Disperse 和 Indirect 是两值哑变量，模型（1）采用 Ordered Logit 回归分析方法，而模型（2）和模型（3）采用 Logit 回归分析方法。为减轻可能的异方差问题，所有回归结果的 Z 值都经过 Huber-White 稳健标准误差调整。

2. 测试变量

IndexMrk 是公司注册地所在省、自治区或直辖市的市场化相对进程指数。根据研究假说 1，这一变量应与因变量显著正相关。在后文的稳健性分析中，我们还将分别考察市场化进程五个方面的分指数与因变量之间的关系，以了解市场化进程与治理结构之间关系的稳定性。这些分指数包括政府与市场关系指数、非国有经济发展指数、产品市场发育指数、要素市场发育指数、中介发育和法律制度环境指数。ReguSize 为公司年末总资产的自然对数，代表公司规模，用以考察国企改革的"抓大放小"策略对治理结构的影响。ReguInd 为哑变量，代表公司所属行业的管制特征，当公司属于管制性行业时，该变量取值为 1，否则为 0。该变量用以考察国企改革的"战略调整"策略对治理结构的影响。根据国有经济战略性调整的原则,我们将"涉及国家安全的行业、自然垄断的行业、提供重要公共产品和服务的行业以及支柱产业和高新技术产业"界定为管制性行业,具体包括以下行业:采掘业(B);石油、化学、塑胶、塑料(C4);金属、非金属(C6);电力、煤气及水的生产和供应业(D);交通运输、仓储业(F);信息技术业(G)。括号内为中国证监会2001年颁布的《上市公司行业分类指引》所确定的行业代码。根据研究假说2,ReguSize 和 ReguInd 应与因变量显著负相关。

3. 控制变量

Develop 为公司注册地所在省、自治区或直辖市当年人均 GDP 的自然对数,用以控制各地区经济发展程度差异对因变量的影响。由于宏观经济变量(如经济发展程度与市场化进程)之间往往相关性较高,将该变量纳入模型,有助于更好地分离出市场化进程对治理结构的影响,防止出现伪回归问题。HaveBH 用以控制公司发行 B 股或 H 股的情况,若当年年末公司已发行 B 股或 H 股,则该变量取值为1,否则为0。由于 B 股或 H 股的发行要求以及发行后的国际影响与 A 股存在很大差异,而这些差异可能导致发行 B 股或 H 股的公司在治理结构上与仅发行 A 股的公司存在差异,因此在模型中纳入这一控制变量。在模型(2)和模型(3)中,增加了 City 和 Province 这两个控制变量,以控制政府级别对政府持股比例和政府持股方式的可能影响。当公司最终被市级政府控制时,City 取值为1,否则为0;当公司最终被省级政府控制时,Province 取值为1,否则为0。政府级别对政府持股比例的影响,有两种可能的方向,一是高级别地方政府有可能更加重视其社会性目标,或者其控制的企业面临的竞争压力更小,因而可能在企业中保持更高的股权比例,以实现其社会性目标;二是高级别政府在股票发行额度制下容易争取到更多的流通股发行额度,从而政府持有的非流通股占全部股份的比例更低。政府级别对持股方式的影响,可能是因为高级别地方政府控制的上市公司较多,为了提高管理效率,而倾向于通过设立国有资产经营公司等方式间接持股。在模型(3)中,还进一步加入了 Disperse 这一变量,以控制政府持股比例对持股方式的影响,该变量的含义与模型(2)中相同。加入该变量可以在一定程度上考察政府持股比例和持股方式这两种放松控制方式是否存在替代效应。

List97_00 和 List01_03 是哑变量,用以控制公司上市期间对治理结构的可能影响。当公司于1997年至2000年期间上市,List97_00 取值为1,否则为0;当公司于2000年之后上市,List01_03 取值为1,否则为0。这两个变量的回归系数分别代表了1997年至2000年期间上市、2000年之后上市的公司相对1997年之前上市的公司,在治理结构上的差别。设置这两个控制变量,主要是因为中国的股票发行制度先后经历了"总量控制、划分额度"阶段(1997 年之前)、"总量控制、限报家数"阶段(1997 年至 2000 年期间)和"核准制"阶段(2000 年之后),而股票发行制度的变化可能会影响公司改制上市时地方政府调整公司治理结构的动机和受到的约束。Year02 和 Year03 为哑变量,用以控制公司治理结构的年度间差异。当样本公司属于 2002 年度时,Year02 取值为 1,否则为 0;当样本公司属于 2003 年度时,Year03 取值为 1,否则为 0。

表 3 给出了检验模型中主要变量的描述性统计结果(样本数均为 1674)。[①]

表 3　主要变量的描述性统计

变量	平均值	标准差	最小值	中位数	最大值	变量	平均值	标准差	最小值	中位数	最大值
ReguSize	21.11	0.90	18.47	21.05	26.64	HaveBH	0.13	0.33	0.00	0.00	1.00
ReguInd	0.34	0.47	0.00	0.00	1.00	List97_00	0.45	0.50	0.00	0.00	1.00
Develop	9.39	0.67	7.97	9.40	10.75	List01_03	0.11	0.31	0.00	0.00	1.00

四、实证检验结果及分析

(一)市场化进程、国企改革策略与政府级别

表 4 给出了模型(1)的 Ordered Logit 回归分析结果,从左至右分别报告了"全样本""剔除深圳和上海公司"以及"工具变量法"三种情况。从"全样本"回归结果可见,在控制了其他变量的影响后,Descend 与 IndexMrk 在 0.01 以下水平显著正相关,与 ReguSize 和 ReguInd 在 0.01 以下水平显著负相关。这说明在市场化进程越快的地区,公司被低级别地方政府控制的可能性越高;大规模公司、管制性行业公司被高级别地方政府控制的可能性更大。这一结果支持研究假说 1 和研究假说 2 中关于政府级别的判断。此外,Descend 与 Develop 在 0.01 以下水平显著负相关,可能是因为经济越发达的地区,地方政府放松对企业控制的经济压力越小。Descend 与 HaveBH 在 0.05 以下水平显著负相关,说明发行 B 股或 H 股的公司被高级别政府控制的可能性更大。这可能是因为高级别地方政府在

---

① 　限于篇幅,并且表 2 和图 1 已经提供了部分变量的情况,表 3 中只给出了其他变量的描述性统计。

获得 B 股或 H 股的发行权上更有优势，或者发行 B 股或 H 股的公司被地方政府放松控制的可能性较低。

表 4　市场化进程、国企改革策略与最终控制人政府级别的 Ordered Logit 回归分析结果

自变量及模型参数	预测符号	因变量：Descend（政府级别序数变量，数值越大级别越低）					
		全样本		剔除深圳和上海公司		工具变量法	
		系数	Z 值	系数	Z 值	系数	Z 值
IndexMrk	＋	0.565	12.19 ***	0.375	6.66 ***	0.428	6.67 ***
ReguSize	－	−0.250	−4.67 ***	−0.355	−4.88 ***	−0.247	−4.49 ***
ReguInd	－	−0.558	−5.49 ***	−0.627	−5.57 ***	−0.540	−5.35 ***
Develop	？	−1.128	−9.48 ***	−0.272	−1.51	−0.924	−7.15 ***
HaveBH	？	−0.309	−2.46 **	−0.196	−1.21	−0.226	−1.80 *
List97_00	？	−0.062	−0.60	−0.095	−0.82	−0.059	−0.58
List01_03	？	−0.009	−0.06	−0.092	−0.51	−0.060	−0.38
Year02	？	0.055	0.48	0.016	0.12	0.041	0.36
Year03	？	0.231	1.95 *	0.080	0.57	0.192	1.62
样本数		1674		1319		1674	
模型 χ^2 值		228.37 ***		140.34 ***		128.34 ***	
Pseudo R^2		0.077		0.052		0.042	

注：***、** 和 * 分别表示在 0.01、0.05 和 0.10 水平以下统计显著（双尾检验）。由于因变量有三个取值，采用 Ordered Logit 回归将有两个 Cut 项，表中未报告这两项的估计系数。在最后一栏"工具变量法"中，市场化进程的工具变量为"公司是否注册于改革开放先行地区"哑变量；在第一阶段 OLS 回归中，IndexMrk 是因变量，除了工具变量外，自 ReguSize 以下的所有变量也作为控制变量纳入模型，结果显示工具变量在 0.01 以下水平统计显著；在第二阶段中，IndexMrk 采用第一阶段 OLS 回归的预测值。

　　由于在改革开放和国企改革上，深圳和上海的做法相对其他地区比较特殊，并且深圳和上海是两个证券交易所的所在地，深圳和上海的公司在治理结构上可能有别于其他地区。同时，在样本公司中，注册于深圳和上海的公司比较多。为了避免研究结果的出现只是由于深圳和上海的公司引起的，我们对剔除深圳和上海公司的情况进行了分析。表 4 中"剔除深圳和上海公司"部分报告了这一结果。从中可见，Descend 仍然与 IndexMrk 在 0.01 以下水平显著正相关，与 ReguSize

和 ReguInd 仍然在 0.01 以下水平显著负相关。这说明，IndexMrk、ReguSize 和 ReguInd 对政府级别的影响，不是由于深圳和上海样本公司的特殊性引起的。Descend 与 Develop、HaveBH 仍然负相关，但回归系数不显著，说明这两个变量上的结果受深圳和上海的公司影响较大。

　　虽然市场化进程可能影响地方政府控制公司的动机，但地方政府的国企改革行为也可能反过来影响市场化进程，为了减轻地区市场化进程变量的内生性问题，我们采用以下哑变量作为地区市场化进程的工具变量：若公司注册在深圳、珠海、汕头、厦门、海南、大连、秦皇岛、天津、烟台、青岛、连云港、南通、上海、宁波、温州、福州、广州、湛江、北海、营口这些经济特区或沿海开放城市的所在省级行政区域内，则取值为 1，否则为 0。自 20 世纪 70 年代末以来，中央政府对部分地区首先实施了改革开放政策，由此在很大程度上造成了各地区市场化进程的不同。这种政策差异主要基于地理位置，表现为沿海地区的改革开放先于其他地区，而理论上，地理位置不直接影响本文所考察的政府级别、政府持股比例和政府持股方式。因此，这一哑变量适合作为地区市场化进程的工具变量[①]。我们采用这一工具变量对模型(1)进行了二阶段回归，表 4 的"工具变量法"部分报告了回归结果。从中可见，Descend 仍然与 IndexMrk 在 0.01 以下水平显著正相关，与 ReguSize 和 ReguInd 仍然在 0.01 以下水平显著负相关。这说明在控制了市场化进程的内生性问题后，市场化进程和国企改革策略对政府级别的影响依然存在。

（二）市场化进程、国企改革策略与政府持股比例

　　在后文的分析中，我们均报告"全样本""剔除深圳和上海公司"以及"工具变量法"三种情况的结果。其中，"工具变量法"均指采用和表 4 中相同的市场化进程工具变量进行分析。表 5 给出了模型(2)的 Logit 回归分析结果。从其中的"全样本"部分可见，Disperse 与 IndexMrk 在 0.05 以下水平显著正相关，与 ReguSize 在 0.05 以下水平显著负相关，与 ReguInd 在 0.01 以下水平显著负相

[①]　1980 年 8 月 26 日，第五届全国人大常委会第十五次会议通过决议，决定在深圳、珠海、汕头、厦门设置经济特区；1984 年 5 月 15 日，中共中央、国务院决定在兴办原有 4 个经济特区的基础上，进一步开放大连、秦皇岛、天津、烟台、青岛、连云港、南通、上海、宁波、温州、福州、广州、湛江、北海等 14 个沿海港口城市；1985 年 3 月，国务院批准营口市享受沿海开放城市政策；1988 年 4 月 13 日，第七届全国人大常委会第一次会议通过原隶属广东省的海南行政区正式改制为省，同时划海南省为经济特区；1990 年 4 月 18 日，中国政府宣布开发、开放上海浦东，同年 6 月正式批准成立浦东新区。与其他地区相比，这些经济特区和开放城市率先享受了减免税、信贷、投资、吸引外资、地方政府决策权等多方面的特殊政策，由此促使其市场化进程普遍高于其他地区。处于沿海的地理位置，则是被中央政府选定为改革开放先行地区的重要因素。

关。这说明在市场化进程越快的地区,政府持有的股权比例更低;在大规模公司、管制性行业公司中,政府持有的股权比例更高。在"剔除深圳和上海公司"以及"工具变量法"部分的结果中,Disperse 与 IndexMrk 依然显著正相关,与 ReguSize 和 ReguInd 依然显著正相关。这说明,市场化进程和国企改革策略对政府持股比例的影响,在考虑了深圳和上海公司的特殊性以及市场化进程的内生性问题后依然存在。这些结果支持研究假说 1 和 2 中关于政府持股比例的判断。

表 5　市场化进程、国企改革策略与政府持股比例的 Logit 回归分析结果

自变量及模型参数	预测符号	因变量:Disperse(政府持股比例哑变量,取值为 1 代表持股比例低于 30%)					
		全样本		剔除深圳和上海公司		工具变量法	
		系数	Z 值	系数	Z 值	系数	Z 值
截距	?	5.090	2.63 ***	7.598	3.38 ***	5.375	2.70 ***
IndexMrk	+	0.126	2.17 **	0.113	1.65 *	0.166	1.95 *
ReguSize	—	−0.202	−2.31 **	−0.311	−3.31 ***	−0.205	−2.32 **
ReguInd	—	−0.370	−2.70 ***	−0.523	−3.52 ***	−0.379	−2.74 ***
City	?	−0.127	−0.72	−0.203	−1.01	−0.142	−0.80
Province	?	−0.540	−2.96 ***	−0.522	−2.41 **	−0.518	−2.76 ***
Develop	?	−0.217	−1.64	−0.222	−1.13	−0.269	−1.70 *
HaveBH	?	−0.847	−3.91 ***	−0.618	−1.97 **	−0.853	−3.92 ***
List97_00	?	−0.661	−5.20 ***	−0.724	−5.17 ***	−0.663	−5.21 ***
List01_03	?	−0.897	−4.00 ***	−1.103	−4.41 ***	−0.905	−4.01 ***
Year02	?	0.053	0.36	0.066	0.40	0.057	0.40
Year03	?	0.191	1.29	0.174	1.04	0.203	1.36
样本数			1 674		1 319		1 674
模型 χ^2 值			83.21		80.24		82.44
Pseudo R^2			0.053		0.064		0.052

注:*** 、** 和 * 分别表示在 0.01、0.05 和 0.10 水平以下统计显著(双尾检验)。在最后一栏"工具变量法"中,市场化进程的工具变量为"公司是否注册于改革开放先行地区"哑变量;在第一阶段 OLS 回归中,IndexMrk 是因变量,除了工具变量外,自 ReguSize 以下的所有变量也作为控制变量纳入模型,结果显示工具变量在 0.01 以下水平统计显著;在第二阶段中,IndexMrk 采用第一阶段 OLS 回归的预测值。

此外，在表 5 的三部分结果中，Disperse 与 City 负相关但不显著，与 Province 显著负相关，说明市级政府持有的股权比例与县级政府没有显著差异，而省级政府持有的股权比例更高。这一结果支持政府级别对持股比例影响的第一种解释，即高级别地方政府有可能更加重视其社会性目标，如就业、社会形象等，或者其控制的企业面临的竞争压力更小，因而可能会在企业中保持更高的股权比例，以实现其社会性目标。Disperse 与 HaveBH 显著负相关，说明在发行 B 股或 H 股的公司中，政府持有的股权比例更高，即控制 B 股或 H 股公司的地方政府更加注重对股权比例的控制。Disperse 与 List97_00 和 List01_03 均显著负相关，说明在后期上市的公司中，政府持有的股权比例更高。这可能是因为地方政府持有较高股权比例的公司更多地在后期上市。

（三）市场化进程、国企改革策略与政府持股方式

表 6 给出了模型（3）的 Logit 回归分析结果。从中可见，在"全样本"部分，Indirect 与 IndexMrk 在 0.10 以下水平显著正相关，在"剔除深圳和上海公司"部分没有显著关系，而在"工具变量法"部分显著负相关。这说明市场化进程对政府持股方式的影响，与深圳和上海样本公司的特殊性以及市场化进程变量的内生性有关。这一结果不支持研究假说 1 和研究假说 2 关于政府持股方式的判断，可能是因为地方政府控制公司的动机主要体现在政府级别和持股比例上，而不是持股方式上。这一结果与 Fan，Wong，and Zhang（2007b）关于上市公司与最终控制人之间层级数的研究结果也不一致，这可能是由于两项研究的样本、控制变量、对特殊地区样本的考虑以及工具变量的不同所致，同时也说明市场化进程与政府持股方式的关系，还有待更深入、更有说服力的研究设计来考察。在表 6 的三部分结果中，Indirect 均与 ReguSize 在 0.01 以下水平显著正相关，与 ReguInd 没有显著关系。这说明大规模公司被政府间接持股的可能性更高，而管制性行业和非管制性行业的公司被政府间接持股的可能性没有显著差异。这一结果不支持研究假说 1 和研究假说 2 关于政府持股方式的判断。可能的原因是中央政府"抓大放小"或"战略调整"的国企改革策略关注的主要是政府级别和持股比例，而不是持股方式。

表 6　市场化进程、国企改革策略与政府持股方式的 Logit 回归分析结果

自变量及模型参数	预测符号	因变量:Indirect(政府持股方式哑变量,取值为 1 代表政府间接持股)					
		全样本		剔除深圳和上海公司		工具变量法	
		系数	Z 值	系数	Z 值	系数	Z 值
截距	?	−8.801	−3.53 ***	−12.113	−4.25 ***	−11.868	−4.45 ***
IndexMrk	+	0.137	1.91 *	−0.015	−0.19	−0.217	−1.86 *
ReguSize	−	0.290	2.73 ***	0.371	3.04 ***	0.294	2.81 ***
ReguInd	−	−0.048	−0.29	0.167	0.94	−0.021	−0.13
City	?	0.025	0.12	0.087	0.39	0.166	0.77
Province	?	1.626	6.37 ***	1.803	6.09 ***	1.459	5.61 ***
Disperse	?	0.115	0.65	0.001	0.01	0.145	0.83
Develop	?	0.268	1.46	0.534	2.26 **	0.836	3.30 ***
HaveBH	?	0.602	2.05 **	−0.110	−0.33	0.668	2.28 **
List97_00	?	0.951	5.76 ***	1.011	5.87 ***	0.946	5.79 ***
List01_03	?	1.046	3.59 ***	1.071	3.62 ***	1.067	3.70 ***
Year02	?	0.135	0.76	0.131	0.69	0.088	0.49
Year03	?	0.392	2.03 **	0.335	1.61	0.270	1.36
样本数		1 674		1 319		1 674	
模型 χ² 值		130.38 ***		134.09 ***		130.16 ***	
Pseudo R²		0.122		0.133		0.123	

注:*** 、** 和 * 分别表示在 0.01、0.05 和 0.10 水平以下统计显著(双尾检验)。在最后一栏"工具变量法"中,市场化进程的工具变量为"公司是否注册于改革开放先行地区"哑变量;在第一阶段 OLS 回归中,IndexMrk 是因变量,除了工具变量外,ReguSize 以下的所有变量也作为控制变量纳入模型,结果显示工具变量在 0.01 以下水平统计显著;在第二阶段中,IndexMrk 采用第一阶段 OLS 回归的预测值。

　　此外,在表 6 的三部分结果中,Indirect 均与 City 没有显著关系,而与 Province 均在 0.01 以下水平显著正相关,这说明县级和市级政府的持股方式没有显著差异,而省级政府间接持股的可能性更高。其原因可能是单个省级政府相对单个县级或市级政府控制的上市公司数目更多,为了更有效地进行管理,更可能采用间接持股的方式。Indirect 与 Disperse 没有显著关系,在一定程度上说明国有股权可转让性和政府间接持股之间不是非此即彼的替代性放松控制方式。

其理由是政府持有的股权比例越高,意味着国有股权转让受到的限制越大,如果政府间接持股是国有股权转让受到限制时的替代性放松控制方式,那么应当观察到 Indirect 与 Disperse 显著负相关。Indirect 与 List97_00 和 List01_03 均显著正相关,说明在后期上市的公司中,政府间接持股的可能性更高。

(四)稳健性分析

为考察研究结果的稳健性,我们对表4至表6的结果做了一系列稳健性分析。其一,分别用市场化进程的五个分指标代替市场化进程指标,检验各分指标对治理结构的影响。其二,改变 Disperse 的定义,分别将其定义为"若公司第一大股东持股比例低于20%、25%、35%、40%、45%、50%时,该变量取值为1,否则为0",以考察 Disperse 的不同定义对研究结果的影响。其三,对模型(1)和模型(2)在政府直接持股和间接持股的公司分组检验。其四,对股票发行制度的"总量控制、划分额度"阶段(1997年之前)、"总量控制、限报家数"阶段(1997至2000年期间)以及"核准制"阶段(2000年之后)上市的样本公司分组检验。其五,对三个样本年度进行分年度回归,以考察可能的变量自相关问题对研究结果的影响。其六,采用上一期公司规模变量代替当期公司规模变量,以减轻公司规模可能的内生性问题。上述稳健性分析结果均显示,表4至表6的主要研究结论不变。此外,由于我们采用的是樊纲、王小鲁(2003)报告的2000年度市场化进程指标数据,而样本期间是2001年至2003年,这样市场化进程变量都是相对于因变量的滞后几期变量,这也减轻了市场化进程变量可能的内生性问题。

五、研究结论和启示

本文以2001年至2003年期间中国地方政府控制的上市公司为对象,考察了地区市场化进程以及中央政府分别基于公司规模和行业特征采取的"抓大放小"和"战略调整"的国企改革策略对公司治理结构(政府级别、政府持股比例以及政府持股方式)的影响。研究发现,在市场化进程越快的地区,上市公司更可能由低级别的地方政府控制、政府持有的股权比例更低,而大规模公司、管制性行业公司更可能由高级别的地方政府控制、政府持有的股权比例更高。但在政府持股方式上,市场化进程的影响并不稳定,而大规模公司由政府直接持股的可能性更小,并且管制性行业与非管制性行业的公司没有显著区别。这些结果表明,地区市场化进程以及中央政府采取的国企改革策略对公司治理结构的形成具有重要影响（主要体现在政府级别和持股比例上）——地区市场化进程减轻了地方政府控制公司的经济动机，而中央政府的国企改革策略使得地方政府具有控制大规模公司和管制性行业公司的政治动机。上述结论在剔除深圳和上海地区的公司以减轻样本特殊性问题、采用工具变量法以减轻内生性问题以及一系列稳健性检验后依然成立。

本文的理论启示是，考察或评估中国上市公司治理结构的种种经济后果（公司绩效、财务政策、会计信息等），需要考虑治理结构的内生性问题。例如，以往研究发现政府级别、政府持股比例、政府持股方式等治理结构变量与公司业绩之间的关系，有可能源自地区市场化进程、公司规模或行业管制特征对公司业绩的影响。本文的政策启示是，国有企业治理结构上的变革需要以变革企业所处的制度环境为基础，而不能仅仅关注治理结构本身。需要说明的是，本文研究对象仅限于地方政府控制的上市公司，因此研究结论不一定适用于非上市公司，也不一定适用于非政府控制或中央政府控制的上市公司。关于这些公司的治理结构是如何形成的，可能有着不同的逻辑，而事实如何尚待未来深入研究。此外，本文考察了市场化进程和国企改革策略对治理结构的影响，但我们无法界定这些影响在多大程度上发生在公司上市之前、上市当时还是上市之后，这是本文的一个局限，也是未来研究可以深化的地方。

参考文献

陈信元，陈冬华，朱凯．股权结构与公司业绩：文献回顾与未来研究方向[J]．中国会计与财务研究，2004(4)：1-47．

樊纲，王小鲁．中国市场化指数——各地区市场化相对进程报告(2001年)[M]．北京：经济科学出版社，2003．

方军雄．市场化进程与资本配置效率的改善[J]．经济研究，2006(05)：50-61．

冯根福，韩冰，闫冰．中国上市公司股权集中度变动的实证分析[J]．经济研究，2002(08)：12-18．

李涛．混合所有制公司中的国有股权：论国有股减持的理论基础[J]．经济研究，2002(08)：19-27．

林毅夫，蔡昉，李周．充分信息与国有企业改革[M]．上海：格致出版社，2014．

尚德琪，牛彦君．国企改革大提速——我省下放省属部分国有工业企业管理权综述[N]．甘肃日报，2003-12-16．

孙铮，刘凤委，李增泉．市场化程度，政府干预与企业债务期限结构——来自我国上市公司的经验证据[J].经济研究,2005,40(05):52-63.

王永钦,张晏,章元,等.中国的大国发展道路——论分权式改革的得失[J].经济研究,2007(01):4-16.

夏立军,方轶强.政府控制,治理环境与公司价值——来自中国证券市场的经验证据[J].经济研究,2005(05):40-51.

张维迎,栗树和.地区间竞争与中国国有企业的民营化[J].经济研究,1998(12):13-22.

郑国坚,魏明海.股权结构的内生性:从我国基于控股股东的内部资本市场得到的证据[J].中国会计评论,2006,04(02):189-204.

周黎安.晋升博弈中政府官员的激励与合作——兼论我国地方保护主义和重复建设问题长期存在的原因[J].经济研究,2004(06):33-40.

Blanchard O, Shleifer A. Federalism with and without political centralization: China versus Russia[J]. IMF economic review, 2001, 48(1):171-179.

Chen C J P, Li Z Q. Rent seeking incentives, political connections and organizational structure: empirical evidence from listed family firms in China[R]. Working paper, 2005.

Daron A, Simon J, Robinson J A. The colonial origins of comparative development: an empirical investigation[J]. American economic review, 2001, 91(5): 1368-1401.

Faccio M. Politically connected firms[J]. American economic review, 2006, 96(1): 369-386.

Fan J P H, Rui O M, Zhao M X. Rent seeking and corporate finance: evidence from corruption cases[R]. Working paper, 2006.

Fan J P H, Wong T J, Zhang T Y. Organizational structure as a decentralization device: evidence from corporate pyramids[J]. Social science electronic publishing, 2007[2009-06-08]. http://papers.ssrn.com/sol3/papers.cfm?abstract_id=963430.

Fan J P H, Wong T J, Zhang T Y. Politically connected CEOs, corporate governance, and the post-IPO performance of China's partially privatized firms[J]. Journal of applied corporate finance, 2014, 26(3): 85-95.

Jensen M C, Heckling W H. Specific and general knowledge and organization structure[J]. Journal of applied corporate finance, 1995, 8(2):4-18.

Jin H H, Qian Y Y, Weingast B R. Regional decentralization and fiscal incentives: federalism, Chinese style[J]. Journal of public economics, 2005, 89(9-10): 1719-1742.

La Porta R, Lopez-De-Silanes F, Shleifer A. Corporate ownership around the world[J]. The journal of finance, 1999, 54(2): 471-517.

La Porta R, Lopez-de-Silanes F, Shleifer A, et al. Law and finance[J]. Journal of political economy, 1998, 106(6): 1113-1155.

Leuz C, Oberholzer-Gee F. Political relationships, global financing, and corporate transparency：evidence from Indonesia[J]. Journal of financial economics，2006，81（2）：411－439.

Li H B，Zhou L A. Political turnover and economic performance：the incentive role of personnel control in China[J]. Journal of public economics，2005，89(9－10)：1743－1762.

Qian Y Y. Enterprise reform in China：Agency problems and political control[J]. Economics of transition，1996，4(2)：427－447.

Roe M J. Political preconditions to separating ownership from corporate control[J]. Stanford law review，2000，53(3)：539－606.

Roe M J. The institutions of corporate governance[M]//Ménard C，Shirley M M. Hand book of new institutional economics. Berlin：Springer，2008.

Williamson O E. The new institutional economics：taking stock，looking ahead[J]. Global jurist，2000，38(3)：595－613.

▶本文系陈信元教授主持的教育部人文社会科学重点研究基地重大项目"政府管制、公司治理与企业价值"（项目批准号：05JJD630028）和国家社会科学基金项目"制度环境、公司治理与会计信息"（项目批准号：06BJY016）的阶段性成果。作者特别感谢两位匿名审稿人以及中国社科院剧锦文研究员、朱恒鹏研究员、复旦大学陆铭副教授、上海财经大学李增泉教授、南京大学陈冬华教授、上海立信会计金融学院张奇峰副教授、中国人民银行方轶强博士等的宝贵意见，但文责自负。

State Ownership, the Institutional Environment, and Auditor Choice: Evidence from China[*]

Abstract: This paper finds that compared with non-state-owned firms, Chinese state-owned enterprises controlled by province, city, or county governments (local SOEs) are more likely to hire small auditors within the same region (small local auditors). In regions with less developed institutions, SOEs controlled by central government (central SOEs) also have such a tendency. However, the tendency of local and central SOEs to hire small local auditors is attenuated as the institutions develop. This auditor choice pattern is likely to be explained by SOEs' lack of demand for large or non-local auditors, small local auditors' superior local knowledge, and SOEs' collusion incentives.

Keywords: auditor choice; state ownership; institutions; corporate governance; transition economies

1. Introduction

This paper studies how institutional features such as the extent of state

---

* 本文选自：Wang Q，Wong T J，Xia L，State Ownership, the Institutional Environment, and Auditor Choice: Evidence from China，*Journal of Accounting and Economics*，2008(46)，112 - 134。本文曾连续多年为中国大陆高校发表的会计学国际期刊的唯一 ESI 高被引论文。并且，在中国资本市场研究领域过去二十年(1999—2018)全球学者发表的 129 篇国际顶级期刊论文中，该文被引次数名列全球第 7，中国大陆高校署名论文中名列第 1(Han et al., 2018, Abacus)。作者按姓氏拼音排序；被 2006 年 8 月 7 日 *South China Morning Post* 专文介绍、被 2009 年 3 月 23 日 *Sing Tao Daily*、*Ming Pao*、*Hong Kong Economic Times* 引用；获上海财经大学第十五届中振科研基金优秀论文奖。

ownership, the level of market and legal institutions' development, and the degree of government power over auditors affect Chinese listed firms' auditor choice decisions. We study the Chinese audit market for both Chinese government involvement in business and China's market and legal institutions vary significantly across regions, creating a natural laboratory to study the relation between political and economic institutions and firm-level auditor choice decisions. This paper is motivated by a growing body of research that examines the role of political and economic institutions on firm behavior (e.g., Shleifer and Vishny, 1994; Shleifer, 1998; Johnson and Mitton, 2003; Faccio, 2006) and on corporate reporting incentives and accounting quality (Ball et al., 2000; Fan and Wong, 2002; Bushman et al., 2004; Leuz and Oberholzer-Gee, 2006).[1]

Despite three recent audit market reforms in China, in particular, ① adoption of international auditing standards in 1995, ② separation of audit firms from government control in 1998, and ③ facilitation of mergers of small auditors in 2000, the market share of the top10 audit firms, which presumably provide better quality and more independent audits, has been declining (DeFond et al., 1999). Indeed, in 2003, 54% of Chinese listed firms hired auditors that are small (non-top-10) and from the same locality (hereafter, small local auditors), whereas only 25% of Chinese listed firms hired top-10 audit firms.[2]

Our paper seeks to address the following questions. Why do Chinese listed firms have a tendency to choose small local auditors? More fundamentally, how do Chinese listed firms choose auditors? The answers to these questions lie in the political and economic institutions of the Chinese audit market. We posit that three institutional factors affect Chinese listed firms' auditor choice: the extent of state ownership, the level of market and legal institutions' development, and the degree of government power over auditors.

---

[1] Other research using cross-country data has shown that a country's legal environment, a broad institutional factor, has significant effects on the quality of accounting information (Ball et al., 2003; Hung, 2000; Leuz et al., 2003) and audit services (Francis et al., 2003; Choi and Wong, 2007).

[2] Market share is computed based on the number of clients. Market share based on total assets audited bottomed out in 1998 and rose again thereafter. However, the rise in market share after 1998 is a result of a few very large firms.

The empirical results support our conjecture that these institutional factors affect auditor choice decisions. Using a sample of Chinese listed firms from 1993 to 2003, we document that compared with non-state-owned firms (hereafter, non-state firms), state-owned enterprises ultimately controlled by local (province, city, or county) governments (hereafter, local SOEs) are more likely to hire small local auditors. In addition, we find that in regions with more local government intervention and a less developed credit market, both local SOEs and SOEs under the control of the central government (hereafter, central SOEs) have a stronger tendency than non-state firms to hire small local auditors. However, the tendency of local and central SOEs to hire small local auditors is significantly attenuated when the state is less involved in controlling the economy and as the market and legal institutions develop.

As the relation between type of firm ownership and auditor choice is likely to be endogenous, we also examine auditor switches in the sub-sample of local and central SOEs that have changed controlling ownership. Specifically, we compare the auditor switches of local and central SOEs whose ownership changed from the government to private control with those of a matched sample of local and central SOEs that have not changed ownership. We find that local SOEs that change from government to private control are more likely to switch from a small local auditor to a non-small local (top-10 or non-local) auditor than are matched firms. This effect of ownership control changes on changes in the type of auditor hired is more pronounced in regions with more local government intervention and less developed market and legal institutions, consistent with the auditor choice gap between state and private ownership being significantly larger in regions with weak institutions. However, to the extent that ownership changes are endogenous, we cannot infer a causal relation between state ownership and choice of small local auditors from our analysis.

Next we analyze three potential arguments that explain how state ownership, market and legal institutions, and state influence (collectively referred to hereafter as political and economic institutions) affect local and central SOEs' auditor choice. Our first argument is related to local and central

SOEs' weaker demand for top-10 and/or non-local auditors (our "demand" argument). Specifically, we posit that local and central SOEs tend to hire small local auditors for SOEs have preferential access to new capital, or SOE investors expect a government bailout when local or central firms fall into financial distress. Our second argument is that small local auditors possess an information advantage: since small local auditors were previously affiliated 1 "local knowledge" argument). Finally, our third argument hypothesizes that local and central SOEs may hire small local auditors for opportunistic reasons, with governments using political pressure to coerce small local auditors to collude with their SOEs (our "collusion" argument).

We explore whether the above, non-mutually exclusive, arguments explain our findings by performing a series of tests, each of which is designed to assess the validity of one or more of the arguments. These tests investigate various aspects of the auditor-client relation that provide insights into which arguments are likely to explain the auditor-client pairings we observe in our primary analysis, and include regression analyses: audit opinion regressions, audit fee regression, auditor choice regression for central SOEs, and valuation effects regressions. The results of these analyses are consistent with the demand, local knowledge and collusion arguments all helping to explain why local and central SOEs tend to choose small local auditors.

Our paper contributes to the auditing literature in several ways. First, by studying the link between state ownership and auditor choice, this paper extends the auditor choice research that focuses mainly on agency cost issues in the U.S. (Palmrose, 1984; Simunic and Stein, 1987; Francis and Wilson, 1988; DeFond, 1992). Second, this paper examines two aspects of auditor location, namely, local knowledge advantage and local government influence, extending prior research that uses auditor location to measure auditors' industry specialization and client dependence (Craswell et al., 1995; Reynolds and Francis, 2001). Third, our results extend Francis et al. (2003) and Choi and Wong (2007), who link legal environments and auditor choice, by demonstrating that in addition to legal institutions, political and economic institutions affect the demand for auditors.

This study is also complementary to a number of recent studies on the effects of institutions on accounting and finance. First, our results suggest that governments may influence firms' accounting properties through their impact on firms' auditor choice decisions (Ball et al., 2000; Bushman et al., 2004; Fan and Wong, 2002; Leuz and Oberholzer-Gee, 2006). Second, while prior studies generally use a cross-country setting, we focus on a single country but analyze the cross-sectional effects of political and economic institutions on accounting using regional differences in the market and legal institutions and in the government's involvement in the economy. This approach enables us to eliminate cross-country confounding factors and to obtain more detailed regional and firm-level information about the effects of institutions. Finally, our findings on the relation between political and economic institutions and the demand for large and more reputable auditors in a transition economy provide supporting evidence on the importance of institutional development for the efficient allocation of resources and economic growth (Rajan and Zingales, 1998; Wurgler, 2000; Bushman and Smith, 2001).

The remainder of this paper proceeds as follows. Section 2 develops our hypotheses and Section 3 presents the data. We report the results and the analyses in Section 4 and Section 5 concludes the paper.

2. Hypothesis Development

In this section, we develop two hypotheses. The first hypothesis examines the relation between state ownership and auditor choice for Chinese listed firms. The second hypothesis examines how the political and economic institutions of the region in which a client firm operates affect the firm's auditor choice decision.

Before describing our hypotheses, we discuss how three institutional features of the Chinese political economy, namely, the extent of state ownership, the level of market and legal institutions' development, and the degree of government power over auditors, affect Chinese listed firms' auditor choice. In particular, we provide three arguments to explain how these features affect auditor choice decisions.

2.1 Demand Argument

2.1.1 Local and Central SOEs' Preferential Access to Capital

One reason local and central SOEs hire small local auditors rather than top-10 or non-local auditors is the preferential treatment these SOEs enjoy, not only in input factor and product markets (McMillan, 1997; Chang and Wang, 1994; Li, 1996; Qian, 1995), but also in the capital market. Stock market regulators give preferential treatment by extending listing privileges to local and central SOEs based on political rather than economic objectives. For example, when applying for listing, the government allows local and central SOEs to report pre-IPO earnings based on estimations in the recent three years because they are typically restructured from a parent company immediately prior to the IPO (Companies Law No. 137 promulgated in July 1994; CSRC Share Issuance Announcement in December 1996). This special provision enables these SOEs to provide favorable profit numbers, helping them qualify for listing and inflate their IPO prices (Aharony et al., 2000). Non-state firms, in contrast, must have been in operation for three years prior to listing and therefore need to report actual earnings.

Similarly, state banks give preferential treatment to local and central SOEs by granting loans based on the political, social, or tax-motivated factors. These SOEs' outside shareholders also contribute to lower demand for top-10 or non-local auditors than those of non-state firms because the former receive political and financial support from the government. Government leaders have incentives to assist local and central SOEs (Kornai, 1993; Qian, 1994) because successful SOE listings bring more resources into local SOEs' regions or central SOEs' ministries, enhancing the government leaders' political capital and increasing their chances for promotion (Li and Zhou, 2005). The government's or state banks' preferential treatment to local and central SOEs is likely to result in these SOEs' lower demand for reputable (presumably large or non-local) auditors to serve as a signal of their quality.

2.1.2   Government Bailout

Another reason for the weak demand for top-10 or non-local auditors is that local and central SOEs receive the government backing that provides financial insurance to outside shareholders. When these SOEs have financial problems, investors are likely to look to the largest shareholder, the government, for a bailout. The Chinese government has incentives to provide such a bailout because worker layoffs might lead to civil unrest. In contrast, without the protection afforded by the government, non-state firms are under more pressure to hire reputable (large or non-local) auditors to mitigate the agency problem and provide an early warning of any possible financial distress. As a result, non-state firms would have more incentives to hire top-10 or non-local auditors instead of small local auditors.

2.2   Local Knowledge Argument

Many auditors in China were closely affiliated with their local governments until they separated themselves from the government in 1998. After the separation, however, most accountants remained in their audit firms, carrying with them specialized knowledge of the local or central SOEs in the same regions. This is a potential reason for local or central SOEs to hire small local auditors. This tendency is perhaps even stronger for local SOEs for local auditors have specialized knowledge of local government units that supervise or hold ownership stakes in the firms. Non-state firms, in contrast, are likely to have less incentive to hire local auditors because they have relatively less local government involvement in their operations and thus they require less specialized knowledge of the government in their audits.

We expect that a local knowledge advantage is likely to be important in auditor choice decisions. Prior research uses the local information advantage argument to explain a home bias in investors' portfolio choices between domestic and foreign stocks (Kang and Stulz, 1997; Covrig et al., 2007). In addition, Bae et al. (2007) find that local analysts have an information advantage over foreign analysts, with the information gap increasing in countries with weaker market institutions. Similarly, we predict that compared with non-local auditors, local auditors have more specialized knowledge of the local or central SOEs from the same regions. This local knowledge advantage is likely to be greater in the regions with weaker market and legal institutions and stronger government involvement in business.

2.3 Collusion Argument

Chinese listed firms have incentives to hire acquiescent auditors to facilitate their meeting the China Securities Regulatory Commission's (CSRC) earnings targets for IPO and seasoned equity offerings or to avoid delisting (Aharony et al., 2000; Chen and Yuan, 2004). An acquiescent auditor would allow its client to manipulate earnings by not issuing a modified opinion that may lead to a share price decline and trigger government sanctions such as delisting and loss of qualifications for seasoned equity offerings (Chen et al., 2000).

Although non-state firms, local and central SOEs all have incentives to collude with auditors, government owners of local SOEs face the least collusion costs because of their political power over local auditors, especially small local auditors.[①] Indeed, despite efforts to separate auditors (financially and operationally) from their local governments, many local auditors remain under strong government influence. Being a major client of the region's local auditors, the local government can threaten these auditors by asking its SOEs not to use their services. Further, many of the local audit firms' partners are ex-bureaucrats of the local governments, and the same governments serve as controlling shareholders of a large portion of these audit firms' clients. Local governments can also exert influence on audit firms through their finance bureaus, audit bureaus, and local CPA institutes in the licensing of audit firms, the administration of qualifying exams, and the regulation of audit firms' day-to-day operations (Zhong, 1998; Tang, 1999). Central SOEs are likely to have higher collusion costs than local SOEs because the central

---

① Using U. S. data, Reynolds and Francis (2001) find that within an audit firm's local office, large clients lower or reduce the auditor's independence.

government does not directly regulate auditors in the regions where its firms operate.

Government owners may also have incentives to hire acquiescent auditors to pursue private gains (Shleifer and Vishny, 1994; Shleifer, 1998), or to pursue social or political goals such as infrastructure development and resolution of the region's fiscal and unemployment challenges (Lin et al., 1996). There is evidence that government officials achieve such objectives by controlling SOEs' boards (Fan et al., 2007a) and setting up corporate structures that facilitate direct intervention (Fan et al., 2007b). Although the market will have price protect against the government officials' pursuit of private benefits, the effect of such price discount is limited because they do not personally own shares in the firms (Fan et al., 2007a; Jian and Wong, 2007).

2.4 Hypotheses

Based on these three arguments of how political and economic institutions in China affect firms' auditor choice decisions, we predict that local and central SOEs have a stronger tendency than non-state firms to hire small local auditors. A formal statement of this hypothesis is as follows。

Hypothesis 1: *Local and central SOEs are more likely than non-state firms to hire small local auditors.*

To further our understanding of how institutions affect firms' auditor choice decisions, the next hypothesis provides a cross-sectional test of the effects of regional institutions on auditor choice. Fiscal decentralization from central to local governments since 1978 has created great heterogeneity in market and institutional quality across localities in China (Qian and Xu, 1993; Huang, 1996; Qian and Weingast, 1997; Jin et al., 2005). We predict that the difference in SOEs' and non-state firms' tendency to hire small local auditors is larger (smaller) in regions with more (less) local government involvement in business and less (more) developed market and legal institutions. This leads to our second hypothesis (again in alternative form):

Hypothesis 2: *The difference in the propensity to choose small local auditors between non-state firms and local or central SOEs is larger in regions with more local government involvement in business and with less developed market and legal institutions.*

To measure the quality of regional institutions, we use three indexes that are related to the three arguments for local and central SOEs' propensity to hire small local auditors: the credit market index, the government decentralization index, and the legal environment index. The demand argument is primarily affected by the level of the region's credit market index and government decentralization index; the legal environment index and government decentralization index will have an impact on the local knowledge and collusion arguments for local and central SOEs' auditor choice across the regions. Appendix 1 presents a detailed description of these indexes and their distribution across China's 30 provincial level regions.[①]

3. Data

To test the hypotheses, and the proposed arguments, above, we begin by collecting auditor choice and audit opinion data of all listed companies in China from 1993 to 2003. We also obtain a sub-sample of audit fees for all years available, i.e., 2001, 2002, and 2003. Information about company background, auditor identities, audit opinions, and audit fees comes from companies' annual reports or summaries of annual reports published in one of the three securities newspapers in China (*China Securities News*, *Shanghai Securities News*, *Securities Times*). The China Stock Market and Accounting Research (CSMAR) database serves as the primary source for our financial data.

Next, we classify our sample audit firms as small *vs.* top-10. Specifically, following DeFond et al. (1999), we classify audit firms as small if they are not

---

①   Data on the institutional indexes are not available annually for the entire sample period. Since the correlation of these indexes is very stable over time (e.g. Pearson correlation of the government decentralization index from 2000 to 2002 ranges from 0.865 to 0.983), we use the year 2000 indexes for our pooled regression analyses.

a top-10 auditor based on total assets audited.[1] We rank top-10 auditors on a national rather than regional basis as the size of the top auditors of each province varies significantly. For example, the mean size of the top auditor based on client assets in each of the bottom 10 provinces (with at least one local auditor) was US $ 5.5 billion in 2003, which is significantly smaller than the mean size of the top-10 auditors in the country in the same year, US $ 43 billion. Also, it is rather easy for the market to distinguish national top-10 auditors from other auditors as the CSRC publishes an annual national top-10 auditors list, which is relatively stable with at most two firms falling off the list annually between 1993 and 2003. Note that the mean size of top-10 auditors based on client assets (US $ 43 billion in 2003) is significantly larger than that of non-top-10 auditors (US $ 4 billion in 2003).

Our tests also call for identifying local versus non-local auditors. A listed firm is considered to have hired a local auditor if the audit firm is located in the same province (or region with provincial status, that is, autonomous administrative region or municipality under the central government) as the listed firm. In China, auditors typically have a single office and thus their locations can be easily identified. While in the early years some top-10 auditors subcontracted auditing work out to smaller auditors that did not have licenses to audit listed firms (DeFond et al., 1999), the signing auditors, not the affiliates, bore all legal and government sanction risks. Accordingly, we identify auditors based on the signing auditors, not the affiliates, in these cases.

Note that when auditors from two or more regions merge to form a new auditor, we treat the original registry regions of the merging auditors and the new registry region of the merged firm as the registry regions of the new audit firm. In other words, if a listed firm hires an auditor that results from a merger of auditors from different regions, this firm is considered as hiring a local auditor if the firm is located in any one of the registry regions of the new auditor. For example, if a Beijing audit firm merges with a Shanghai audit

---

[1] We experiment with different definitions of top auditors (top-10 auditors based on number of clients; Big-4 international or Top-10 domestic auditors, based on total assets audited or number of clients), and our inferences don't change.

firm, the new merged firm will have a Beijing office and a Shanghai office and thus is considered a local auditor for any Beijing or Shanghai client firm. We classify a local auditor in this way because the new auditor can potentially be influenced by the local governments of both the new registry region of the merged firm and the registry regions of the original firms prior to the merger. During the sample period, there are 26 mergers, of which 16 involved audit firms from different regions. The percentage of sample observations audited by merged firms is 19.27%, and merged firms from different regions audit approximately 10.78% of the total sample. For robustness we use alternative treatments for merged firms such as using the location of the lead office (in terms of size prior to the merger) to measure the merged audit firm's locality and deleting all the merged firms from our sample; the results remain unchanged.

Finally, we must separate the sample into three ownership categories: non-state firms, whose ultimate owners are non-government units such as entrepreneurs, townships and villages, and foreign companies; local SOEs, which are owned by local governments (e.g., the Bureau of State Assets Management and the Finance Bureau); central SOEs, which are owned by the central government (e.g., the Ministry of Finance and the Central Industrial Enterprises Administration Committee). If two or more types of owners control a listed firm, we classify the firm's ownership type based on the identity of the owner that has the largest ownership control in the firm. We obtain ownership information from annual reports for years since 2001; the first year firms were subject to mandatory reporting of the ultimate owners. For years prior to 2001, we treat the ultimate owner to be the same as that in 2001 unless there is a change in the controlling owner. In the latter case, we use the information of the controlling owner in the annual reports prior to the change to ascertain the ultimate ownership type. At the end of 2003, 72% of Chinese listed firms are SOEs with the largest shareholder a government entity that owns more than 20% of the firm's stock. Another 4% are also SOEs, but the controlling government entity owns less than 20% of the firm's shares. Of the 76% (72%+4%) of firms that are government-owned, local governments own 53% and the central government the remaining 23% (76%~53%).

As reported in Table 1, a number of firms are excluded from our sample. Firms that issue shares to foreign investors, termed B-shares or H-shares, are excluded from the sample because these firms' financial characteristics and regulatory environments are different from those of firms that only issue domestic shares (termed A-shares). We also exclude firm-year observations for the years in which the firm's region does not have a local auditor. The regions that do not have local auditors in any one year between 1993 and 2003 are: Guangxi, Guizhou, Hebei, Henan, Jiangxi, Inner Mongolia, Ningxia, Qinghai, Shaanxi, Shanxi, Tibet, and Xinjiang; Tibet does not have an auditor over the entire sample period. Further, firms without sufficient information to identify the ownership type of the ultimate controlling shareholders and/or firms with missing financial information are not included in the sample. The final sample includes 67% of all listed firms in China from 1993 to 2003.

Table 2 reports the sample distribution and choice of auditors by firm ownership type. The first column (all years combined) shows that compared with 51% of non-state firms and central SOEs choosing small local auditors, 63% of local SOEs choose small local auditors. In addition, the first row (full sample) reports that from 1993 to 1997, the ratio of all companies choosing small local auditors increases each year from 48% to 62%, whereas in the period from 1998 to 2003, the increasing trend no longer persists with the ratio dropping from 59% to 54%.

Table 2 further reports by ownership type the ratio of companies choosing small local auditors from 1993 to 2003. From 1993 to 1997, the ratio of all three types of companies increased (33% to 63% for non-state firms, 30% to 56% for central SOEs, and 52% to 64% for local SOEs). From 1998 to 2003, the ratio of non-state firms and central SOEs choosing small local auditors decreased from 59% to 45% and 58% to 47%, respectively. However, local SOEs continued to choose a higher ratio of small local auditors with 60% in 1998 and 62% in 2003. This is consistent with the conjecture that the reforms separating audit firms from local governments and the mergers of small auditors affect non-state firms and central SOEs, but not local SOEs, in their choice of small local auditors.

Table 1   Sample Selection Process

	1993—2003	1993	1994	1995	1996	1997	1998	1999	2000	2001	2002	2003
Population	8627	183	291	323	530	744	851	949	1088	1160	1223	1285
step 1: exclude firms having B-shares or H-shares	1205	45	64	81	99	118	124	127	133	137	138	139
step 2: exclude firms in a region where there is no auditor	112	4	9	8	11	12	12	13	7	21	8	7
step 3: exclude firms without information on ultimate controlling shareholders	1483	21	34	37	81	137	163	180	198	191	213	228
step 4: exclude firms without financial information	68	1	3	0	0	0	3	7	8	14	14	18
Sample	5759	112	181	197	339	477	549	622	742	797	850	893
Sample/Population (%)	67	61	62	61	64	64	65	66	68	69	70	69

This table reports the steps we take to select our final sample. B-shares and H-shares are shares issued to non-domestic investors. The regions that do not have any auditors in any one year of our sample period between 1993 and 2003 are: Guangxi, Guizhou, Hebei, Henan, Jiangxi, Inner Mongolia, Ningxia, Qinghai, Shaanxi, Shanxi, Tibet, and Xinjiang. Tibet does not have an auditor over the entire sample period.

Table 2 Sample by Ownership Type and Auditor Type

	1993—2003	1993	1994	1995	1996	1997	1998	1999	2000	2001	2002	2003
Total Sample Total Number of Clients	5759	112	181	197	339	477	549	622	742	797	850	893
Ratio Choosing Small Local Auditors	58%	48%	54%	55%	57%	62%	59%	63%	62%	58%	57%	54%
Local SOE Clients Total Number of Clients	3601	93	149	160	250	323	357	391	442	472	485	479
Ratio Choosing Small Local Auditors	63%	52%	56%	56%	59%	64%	60%	67%	68%	64%	65%	62%
Central SOE Clients Total Number of Clients	1158	10	16	20	47	87	109	132	162	178	194	203
Ratio Choosing Small Local Auditors	51%	30%	44%	50%	53%	56%	58%	55%	52%	51%	47%	47%
Non-state Firm Clients Total Number of Clients	1000	9	16	17	42	67	83	99	138	147	171	211
Ratio Choosing Small Local Auditors	51%	33%	50%	53%	48%	63%	59%	60%	57%	47%	44%	45%

This table reports the number of clients (first row) and the percentage of clients choosing small local auditors (second row) by ownership type. Local SOEs, central SOEs, and non-state firms refer to the listed firms whose ultimate shareholders are local government entities (any department in the local government, such as Bureau of State Assets Management or Finance Bureau), central government (any central government unit, such as Ministry of Finance or Central Industrial Enterprises Administration Committee), and non-government units (individuals, townships and villages, or foreign companies), respectively. Small local auditors: if a client's registry province or provincial level region is the same as that of its auditor who is not a top-10 auditor in terms of assets audited, then this client is considered to be hiring a small local auditor. In the case of mergers, the merged firms are considered to have multiple registry regions, comprising all the registry regions of merging firms before the merger and the registry region of the merged firm after the merger.

4. Results and Analyses

4.1 State Ownership，Institutional Development，and Auditor Choice

We test Hypothesis 1 by regressing a dummy variable indicating whether the auditor is a small local auditor on the following three sets of variables: two ownership type variables, Local SOEs and Central SOEs; three index variables, Credit Market Index, Government Decentralization Index, and Legal Environment Index; and firm characteristic and financial control variables. Our controls are based on the work of Francis and Wilson (1988) and DeFond et al. (1999), which demonstrates that these firm characteristics and financial variables are related to auditor choice. In particular, we include Growth and Equity Issuance to capture the effect of a firm's capital needs on the demand for auditing. Log of Client Assets and Return on Assets are used to capture the effects of size and performance, and Total Debt / Total Assets and Current Assets / Current Liabilities are included to control for risk. To control for firm complexity, we include Receivables / Total Assets and Inventory / Total Assets. Finally, we include dummy variables for years and for clients' industrial sectors, including industrial manufacturers, financial services, utilities, real estate, conglomerates, and commerce. Table 3 summarizes the definitions of all variables used in all our regression analyses.

With the exception of Growth, which is winsorized at the top and bottom 1%, the rest of the financial variables are generally distributed within reasonable ranges and are not winsorized.[①] As a diagnostic check in Appendix 2, we winsorize all financial variables at the top and bottom 1% or 2%.

---

① We also perform all our analyses without winsorizing *Growth*; our results remain the same.

Table 3 Definition of Variables

Variables on Auditor Type, Audit Opinions, Auditor Switches, Audit Fees, and Market-to-Book Assets	
Small Local Auditors	Dummy variable, which equals 1 if a client's registry province or provincial-level region is the same as that of its auditor who is not a Top-10 auditor based on assets audited, and 0 otherwise. In the case of mergers, the merged firms are considered to have multiple registry regions, comprising all the registry regions of merging firms before the merger and the registry region of the merged firm after the merger
Audit Opinion	Dummy variable, which equals 1 if the audit opinion is modified, and 0 otherwise. Following Chen et al., 2000 and 2001, we classify unqualified opinions with an explanatory paragraph, qualified opinions, disclaimers, and adverse opinions as "modified opinions"
Auditor Switch	Ordered variable, which equals 1, 2, and 3 if the client switches its auditor from a small local auditor to another type of auditor, does not switch its auditor or switches within the same type of auditors, and switches its auditor from another type of auditor to a small local auditor, respectively
Log of Audit Fee	The natural logarithm of annual audit fee (in ten thousand RMB Yuan) in years 2001, 2002, and 2003, when the data were disclosed publicly
Market-to-Book Assets	The market value of owners' equity and book value of total liabilities all divided by book value of total assets. The market value of tradable shares is calculated based on the market price in the secondary markets. For non-tradable shares, we set their market price at book value because they are usually transacted at a price benchmarked against book value
Variables on Ownership Type and Change	
Local SOEs	Dummy variable, which equals 1 if a firm's ultimate shareholder is a local government (any department in the local government, such as Bureau of State Assets Management or Finance Bureau), and 0 otherwise

(continued)

Variables on Ownership Type and Change	
Central SOEs	Dummy variable, which equals 1 if a firm's ultimate shareholder is central government (any central government unit, such as Ministry of Finance or Central Industrial Enterprises Administration Committee), and 0 otherwise
Local SOEs to Non-state Firms	Dummy variable, which equals 1 if a firm's ultimate shareholder changes from a local government (any department in the local government, such as Bureau of State Assets Management or Finance Bureau) to non-state entity, and 0 otherwise
Central SOEs to Non-state Firms	Dummy variable, which equals 1 if a firm's ultimate shareholder changes from central government (any central government unit, such as Ministry of Finance or Central Industrial Enterprises Administration Committee) to non-state entity, and 0 otherwise
Variables on Institutions Across Regions	
Credit Market Index	The index, constructed by Fan and Wang (2003), measures the percentage of deposits taken by non-state financial institutions and the percentage of short-term loans to the non-state sector for each province or provincial level region in 2000
Government Decentralization Index	The index, constructed by Fan and Wang (2003), is based on government spending as a percentage of GDP, the tax rates in a province, and the amount of government administrative regulations for each province in 2000. Higher index suggests less government involvement
Legal Environment Index	The degree of legal environment development, measured by the number of lawyers as a percentage of the population, the efficiency of the local courts and protection of property rights, for each province or provincial level region in 2000 from Fan and Wang (2003)

(continued)

Variables on Client Characteristics

Growth	(Total sales of next year divided by total sales of current year) $-$ 1
Equity Issuance	Dummy variable, which equals 1 if a firm issues equity next year and 0 otherwise
Loss	Dummy variable, which equals 1 if a firm's net income is below zero and 0 otherwise
Stock Return	Yearly market-adjusted stock returns during the fiscal year
S. D. of Residuals	The standard deviation of residuals from the market model estimated by daily returns during the year
Log of Client Assets	The natural logarithm of year-end total assets (RMB Yuan)
Return on Assets	Net income divided by year-end total assets
Total Debt / Total Assets	Year-end total debt divided by year-end total assets
Current Assets / Current Liabilities	Year-end total current assets divided by year-end total current liabilities
Receivables / Total Assets	Year-end total receivables divided by year-end total assets
Inventory / Total Assets	Year-end inventory divided by year-end total assets
Clients ⩾ 3 Years Old	Dummy variable, which equals 1 if the firm has been listed for three years or more, and 0 otherwise
Located in Beijing	Dummy variable, which equals 1 if the firm registers in Beijing, the capital of China, and 0 otherwise
Ratio of Tradable Shares	The ratio of the number of tradable shares of a firm over its number of total shares
Ownership of the Largest Shareholder	The ratio of the number of shares held by the largest shareholder over the number of total shares of the firm

Table 4，Panel A reports the summary statistics of the three institutional indexes and the control variables for the auditor choice regressions across the three sub-samples based on ownership type and the difference in mean and median between each state ownership group and the non-state firms. For the institutional indexes，the higher credit market index scores refer to more developed credit markets，higher government decentralization index scores refer to less government intervention，and higher legal environment index scores refer to more developed legal institutions. Consistent with expectations，local and central SOEs' median credit market index and government centralization index are significantly lower than those of the non-state firms. This indicates that local and central SOEs are more likely than non-state firms to be operating in regions with more government intervention and less developed credit markets. In addition，compared with that of non-state firms，local SOEs' mean and median legal environment index are significantly lower，while central SOEs' mean and median legal environment index are significantly higher. This suggests that local SOEs are more likely than non-state firms to be in regions with less developed legal institutions，whereas central SOEs tend to operate in more developed legal environments. One reason is that a significant percentage （16.53%） of central SOEs registers in Beijing，which is a region with the highest legal index in China （see Appendix 1）.

There is no significant difference in the first two control variables，Growth and Equity Issuance，between SOEs and non-state firms，though local SOEs experience lower Growth than non-state firms. This pattern remains the same if we use the average three-year-ahead growth and equity issuance measures instead of the one-year-ahead numbers in Table 4. Both central and local SOEs are significantly larger （Log of Client Assets） and report weaker accounting performance （Return on Assets） than non-state firms. Also，compared with non-state firms，central SOEs have lower risk，as indicated by their lower mean and median Total Debt / Total Assets，higher median Current Assets / Current Liabilities，and lower asset complexity，as indicated by Receivables / Total Assets and Inventory / Total Assets. The results are mixed for local SOEs. Compared with non-state firms, local SOEs have lower median Current Assets / Current Liabilities but no difference in Total Debt / Total Assets, and in terms of asset complexity local SOEs have lower mean and median Receivables / Total Assets but higher mean and median Inventory / Total Assets than non-state firms.

Table 4, Panel B presents the results of the logistic regression equations without the three index variables in model (1), with each of the three indexes separately in models (2) to (4), and with all three indexes together in model (5). Before discussing the results, note that in this study, except for the auditor switches regression in Table 5, all Z-statistics in the logistic regressions and t-statistics in the OLS regressions are computed using Newey-West robust standard errors with a one-year lag.[1] As a robustness check for potential cross-correlation of residuals that would overstate the test statistics of the three institutional indexes, we use standard errors clustered by year in addition to the Newey-West adjustment; the regression results remain qualitatively unchanged and are discussed in Appendix 2. Year and industry dummies are included in the regressions, but for brevity are not tabulated.

Our regression results show that local SOEs are more likely than non-state firms to choose small local auditors. Specifically, in model (1) of Table 4, Panel B, we report results from a regression including ownership type and the financial characteristics of the client firms. The coefficient on Local SOEs is positive and statistically significant at the 1% level, while that on Central SOEs is positive but statistically insignificant. This suggests that local SOEs have the strongest propensity to hire small local auditors, while central SOEs are not different from non-state firms in their likelihood of hiring small local auditors. The change in odds for Local SOEs indicates that local SOEs' odds (the ratio of the probability of hiring small local auditors over that of hiring other auditors) are 84.5% greater than that of non-state firms. Further, the Chi-square test (not reported) shows that the coefficient on local SOEs is

---

① We re-run the tests by using the standard Fama-Macbeth (annual) regressions. The results still hold and are discussed in Appendix 2.

significantly greater than that on central SOEs, with a p-value below 0.001. This provides support to the conjecture that local governments have more direct political power than the central government over small local auditors.

As mentioned above, in Panel B we also examine whether the institutional environment, measured by the three institutional indexes, has a direct impact on auditor choice by examining each institutional index separately in models (2) to (4), and all three indexes together in model (5). Consistent with our expectation that Chinese listed firms have a weaker tendency to hire small local auditors in regions with a better institutional environment, the coefficient on each index is significantly negative, and at the 1% level in models (2) to (4). The change in odds ranges from −21.5% to −32.4%, suggesting that the decrease in odds of hiring small local auditors for each one standard deviation increase in regional institutions is economically significant. The coefficient on the government decentralization index is negative but insignificant while the coefficients on the other two indexes remain significantly negative in model (5). This suggests that although there is multicollinearity among the three indexes, the credit market index and the legal environment index are able to capture unique aspects of a province's institutions that are distinct from the other indexes.

Next we test Hypothesis 2, i.e., whether the effect of government ownership on auditor choice varies with the quality of institutions. In Table 4, Panel C, we add the interaction terms between government ownership (Local SOEs and Central SOEs) and the three institutional indexes to the regression model. Hypothesis 2 predicts that when market and legal institutions are more developed or when the government intervenes less, local and central SOEs are more likely to behave the same as non-state firms in choosing auditors. We expect the coefficients on these interaction terms to be negative.

The regression results for local SOEs reported in models (1) to (4) of Panel C support our predictions. The coefficient on Local SOEs is significantly positive, while the coefficient on the interaction between Local SOEs and each of the three indexes in models (1) to (3) is significantly negative. This result is consistent with our prediction that when institutions develop, the positive effect of local government ownership on the choice of small local auditors decreases. When the three indexes are included in the same regression in model (4), the coefficients on the three interaction terms with Local SOEs remain negative but only the one with Credit Market Index is statistically significant, indicating that the three index variables are likely to be capturing similar underlying institutional factors.

Turning to central SOEs, we find that in contrast with the results in Panel B, the coefficient on Central SOEs is significantly positive and the coefficient on the interaction term is significantly negative when the Credit Market Index and Government Decentralization Index are used in models (1) and (2) of Panel C. The coefficients on the interaction terms remain marginally significantly negative for Credit Market Index (Z-stat $= -1.50$) and significantly negative for Government Decentralization Index (Z-stat $= -1.81$) in model (4). These results indicate that although central SOEs as a whole do not exhibit a significantly stronger tendency than non-state firms to hire small local auditors, the former are more likely to hire small local auditors in regions with less developed institutions. One puzzling result is that contrary to our prediction, the coefficient on Central SOEs $\times$ Legal Environment Index is significantly positive in models (3) and (4). As it will be analyzed in Subsection 4.3.3, we find that due to collusion incentives, central SOEs located in Beijing are more likely to hire small local auditors than central SOEs located in other regions. This indicates that the collusion incentives probably outweigh the legal institutions effect of the Beijing location. Consistent with this result, the coefficient on Central SOEs $\times$ Legal Environment Index becomes significantly negative (Z-stat $= -2.26$) and marginally significantly negative (Z-stat $=-1.62$) in models (3) and (4), respectively, when a dummy variable Located in Beijing, which equals 1 when the firm registers in Beijing and 0 otherwise, Local SOEs $\times$ Located in Beijing and Central SOEs $\times$ Located in Beijing are included in the regressions.

It is worth noting that a few other variables in models of Panels B and C also help explain auditor choice. The coefficient on Log of Client Assets is negative and significant, suggesting that large companies are less likely to choose small local auditors. This is reasonable since large companies usually require scale economies and more sophisticated auditing services, which small local auditors are unlikely to offer. In addition, the statistically significantly negative coefficients on Total Debt / Total Assets and Receivable / Total Assets indicate that firms with more leverage, higher risk and more complexity tend to hire top-10 or non-local auditors.

In contrast, we find that Growth and Equity Issuance are not significantly related to auditor choice. High growth firms are likely to be small in size (as indicated by Pearson correlation, not reported), and the negative relation between client size and small local auditors may confound the result. The insignificant coefficient on Equity Issuance suggests that share issuance in China does not create a strong demand for top-10 or non-local auditors. In addition, as reported in Panel A of Table 4, we do not find that local and central SOEs engage in fewer stock issuances than non-state firms. This result fails to support the argument that compared with non-state firms, local and central SOEs' tendency to hire small local auditors is driven by their infrequent share issuances and low growth opportunities.

In summary, results in Table 4 support our Hypotheses 1 and 2. However, care must be taken in drawing inferences from the results because they are potentially subject to an endogeneity problem. In particular, we cannot infer causality in the relation between client firms' ownership types and auditor choice. In the next analysis, we use a sub-sample of firms that have switched controlling owners to examine the effects of a change in ownership control on auditor choice and to examine whether these effects differ across regions with various levels of institutional development. To the extent that an ownership change is caused by exogenous factors that do not affect auditor choice, this analysis mitigates the potential endogeneity problem of Table 4.

Table 4

Panel A: Summary Statistics of Variables Partitioned by Ownership Type

Variables	Ownership Type	Mean	S.D.	Min	25%	Median	75%	Max
		Auditor choice regression variables						
Credit Market Index	Non-state Firms	5.606	2.271	0.350	4.210	6.370	7.680	7.940
	Local SOEs	5.372 ***	2.225	0.350	3.850	5.880 ***	7.670	7.940
	Central SOEs	5.462	2.043	0.350	3.850	5.900 ***	7.670	7.940
Government Decentralization Index	Non-state Firms	6.869	1.486	3.040	5.980	7.430	7.990	8.370
	Local SOEs	6.718 ***	1.327	3.040	5.730	7.380 ***	7.490	8.370
	Central SOEs	6.653 ***	1.192	3.040	6.020	6.400 ***	7.490	8.370
Legal Environment Index	Non-state Firms	5.905	1.225	2.620	5.050	6.240	6.980	7.970
	Local SOEs	5.705 ***	1.275	2.620	4.920	5.630 ***	6.980	7.970
	Central SOEs	6.103 ***	1.401	2.620	5.050	6.290 *	7.290	7.970
Growth	Non-state Firms	0.315	0.748	−0.767	−0.029	0.175	0.459	3.909
	Local SOEs	0.206 ***	0.570	−0.767	−0.050	0.116 ***	0.325	3.909
	Central SOEs	0.277	0.584	−0.767	−0.019	0.163	0.418	3.909
Equity Issuance	Non-state Firms	0.127	0.333	0	0	0	0	1
	Local SOEs	0.137	0.344	0	0	0	0	1
	Central SOEs	0.110	0.313	0	0	0	0	1

(continued)

Variables	Ownership Type	Mean	S.D.	Min	25%	Median	75%	Max
Log of Client Assets	Non-state Firms	20.665	0.891	17.707	20.130	20.620	21.140	26.612
	Local SOEs	20.769 ***	0.892	17.794	20.158	20.716 **	21.279	26.640
	Central SOEs	20.875 ***	0.968	18.651	20.232	20.777 ***	21.427	26.946
Return on Assets	Non-state Firms	0.035	0.135	−3.098	0.020	0.047	0.075	0.317
	Local SOEs	0.036	0.064	−0.898	0.017	0.041 ***	0.065	0.272
	Central SOEs	0.043 *	0.061	−0.896	0.020	0.044	0.068	0.377
Total Debt / Total Assets	Non-state Firms	0.215	0.150	0.000	0.086	0.206	0.321	0.674
	Local SOEs	0.223	0.139	0.000	0.118	0.215	0.315	0.752
	Central SOEs	0.182 ***	0.136	0.000	0.069	0.172 ***	0.272	0.583
Current Assets / Current Liabilities	Non-state Firms	1.987	1.745	0.094	1.092	1.505	2.236	19.471
	Local SOEs	1.898	2.418	0.091	1.061	1.419 **	1.995	47.134
	Central SOEs	2.104	1.960	0.222	1.220	1.633 ***	2.338	36.247
Receivables / Total Assets	Non-state Firms	0.259	0.158	0.006	0.141	0.232	0.345	1.285
	Local SOEs	0.228 ***	0.137	0.000	0.125	0.206 ***	0.309	0.909
	Central SOEs	0.245 **	0.139	0.000	0.139	0.228	0.333	0.703
Inventory / Total Assets	Non-state Firms	0.139	0.117	0.000	0.061	0.110	0.179	0.799
	Local SOEs	0.147 *	0.133	0.000	0.057	0.120 **	0.198	0.838
	Central SOEs	0.130 ***	0.097	0.000	0.057	0.117	0.188	0.704

This table reports the summary statistics of the main variables used in our regression analyses by ownership type. For each variable, we report mean, standard error (S.D.), minimum value (Min), 25th percentile (25%), median, 75th percentile (75%), and maximum value (Max). We also report whether the mean and median values of local SOEs and central SOEs are significantly different from those of non-state firms. ***, **, and * indicate statistical significance at the 1%, 5%, and 10% levels respectively (two-tailed) of the mean or median tests (compared with non-state firms). All variable definitions are presented in Table 3. N=1000, 3601 and 1158 for Non-state firms, Local SOEs and Central SOEs, respectively.

Table 4 (continued)

Panel B: Logistic Regressions Examining the Choice of Small Local Auditors with Ownership Type and Institution Variables

Dependent Variable: Small Local Auditors

Independent Variables	(1) Change in Odds (%)	(1) Coeff.	(1) Z-stat	(2) Change in Odds (%)	(2) Coeff.	(2) Z-stat	(3) Change in Odds (%)	(3) Coeff.	(3) Z-stat	(4) Change in Odds (%)	(4) Coeff.	(4) Z-stat	(5) Change in Odds (%)	(5) Coeff.	(5) Z-stat
Intercept	n/a	3.337	4.55***	n/a	3.587	4.85***	n/a	4.501	5.98***	n/a	3.794	5.11***	n/a	3.974	5.29***
Local SOEs	84.5	0.613	8.14***	77.3	0.573	7.53***	77.3	0.573	7.54***	70.4	0.533	6.87***	67.9	0.518	6.63***
Central SOEs	5.8	0.057	0.64	3.3	0.033	0.37	1.1	0.011	0.12	10.7	0.102	1.12	8.1	0.078	0.84
Credit Market Index				−21.5	−0.110	−7.71***							−11.6	−0.056	−3.27***
Government							−21.5	−0.182	−7.68***						
Decentralization Index										−21.5	−0.182	−7.68***	−2.7	−0.020	−0.67

（continued）

Independent Variables	Dependent Variable: Small Local Auditors														
	(1)			(2)			(3)			(4)			(5)		
	Change in Odds (%)	Coeff.	Z-stat	Change in Odds (%)	Coeff.	Z-stat	Change in Odds (%)	Coeff.	Z-stat	Change in Odds (%)	Coeff.	Z-stat	Change in Odds (%)	Coeff.	Z-stat
Legal Environment Index										−32.4	−0.300	−13.38***	−28.5	−0.258	−10.51***
Growth	0.0	0.000	0.00	0.7	0.012	0.25	0.1	0.002	0.04	1.1	0.018	0.37	1.3	0.022	0.45
Equity Issuance	13.1	0.124	1.44	13.7	0.128	1.48	10.8	0.103	1.18	14.2	0.133	1.51	14.0	0.131	1.49
Log of Client Assets	−14.8	−0.176	−5.01***	−13.0	−0.153	−4.24***	−14.0	−0.166	−4.62***	−9.0	−0.104	−2.88***	−8.8	−0.101	−2.78***
Return on Assets	−2.2	−0.279	−0.75	−2.0	−0.251	−0.67	−2.4	−0.300	−0.80	−3.8	−0.476	−1.27	−3.4	−0.437	−1.16
Total Debt / Total Assets	−8.3	−0.617	−2.78***	−8.6	−0.640	−2.93***	−8.3	−0.616	−2.77***	−8.6	−0.639	−2.90***	−8.7	−0.647	−2.95***
Current Assets / Current Liabilities	−2.7	−0.012	−0.84	−2.6	−0.012	−0.84	−3.0	−0.014	−0.98	−1.2	−0.005	−0.39	−1.4	−0.007	−0.47
Receivables / Total Assets	−4.9	−0.355	−1.68*	−6.3	−0.456	−2.14**	−6.0	−0.437	−2.07**	−4.9	−0.353	−1.62	−5.7	−0.414	−1.91*
Inventory / Total Assets	−4.6	−0.378	−1.50	−4.1	−0.336	−1.36	−3.9	−0.324	−1.30	−4.2	−0.345	−1.34	−3.9	−0.320	−1.27
Industry Dummies	yes			yes			yes			yes			yes		

(continued)

Independent Variables	Dependent Variable: Small Local Auditors														
	(1)			(2)			(3)			(4)			(5)		
	Change in Odds (%)	Coeff.	Z-stat	Change in Odds (%)	Coeff.	Z-stat	Change in Odds (%)	Coeff.	Z-stat	Change in Odds (%)	Coeff.	Z-stat	Change in Odds (%)	Coeff.	Z-stat
Year Dummies		yes			yes			yes			yes			yes	
Number of Obs.		5759			5759			5759			5759			5759	
Pseudo R-Square		0.025			0.035			0.035			0.048			0.051	
Chi Square		192.64			240.72			245.79			363.03			372.02	
p-value		<0.001			<0.001			<0.001			<0.001			<0.001	

This table reports the logistic regression results on the choice of small local auditors by non-state firms, local SOEs, and central SOEs. All variable definitions are presented in Table 3. The change in odds equals $[\exp (s_i \beta_i) - 1]$, where s_i is the sample standard deviation of continuous variable i, or 1 for dummy variable i, and β_i is the estimated regression coefficient for variable i. Z-statistics are computed based on Newey-West standard errors with a one-year lag. ***, **, and * represent statistical significance at the 1%, 5%, and 10% levels respectively, two-tailed.

Table 4 (continued)

Panel C: logistic regressions examining the choice of small local auditors with ownership type and institution variables, and their interaction terms

Independent Variables	Dependent Variable: Small Local Auditors											
	(1)			(2)			(3)			(4)		
	Change in Odds (%)	Coeff.	Z-stat	Change in Odds (%)	Coeff.	Z-stat	Change in Odds (%)	Coeff.	Z-stat	Change in Odds (%)	Coeff.	Z-stat
Intercept	n/a	3.176	4.20***	n/a	3.926	4.98***	n/a	3.133	3.87***	n/a	3.125	3.75***
Local SOEs	198.6	1.094	5.24***	233.5	1.205	3.16***	303.4	1.395	3.84***	334.5	1.469	3.48***
Central SOEs	69.9	0.530	2.08**	213.7	1.143	2.29**	-45.8	-0.612	-1.47	62.8	0.487	0.92
Credit Market Index	-7.8	-0.037	-1.31							4.1	0.018	0.48
Local SOEs×Credit Market Index	-18.6	-0.093	-2.71***							-15.4	-0.076	-1.71*
Central SOEs×Credit Market Index	-17.7	-0.089	-2.08**							-16.2	-0.081	-1.50
Government Decentralization Index				-12.4	-0.099	-2.25**	-0.4	-0.003		1.0	0.008	0.12
Local SOEs×Government Decentralization Index				-11.5	-0.092	-1.70*				-0.04		

(continued)

Dependent Variable: Small Local Auditors

Independent Variables	(1)			(2)			(3)			(4)		
	Change in Odds (%)	Coeff.	Z-stat	Change in Odds (%)	Coeff.	Z-stat	Change in Odds (%)	Coeff.	Z-stat	Change in Odds (%)	Coeff.	Z-stat
Central SOEs×Government Decentralization Index				−19.9	−0.167	−2.31**				−21.1	−0.178	−1.81*
Legal Environment Index							−27.7	−0.249	−4.75***	−29.7	−0.270	−4.18***
Local SOEs×Legal Environment Index							−17.6	−0.148	−2.47**	−10.8	−0.087	−1.22
Central SOEs×Legal Environment Index							16.0	0.114	1.68*	30.1	0.202	2.57***
Growth	0.8	0.013	0.27	0.1	0.002	0.05	1.0	0.017	0.35	1.3	0.021	0.45
Equity Issuance	13.4	0.126	1.46	10.3	0.098	1.13	14.9	0.139	1.58	13.9	0.130	1.48
Log of Client Assets	−13.0	−0.153	−4.23***	−14.0	−0.166	−4.71***	−7.5	−0.085	−2.34**	−7.4	−0.085	−2.33**
Return on Assets	−2.2	−0.274	−0.74	−2.5	−0.312	−0.83	−4.0	−0.501	−1.34	−4.1	−0.525	−1.39
Total Debt / Total Assets	−8.1	−0.600	−2.67***	−7.9	−0.579	−2.64***	−8.5	−0.627	−2.82***	−7.7	−0.569	−2.53**
Current Assets / Current Liabilities	−2.5	−0.011	−0.78	−2.9	−0.013	−0.94	−0.8	−0.004	−0.26	−1.0	−0.005	−0.33

(continued)

Dependent Variable: Small Local Auditors

Independent Variables	(1)			(2)			(3)			(4)		
	Change in Odds (%)	Coeff.	Z-stat	Change in Odds (%)	Coeff.	Z-stat	Change in Odds (%)	Coeff.	Z-stat	Change in Odds (%)	Coeff.	Z-stat
Receivables / Total Assets	−6.1	−0.445	−2.10**	−5.7	−0.416	−1.94*	−5.4	−0.390	−1.78*	−5.7	−0.411	−1.89*
Inventory / Total Assets	−4.4	−0.363	−1.47	−3.9	−0.324	−1.30	−3.8	−0.314	−1.22	−3.7	−0.307	−1.19
Industry Dummies		yes			yes			yes			yes	
Year Dummies		yes			yes			yes			yes	
Number of Obs.		5759			5759			5759			5759	
Pseudo R-Square		0.036			0.036			0.052			0.056	
Chi Square		236.24			249.64			376.30			397.78	
p-value		<0.001			<0.001			<0.001			<0.001	

This table reports the logistic regression results on the choice of small local auditors by non-state firms, local SOEs, and central SOEs. All variable definitions are presented in Table 3. The change in odds equals $[\exp(s_i \beta_i) - 1]$, where s_i is the sample standard deviation of continuous variable i, and β_i is the estimated regression coefficient for variable i. Z-statistics are computed based on Newey-West standard errors with a one-year lag. ***, **, and * represent statistical significance at the 1%, 5%, and 10% levels respectively, two-tailed.

4.2   Change in Ownership Control and Auditor Choice

To further examine Hypotheses 1 and 2, we look at the sub-sample of 62 SOEs, 50 local SOEs, and 12 central SOEs that have changed controlling ownership (from government to private owners) during the sample period.[①] For the control group, we match each of the 62 SOEs in the year before the ownership change with another SOE that has the same ownership type, operates in the same region and industry, and is closest in total assets.

Using the above sub-sample and control group, we run an ordered logistic regression with the dependent variable Auditor Switch, which equals 1 when the firm switches from a small local auditor to a non-small local auditor, 2 when the firm either does not switch auditor or switches auditor within the same auditor type (small local auditor vs. non-small local auditor), and 3 when the firm switches from a non-small local auditor to a small local auditor. The test variables include two ownership change variables, Local SOEs to Non-state Firms and Central SOEs to Non-state Firms, the three institutional indexes, and the interaction terms between the two ownership change variables and the three indexes. We define Local (Central) SOEs to Non-state Firms to be equal to 1 when the firm changes its control ownership from a local (the central) government to a private owner, and 0 otherwise. All the control variables are the same as those in Table 4 except that we measure them in terms of changes (switch year minus the year before) instead of levels.

The results in Table 5 show that the coefficient on Local SOEs to Non-state Firms in models (1) to (4) is consistently negative and statistically significant. This indicates that compared with the matched sample that has no ownership change, local SOEs that change control ownership to private owners are more likely to switch from small local auditors to non-small local auditors. Consistent with our conjecture that institutional development lowers this negative association between change in ownership control and an auditor

---

① Four firms are dropped from the sub-sample due to a lack of good matching firms and another eight firms are excluded because they switched ownership control from non-state to state.

switch, we find that the coefficients on Local SOEs to Non-state Firms $\times$ Credit Market Index, Local SOEs to Non-state Firms $\times$ Government Decentralization Index, and Local SOEs to Non-state Firms $\times$ Legal Environment Index are all significantly positive when they are included separately in models (1), (2), and (3), respectively.[①] However, the three coefficients remain positive but are statistically insignificant when the three indexes are included together in model (4), suggesting that there is possibly strong multicollinearity among the interaction terms. For central SOEs, we find that the coefficient on Central SOEs to Non-state Firms is only significantly negative for model (3), and the coefficient on the interaction between Central SOEs to Non-state Firms and the institutional index is only significantly positive for models (3) and (4), when the legal environment index is included in the regression model.

In summary, the evidence in Table 5 provides further support for Hypotheses 1 and 2. However, these models rely on the assumption that the change in controlling ownership is exogenous. To the extent that ownership switches and auditor choice are endogenously determined, the results in Table 5 may still be subject to the endogeneity problem discussed in relation to Table 4.

---

① The reason that the change in odds of the three coefficients are large, ranging from 186.7% to 448.5%, is the probability of the control firms that switch from small local auditors to non-small local auditors (the numerator of the odds ratio) is likely to be much smaller than one.

Table 5 Ordered Logistic Regressions Examining Auditor Switches for the Ownership Change Sample

Independent Variables	Dependent Variable: Auditor Switch											
	(1)			(2)			(3)			(4)		
	Change in Odds (%)	Coeff.	Z-stat	Change in Odds (%)	Coeff.	Z-stat	Change in Odds (%)	Coeff.	Z-stat	Change in Odds (%)	Coeff.	Z-stat
Local SOEs to Non-state Firms	-99.4	-5.117	-2.93***	-99.9	-7.424	-2.25**	-99.7	-5.935	-2.58***	-100.0	-8.434	-2.46**
Central SOEs to Non-state Firms	-49.3	-0.679	-0.28	3414.1	3.559	0.62	-100.0	-11.252	-2.31**	-100.0	-12.753	-1.61
Credit Market Index	-44.4	-0.256	-0.85							-39.5	-0.219	-0.67
Local SOEs to Non-state Firms × Credit Market Index	448.5	0.741	2.12**							273.7	0.574	1.24
Central SOEs to Non-state Firms × Credit Market Index	-48.3	-0.287	-0.53							-27.2	-0.138	-0.26
Government Decentralization Index				-17.6	-0.142	-0.36				2.7	0.020	0.04

(continued)

Dependent Variable: Auditor Switch

Independent Variables	(1)			(2)			(3)			(4)		
	Change in Odds (%)	Coeff.	Z-stat	Change in Odds (%)	Coeff.	Z-stat	Change in Odds (%)	Coeff.	Z-stat	Change in Odds (%)	Coeff.	Z-stat
Local SOEs to Non-state Firms × Government Decentralization Index				240.4	0.902	1.71*				76.0	0.416	0.59
Central SOEs to Non-state Firms × Government Decentralization Index				−67.1	−0.819	−0.87				20.4	0.137	0.16
Legal Environment Index							−8.6	−0.069	−0.31	−10.9	−0.089	−0.26
Local SOEs to Non-state Firms × Legal Environment Index							186.7	0.810	1.83*	34.1	0.226	0.54
Central SOEs to Non-state Firms × Legal Environment Index							592.6	1.489	2.05**	796.2	1.687	2.14**
Change in Growth	296.1	1.104	2.88***	254.1	1.014	2.62***	229.3	0.955	2.60***	314.5	1.140	2.74***

(continued)

Dependent Variable: Auditor Switch

Independent Variables	(1)			(2)			(3)			(4)		
	Change in Odds (%)	Coeff.	Z-stat	Change in Odds (%)	Coeff.	Z-stat	Change in Odds (%)	Coeff.	Z-stat	Change in Odds (%)	Coeff.	Z-stat
Change in Equity Issuance	−28.9	−0.877	−1.42	−24.2	−0.712	−1.45	−26.6	−0.796	−1.29	−30.8	−0.946	−1.45
Change in Log of Client Assets	150.5	2.674	1.48	76.0	1.645	1.11	125.4	2.367	1.30	138.3	2.529	1.39
Change in Return on Assets	1896.7	10.565	1.71*	1065.5	8.666	1.62	1065.6	8.666	1.66*	1778.5	10.350	1.49
Change in Total Debt / Total Assets	62.6	5.013	1.27	62.6	5.014	1.29	50.5	4.219	1.05	52.5	4.354	1.31
Change in Current Assets / Current Liabilities	−98.1	−1.588	−2.04**	−96.2	−1.315	−1.95*	−95.8	−1.281	−2.02**	−98.0	−1.569	−1.76*
Change in Receivables / Total Assets	19.6	1.307	0.39	29.2	1.870	0.56	−4.3	−0.324	−0.11	43.5	2.638	0.68
Change in Inventory / Total Assets	221.0	13.118	2.61***	178.6	11.523	2.86***	123.1	9.027	1.90*	259.8	14.400	2.85***
Industry Dummies	yes			yes			yes			yes		

(continued)

Dependent Variable: Auditor Switch

Independent Variables	(1) Coeff.	(1) Z-stat	(1) Change in Odds (%)	(2) Coeff.	(2) Z-stat	(2) Change in Odds (%)	(3) Coeff.	(3) Z-stat	(3) Change in Odds (%)	(4) Coeff.	(4) Z-stat	(4) Change in Odds (%)
Year Dummies	yes			yes			yes			yes		
Number of Obs.	124			124			124			124		
Pseudo R-Square	0.437			0.435			0.432			0.481		
Chi Square	63.66			83.76			61.41			82.74		
p-value	<0.001			<0.001			<0.001			<0.001		

This table reports the ordered logistic regression results on auditor switches for the ownership change sample with a matched control sample. All variable definitions are presented in Table 3. The change in odds equals $[\exp(s_i \beta_i) - 1]$, where s_i is the sample standard deviation of continuous variable i, and β_i is the estimated regression coefficient for variable i. ***, **, and * represent statistical significance at the 1%, 5%, and 10% levels respectively, two-tailed. Change in Growth, Change in Equity Issuance, Change in Log of Client Assets, Change in Return on Assets, Change in Total Debt/ Total Assets, Change in Current Assets/ Current Liabilities, Change in Receivables/ Total Assets, and Change in Inventory/ Total Assets denote the corresponding variables in the current year less those of the previous year.

4.3   Additional Analyses

We now turn to several tests that analyze whether the three arguments discussed in Section 2 explain our results for Hypotheses 1 and 2. Specifically, we conduct four separate regression analyses: audit opinion regressions in Table 7, audit fee regression in Table 8, auditor choice regression for central SOEs in Table 9, and valuation effects regressions in Table 10. Note that except for the local knowledge argument, the other two arguments are evaluated by more than one of these tests. Thus, in relation to the results in Tables 7 through 10, the discussion on each argument will draw from several of these tables. Table 6 presents a summary of which regression analyses test which arguments, and the tables that report the corresponding results.

4.3.1   Audit opinions

To evaluate the proposed arguments for Hypotheses 1 and 2, we first use two separate tests of the likelihood of small local auditors to issue modified opinions by regressing audit opinion on auditor type and other control variables.

In the first test, we predict that small local auditors are generally less likely to issue a modified opinion for Chinese listed firms than large or non-local auditors. That is, as indicated in Table 6, the sign of the regression coefficient on Small Local Auditors is expected to be negative. The significantly negative coefficient on Small Local Auditors can be interpreted as small local auditors having less ability to find errors or being less willing to report errors when they are found. The former interpretation is consistent with the demand argument, which suggests that Chinese listed firms have incentives to hire small local auditors even though they may be less capable, while the latter supports the collusion argument. We do not have any prediction for the local knowledge argument in the context of this test because an information advantage can either increase small local auditors' ability to discover problems, thereby leading to *more* modified opinions, or discourage firms from engaging in opportunistic activities in the first place, thereby leading to *fewer* chances to issue modified opinions.

Table 6   Summary of Results for the Three Arguments

Tests	Tables	Demand for Large or Non-local Auditors	Local Knowledge of Small Local Auditors	Collusion Incentives in Hiring Small Local Auditors
Audit Opinion Regressions	Test 1 in Table 7. Models (1) and (2):			
	Coefficient on Small Local Auditors	Expected sign: − Supported		Expected sign: − Supported.
	Test 2 in Table 7. Model (3):			
	Coefficient on Local SOEs × Small Local Auditors			Expected sign: − Weakly supported
	Coefficient on Central SOEs × Small Local Auditors			Expected sign: − Weakly supported
Audit Fee Regression	Table 8:			
	Coefficient on Local SOEs × Small Local Auditors	Expected sign: + Not supported		
	Coefficient on Central SOEs × Small Local Auditors	Expected sign: + Supported		
Auditor Choice Regression for Central SOEs	Table 9: Coefficient on Located in Beijing			Expected sign: + Supported

(continued)

Tests	Tables	Demand for Large or Non-local Auditors	Local Knowledge of Small Local Auditors	Collusion Incentives in Hiring Small Local Auditors
	Table 10, Model (3):			
Valuation Effects	Coefficient on Local SOEs × Small Local Auditors	Expected sign: 0/+ Not supported	Expected sign: 0/+ Not supported	Expected sign: — Supported
Regressions	Coefficient on Central SOEs × Small Local Auditors	Expected sign: 0/+ Supported	Expected sign: 0/+ Supported	Expected sign: — Not supported

Table 7

Panel A: Auditor Opinion by Ownership Type and Auditor Type

		1993—2003	1993	1994	1995	1996	1997	1998	1999	2000	2001	2002	2003
All Sample	All Auditors	5759	112	181	197	339	477	549	622	742	797	850	893
		11%	4%	4%	12%	11%	13%	15%	16%	14%	12%	11%	6%
	Small Local Auditors	3362	54	98	109	193	298	326	393	462	462	481	486
		11%	0%	2%	6%	7%	12%	15%	15%	15%	11%	8%	5%
	Other Auditors	2397	58	83	88	146	179	223	229	280	335	369	407
		13%	7%	7%	18%	15%	13%	15%	17%	13%	14%	14%	7%

(continued)

		1993 – 2003	1993	1994	1995	1996	1997	1998	1999	2000	2001	2002	2003
Local SOEs	Small Local Auditors	2263	48	83	90	148	207	214	262	299	303	313	296
		10%	0%	2%	7%	7%	13%	14%	16%	15%	11%	7%	5%
	Other Auditors	1338	45	66	70	102	116	143	129	143	169	172	183
		13%	7%	5%	14%	15%	16%	16%	16%	15%	17%	15%	7%
Central SOEs	Small Local Auditors	591	3	7	10	25	49	63	72	84	90	92	96
		7%	0%	0%	0%	4%	8%	13%	7%	6%	8%	10%	3%
	Other Auditors	567	7	9	10	22	38	46	60	78	88	102	107
		10%	0%	11%	30%	18%	11%	15%	13%	8%	9%	9%	5%
Non-state firms	Small Local Auditors	508	3	8	9	20	42	49	59	79	69	76	94
		16%	0%	0%	11%	10%	17%	20%	24%	24%	14%	11%	10%
	Other Auditors	492	6	8	8	22	25	34	40	59	78	95	117
		15%	17%	25%	38%	14%	4%	12%	25%	15%	15%	17%	9%

This table reports the number of clients and the percentage of clients receiving modified opinions by year, auditor type (small local auditors vs. other auditors), and ownership type. All variable definitions are presented in Table 3.

Table 7 (continued)

Panel B: Logistic Regressions Examining Auditor Opinion with Auditor Type and Ownership Type

Independent Variables	Dependent Variable: Audit Opinion								
	(1)			(2)			(3)		
	Change in Odds (%)	Coeff.	Z-stat	Change in Odds (%)	Coeff.	Z-stat	Change in Odds (%)	Coeff.	Z-stat
Intercept	n/a	-2.395	-1.58	n/a	-2.535	-1.66 *	n/a	-2.657	-1.74 *
Small Local Auditors	-21.2	-0.238	-2.47 **	-21.0	-0.236	-2.41 **	3.8	0.037	0.18
Local SOEs				-24.3	-0.279	-2.28 **	-11.3	-0.120	-0.69
Central SOEs				-46.0	-0.615	-3.89 ***	-32.5	-0.393	-1.87 *
Small Local Auditors × Local SOEs							-27.0	-0.315	-1.32
Small Local Auditors × Central SOEs							-37.3	-0.467	-1.51
Credit Market Index	1.8	0.008	0.31	2.1	0.009	0.37	1.8	0.008	0.32
Government Decentralization Index	-4.4	-0.034	-0.72	-5.1	-0.039	-0.86	-5.2	-0.040	-0.87
Legal Environment Index	12.8	0.093	2.17 **	14.5	0.104	2.34 **	14.6	0.105	2.34 **
Loss	91.3	0.649	2.59 ***	93.1	0.658	2.57 ***	94.2	0.664	2.59 ***
Stock Return	-10.4	-0.274	-1.82 *	-10.8	-0.284	-1.90 *	-11.0	-0.288	-1.92 *
S. D. of Residuals	21.5	25.724	3.02 ***	21.9	26.112	2.73 ***	22.1	26.373	2.81 ***
Log of Client Assets	-10.1	-0.117	-1.71 *	-8.6	-0.099	-1.45	-8.6	-0.099	-1.44
Return on Assets	-44.5	-7.329	-4.53 ***	-44.9	-7.413	-4.45 ***	-44.8	-7.396	-4.44 ***

(continued)

Independent Variables	Dependent Variable: Audit Opinion								
	(1)			(2)			(3)		
	Change in Odds (%)	Coeff.	Z-stat	Change in Odds (%)	Coeff.	Z-stat	Change in Odds (%)	Coeff.	Z-stat
Total Debt / Total Assets	28.0	1.750	4.51***	26.8	1.679	4.25***	26.6	1.668	4.22***
Current Assets / Current Liabilities	4.4	0.019	0.74	4.4	0.019	0.74	4.1	0.018	0.69
Receivables / Total Assets	50.1	2.858	8.59***	50.9	2.896	8.76***	50.9	2.894	8.60***
Inventory / Total Assets	−17.0	−1.501	−3.10***	−16.3	−1.435	−3.04***	−16.1	−1.420	−3.01***
Clients ≥ 3 Years Old	25.3	0.454	3.75***	23.1	0.420	3.47***	23.0	0.417	3.43***
Industry Dummies	yes			yes			yes		
Year Dummies	yes			yes			yes		
Number of Obs.	5759			5759			5759		
Pseudo R-Square	0.201			0.205			0.205		
Chi Square	583.37			588.07			572.05		
p-value	<0.001			<0.001			<0.001		

Columns (1) − (3) of this table report the logistic regression results on the auditor opinion by auditor type and ownership type. The change in odds equals $[\exp(s_i\beta_i)-1]$, where s_i is the sample standard deviation of continuous variable i, or 1 for dummy variable i, and β_i is the estimated regression coefficient for variable i. Z-statistics are computed based on Newey-West standard errors with a one-year lag. All variable definitions are presented in Table 3. ***, **, and * represent statistical significance at the 1%, 5%, and 10% levels respectively, two-tailed.

Table 8   OLS Regression Examining the Determinants of Audit Fee

Independent Variables	Dependent Variable: Log of Audit Fee	
	Coeff.	t-stat
Intercept	−3.408	−15.06 ***
Small Local Auditors	−0.084	−2.54 **
Local SOEs	−0.052	−1.78 *
Central SOEs	−0.095	−2.74 ***
Small Local Auditors×Local SOEs	−0.028	−0.71
Small Local Auditors×Central SOEs	0.116	2.44 **
Credit Market Index	−0.004	−1.13
Government Decentralization Index	0.015	2.20 **
Legal Environment Index	0.029	4.11 ***
Loss	0.007	0.24
Stock Return	−0.074	−1.94 *
S. D. of Residuals	3.885	1.87 *
Log of Client Assets	0.324	31.39 ***
Return on Assets	−0.103	−1.67 *
Total Debt / Total Assets	0.163	2.68 ***
Current Assets / Current Liabilities	−0.001	−0.24
Receivables / Total Assets	0.182	2.84 ***
Inventory / Total Assets	−0.161	−2.42 **
Clients ⩾ 3 Years Old	−0.057	−3.14 ***
Industry Dummies		yes
Year Dummies		yes
Number of Obs.		2263
Adjusted R-Square		0.377
F-statistics		54.98
p-value		<0.001

This table reports the OLS regression results on auditor fee by auditor type and by ownership type. All variable definitions are presented in Table 3. Z-statistics are computed based on Newey-West standard errors with a one-year lag. ***, **, and * represent statistical significance at the 1%, 5%, and 10% levels respectively, two-tailed.

Table 9   Logistic Regression Examining the Choice of Small Local Auditors for the Central Soes Sample

Independent Variables	Dependent Variable: Small Local Auditors		
	Change in Odds (%)	Coeff.	Z-stat
Intercept	n/a	7.852	4.53 ***
Located in Beijing	601.7	1.948	7.37 ***
Credit Market Index	14.8	0.067	1.58
Government Decentralization Index	−13.0	−0.117	−1.60
Legal Environment Index	−45.6	−0.435	−6.36 ***
Growth	3.7	0.062	0.56
Equity Issuance	22.9	0.206	0.96
Log of Client Assets	−24.9	−0.296	−4.02 ***
Return on Assets	−2.7	−0.444	−0.35
Total Debt / Total Assets	6.5	0.462	0.85
Current Assets / Current Liabilities	5.2	0.026	0.79
Receivables / Total Assets	2.6	0.187	0.36
Inventory / Total Assets	9.6	0.950	1.37
Industry Dummies		yes	
Year Dummies		yes	
Number of Obs.		1158	
Pseudo R-Square		0.078	
Chi Square		117.98	
p-value		<0.001	

This table reports the logistic regression results on auditor choice by central SOEs. All variable definitions are presented in Table 3. The change in odds equals $[\exp(s_i \beta_i) - 1]$, where s_i is the sample standard deviation of continuous variable i or 1 for dummy variable i, and β_i is the estimated regression coefficient for variable i. Z-statistics are computed based on Newey-West standard errors with a one-year lag. ***, **, and * represent statistical significance at the 1%, 5%, and 10% levels respectively, two-tailed.

Table 10　OLS Regressions Examining Market-to-Book Assets with

Auditor Type and Ownership Type

Independent Variables	Dependent Variable: Market-to-Book Assets					
	(1)		(2)		(3)	
	Coeff.	t-stat	Coeff.	t-stat	Coeff.	t-stat
Intercept	6.461	48.49 ***	6.485	48.89 ***	6.466	48.80 ***
Small Local Auditors	−0.035	−4.11 ***	−0.027	−3.11 ***	0.034	1.38
Local SOEs			−0.081	−6.00 ***	−0.029	−1.54
Central SOEs			−0.008	−0.48	−0.002	−0.08
Small Local Auditors × Local SOEs					−0.095	−3.59 ***
Small Local Auditors × Central SOEs					−0.012	−0.39
Credit Market Index	0.000	0.06	0.000	−0.14	−0.001	−0.27
Government Decentralization Index	0.001	0.14	0.002	0.45	0.002	0.59
Legal Environment Index	0.016	4.24 ***	0.013	3.30 ***	0.012	3.06 ***
Growth	0.031	3.97 ***	0.028	3.63 ***	0.028	3.58 ***
Equity Issuance	0.038	2.83 ***	0.037	2.78 ***	0.036	2.72 ***
Log of Client Assets	−0.264	−39.20 ***	−0.262	−39.09 ***	−0.262	−39.24 ***
Return on Assets	0.919	5.31 ***	0.886	5.20 ***	0.888	5.26 ***
Total Debt / Total Assets	−0.214	−5.68 ***	−0.190	−5.06 ***	−0.188	−5.06 ***
The Ratio of Tradable Shares	0.763	15.16 ***	0.773	15.39 ***	0.773	15.44 ***
Ownership of the Largest Shareholder	−0.035	−1.22	−0.007	−0.23	−0.003	−0.10
Industry Dummies		yes		yes		yes
Year Dummies		yes		yes		yes
Number of Obs.		5665		5665		5665
Adjusted R-Square		0.508		0.514		0.516

(continued)

Independent Variables	Dependent Variable: Market-to-Book Assets					
	(1)		(2)		(3)	
	Coeff.	t-stat	Coeff.	t-stat	Coeff.	t-stat
F-statistics		155.73		147.78		141.30
p-value		<0.001		<0.001		<0.001

This table reports the OLS regression results on market-to-book assets of non-state firms, local SOEs, and central SOEs that choose small local auditors. All variable definitions are presented in Table 3. T-statistics are computed based on Newey-West standard errors with a one-year lag. ***, ** and * represent statistical significance at the 1%, 5%, and 10% levels respectively, two-tailed.

Table 7, Panel A, presents the ratios of modified audit opinions issued by local versus top-10 or non-local auditors. The panel shows that from 1993 to 2003, the ratio of modified opinions issued by small local auditors was 11%, which was 2% lower than that issued by top-10 or non-local auditors in the overall sample. Table 7, Panel B, which presents audit opinion regressions, shows that the coefficient on Small Local Auditors is significantly negative, with a change in odds of −21.2% for model (1) and −21.0% for model (2), in which Local SOEs and Central SOEs are included to capture any differences in the return-risk structure related to client firms' ownership types.

Turning to the control variables, the performance variables (Loss, Stock Return and Return on Assets), risk variables (S.D. of Residuals and Total Debt / Total Assets), and asset complexity variable Receivables / Total Assets are significantly associated with modified opinions in the predicted directions. In contrast, and inconsistent with prior U.S. evidence but consistent with Chen et al. (2007) for China, the coefficient on Inventory / Total Assets is significantly negative in the audit opinion regressions. This is not surprising, as in China inventory is less associated with audit risk because listed firms prefer to use methods other than inventory manipulation to manage earnings. Moreover, a high level of inventory does not necessarily signal poor performance because firms in regions with weak logistical support need to stock inventory to meet volatile product demand. In summary, the results of this first test are generally consistent with small local auditors being less likely to issue a modified opinion, and lend support to our demand and collusion arguments.

In the second test, we examine whether small local auditors have a different propensity to issue modified opinions to SOE (local or central) versus non-state clients. The collusion argument predicts that small local auditors are less likely to issue modified opinions to local and central SOE than non-state clients because of collusion incentives. That is, the predicted sign of the coefficients on Small Local Auditors×Local SOEs and Small Local Auditors× Central SOEs are negative as indicated in Table 6. The local knowledge and demand arguments do not have any prediction for the difference in modified opinions between the two types of clients. Table 7, Panel A shows that the percentage of modified opinions of small local auditors is 3% smaller than that of top-10 or non-local auditors for local and central SOEs, but small local auditors issue a greater number of modified opinions (by 1%) than top-10 or non-local auditors for non-state firms in the same period. In a more formal test, model (3) of Table 7, Panel B shows that the coefficients on Small Local Auditors×Local SOEs and Small Local Auditors×Central SOEs are negative but only marginally significant (Z-statistics of -1.32 and -1.51, respectively), weakly supporting the collusion argument.① It is important to note that we assume the probability of the existence of a problem that leads to a modified opinion is equal across ownership types. To the extent that such probability is endogenous to ownership types, we have to interpret this audit opinion analysis with caution.

4.3.2　Audit Fees

As reported in Table 6, we run a standard fee regression using annual audit fee data from 2001 to 2003 to test whether the demand argument can

①　Using a sample of firms switching from non-local auditors to local auditors, Chan et al. (2006) document that local auditors are more likely to issue clean opinions to local SOEs.

explain our results.[①] Consistent with our underlying assumption that small local auditors are less capable in detecting accounting errors, we expect the coefficient on Small Local Auditors to be negative because such auditors are unable to charge as high a fee as top-10 or non-local auditors. To test the demand argument, we predict that this fee discount will be smaller for SOEs than non-state firms if the former have weaker demand for top-10 or non-local auditors. This reduction in fee discount would be reflected in positive coefficients on Small Local Auditors×Local SOEs and Small Local Auditors× Central SOEs. We do not have a prediction for the local knowledge or collusion arguments for the interaction terms: small local auditors' information advantage, if any, may result in better service and a fee premium or improved cost efficiency and a fee discount, and bribes can be paid in the form of an audit fee, increasing the fee, or through other channels, decreasing the fee.

As shown in Table 8, the coefficient on Small Local Auditors is significantly negative, while the coefficient on Central SOEs × Small Local Auditors is positive and significant and that on Local SOEs × Small Local Auditors is not significantly different from zero. This suggests that small local auditors generally charge a price discount. Compared with non-state firms, the discount is smaller for central SOEs but not for local SOEs, consistent with our demand argument for central SOEs but not for local SOEs.

The results for three control variables are worth noting. First, the relation between client size (Log of Client Assets) and audit fees may not follow a log-linear relation. We conduct a robustness check (untabulated) by adding the square root of client assets, client assets, and the square and cube of client assets in the audit fee model (using audit fee instead of log of audit fee as the dependent variable); the main results remain the same. The coefficients on the square root of client assets and on client assets are significantly positive and negative, respectively, and the coefficients on the square and the cube of client assets are not statistically significant. Second, the coefficient on

---

① We exclude 14 observations with audit fees larger than three standard deviations from the sample mean in Table 9. The results remain unchanged if we include these observations in the regressions.

Inventory / Total Assets remains significantly negative, further suggesting that it is unlikely to capture audit risk as discussed previously. Third, the age variable (Clients $\leqslant$ 3 Years Old) is positively associated with modified opinions (Table 7), indicating that the post-IPO earnings decline increases firm risk (Aharony et al., 2000). However, the coefficient on the age variable is negatively associated with audit fees. This indicates that for older firms, the decline in audit fees due to longer tenure outweighs any possible fee premium for the decline in performance.

4.3.3 Auditor Choice by Central SOEs

Next, we use the auditor choice decisions of central SOEs to further examine whether the hiring of small local auditors is motivated by collusion incentives. More specifically, we investigate whether the likelihood of central SOEs to hire small local auditors is greater for firms headquartered in Beijing than for those headquartered in other provinces. By focusing on one ownership type (central SOEs) and comparing auditor choice decisions between central SOEs headquartered in Beijing and those headquartered in other regions, the analysis is not confounded by a possible endogenous relation between various ownership types and auditor choice. Also, this test allows us to isolate the collusion argument because central SOEs' demand for audit service and small local auditors' knowledge of local markets and regulatory environments are presumably quite similar across regions. In case the local knowledge advantage is different between Beijing and other regions, we include the three institutional indexes in the regression to control for this potential variation. We predict that relative to local auditors in other regions, the central government can exert more direct influence on local auditors in Beijing because of their location and the central government's market power through supplying all the major clients of local auditors in the capital city. If we find that the choice of small local auditors is significantly more prevalent in Beijing than in other regions, we could attribute the result to the higher degree of the central government's influence on small local auditors in Beijing than on small local auditors in other regions.

Using a sub-sample of central SOEs, we repeat the auditor choice regression of model (5) in Table 4, Panel B by adding the dummy variable Located in Beijing, which equals 1 when the central SOE is headquartered in Beijing and 0 otherwise. Our collusion argument predicts that the coefficient on Located in Beijing is positive and statistically significant. The results, presented in Table 9, show that the coefficient on Located in Beijing is significantly positive, which suggests that the likelihood with which central SOEs headquartered in Beijing hire small local auditors is larger than that of central SOEs in other regions. This result also indicates that decision of central SOEs to hire small local auditors is likely to be explained by the collusion story.

4.3.4　Valuation Effects of Choosing Small Local Auditors

We further test the collusion story by analyzing the firm valuation effects of auditor choice. If the gap in the auditor choice between SOEs and non-state firms is driven by the local knowledge argument or the demand argument rather than the collusion argument, then the hiring of small local auditors by SOEs should not cause price discounts by investors. On the other hand, if the auditor choice is motivated by collusion objectives, we expect to observe a price discount for SOEs when they hire small local auditors.

We regress the client firm's Market-to-Book Assets on Small Local Auditors (auditor type), Local SOEs and Central SOEs (control ownership type), the interaction terms between auditor type and ownership type, Growth, Equity Issuance, the three institutional indexes, and a set of other control variables. In our calculation of Market-to-Book Assets, as defined in Table 3, we use book value to proxy for the market price of non-tradable shares. To the extent that book value fails to capture the true market value of these shares, we include Ratio of Tradable Shares as an additional explanatory variable in the regression. We find that the coefficient is significantly positive, indicating that these non-tradable shares are likely to have a market price that is higher than book value. As summarized in Table 6, the collusion argument predicts the coefficients on Local SOEs × Small Local Auditors and Central SOEs × Small Local Auditors to be negative and statistically significant. On the other hand, the demand argument or local knowledge argument predicts that the two coefficients are zero or significantly positive.

The results of models (1) and (2) in Table 10 show that the coefficient on Small Local Auditors is negative and statistically significant, suggesting that investors discount the share prices of small local auditors' clients. Consistent with the collusion argument, we find that compared with non-state firms, local SOEs are subject to a larger price discount for hiring small local auditors as indicated by the significantly negative coefficient on Small Local Auditors× Local SOEs in model (3).[1] However, we do not find that central SOEs' price discount is larger than that of non-state firms when they hire small local auditors. This suggests that central SOEs' auditor choice is consistent with the demand argument or local knowledge argument.

Note that in addition to the collusion story, one possible explanation for local SOEs' larger price discount is that high growth local SOEs have large market-to-book assets and are more likely to hire large and/or non-local auditors for equity issuance. We include Growth and Equity Issuance in the regression to control for this potential endogeneity problem. Also, the auditor choice results in Tables 4 and 5 do not show that high growth and equity-issuing firms are more likely to hire top-10 or non-local auditors in China.[2] To the extent that this spurious effect is not properly controlled for in the model, we have to take caution in drawing conclusions from the results.

4.3.5　Summary of Results for the Three Arguments

As suggested in Table 6, which summarizes our tests of the three arguments for our hypotheses, the results above are consistent with our three arguments and these arguments are not mutually exclusive in explaining Hypotheses 1 and 2. The evidence corresponding to the audit opinion analysis is generally consistent with the demand argument, and it is also weakly supportive of the collusion argument. The evidence for the valuation effects

---

[1]　We exclude 86 observations with a market-to-book ratio larger than three standard deviations from the sample mean in Table 10. The results remain unchanged if we include these observations in the regressions.

[2]　We use the average three-year-ahead Growth and Equity Issuance in the model and the results remain identical. We also partition the sample into high and low growth based on sample median sales growth, and into firms with and without equity issuance based on the variable Equity Issuance, and re-run the regressions. The interaction term Small Local Auditors× Local SOEs remains negative and statistically significant in both sub-samples using either partitioning variable.

regressions is consistent with the collusion argument for local SOEs, while for central SOEs the results are inconsistent with the collusion argument but are consistent with the demand and local knowledge arguments. The fee results corresponding to central SOEs support the demand argument. However, in test for central SOEs' auditor choice, the evidence is consistent with collusion incentives.

In summary, the results support the view that the three arguments discussed in Section 2 help explain Chinese SOEs' auditor choice pattern. Further, results from the tests above provide suggestive evidence that local SOEs' auditor choice decisions are likely driven primarily by collusion incentives, while central SOEs' motivations are likely driven by multiple factors. Perhaps local governments have more direct political influence than the central government to coerce small local auditors to acquiesce. Further research should explore in greater depth how local and central SOEs' incentives and political influence on small local auditors affect their choices of auditors in China.

4.3.6　Supply-Side Arguments for Chinese Firms' Auditor Choice

We briefly note that our evidence is inconsistent with two supply-side arguments for Chinese firms' auditors' choice. First, Top-10 or non-local auditors may face capacity constraints that prevent them from serving local SOE clients. However, if the capacity constraint argument were to hold, Top-10 or non-local auditors would be more likely to first give up non-state clients, which on average are smaller in size than local SOEs (Table 4, Panel A). In addition, our auditor switches regression results in Table 5 also cast doubt on the capacity constraint story, which does not explain why the difference in likelihood of hiring small local auditors between non-state firms and local SOEs changes with the region's institutional environment.

A second supply-side argument suggests that Top-10 or non-local auditors may choose not to supply audit services to SOEs by charging them significant fee premiums relative to non-state firm clients. This argument predicts the coefficients on Small Local Auditors × Local SOEs and Small Local Auditors × Central SOEs to be negative in Table 8. However, the results do not support this prediction.

5. Conclusions

This paper analyzes how political and economic institutions affect the choice of auditors in China. Using a sample of firms covering the period from 1993 to 2003, we find that local SOEs are more likely than non-state firms to hire small local auditors. In addition to local SOEs, we find that central SOEs are also more likely than non-state firms to hire small local auditors in regions where institutions are less developed, but this tendency of local and central SOEs to hire small local auditors is significantly attenuated in regions with more developed institutions.

Additional analyses show that local and central SOEs' tendency to hire small local auditors is consistent with three arguments. The first argument is that local and central SOEs have less demand for top-10 or non-local auditors due to preferential access to capital or government bailouts in times of financial distress. Local and central SOEs' likelihood to hire small local auditors can also be explained by collusion incentives or local auditors' superior local knowledge.

Interpretation of our results is subject to a few important caveats. First, client firms' ownership types and auditor choice are likely to be endogenously determined by institutional factors. Therefore, we cannot infer causality from our analyses in Table 4. Second, while the ownership change sample can potentially alleviate the endogeneity problem, switches in ownership control can also be endogenously determined, which, again, would affect inferences from our analysis. Third, to the extent that the choice of small local auditors by local or central SOEs is endogenously related to audit opinions, audit fees, and market-to-book assets, care must be taken in making inferences in our additional analyses.

In spite of the above limitations, our paper represents a first step toward understanding the relation between political and economic institutions and the derived demand for auditors in a transition economy such as China. Future research can focus on gaining better understanding of government owners' as well as private owners' incentives in choosing auditors and of how political and economic institutions affect their respective incentives.

Appendix 1

Credit market index，government decentralization index，legal environment index，and the number of observations for each region

Regions	Credit Market Index	Government Decentralization Index	Legal Environment Index	Number of Observations （Total：5759）
ANHUI	5.24	7.43	5.32	86
BEIJING	3.85	6.40	7.97	318
CHONGQING	6.33	7.61	3.83	136
FUJIAN	3.74	7.12	6.32	260
GANSU	4.70	5.94	3.98	69
GUANGDONG	6.37	7.99	7.29	697
GUANGXI	3.46	7.89	4.92	70
GUIZHOU	4.89	5.43	4.36	47
HAINAN	5.25	6.02	6.33	111
HEBEI	7.20	7.13	5.15	97
HENAN	5.80	5.54	4.93	111
HEILONGJIANG	1.89	3.60	5.34	154
HUBEI	4.21	5.11	5.05	257
HUNAN	5.90	5.73	2.62	173
INNER MONGOLIA	3.42	3.27	4.93	66
JILIN	5.37	5.70	5.81	195
JIANGSU	7.67	8.12	6.29	305
JIANGXI	4.69	6.15	4.78	94
LIAONING	6.16	6.14	5.53	246
NINGXIA	4.36	3.79	5.16	40
QINGHAI	0.35	3.04	4.69	32

(continued)

Regions	Credit Market Index	Government Decentralization Index	Legal Environment Index	Number of Observations (Total: 5759)
SHAANXI	5.88	5.30	3.21	154
SHANDONG	7.74	7.38	5.63	266
SHANXI	1.08	4.54	5.53	72
SHANGHAI	7.94	7.49	6.98	730
SICHUAN	0.70	7.43	4.69	382
TIANJIN	5.34	6.05	6.96	88
XINJIANG	0.90	3.16	4.10	106
YUNNAN	4.75	6.56	3.87	89
ZHEJIANG	7.68	8.37	6.24	308

This table reports the credit market index, government decentralization index, and legal environment index. The credit market development index measures the percentage of deposits taken by non-state financial institutions and the percentage of short-term loans to the non-state sector. The government decentralization index is constructed based on the following information: ① the provincial government's spending as a percentage of provincial GDP; ② the tax rates in the province; ③ the time spent by entrepreneurs in dealing with the bureaucracy; and ④ the time needed for firm registration and to obtain various licenses. The legal environment index has the following components: ① the number of lawyers as a percentage of the provincial population; ② the efficiency of local courts (percentage of lawsuits pursued by the courts); and ③ protection of property rights. These three institutional indexes are obtained from the National Economic Research Institute (NERI) Index of Marketization of China's provinces in 2000 to measure the quality of market-supporting institutions at the provincial level. The NERI Index project was sponsored by the National Economic Research Institute and the China Reform Foundation and conducted by Fan and Wang (2003). The NERI indices capture the progress of the institutional transition in China's 30 provinces (excluding Tibet, due to lack of data). Appraisals of the regional institutions are made along several dimensions, namely, the relationship between the government and the market, the development of the non-state sector, the development of the factor markets, the development of the product markets, and the development of market intermediaries and the legal environment.

Appendix 2

Robustness Checks

The results for Hypotheses 1 and 2 continue to hold qualitatively when we perform the following robustness checks. First, we use alternative definitions of large auditors, namely, top-10 auditors based on number of clients and Big-4 international or top-10 domestic auditors based on total assets audited or number of clients. Second, we define local auditors as auditors in the same region in which the firm is located or the ultimate owner is located. This alternate definition alleviates the concern that ultimate owners may tend to collude with auditors in their region. We also use alternative definitions for local auditors to determine whether auditor mergers affect our results. In addition to requiring the client's registry region to be the same as that of its auditor, we add either one of these criteria: ① the auditor has more than 50% of total client assets audited in its registry region, or ② the auditor has more than 50% of the total number of clients audited in its registry region. Third, we delete firms that are not under the effective control of their largest shareholders (state or non-state) holding less than 10% (or 20% or 30%) of the shares. Fourth, we sequentially exclude the top or bottom one to five provinces for each of the three indexes to check if the results are driven by provinces with an extreme index value. Fifth, we re-run our tests by excluding two provincial level regions, Jiangxi and Tianjin, that do not have non-state firms. Sixth, to remove any possible initial public offering effect, we exclude firms that had been listed for less than one year. Seventh, we winsorize all financial variables at the top and bottom 1% or 2%. Next, we use standard error clustering by year together with Newey-West with a one-year lag to control for cross-correlation and autocorrelation of residuals in the regressions. Ninth, we re-run the tests by using the standard Fama-Macbeth (annual) regressions.

In addition, we try to disentangle small versus top-10 and local vs. non-local effects by separately running the auditor choice regressions using auditor size (top-10 versus other auditors) and locality (local versus non-local auditors) as dependent variables. In the auditor locality regression, we exclude the few regions (Shanghai, Beijing, and Guangdong from 1993 to 2003; Sichuan from 1994 to 1998; Zhejiang from 1998 to 2003; and Liaoning in 1993) that have top-10 auditors to avoid the confounding effect that client firms are choosing a local top-10 auditor because of its size or reputation, not its locality. The main results remain unchanged. We provide further analysis for the auditor size regression by dividing auditor type into three groups, namely, Big-4 international, top-10 non-Big-4 international, and all others, and the results show that local SOEs are most (least) likely to choose non-Big-4 international auditors (Big-4 international auditors). Finally, some of the Pearson correlations among the independent variables such as the three institutional indexes ranging from 0.341 to 0.596 are high. However, the variance inflation factors described in Belsley et al. (1980) for the test and control variables in our regressions indicate that there is no serious multicollinearity problem in our regressions.

References

曹海丽，黄山. 德勤联姻北京天健[J]. 财经，2005，(007)：40.

《公开发行证券的公司信息披露编报规则》第 14 号——非标准无保留审计意见及其涉及事项的处理[J]. 财会通讯，2002(01)：64.

胡舒立，张继伟. 周小川谈利率[J]. 财经，2004，(022)：32 – 41.

朱红军，夏立军，陈信元. 转型经济中审计市场的需求特征研究[J]. 审计研究，2004，(5)：53 – 62.

Aharony J，Lee J，Wong T J. Financial packaging of IPO firms in China[J]. Journal of accounting research，2000，38(1)：103 – 126.

Bae，K H，Stulz R M，Tan H P. Do local analysts know more? A cross-country study of the performance of local analysts and foreign analysts[J]. Journal of financial economics，2008，88(3)：581 – 606.

Ball R，Kothari S P，Robin A. The effect of international institutional factors on properties of accounting earnings[J]. Journal of accounting and economics，1999，30(2)：1 – 51.

Ball R，Robin A，Wu J S. Incentives versus standards：properties of accounting income in four East Asian countries[J]. Journal of accounting and economics，2004，36(1 – 3)：235 – 270.

Belsley D A，Kuh E，Welsch R E. Regression diagnostics[M]. New York：Wiley，1980.

Bushman R M，Piotroski J D，Smith A J. What determines corporate transparency? [J]. Journal of accounting research，2004，42(2)：207 – 252.

Bushman R M，Smith A J. Financial accounting information and corporate governance [J]. Communication of finance and accounting，2007，32(1)：237 – 333.

Asthana S C，Sami H，Ye Z. Auditor failure and market reactions：evidence from China [J]. International journal of accounting，auditing and performance evaluation，2009，5(4)：408 – 441.

Chan K H，Lin K Z，Mo L L. A political-economic analysis of auditor reporting and auditor switches[J]. Review of accounting studies，2006，11(1)：21 – 48.

Che J H，Qian Y Y. Institutional environment，community government，and corporate governance：understanding China's township-village enterprises[J]. The journal of law，economics，& organization，1998，14(1)：1 – 23.

Chen C J P，Su X J，Zhao R. An emerging market's reaction to initial modified audit opinions：evidence from the Shanghai Stock Exchange [J]. Contemporary accounting research，2000，17(3)：429 – 455.

Chen C J P，Chen S M，Su X J. Profitability regulation，Earnings management，and modified audit opinions：evidence from China[J]. Auditing：a journal of practice & theory，2001，20(2)：9 – 30.

Chen C J P，Su X J，Wu X. Market competitiveness and Big 5 pricing：evidence from China's binary market[J]. International journal of accounting，2007，42(1)：1 – 24.

Chen C W，Yuan H Q. Earnings management and capital resource allocation：evidence from China's accounting-based regulation of rights issues[J]. Accounting review，2004，79(3)：645 – 665.

Chun，Wang Y J. The nature of the township-village enterprise [J]. Journal of comparative economics，1994，19(3)：434 – 452.

Choi J H, Wong T J. Auditors' governance functions and legal environments: an international investigation[J]. Contemporary accounting research, 2010, 24(1):13 – 46.

Clarke D. The creation of a legal structure for market institutions in China[M]// McMillan J, Naughton B. Reforming Asian socialism: the growth of market institutions. Ann Arbor: University of Michigan Press, 1996.

Craswell A T, Francis J R, Taylor S L. Auditor brand name reputations and industry specializations[J]. Journal of accounting and economics, 1995, 20(3): 297 – 322.

Craswell A, Stokes D J, Laughton J. Auditor independence and fee dependence[J]. Journal of accounting and economics, 2002, 33(2): 253 – 275.

Covrig V M, Defond M L, Hung M. Home bias, foreign mutual fund holdings, and the voluntary adoption of international accounting standards[J]. Journal of accounting research, 2007, 45(1): 41 – 70.

DeAngelo L E. Auditor size and audit quality[J]. Journal of accounting and economics, 1981, 3(3): 183 – 199.

DeFond M L. The association between changes in client firm agency costs and auditor switching[J]. Auditing, 1992, 11(1): 16 – 31.

DeFond Mark L, Wong T J, Li S H. The impact of improved auditor independence on audit market concentration in China[J]. Journal of accounting and economics, 1999, 28(3): 269 – 305.

Dye R A. Auditing standards, legal liability, and auditor wealth[J]. Journal of political economy, 1993, 101(5): 887 – 914.

Faccio M. Politically connected firms[J]. American economic review, 2006, 96(1): 369 – 386.

Fan G, Wang X L. China marketization index: report on the relative progress of marketization in various regions in 2001[M]. Beijing: Economic Science Press, 2003.

Fan J P H, Wong T J. Corporate ownership structure and the informativeness of accounting earnings in East Asia[J]. Journal of accounting and economics, 2002, 33(3): 401 – 425.

Fan J P H, Wong T J, Zhang T. Organizational structure as a decentralization device: evidence from corporate pyramids[R]. Working paper, 2007a.

Fan J P H, Wong T J, Zhang T. Politically connected CEOs, corporate governance, and post-IPO performance of China's newly partially privatized firms[J]. Journal of financial economics, 2007b, 84(2): 330 – 357.

Fisman R. Estimating the value of political connections[J]. American economic review, 2001, 91(4): 1095 – 1102.

Francis J R, Khurana I K, Pereira R. The role of accounting and auditing in corporate governance and the development of financial markets around the world[J]. Asia-Pacific journal of accounting & economics,2003,10(1):1 - 30.

Francis J R,Wilson E R. Auditor changes:a joint test of theories relating to agency costs and auditor differentiation[J]. Accounting review,1988,63(4):663 - 682.

Hay J R,Shleifer A. Private enforcement of public laws:a theory of legal reform[J]. The American economic review,1998,88(2):398 - 403.

Huang Y S. Inflation and investment controls in China[M]. Cambridge:Cambridge University Press,1996.

Hung M. Accounting standards and value relevance of financial statements:an international analysis[J]. Journal of accounting and economics,2000,30(3):401 - 420.

Jian M,Wong T J. Earnings management and tunneling through related party transactions:evidence from Chinese corporate groups[D]. Hong Kong:Hong Kong University of Science and Technology,2003.

Jin H H,Qian Y Y. Public versus private ownership of firms:evidence from rural China [J]. The quarterly journal of economics,1998,113(3):773 - 808.

Jin H H,Qian Y Y,Weingast B R. Regional decentralization and fiscal incentives: federalism,Chinese style[J]. Journal of public economics,2005,89(9 - 10):1719 - 1742.

Johnson S,Mitton T. Cronyism and capital controls:evidence from Malaysia[J]. Journal of financial economics,2003,67(2):351 - 382.

Johnson S,McMillan J,Woodruff C. Property rights and finance[J]. American economic review,2002,92(5):1335 - 1356.

Johnson S,McMillan J,Woodruff C. Courts and relational contracts[J]. Journal of law, economics,and organization,2002,18(1):221 - 277.

Kang J K. Why is there a home bias? An analysis of foreign portfolio equity ownership in Japan[J]. Journal of financial economics,1997,46(1):3 - 28.

Kornai J. The evolution of financial discipline under the postsocialist system[J]. Kyklos, 1993,46(3):315 - 336.

La Porta R,Lopez-de-Silanes F,Shleifer A. Corporate ownership around the world[J]. The journal of finance,1999,54(2):471 - 517.

La Porta R,Lopez-de-Silanes F,Shleifer A,et al. The quality of government[J]. The journal of law,economics,and organization,1999,15(1):222 - 279.

Leuz C,Oberholzer-Gee F. Political relationships,global financing,and corporate transparency:evidence from Indonesia[J]. Journal of financial economics,2006,81(2): 411 - 439.

Leuz C,Nanda D,Wysocki P D. Earnings management and investor protection:an international comparison[J]. Journal of financial economics, 2003, 69(3): 505 – 527.

Li D D. A theory of ambiguous property rights in transition economies: the case of the Chinese non-state sector[J]. Journal of comparative economics, 1996, 23(1): 1 – 19.

Li H, Meng L, Zhang J. Why do entrepreneurs enter politics? Evidence from China[J]. Economic inquiry, 2006, 44(3): 559 – 578.

Li H, Zhou L A. Political turnover and economic performance: the incentive role of personnel control in China[J]. Journal of public economics, 2005, 89(9 – 10): 1743 – 1762.

Lin Y F, Cai F, Li Z. The China miracle: development strategy and economic reform [M]. Hong Kong: Chinese University Press, 1996.

McMillan J. Markets in transition[M]//Kreps D M, Wallis K F. Advances in economics and econometrics. Cambridge: Cambridge University Press, 1997.

Palmrose Z. The demand for quality-differentiated audit services in an agency-cost setting: an empirical investigation[C]. Auditing Research Symposium. University of Illinois Urbana Champaign, 1984, 229: 252.

Petersen M A. Estimating standard errors in finance panel data sets: comparing approaches[J]. The review of financial studies, 2009, 22(1): 435 – 480.

Qian Y Y. A theory of shortage in socialist economies based on the "Soft Budget Constraint"[J]. The American economic review, 1994, 84(1): 145 – 156.

Qian Y Y. Reforming corporate governance and finance in China[M]//Aoki M, Kim H K. Corporate governance in transition economies: insider control and the role of banks. Washington DC: The World Bank Press, 1995.

Qian Y Y, Weingast B R. Federalism as a commitment to reserving market incentives[J]. Journal of economic perspectives, 1997, 11(4): 83 – 92.

Qian Y Y, Xu C G. Why China's economic reforms differ: the M-form hierarchy and entry/expansion of the non-state sector[J]. Economics of transition, 1993, 1(2): 135 – 170.

Rajan R G, Zingales L. Financial dependence and growth[J]. The American economic review, 1998, 88(3): 559 – 586.

Reynolds J K, Francis J R. Does size matter? The influence of large clients on office-level auditor reporting decisions[J]. Journal of accounting and economics, 2000, 30(3): 375 – 400.

Shleifer A. State versus private ownership[J]. Journal of economic perspectives, 1998, 12 (4): 133 – 150.

Shleifer A, Vishny R W. A survey of corporate governance[J]. The journal of finance, 1997, 52(2): 737 – 783.

Shleifer A, Vishny R W. Politicians and firms[J]. The quarterly journal of economics, 1994, 109(4): 995 – 1025.

Simunic D A，Stein M T. Product differentiation in auditing：auditor choice in the market for unseasoned new issues［R］. Vancouver：The Canadian Certified General Accountants' Research Foundation，1987.

Tang Y W. Issues in the development of the accounting profession in China［J］. China accounting and finance review，1999，1(1)：21 - 36.

Willenborg M. Empirical analysis of the economic demand for auditing in the initial public offerings market［J］. Journal of accounting research，1999，37(1)：225 - 238.

Wurgler J. Financial markets and the allocation of capital［J］. Journal of financial economics，2000，58(1 - 2)：187 - 214.

Zhong H. Analysis of the answers to survey questions by Chinese CPAs［J］. CPA News，1998，1：59 - 64.

▶This study was funded by grants from the Research Grants Council of the Hong Kong SAR Government （HKUST 6024/00H），and the National Natural Science Foundation of China （No. 70572105，70772101）. We appreciate helpful comments from Jim Brickley，Xinyuan Chen，Mark DeFond （the referee），Joseph Fan，Mingyi Hung，Hongbin Li，Yue Li，Jing Liu，Gordon Richardson，Ann Vantraelen，Joanna Wu，Jason Xiao，Amy Zhang，Tianyu Zhang，Weiguo Zhang，Jerry Zimmerman （the editor），and workshop participants at the Chinese University of Hong Kong （CUHK），University of Rochester，University of Southern California，the 2005 AAA International Symposium on Auditing Research，and the Panel Discussion titled "Corporate Governance，Accounting Research for Asia and China" at the 2005 American Accounting Association Annual Meeting，the 2006 China Research Conference at CUHK，the 2007 European Accounting Association Annual Congress，and the Cheung Kong Graduate School of Business Summer Conference 2007. Mochou Li and Hongjun Zhu's help in our data collection is greatly appreciated.

政企纽带与跨省投资
——来自中国上市公司的经验证据[*]

内容提要：本文运用中国上市公司数据研究了高管（董事长或总经理）的政府任职背景这一政企纽带（political connection）对企业异地投资的影响。我们发现企业高管拥有的政企纽带能够帮助企业到注册地以外的其他省份去开设下属企业（子公司、联营企业或分公司），但这种影响出现的条件是政企纽带达到较高的级别（厅局级以上），而低级别的政企纽带不起作用，并且这种影响主要存在于地方政府控制的公司中。同时，我们发现在非政府控制的公司中，高管在中央政府部门的任职经历也有助于企业跨省投资。而在中央政府控制的公司中，高管的政企纽带对异地投资没有显著影响。

关　键　词：政企纽带；异地投资；市场分割；经济增长

一、引言

随着经济发展，统一的国内市场和规模经济变得越来越重要，但国家之间和地区之间的行政边界却往往成为统一市场的障碍。市场分割有碍于公平竞争，降低资源配置效率。对中国这样一个快速成长的经济体而言，市场分割正逐渐成为制约规模经济效应的重要因素，不利于经济的持续增长。

在既有文献中，中国被当作一个国内市场零碎分割的经济体（例如 Young，2000；Poncet，2002）。但是，既有文献关注的焦点是商品市场，鲜有研究关注中国

＊ 本文选自：夏立军、陆铭、余为政：政企纽带与跨省投资——来自中国上市公司的经验证据，《管理世界》，2011 年第 7 期，第 128－140 页。

的资本市场是否同样存在地区间的分割。同时,既有文献也未研究:是所有的企业都在面临市场分割的障碍,还是部分企业拥有突破市场分割的特殊资源?研究这些问题对于理解中国市场分割的形成以及未来市场整合的进程非常重要。本文将以中国企业的跨省投资行为作为研究对象,考察高管的政企纽带对企业跨省投资的影响。我们预期,如果市场分割是由地方政府的保护行为这类制度因素导致的,那么企业与政府之间的纽带就可以帮助企业突破省际的行政边界,进行异地投资。相反,如果市场分割只是由于交通成本、通信技术这样的自然地理或技术因素所致,那么政企纽带与异地投资之间就应该没有联系。

具体来说,本文运用 1997 年至 2003 年首次发行股票的中国上市公司(即 IPO 公司)的数据研究了企业高管(董事长或总经理)的政府任职背景对企业跨越省界进行异地投资的影响。我们发现企业高管拥有的政企纽带能够帮助企业到其他省份去开设下属企业(子公司、联营企业或分公司),但这种影响出现的条件是政企纽带达到较高的级别(厅局级以上),而较低级别的政企纽带不起作用,并且这种影响主要存在于地方政府控制的公司中。同时,我们发现在非政府控制的公司中,高管在中央政府部门的任职经历也有助于企业异地投资。而在中央政府控制的公司中,高管的政企纽带对异地投资没有显著影响。

基于这些研究发现,我们可以进行这样的推断:中国地区之间的市场分割的确在一定程度上是政府行为所致。由于市场分割所形成的经济租金一部分被那些具有政企纽带的企业所获得,中国的市场经济体制在制造企业间的投资机会仍然不均等。因此,通过制度构建来规范地方政府行为,对于促进市场整合和公平竞争是至关重要的。本文不仅对研究中国企业政治联系的后果的相关文献有所发展,更重要的是从跨地区投资这一角度揭示了中国资本市场的地区间分割这一重要问题。而以往文献几乎没有研究资本市场的地区间分割,也少有研究揭示出市场分割给企业带来的投资机会不平等。

下文的结构安排如下:第二部分对相关文献进行评述;第三部分结合中国的制度背景对研究问题进行理论分析,并提出研究假说;第四部分是研究方法设计,包括样本选择和数据来源、检验模型和变量设定等;第五部分是实证结果和解释;第六部分是结论和政策含义。

二、文献评述

自 Young(2000)的研究以来,大量文献研究了中国国内市场地区分割的演变趋势、原因及后果。虽然有文献认为中国国内市场正在走向整合（Naughton，2000；桂琦寒等，2006），但中国国内市场仍然存在着较为严重的地区分割却是不争的共识（Poncet，2002；Naughton，2000；Xu，2002；白重恩等，2004；Fan and Wei，2006；桂琦寒等，2006；陆铭、陈钊，2006）。市场分割不利于竞争，对本地企业则形成了"市场力量"和相应的租金，受保护的更多是利税率高的企业，或者是国有企业（白重恩等，2004）。在失业率高或政府干预强的地区，市场分割现象也更为严重（Poncet，2005）。林毅夫、刘培林（2004）认为，重工业优先发展的赶超战略背离了中国地方经济的比较优势，改革以来，在分权式改革之下，地方政府当然有动力去保护那些没有市场竞争力的企业。中国的经济开放过程对市场分割而言是一把双刃剑，一方面，开放有利于市场竞争，促进市场整合（Li，Qiu，and Sun，2003），另一方面，在经济更为开放的地区，当地越是可能在参与国际市场的过程中放弃国内市场，特别是在经济开放的早期，地方政府更是可能一边加入国际市场，一边放弃国内市场（陈敏等，2007）。

在发达国家内部，通常不存在制度层面的市场分割，甚至在欧盟的不同国家之间，统一市场的努力都一直没有被中断过。与此形成对照的是，在中国，来自地方政府的保护主义政策所造成的市场分割始终是不可忽视的。虽然站在地方本位的角度，市场分割可能保护了本地企业，从而对本地经济增长有利，但总体来说，整个中国却可能因为市场分割而陷于"囚徒困境"的局面，失去经济增长的规模经济（陆铭、陈钊，2009）。具体来说，国内市场分割对分工、专业化及经济发展均有负面影响（白重恩等，2004；Poncet，2003；郑毓盛、李崇高，2003；刘培林，2005）。

值得注意的是，以往文献多使用地区层面的数据考察商品市场，却很少研究要素市场的分割。相比之下，本文将使用企业层面的数据，考察企业的跨省投资行为，实际上就是在研究资本市场是否存在地区分割。从经济理论来说，要素市场的分割是比商品市场分割更为根本的问题。如果要素市场是分割而不是完全竞争的，那么要素的配置效率必然被扭曲，商品市场的竞争也难以形成。在企业投资时，如果异地市场是完全自由进入的，或者市场分割仅仅是因为交通成本、通信技术这样的自然地理或技术因素所致，那么企业是否拥有政企纽带就应该不影响企业的异地投资行为，而且此类市场分割对每个市场活动参与者是没有歧视的。但是，如果市场分割是由地方政府的保护主义政策所造成的，那么这实际上是一种"设租"行为，它减少了本地企业所面临的竞争，这时企业所拥有的政企纽带就可能成为企业获取租金的渠道。

　　企业的政企纽带(或政治联系)的形成原因及经济后果也是近年来的研究热点,并且已经形成了相当丰富的文献。多数文献发现,具有政企纽带的企业获得了"租金",这些租金包括公司价值的提升(Fisman,2001;Faccio and Parsley,2009)、更多的政府补贴和救助(Johnson and Mitton,2003;Faccio,Masulis and Mcconnell,2006)、更多的贷款和更优厚的贷款条件(Faccio,2006;Khwaja and Mian,2005;Charumilind,Kali,and Wiwattanakantang,2006;Claessens,Feijen,and Laeven,2008;Fan,Rui,and Zhao,2008;余明桂、潘红波,2008)、更低的税率(Faccio,2006;Adhikari,Derashid,and Zhang,2006;吴文锋、吴冲锋、芮萌,2009)、更多的市场份额和政府采购合同(Faccio,2006;Goldman,Rocholl and So,2013)、更高的产品价格(Cingano and Pinotti,2009)和更多的跨地区产品销售(巫景飞等,2008;Lu,2008)、更高的产业进入能力(胡旭阳,2006;胡旭阳、史晋川,2008;Fan et al.,2009;罗党论、刘晓龙,2009;张敏、黄继承,2009)、更弱的监管约束和法律制裁(Correia,2012;陈信元等,2009)。

　　为了获得并掩盖"租金",具有政企纽带的企业相对其他企业而言,会计信息更不透明(Riahi-Belkaoui,2004;Wang,Wong,and Xia,2008;Chaney,Faccio,and Parsley,2009;Ramanna and Roychowdhury,2009)。Faccio(2006)的跨国研究还发现,当公司运营在一个高度腐败、产权保护弱、政府干预强或者非民主政府的国家中时,政企纽带给企业带来的融资、税收及市场力量上的利益更为明显。此外,一些文献也发现了政企纽带给企业带来的负面影响,例如 Fan,Wong,and Zhang(2007)对中国 790 家 IPO 公司的研究发现,政府更有能力通过那些有政府任职背景的 CEO 来干预企业,进而损害了这些企业的长期绩效。Hung,Wong,and Zhang(2008)对中国部分民营化的国有企业在海外上市情况的研究发现,强有力的政企纽带削弱了海外上市对企业投资效率及上市后股票绩效的正面影响。从现有文献来看,关于政企纽带如何影响企业投资行为——尤其是跨地区投资行为——之类的研究还很少,因此,本文也对研究政企纽带的文献有所发展。

三、理论分析和研究假说

　　根据以往的文献,在中国国内市场上,企业跨省经营行为(涉及产品市场、要素市场、投融资市场或劳动力市场等)可能会受到种种限制。由于现代交通和通信技术的发展,自然地理或技术因素对企业跨省经营行为的限制变得越来越小,而制度性因素则变得相对更为重要。尤其是,中国地方官员晋升是基于相对绩效考核的锦标赛体制(Li and Zhou，2005；周黎安，2004、2007)，这可能会强化地方政府的地区分割行为，以追求本地的短期经济增长目标(王永钦等，2007)。

从本文关心的企业跨省投资行为来看，制度性因素同样会导致跨省投资上的地区分割。地方政府有激励出于 GDP、税收、就业、产业发展等方面的原因，限制本地的企业进行跨省投资，或限制外地的企业来本地投资。一方面，注册于 A 省的企业如果在 B 省投资设立下属企业，其税收、GDP、就业通常归属到下属企业的属地，即 B 省。因此，出于保护本省的利益，A 省的政府不可能希望本省企业到省外投资设立下属企业。我们在调研中发现过这样的案例，地方政府有能力限制本地企业到外地投资，比如说，平时企业或多或少地存在偷税漏税的现象，当政府获知企业有异地投资的计划时，便将企业负责人找来，威胁说要对企业的税收状况进行核查。

另一方面，从 B 省来说，虽然接受外省企业到本省投资设立下属企业能够带来一定的税收、GDP、就业方面的利益，却可能有助于外省的企业扩张和产业发展，甚至挤出本地企业原本可以带来的 GDP、税收、就业和市场份额，因此 B 省的政府可能同样不希望接受外省企业到本省进行投资。尤其是，中国地方政府官员的政绩考核是一种基于相对绩效表现的锦标赛体制(周黎安，2004、2007；王永钦等，2007)，地方官员关注的是当地经济发展速度与其他地区经济发展速度的相对位置。如果来自 A 省的投资对 B 省经济发展的促进程度小于其对 A 省经济发展的促进程度，则可能降低 B 省相对 A 省的经济发展排位，因而 B 省可能不愿意接受这样的投资。① 换言之，企业进行跨省投资设立下属企业，不仅可能面临来自本省政府部门的限制，也可能面临投资目标所在地政府的限制。现实中，这样的例子也有很多。例如，2009 年开始推行的十大产业调整振兴计划已经明确提出了一些产业重组目标，但"对于汽车、钢铁、造船等各地政府的支柱产业而言，任一企业被重组、被并购，当地政府都不可能心甘情愿，因为这涉及许多方面的利益，包括就业，包括税收，包括 GDP……地方政府是否支持重组，目前成为各行业重组是否能够顺利开展的关键。"②

① 虽然在现实中各地都将招商引资作为一个重要的政治和经济目标对待，但招商引资时并非不考虑其对本省和对外省经济发展的相对影响。如果一项引资对外省经济的贡献超过对本省经济的贡献，则有可能损害本省经济相对外省经济发展速度的相对位置，引资的积极性可能下降。此外，各地政府实际上更加看重的是引进港澳台和外国资本，这种招商引资既能发展本省经济，又不增进外省经济发展，还减少了外省引进这类资本的可能性，从而有助于本省在省际之间的 GDP 锦标赛中胜出。所以，招商引资的积极性和地区分割实际上并不矛盾，即所谓的"对国内分割、对国外开放"。
② 参见 2009 年 4 月 3 日《解放日报》的一则题为"产业重组面临障碍"的报道。

地方政府也可能采取一些其他手段来降低企业异地投资的积极性。我们曾经在调研中发现这样的案例，一些地方政府仅仅将总部注册在本地的企业当作真正本地的企业，在地方的一些扶持企业发展的政策下，地方政府仅将"本地企业"作为扶持对象，这样一来，外来企业就受到了歧视，企业进行异地投资的积极性也将受挫。

当企业跨省投资行为受到地方政府（投出地或接收地的地方政府）的限制时，高管（董事长或总经理）的政府任职背景这一政企纽带便有可能帮助企业突破这些限制。相对于不具有政企纽带的企业，具有政企纽带的企业可能更有能力借助其与当地政府部门的关系，了解政府（既包括本地政府也包括外地政府）在跨省投资上的政策和偏好，对政府部门和官员进行游说，进而获得本省政府及投资目标所在地政府的批准而进行异地投资。同时，具有政企纽带的企业也更有能力和关系去保护其在异地投资所设立下属企业的产权，克服异地投资过程中的信息不对称、政策风险等种种障碍。高管的政府任职背景虽然主要发生于本地，但中国政府官员之间的跨地区交流和考察非常频繁，官员的级别越高，就越有可能与异地官员互相熟识并建立关系，并且在政府部门的任职背景也有助于高管更好地理解政府系统的运作模式和政策偏好，而这无疑可以减轻异地投资中的风险和障碍。由于我们研究的是跨省投资，高级别的政企纽带以及中央政府部门政企纽带应该更有可能发挥作用。根据以上分析，我们提出下面的 H1 和 H2 研究假说。[①]

H1：相对于不具有政企纽带的企业，具有政企纽带及政企纽带级别较高的企业，异地（省级行政区以外）投资的可能性越大；

H2：相对不具有政企纽带的企业，具有中央政府部门政企纽带的企业，异地（省级行政区以外）投资的可能性越大。

四、研究方法设计

（一）样本选择和数据来源

为检验上文提出的研究假说，我们以 1997 年至 2003 年期间首次在沪深证券交易所发行股票并上市的公司（IPO 公司）为对象，收集了 IPO 当年年末相应的数据资料。以这些公司为研究对象，是因为其数据资料受证券监管部门严格监

---

① 政企纽带在不同产权类型的企业中对异地投资所起的作用可能不同，但由于我们先验地不清楚会有怎样的不同，我们未对此进行理论分析并提出研究假说，而将其留作一个实证问题并分别对不同产权类型的企业进行检验。

管、财务数据经过注册会计师审计,从而相对非上市公司而言数据资料更为完备、准确。而且,这些公司往往是各地区经济发展的主体,相对非上市公司来说对当地经济的影响更大。此外,考察 IPO 当年年末的情况也有助于更好地反映上市之初的初始状态。之所以没有使用上市后的数据,是因为上市会给企业带来大量的新增资本,企业规模迅速扩张,这时企业聘用有政府任职背景的管理人员和进行跨省投资可能都是上市带来的企业扩张的结果。相比之下,IPO 当年的数据主要反映的是企业上市之初的信息。不管企业是跨省开设下属企业还是进行了跨省的兼并重组,本质上都是一种跨省的投资行为,而且都发生在上市前或上市之初,这就避免了政企纽带和跨省投资之间的关系只是因为它们都是上市带来的结果。以 1997 年为研究样本的开始年份,是因为财政部于 1997 年颁布实施了《企业会计准则——关联方关系及其交易的披露》,因而上市公司自 1997 年开始披露关联方信息,这是我们确定公司下属企业个数及所在地区的基础。同时,中国股票市场于 1990 年设立,早期上市公司信息披露质量较低。以 2003 年为样本期间的结束年份,是因为我们手工收集了截至 2003 年度的高管政府任职背景和股权性质数据,并且我们在考察异地投资对企业绩效的影响时使用的绩效衡量指标是公司上市后 1 年至 3 年的股价表现。我们认为 1997 年至 2003 年期间长达七年的数据资料足以反映高管政府任职背景与企业异地投资的关系。

　　高管政府任职背景(是否有政府部门任职经历、职务级别、是否有中央政府部门任职经历)、股权性质(政府控制还是非政府控制)、异地投资数据分别根据公司 IPO 当年的年度报告披露的高管详细简历、最终控制人、关联方情况手工整理而得。遇到 IPO 当年的年度报告披露不详或未披露相关信息的情况,我们再根据公司招股说明书和上市后披露的各年年度报告进行核对和补充。公司股权结构、财务指标、行业类型数据来自国泰安信息技术有限公司开发的 CSMAR 中国股票市场研究数据库这一研究中国股票市场的常用数据库。我们将这些数据与 Wind 中国金融数据库中的相应数据进行了校对,以确保数据准确无误。各省级行政区的市场化程度指数来自樊纲、王小鲁(2003)报告的 2000 年度数据,这个市场化指数主要用于度量截面意义上的地区间市场化进程差异,不同地区的市场程度都在提高,其排序在不同的年份间变化并不大。[①]

　　表 1 列示了样本筛选过程。我们以 1997 年至 2003 年期间发行 A 股的 IPO

---

① 我们也尝试采用了樊纲等人于 2010 年出版的报告(樊纲、王小鲁、朱恒鹏,2010)中给出的 1997—2007 年各地区市场化指数来代替我们原本采用的 2000 年数据,结果没有实质性变化。

公司为初选样本,依次剔除公司最终控制人类型不详、董事长或总经理的政府任职背景不详及无投资设立下属企业情况的 IPO 公司。剔除无投资设立下属企业情况的公司,是因为这些公司可能出于某些原因而缺乏设立下属企业的动机或能力,剔除这些公司可以增加样本公司在异地投资行为上的可比性。经过上述筛选程序,最后的样本公司为 297 家,这些公司较为均匀地分布于 1997 年至 2003 年期间。

表 1　样本筛选过程

样本类型	1997 年	1998 年	1999 年	2000 年	2001 年	2002 年	2003 年	合计
各年发行 A 股 IPO 公司数	209	104	97	133	75	71	67	756
剔除:公司类型一	62	26	21	30	25	21	12	197
公司类型二	11	1	0	0	0	0	1	13
公司类型三	74	39	45	43	20	15	13	249
最终样本	62	38	31	60	30	35	41	297
最终样本占 A 股 IPO 公司比例(%)	29.7	36.5	32.0	45.1	40.0	49.3	61.2	39.3

注:公司类型一、二、三分别为最终控制人类型不详、董事长或总经理政府任职背景不详、无投资设立下属企业情况的公司。

(二)检验模型和变量设定

根据上文的分析,我们采用以下模型,并使用 OLS 回归分析来检验研究假说:

$$
\begin{aligned}
AFF\_NLOCAL_i = {} & \beta_0 + \beta_1 * PC_i + \beta_2 * LOCAL\_SOE_i + \\
& \beta_3 * CENTRAL\_SOE_i + \beta_4 * AFF\_NUMB_i + \\
& \beta_5 * REG\_IND_i + \beta_6 * TOP1_i + \beta_7 * MBRATIO_i + \\
& \beta_8 * LEVERAGE_i + \beta_9 * SIZE_i + \\
& \beta_{10} * INDEX\_MRK_i + \varepsilon
\end{aligned}
$$

其中,β_0 为截距,$\beta_1 \sim \beta_{10}$ 为系数,ε 为残差。除 $INDEX\_MRK_i$ 以外,模型中其他所有变量的取值均为 IPO 当年年末(或 IPO 当年)的情况,这样可以减少联立性偏误的影响。模型中各变量的含义如下:

1. 因变量

AFF_NLOCAL_i 为公司 i 在注册地省级行政区以外的中国大陆地区投资设

立下属企业(子公司、联营企业或分公司)数目占其在中国大陆设立下属企业总数比重。受限于公司对外投资资产规模方面的数据缺乏,我们不能计算公司异地投资规模占其对外投资总规模的比重。但由于公司对外投资一般以设立下属企业形式进行,该变量可以较好地体现公司在异地投资设立下属企业数目占其设立下属企业总数的比重,进而反映公司进行异地投资的能力。公司设立下属企业的数目和地址根据公司公开披露的 IPO 当年年度报告中的"关联方情况"获得。根据中国企业会计准则和上市公司有关信息披露规则的规定,子公司、联营企业、分公司均属于企业的关联方,因此上市公司通常都会披露这些关联方的名称、地址等基本情况。

2. 解释变量

PC_i 代表公司高管政企纽带变量的统称。为了具体检测政企纽带的强度对公司异地投资能力的影响,我们分别使用 PC_T_i、PC_TLVL_i、PC_TCNTY_i、PC_TCITY_i、PC_ICEN_i 这五个变量来刻画高管的政企纽带。

PC_T_i 为哑变量,若公司 i 的董事长或总经理曾经或正在政府机构任职,则取值为 1,否则为 0。该变量用以反映公司高管是否具有政企纽带,而不考虑这一纽带的类型和级别。PC_TLVL_i 为数值变量,若公司 i 的董事长和总经理均无政府机构任职经历,则取值为 0;若 IPO 当年年末公司董事长或总经理的曾任或现任政府机构职务最高级别为正县处级以下(包括正县处级)、副厅局级以上(包括副厅局级),则取值分别为 1 和 2。该变量用以反映高管政企纽带的级别,变量取值从 0 至 2 依次代表高管没有政企纽带到高管政企纽带的级别达到副厅局级以上的三种情况。①

PC_TCNTY_i、PC_TCITY_i 为刻画高管政企纽带级别的哑变量。若公司 i 的董事长或总经理具有政府机构任职经历且任职职务最高级别为正县处级以下(包括正县处级),则 PC_TCNTY 取值为 1,否则为 0。若公司 IPO 当年末董事长或总经理的曾任或现任政府机构职务最高级别为副厅局级以上(包括副厅局级),则 PC_TCITY 取值为 1,否则为 0。这两个变量同时纳入模型可以检测高管政企纽带的具体级别对异地投资的影响。需要说明的是,由于在样本公司中,高管政府任职职务为副省部级以上的公司仅有四家(其中地方政府控制的公司为一家,中央政府控制的公司为三家),我们未单独考察省部级的政企纽带,而是通过 PC_TCITY 来刻画较高级别(厅局级以上)的政企纽带的影响。

---

① 在本文中,若不具体指明,则政企纽带级别县处级包括正、副县处级,厅局级包括正、副厅局级。

PC_ICEN_i 为哑变量,若公司 i 的董事长或总经理曾经或正在中央政府部门任职,则取值为 1,否则为 0。与前五个政企纽带变量反映高管任职职务的级别不同,该变量代表公司高管是否具有中央政府部门任职经历,反映了高管任职部门的级别。

通过将这五个刻画政企纽带的变量单个或组合地放入检验模型,可以检验政企纽带及其强度对企业异地投资的影响。

3.控制变量

$LOCAL\_SOE_i$、$CENTRAL\_SOE_i$ 为哑变量,若公司 i 的最终控制人为地方政府、中央政府,则分别取值为 1,否则为 0。这两个变量用以控制公司产权类型对其异地投资的影响。相对非政府控制的公司而言,地方政府控制的公司可能在本地市场具有垄断优势而欠缺异地投资的动机,或更可能遭遇异地政府设置的市场分割而难以进入异地设立下属企业;相对非政府控制的公司而言,中央政府控制的公司则更有动机或能力离开其注册地到全国各地进行投资。

AFF_NUMB_i 为公司 i 在中国大陆设立下属企业(子公司、联营企业或分公司)数。该变量用以控制公司设立下属企业的动机对其异地投资比重的影响。公司投资扩张的意愿越强,其异地投资的动机可能也越强。

REG_IND_i 为哑变量,若公司 i 属于管制性行业(自然资源、公用事业、金融保险、房地产),则取值为 1,否则为 0。这一界定管制性行业的标准与 Fan,Wong,and Zhang(2007)在研究中国 IPO 公司的政企纽带与企业绩效关系时使用的标准一致。该变量用以控制公司行业特征对其异地投资的影响。当公司处于管制性行业时,其在注册地的垄断性较强,到异地投资设立下属企业的动机可能减弱。

$TOP1_i$ 为公司 i 的第一大股东持股比例。该变量用以控制股权结构对异地投资的可能影响。一方面,由于异地投资的风险较大,第一大股东持股比例越高,公司决策越集权,可能越容易做出异地投资决策;另一方面,股东的分散化有利于公司利用股东的背景进入更多的产业和地区。

$MBRATIO_i$ 为 IPO 当年年末公司 i 的股票总市值与账面净资产的比重。该变量用以控制公司的成长性对异地投资的影响,成长性越高的企业,可能越有动机通过异地投资进行市场扩张。

$LEVERAGE_i$ 为 IPO 当年年末公司 i 的账面负债总额与 IPO 当年主营业务收入的比重。该变量用以控制公司财务状况对异地投资的影响,公司负债比例越高,通过异地投资进行市场扩张的能力可能越低。

SIZE$_i$为 IPO 当年年末公司 i 的账面总资产的自然对数值。该变量用以控制公司规模对异地投资的影响,通常越大的企业越有突破本地市场局限进行异地投资的动机和能力,这对于企业实现规模经济有利。此外,还有两个机制可能使得企业规模与异地投资倾向相关:一方面,小规模企业相对大规模企业而言在当地市场的垄断性可能更小,进行异地投资的动机可能更强;另一方面,小规模企业相对大规模企业而言融资能力可能更小,进行异地投资的能力可能更弱。

INDEX_MRK$_i$为公司 i 所在省级行政区 2000 年度的市场化程度指数,数据来自樊纲、王小鲁(2003)。由于本文样本公司所处区间为 1997 年至 2003 年,而樊纲、王小鲁(2003)报告了 2000 年和 2001 年的各地区市场化进程数据,因而我们采用他们报告的 2000 年度数据。该变量用以控制企业所在地区的市场化程度对异地投资的影响。在市场化程度高的地区,市场发展可能更好,当地市场容量可能更大,从而降低当地企业进行异地投资的动机。同时,在市场化程度高的地区,政府设置市场分割的行为可能更少,可能更愿意接受来自外地的投资,这也会使得市场化程度低的地区的企业更有可能到市场化程度高的地区进行投资,而不是相反。

表 2 汇总了检验模型中各个变量的定义。除了这些变量以外,我们还在模型中加入了年度哑变量以控制年度固定效应,但为了简洁起见,我们未在实证结果中报告年度哑变量的系数。

表 2　变量定义

因变量	
AFF_NLOCAL	公司截至 IPO 当年年末在注册地省级行政区以外的中国大陆地区投资设立下属企业(子公司、联营企业或分公司)数目占公司在中国大陆设立下属企业总数比重。
解释变量	
PC_T	哑变量,若公司 IPO 当年年末董事长或总经理曾经或正在政府机构任职,则取值为 1,否则为 0
PC_TLVL	数值变量,若公司 IPO 当年年末董事长和总经理均无政府机构任职经历,则取值为 0;若公司 IPO 当年年末董事长或总经理的曾任或现任政府机构职务最高级别为正县处级以下(包括正县处级)、副厅局级以上(包括副厅局级),则取值分别为 1 和 2

（续表）

解释变量	
PC_TCNTY	哑变量,若公司 IPO 当年年末董事长或总经理具有曾任或现任政府机构经历且任职职务最高级别为正县处级以下(包括正县处级),则取值为 1,否则为 0
PC_TCITY	哑变量,若公司 IPO 当年年末董事长或总经理的曾任或现任政府机构职务最高级别为副厅局级以上(包括副厅局级),则取值为 1,否则为 0
PC_ICEN	哑变量,若公司 IPO 当年年末董事长或总经理曾经或正在中央政府部门任职,则取值为 1,否则为 0

控制变量	
LOCAL_SOE	哑变量,若公司 IPO 当年年末最终控制人为地方政府,则取值为 1,否则为 0
CENTRAL_SOE	哑变量,若公司 IPO 当年年末最终控制人为中央政府,则取值为 1,否则为 0
AFF_NUMB	公司截至 IPO 当年年末已在中国大陆设立下属企业(子公司或分公司)数
REG_IND	哑变量,若公司 IPO 当年年末属于管制性行业(自然资源、公用事业、金融保险、房地产),则取值为 1,否则为 0
TOP1	公司 IPO 当年年末第一大股东持股比例
MBRATIO	公司 IPO 当年年末股票总市值与账面净资产的比重
LEVERAGE	公司 IPO 当年年末账面负债总额与 IPO 当年主营业务收入的比重
SIZE	公司 IPO 当年年末账面总资产的自然对数值
INDEX_MRK	公司所在省级行政区 2000 年度的市场化程度指数,数据来自樊纲、王小鲁(2003)

（三）变量描述性统计

表 3 的 Panel A 给出了样本公司的变量描述性统计。因变量 AFF_NLOCAL 的均值、最小值和最大值分别为 0.30、0.00 和 1.00,表明在样本公司中,异地投资比重的平均值为 0.30,异地投资比重最小的公司未在异地投资设立下属企业,异地投资比重最大的公司则设立的下属企业都在异地。从解释变量来看,PC_T 的均值为 0.35,表明 35% 的样本公司高管具有政企纽带,即董事长或总经理曾经或在 IPO 时正在政府部门任职。PC_TLVL 的均值为 0.48、中位数为 0,

表明样本公司平均的政企纽带级别为正县处级以下,并且一半以上的公司政企纽带级别为 0,即不具有政企纽带。PC_ICEN 的均值为 0.06,说明 6% 的样本公司的董事长或总经理具有中央政府部门任职经历。PC_TCNTY、PC_TCITY 的均值分别为 0.22 和 0.13,表明 22% 和 13% 的样本公司分别具有县处级以下和厅局级以上政企纽带。

在控制变量上,LOCAL_SOE、CENTRAL_SOE 的均值分别为 0.53 和 0.25,表明 53% 的样本公司最终被地方政府控制、25% 的样本公司最终被中央政府控制,而非政府控制的公司比例为 22%(=100%−53%−25%)。这是因为在样本期间,中国股票市场还是以服务国有企业改革为主要目标,从而大部分 IPO 公司是国有企业改制而来。AFF_NUMB 的最小值为 1、最大值为 34、均值为 4.77,表明在样本公司中,设立下属企业最少的公司设立了 1 家下属企业①,设立下属企业最多的公司设立了多达 34 家的下属企业,平均而言设立下属企业的数目为4.77家。REG_IND 的均值为 0.11,表明 11% 的样本公司属于管制性行业。TOP1 的均值为 0.47,最小值和最大值分别为 0.06 和 0.85,表明样本公司第一大股东持股比例的平均值为 47%,最小值和最大值分别为 6% 和 85%。其他各变量的分布情况也都未见异常。

表 3 的 Panel B、Panel C、Panel D 分别给出了非政府控制的公司、地方政府控制的公司及中央政府控制的公司这三个子样本中的变量描述性统计。

表 3　变量描述性统计

变量	观测数	均值	标准差	最小值	中位数	最大值
Panel A:全部样本公司						
AFF_NLOCAL	297	0.30	0.37	0.00	0.08	1
PC_T	297	0.35	0.48	0	0	1
PC_TLVL	297	0.48	0.72	0	0	2
PC_ICEN	297	0.06	0.24	0	0	1
PC_TCNTY	297	0.22	0.41	0	0	1
PC_TCITY	297	0.13	0.34	0	0	1
LOCAL_SOE	297	0.53	0.50	0	1	1

---

① 这是因为我们在样本筛选过程中剔除了未设立下属企业的公司。

（续表）

变量	观测数	均值	标准差	最小值	中位数	最大值
CENTRAL_SOE	297	0.25	0.44	0	0	1
AFF_NUMB	297	4.77	5.06	1	3	34
INDEX_MRK	297	6.54	1.36	3.15	6.40	8.41
REG_IND	297	0.11	0.31	0	0	1
TOP1	297	0.47	0.18	0.06	0.48	0.85
MBRATIO	297	4.65	2.02	1.44	4.31	14.08
LEVERAGE	297	0.37	0.41	0.00	0.25	2.95
SIZE	297	20.63	0.74	18.90	20.52	25.73

Panel B:非政府控制的公司

变量	观测数	均值	标准差	最小值	中位数	最大值
AFF_NLOCAL	64	0.32	0.38	0	0.09	1
PC_T	64	0.20	0.41	0	0	1
PC_TLVL	64	0.22	0.45	0	0	2
PC_ICEN	64	0.03	0.18	0	0	1
PC_TCNTY	64	0.19	0.39	0	0	1
PC_TCITY	64	0.02	0.13	0	0	1
AFF_NUMB	64	4.13	4.48	1	3	29
INDEX_MRK	64	7.29	1.21	4.15	7.9	8.41
REG_IND	64	0.02	0.13	0	0	1
TOP1	64	0.39	0.16	0.06	0.41	0.72
MBRATIO	64	4.51	1.88	1.86	4.09	11.27
LEVERAGE	64	0.29	0.31	0.00	0.23	1.51
SIZE	64	20.46	0.55	19.25	20.46	21.71

Panel C:地方政府控制的公司

变量	观测数	均值	标准差	最小值	中位数	最大值
AFF_NLOCAL	158	0.20	0.31	0	0	1
PC_T	158	0.40	0.49	0	0	1
PC_TLVL	158	0.53	0.71	0	0	2
PC_ICEN	158	0.02	0.14	0	0	1

（续表）

变量	观测数	均值	标准差	最小值	中位数	最大值
PC_TCNTY	158	0.27	0.45	0	0	1
PC_TCITY	158	0.13	0.33	0	0	1
AFF_NUMB	158	5.11	5.36	1	3	34
INDEX_MRK	158	6.41	1.45	3.15	6.39	8.41
REG_IND	158	0.13	0.33	0	0	1
TOP1	158	0.49	0.17	0.12	0.53	0.85
MBRATIO	158	4.51	1.78	1.61	4.31	10.51
LEVERAGE	158	0.42	0.45	0.00	0.28	2.95
SIZE	158	20.66	0.66	18.9	20.62	22.71

Panel D：中央政府控制的公司

变量	观测数	均值	标准差	最小值	中位数	最大值
AFF_NLOCAL	75	0.50	0.40	0	0.5	1
PC_T	75	0.36	0.48	0	0	1
PC_TLVL	75	0.60	0.85	0	0	2
PC_ICEN	75	0.17	0.38	0	0	1
PC_TCNTY	75	0.12	0.33	0	0	1
PC_TCITY	75	0.24	0.43	0	0	1
AFF_NUMB	75	4.63	4.88	1	3	30
INDEX_MRK	75	6.19	1.01	4.15	5.74	8.41
REG_IND	75	0.15	0.36	0	0	1
TOP1	75	0.50	0.19	0.11	0.54	0.83
MBRATIO	75	5.07	2.51	1.44	4.4	14.08
LEVERAGE	75	0.32	0.38	0.00	0.17	2.28
SIZE	75	20.71	0.98	19.29	20.53	25.73

五、实证结果和解释

（一）政企纽带与异地投资关系的多元回归分析

为了减轻回归模型可能存在的变量异方差问题对系数显著性的影响，我们在所有的 OLS 多元回归分析中报告 Robust-T（稳健 T 值）统计量。表 5 给出了检验模型的 OLS 多元回归分析结果。在表 4 的所有回归分析中，因变量为 AFF_NLOCAL，即公司在注册地所在省级行政区以外的中国大陆地区设立下属企业数目占其在中国大陆设立下属企业总数的比重。为了考察政企纽带与异地投资的关系是否受公司产权属性影响，表 4 除了报告"全体样本公司"的结果，还报告了"非政府控制的公司""地方政府控制的公司""中央政府控制的公司"这三个子样本上的结果。此外，在每一种样本下，我们都分别报告 PC_T、PC_TLVL 作为解释变量以及 PC_TLVL 和 PC_ICEN 同时作为解释变量的情况，由此一共形成了模型(1)至模型(12)这 12 个模型。

在"全体样本公司"中，从模型(1)可见，PC_T 的系数为正但不显著，说明公司是否具有政企纽带与异地投资比重没有显著关系。从模型(2)可见，PC_TLVL 的系数为正并且稳健 T 值只有 1.18，说明公司政企纽带级别越高，其异地投资比重越大，但这种关系不显著，并且我们依然不知道政企纽带达到何种级别时会对异地投资产生影响。从模型(3)可见，PC_ICEN 的系数为正并且在 0.10 以下水平显著，说明在公司高管的政府部门任职职务级别以外，公司高管的中央政府部门任职经历对异地投资具有正向影响。此外，在模型(1)至(3)中，LOCAL_SOE 的系数均为负且在 0.05 以下水平显著，CENTRAL_SOE 的系数均为正且在 0.05 以下水平显著，这说明相对非政府控制的公司而言，地方政府控制的公司异地投资可能性更低，中央政府控制的公司异地投资可能性更高。

模型(1)至(3)给出了全体样本公司的情况，接下来我们进一步分析在不同产权属性的公司中，政企纽带与企业异地投资的关系，以了解政企纽带对异地投资的影响来自哪种产权属性的公司。模型(4)至(6)反映了非政府控制的公司的情况。在模型(4)中，PC_T 的系数为负但不显著；在模型(5)中，PC_TLVL 的系数为负但不显著。这说明在非政府控制的公司中，公司是否具有政企纽带以及政企纽带的级别对异地投资没有显著影响。在模型(6)中，PC_TLVL 的系数为负且在 0.05 以下水平显著，PC_ICEN 的系数为正且在 0.01 以下水平显著，说明在非政府控制的公司中，高管具有中央政府部门任职经历这种类型的政企纽带有助于企业进行异地投资，并且在考虑了这种政企纽带的作用后，高管政府部门任职职务级别不仅无助于异地投资，甚至出现了反向的作用。这可能是因为本研究中企业高管的政府任职经历基本上都是在本省的任职经历，而这些非政府控制的公司其高管的政府任职级别最高仅是厅局级，这些企业的高管更可能服从于本省政府限制企业跨省进行投资的意图。

模型(7)至(9)是地方政府控制的公司的模型。在模型(7)中,PC_T 的系数为正但不显著;在模型(8)中,PC_TLVL 的系数为正且在 0.05 以下水平显著。这说明在地方政府控制的公司中,公司是否具有政企纽带对异地投资没有显著影响,但政企纽带的级别对异地投资有正向作用。在模型(9)中,PC_TLVL 的系数为正且在 0.05 以下水平显著,PC_ICEN 的系数为正但不显著,说明在地方政府控制的公司中,对异地投资有正向影响的主要是高管政府部门任职职务的级别,而非高管在中央政府部门的任职经历。

中央政府控制的公司的情况反映在模型(10)至(12)中,PC_T、PC_TLVL、PC_ICEN 的系数均不显著,说明在此类公司中,高管是否具有政企纽带以及政企纽带的级别对异地投资没有显著影响。这可能是因为中央政府控制的公司背后有着中央政府的支持,高管是否具有政企纽带对于到注册地以外投资设立下属企业变得不重要。当然,这里的结果尚不能排除在中央政府控制的公司中,较高级别的政企纽带可能仍然对异地投资有正向作用。

从控制变量来看,在模型(7)至(9)中,AFF_NUMB 的系数为正且在 0.05 以下水平显著,说明在地方政府控制的公司中,投资意愿越强(设立下属企业个数越多)的公司异地投资的比重越高;INDEX_MRK 的系数为负且在 0.05 以下水平显著,说明在市场化进程越快的地区以及管制性行业,公司异地投资的比重越低,这可能是因为在市场化进程越快的地区,本地市场发展较好,市场容量较大,从而异地投资的需求降低,同时也可能是因为进入市场化进程慢的地区投资设立下属企业受到阻碍;REG_IND 的系数为负且在 0.01 以下水平显著,说明处于管制性行业的公司更不需要进行异地投资。有趣的是,这三个变量的系数在非政府控制的公司及中央政府控制的公司中都不显著,显示出企业投资意愿、地区市场化程度及行业管制性对异地投资的影响与地方政府的行为有关。

在模型(4)至(6)中,TOP1 的系数均为负且在 0.01 以下水平显著,说明在非政府控制的公司中,第一大股东持股比例越高,异地投资比重越小。这可能是因为在非政府控制的公司中,分散的股权结构有利于公司利用股东的多元化背景进入更多的地区。而在政府控制的公司中,作为大股东的政府具有强势地位,即使股权分散,公司可能也难以利用股东多元化的背景进行异地投资,因而股权集中度与异地投资没有显著关系。在模型(4)至(6)及模型(10)至(12)中,LEVERAGE 的系数均为负且在 0.01 以下水平显著,而在模型(7)至(9)中该变量的系数不显著,说明在非政府控制及中央政府控制的公司中,公司负债程度越高,异地投资能力越低,体现了债务对异地投资扩张的约束,而地方政府控制的公司可能由于银行对其贷款时的预算软约束相对较强而不存在这一效应。此外，在所有模型中，MBRATIO 和 SIZE 的系数均不显著，说明异地投资与公司成长性及规模没有显著关系。

（二）政企纽带的具体级别与异地投资关系的多元回归分析

由于政企纽带的级别与异地投资之间可能存在非线性关系，即政企纽带达到特定级别可能才会对异地投资产生影响，而表 4 的回归模型无法揭示这种关系，我们接下来进一步考察政企纽带的具体级别与异地投资的关系，相应的结果报告于表 5 中。

从表 5 的模型（1）可见，PC_TCNTY 的系数为负但不显著，PC_TCITY 的系数为正且在 0.10 以下水平显著，说明在全体样本公司中，相对高管不具有政企纽带的情况，高管政府部门任职职务级别为正县处级以下的政企纽带对异地投资没有显著影响，但高管政府部门任职职务级别达到厅局级以上的政企纽带则对异地投资有显著的正向作用。从模型（2）可见，PC_ICEN 的系数为正且在 0.05 以下水平显著，说明当不考虑高管的政府任职职务级别时，高管的中央政府部门任职经历也有助于企业异地投资。从模型（3）可见，PC_TCNTY、PC_TCITY 的系数均不显著，而 PC_ICEN 的系数为正且在 0.10 以下水平显著，说明在不区分产权属性的混合样本中，对异地投资有影响的主要是高管的中央政府部门任职经历。

表 5 的模型（1）至（3）反映了样本公司总体的情况，模型（4）至（12）则进一步反映了不同产权属性的公司中政企纽带与异地投资的关系。模型（4）至（6）反映的是非政府控制的公司的情况，从模型（4）可见，PC_TCNTY 的系数不显著，PC_TCITY 的系数为正且在 0.01 以下水平显著，说明在非政府控制的公司中，高管政企纽带达到厅局级以上时对企业异地投资有显著影响。从模型（5）可见，PC_ICEN 的系数为正且在 0.01 以下水平显著，说明在非政府控制的公司中，高管的中央政府部门任职经历有助于企业异地投资。模型（6）同时纳入了高管政企纽带的级别和高管的中央政府部门任职经历变量，此时 PC_TCITY 的系数不显著，PC_TCNTY 的系数甚至显著为负，而 PC_ICEN 的系数依然为正且在 0.01 以下水平显著，这说明在非政府控制的公司中，影响异地投资的主要是高管的中央政府部门任职经历，而不是高管的政府部门任职职务级别。这可能是因为非政府控制的公司在异地投资时更多的是面临与产业政策有关的障碍，而非异地政府自身设置的障碍，高管的中央政府部门任职经历更有助于突破前一方面的障碍。

表 4　政治联系与异地投资关系的 OLS 回归分析（因变量为 AFF_NLOCAL）

自变量及模型参数	全部样本公司			非政府控制的公司			地方政府控制的公司			中央政府控制的公司		
	(1)	(2)	(3)	(4)	(5)	(6)	(7)	(8)	(9)	(10)	(11)	(12)
截距项	0.497	0.565	0.622	−0.784	−0.877	−0.703	0.920	1.085	1.078	0.024	0.019	0.214
	(0.72)	(0.83)	(0.92)	(−0.39)	(−0.43)	(−0.37)	(1.04)	(1.26)	(1.25)	(0.02)	(0.02)	(0.18)
PC_T	0.015			−0.126			0.081			−0.013		
	(0.34)			(−1.11)			(1.58)			(−0.11)		
PC_TLVL		0.038	0.011		−0.056	−0.224 **		0.096 **	0.090 **		0.006	−0.062
		(1.18)	(0.31)		(−0.44)	(−2.51)		(2.35)	(2.20)		(0.09)	(−0.71)
PC_ICEN			0.199 *			0.938 ***			0.192			0.223
			(1.83)			(5.85)			(1.11)			(1.22)
LOCAL_SOE	−0.115 **	−0.121 **	−0.114 **									
	(−2.13)	(−2.25)	(−2.18)									
CENTRAL _SOE	0.173 **	0.164 **	0.143 **									
	(2.55)	(2.39)	(2.10)									
AFF_NUMB	0.005	0.005	0.005	−0.007	−0.007	−0.005	0.010 **	0.010 **	0.010 **	−0.001	−0.001	0.000
	(1.38)	(1.39)	(1.45)	(−0.61)	(−0.63)	(−0.47)	(2.25)	(2.35)	(2.34)	(−0.13)	(−0.15)	(0.03)
INDEX_MRK	−0.032 **	−0.031 **	−0.031 **	−0.029	−0.026	−0.003	−0.042 **	−0.042 **	−0.043 **	−0.033	−0.031	−0.038
	(−2.02)	(−2.03)	(−2.02)	(−0.75)	(−0.66)	(−0.09)	(−2.35)	(−2.42)	(−2.51)	(−0.63)	(−0.62)	(−0.74)

（续表）

自变量及模型参数	全部样本公司			非政府控制的公司			地方政府控制的公司			中央政府控制的公司		
	(1)	(2)	(3)	(4)	(5)	(6)	(7)	(8)	(9)	(10)	(11)	(12)
REG_IND	-0.019	-0.025	-0.008	-0.071	-0.060	-0.049	-0.166**	-0.190***	-0.184***	0.079	0.078	0.119
	(-0.27)	(-0.35)	(-0.11)	(-0.40)	(-0.33)	(-0.28)	(-2.45)	(-2.81)	(-2.72)	(0.48)	(0.47)	(0.77)
TOP1	-0.270**	-0.278**	-0.253**	-0.886***	-0.891***	-0.776***	-0.104	-0.122	-0.097	-0.145	-0.152	-0.103
	(-2.19)	(-2.24)	(-1.99)	(-3.48)	(-3.46)	(-2.95)	(-0.68)	(-0.81)	(-0.63)	(-0.46)	(-0.48)	(-0.32)
MBRATIO	-0.009	-0.009	-0.009	0.034	0.036	0.027	-0.021	-0.021	-0.022	-0.005	-0.003	-0.008
	(-0.86)	(-0.78)	(-0.85)	(1.17)	(1.26)	(0.97)	(-1.33)	(-1.36)	(-1.37)	(-0.22)	(-0.16)	(-0.39)
LEVERAGE	-0.145***	-0.146***	-0.144***	-0.467***	-0.462***	-0.375***	0.000	0.011	0.009	-0.393***	-0.401***	-0.358***
	(-3.12)	(-3.09)	(-3.14)	(-3.25)	(-3.19)	(-2.74)	(0.01)	(0.23)	(0.20)	(-3.31)	(-3.31)	(-2.77)
SIZE	0.011	0.007	0.004	0.083	0.086	0.067	-0.016	-0.024	-0.024	0.039	0.038	0.029
	(0.33)	(0.22)	(0.12)	(0.87)	(0.89)	(0.75)	(-0.35)	(-0.56)	(-0.55)	(0.63)	(0.62)	(0.49)
年度哑变量	纳入	纳入	纳入	纳入	纳入	纳入	纳入	纳入	纳入	纳入	纳入	纳入
观测数	297	297	297	64	64	64	158	158	158	75	75	75
R^2	0.18	0.18	0.19	0.31	0.30	0.42	0.14	0.17	0.18	0.17	0.17	0.19

注：变量定义见表2。括号内为稳健 T 值；*、**、*** 分别表示在 0.10、0.05 和 0.01 以下水平统计显著。

表5　各级别政治联系与异地投资关系的 OLS 回归分析(因变量为 AFF_NLOCAL)

自变量及模型参数	全部样本公司			非政府控制的公司			地方政府控制的公司			中央政府控制的公司		
	(1)	(2)	(3)	(4)	(5)	(6)	(7)	(8)	(9)	(10)	(11)	(12)
截距项	0.734	0.607	0.788	−1.199	−1.191	−0.790	1.215	0.830	1.209	0.196	0.177	0.583
	(1.09)	(0.90)	(1.19)	(−0.63)	(−0.62)	(−0.42)	(1.45)	(0.92)	(1.44)	(0.15)	(0.15)	(0.47)
PC_TCNTY	−0.048		−0.074	−0.178		−0.234 **	−0.000		−0.007	−0.073		−0.222
	(−0.94)		(−1.47)	(−1.68)		(−2.49)	(−0.00)		(−0.14)	(−0.39)		(−0.89)
PC_TCITY	0.128 *		0.074	0.610 ***		−0.258	0.262 ***		0.250 **	0.024		−0.130
	(1.75)		(0.92)	(3.05)		(−1.02)	(2.67)		(2.56)	(0.18)		(−0.72)
PC_ICEN		0.212 **	0.197 *		0.668 ***	0.848 ***		0.264	0.200		0.149	0.269
		(2.18)	(1.86)		(6.19)	(5.98)		(1.34)	(1.37)		(1.15)	(1.40)
LOCAL_SOE	−0.119 **	−0.112 **	−0.112 **									
	(−2.25)	(−2.15)	(−2.18)									
CENTRAL_SOE	0.148 **	0.144 **	0.127 *									
	(2.14)	(2.13)	(1.83)									
AFF_NUMB	0.006	0.005	0.006 *	−0.002	−0.004	−0.004	0.011 ***	0.010 **	0.011 ***	−0.001	−0.001	0.001
	(1.61)	(1.46)	(1.66)	(−0.16)	(−0.39)	(−0.36)	(2.83)	(2.36)	(2.82)	(−0.14)	(−0.08)	(0.08)
INDEX_MRK	−0.033 **	−0.031 **	−0.032 **	−0.022	0.003	−0.004	−0.043 **	−0.044 **	−0.044 **	−0.032	−0.032	−0.041
	(−2.09)	(−2.02)	(−2.08)	(−0.58)	(0.08)	(−0.12)	(−2.51)	(−2.49)	(−2.60)	(−0.61)	(−0.63)	(−0.73)

（续表）

自变量及模型参数	全部样本公司			非政府控制的公司			地方政府控制的公司			中央政府控制的公司		
	(1)	(2)	(3)	(4)	(5)	(6)	(7)	(8)	(9)	(10)	(11)	(12)
REG_IND	-0.029	-0.005	-0.012	-0.084	-0.026	-0.055	-0.214***	-0.150**	-0.209***	0.098	0.105	0.165
	(-0.39)	(-0.07)	(-0.16)	(-0.49)	(-0.14)	(-0.31)	(-3.04)	(-2.18)	(-2.97)	(0.56)	(0.66)	(0.93)
TOP1	-0.288**	-0.249**	-0.264**	-0.830***	-0.801***	-0.774***	-0.157	-0.074	-0.131	-0.128	-0.136	-0.046
	(-2.32)	(-1.99)	(-2.07)	(-3.16)	(-2.88)	(-2.91)	(-1.03)	(-0.48)	(-0.85)	(-0.41)	(-0.42)	(-0.14)
MBRATIO	-0.011	-0.010	-0.012	0.038	0.038	0.028	-0.025	-0.023	-0.025	-0.005	-0.002	-0.012
	(-0.98)	(-0.89)	(-1.05)	(1.23)	(1.36)	(0.97)	(-1.60)	(-1.44)	(-1.60)	(-0.22)	(-0.12)	(-0.55)
LEVERAGE	-0.148***	-0.143***	-0.146***	-0.450***	-0.379**	-0.381***	0.021	-0.005	0.020	-0.408***	-0.397***	-0.362***
	(-3.02)	(-3.16)	(-3.07)	(-3.10)	(-2.62)	(-2.77)	(0.41)	(-0.12)	(0.38)	(-3.34)	(-3.64)	(-2.81)
SIZE	0.001	0.005	-0.003	0.098	0.086	0.071	-0.028	-0.010	-0.028	0.029	0.028	0.011
	(0.02)	(0.15)	(-0.08)	(1.08)	(0.95)	(0.79)	(-0.66)	(-0.22)	(-0.66)	(0.47)	(0.47)	(0.19)
年度哑变量	纳入	纳入	纳入	纳入	纳入	纳入	纳入	纳入	纳入	纳入	纳入	纳入
观测数	297	297	297	64	64	64	158	158	158	75	75	75
R²	0.19	0.19	0.20	0.36	0.37	0.42	0.20	0.14	0.20	0.17	0.18	0.21

注：变量定义见表2。括号内为稳健T值；*、**、*** 分别表示在0.10、0.05和0.01以下水平统计显著。

模型(7)至(9)是地方政府控制的公司的情况,PC_TCNTY 的系数均不显著,
PC_TCITY 的系数均为正且在 0.05 以下水平显著,PC_ICEN 的系数均为正但不
显著,说明在地方政府控制的公司中,厅局级以上的高管政企纽带有助于企业异
地投资,同时高管的中央政府部门任职经历对异地投资没有显著影响。这可能是
因为与非政府控制的公司不同,地方政府控制的公司在异地投资时可能更多的是
面临来自异地政府而非产业政策方面的障碍。中央政府控制的公司反映在模型
(10)至(12)中,PC_TCNTY、PC_TCITY、PC_ICEN 的系数均不显著,这与表 4
中模型(10)至(12)的结果一致,说明在中央政府控制的公司中,高管的政府部门
任职职务级别以及高管的中央政府部门任职经历对异地投资没有显著影响。可
能的原因是中央政府控制的公司依靠中央政府的支持即可以突破异地投资时面
临的障碍,而不需要依靠高管的政企纽带。

(三)异地投资与企业绩效关系的多元回归分析

如果异地投资对企业绩效有正面影响,那么根据上文的结果,政企纽带便真
的帮助了一些企业进行异地投资,从而获取了市场分割带来的"租金"。为了检验
政企纽带是否通过影响异地投资使部分企业获得了"租金",我们接下来对异地投
资与企业绩效的关系进行分析。需要说明的是,正如 Fisman(2001)所指出的,由
于寻租活动需要耗费资源,即使具有政企纽带的公司能够获得巨额"租金",在均
衡状态下,这些企业的绩效未必更好。因此,我们对异地投资与企业绩效关系的
分析只是为了获得一些启示性结果。

表 6 是异地投资与企业绩效关系的 OLS 多元回归分析结果。其中因变量为
CAR1、CAR2、CAR3,分别为公司上市当月的下月起第一、第二、第三个年度的按
月累计的超额股票回报,即个股累计月度回报扣除累计月度等权平均市场回报。
这些变量与 Fan,Wong,and Zhang(2007)在研究中国 IPO 公司的业绩表现时
所用的衡量指标一致。表 6 中的控制变量与表 4、表 5 完全相同。为了减轻可能
的变量异方差问题,我们在表 6 中报告了与回归系数对应的稳健 T 值和显著性。

从表 6 可见,无论在回归模型中控制政企纽带的作用与否,在 CAR1、CAR2
作因变量时,AFF_NLOCAL 的系数都为正且在 0.10 以下水平显著,并且在
CAR3 作因变量时,AFF_NLOCAL 的系数为正且显著性水平接近 0.10,说明异
地投资比重越高的公司,上市后三年中尤其是上市后前两年的股价表现更好。在
表 6 中,所有政企纽带变量 PC_TCNTY、PC_TCITY、PC_ICEN 的系数都为负,

但均不显著,说明除了通过异地投资以外,政企纽带本身对公司绩效没有显著的正面影响。AFF_NUMB 的系数虽然都为正,但均不显著,表明公司投资设立下属企业的总数目对绩效没有影响。如果异地投资只是和本地投资类似的普通投资,那么异地投资对绩效应该也没有显著影响。因此,结合异地投资比重 AFF_NLOCAL 上的结果可以进一步推断,异地投资能够帮助企业获得"租金"。其他控制变量上的结果基本和预期一致,未见异常。

表 6　异地投资与公司上市后股价表现关系的 OLS 回归分析

自变量及模型参数	未控制政企纽带的作用			控制政企纽带的作用		
	CAR1	CAR2	CAR3	CAR1	CAR2	CAR3
截距项	−0.577	1.061	2.204 *	−0.644	1.032	2.139 *
	(−1.03)	(1.24)	(1.80)	(−1.12)	(1.19)	(1.77)
AFF_NLOCAL	0.088 *	0.117 *	0.129	0.095 *	0.119 *	0.129
	(1.80)	(1.80)	(1.49)	(1.90)	(1.79)	(1.44)
PC_TCNTY				−0.053	−0.075	−0.040
				(−1.39)	(−1.24)	(−0.53)
PC_TCITY				−0.063	−0.067	−0.104
				(−1.18)	(−0.94)	(−1.03)
PC_ICEN				−0.053	−0.075	−0.040
				(−1.39)	(−1.24)	(−0.53)
LOCAL_SOE	0.014	−0.064	−0.035	0.022	−0.055	−0.025
	(0.35)	(−1.02)	(−0.42)	(0.55)	(−0.87)	(−0.30)
CENTRAL_SOE	−0.046	−0.166 **	−0.044	−0.033	−0.158 **	−0.041
	(−0.90)	(−2.37)	(−0.48)	(−0.65)	(−2.18)	(−0.45)
AFF_NUMB	0.002	0.004	0.004	0.002	0.004	0.004
	(0.55)	(0.70)	(0.60)	(0.54)	(0.74)	(0.59)
INDEX_MRK	0.019	0.013	0.036	0.019	0.012	0.036
	(1.47)	(0.68)	(1.59)	(1.46)	(0.65)	(1.59)
REG_IND	0.018	0.112	0.266 **	0.022	0.118	0.282 **
	(0.39)	(1.56)	(2.42)	(0.48)	(1.64)	(2.53)

（续表）

自变量及	未控制政企纽带的作用			控制政企纽带的作用		
模型参数	CAR1	CAR2	CAR3	CAR1	CAR2	CAR3
TOP1	0.122	0.011	0.084	0.127	0.017	0.105
	(1.20)	(0.08)	(0.49)	(1.22)	(0.12)	(0.60)
MBRATIO	0.034 ***	−0.008	−0.032	0.032 ***	−0.011	−0.033
	(3.18)	(−0.52)	(−1.53)	(3.02)	(−0.66)	(−1.56)
LEVERAGE	0.078 *	0.046	−0.089	0.078 *	0.046	−0.087
	(1.94)	(0.90)	(−1.27)	(1.93)	(0.89)	(−1.24)
SIZE	0.011	−0.052	−0.114 *	0.015	−0.049	−0.111 *
	(0.41)	(−1.23)	(−1.93)	(0.55)	(−1.15)	(−1.89)
IPO 年度哑变量	纳入	纳入	纳入	纳入	纳入	纳入
R^2	0.08	0.08	0.12	0.10	0.09	0.13

注:表中各模型观测数均为 297。括号内为稳健 T 值;*、**、*** 分别表示在 0.10、0.05 和 0.01以下水平统计显著。

（四）稳健性分析

在上文的分析中,我们衡量企业高管的政企纽带时,未考虑高管曾任和现任政府部门职务的差别,也未考虑高管任职本省和外省政府部门的差别。为了考察这些差别对研究结果的影响,我们对样本公司进行了检查,发现仅有 6 家公司高管具有现任政府部门职务的情况,10 家公司高管具有公司注册地所在省份以外政府部门任职经历(高管的中央政府部门任职经历不算作外省任职),不足以对这些公司进行单独的实证检验。我们分别剔除高管具有现任政府部门职务的 6 家公司和高管具有外省政府部门任职经历的 10 家公司,对表 5 至表 7 的结果进行了重新检验,研究结论没有实质性改变。换言之,本文发现的政企纽带与异地投资的关系主要是由高管曾任本省政府部门职务及曾任中央政府部门职务引起的。

六、结论和政策含义

本文运用中国上市公司数据研究了高管(董事长或总经理)的政府任职背景对企业异地投资的影响。我们发现企业高管拥有的政企纽带能够帮助企业到其他省份去开设下属企业(子公司、联营企业或分公司),但这种影响出现的条件是政企纽带达到较高的级别(厅局级以上),而更低级别的政企纽带不起作用,并且这种影响主要存在于地方政府控制的公司中。同时,我们发现在非政府控制的公司中,高管曾在中央政府部门任职也有助于企业异地投资。而在中央政府控制的公司中,高管的政企纽带对异地投资没有显著影响。遗憾的是,受制于数据,我们未能对上述发现的理论解释给出直接的经验证据。进一步分析发现,进行异地投资的企业也的确在某种程度上获得了有利于企业盈利的租金,但在控制了异地投资之后,政企纽带对企业绩效没有显著的影响。总体上来说,政企纽带与异地投资之间的联系是资本市场分割和低效率的表现,同时也加剧了企业之间的不平等。

本文的研究说明,中国的省际资本市场分割在一定程度上是由地方政府行为所致。换句话说,市场分割在中国更是一个制度问题,而不是自然地理或技术问题。由制度所造成的问题,需要借助于法律规范来解决,为此,《中华人民共和国反垄断法》中的第三十三条已经对商品市场上的分割行为进行了规范,"行政机关和法律、法规授权的具有管理公共事务职能的组织不得滥用行政权力,……妨碍商品在地区之间的自由流通"。相比之下,中国却没有任何一部法律对资本市场的地区间分割进行规范,例如,没有法律规定地方政府不得限制企业的异地投资行为。相关立法不足的状况应尽早改变,同时制定出来的法律要真正能够约束地方政府的行为,这比制定法律本身来得更重要。

虽然从单个企业来看,企业家的政企纽带有助于企业突破省界进行异地投资,但对于更多的企业来说,却可能失去了公平竞争的机会。更为重要的是,如果国内市场逐步走向整合,那么中国将可能因其人口众多和疆域辽阔而得益。否则,省际的市场分割将使中国难以获得一个大国本应拥有的规模经济效应。对于中国未来的经济增长而言,国内统一市场带来的规模经济是国家竞争力的关键来源。当欧盟为了获得国际竞争力而走向统一的时候,如果中国因为市场分割而制约其竞争力,将是非常遗憾的。

参考文献

白重恩,杜颖娟,陶志刚,等.地方保护主义及产业地区集中度的决定因素和变动趋势[J].经济研究,2004(04):29-40.

陈敏,桂琦寒,陆铭,等.中国经济增长如何持续发挥规模效应?——经济开放与国内商品市场分割的实证研究[J].经济学(季刊),2007(1):125-150.

陈信元,李莫愁,芮萌,等.司法独立性与投资者保护法律实施——最高人民法院1/15通知的市场反应[J].经济学(季刊),2009(4):1-28.

樊纲,王小鲁.中国市场化指数——各地区市场化相对进程报告(2001年)[M].北京:经济科学出版社,2003.

樊纲,王小鲁,朱恒鹏.中国市场化指数——各地区市场化相对进程2009年报告[M].北京:经济科学出版社,2010.

桂琦寒,陈敏,陆铭,等.中国国内商品市场趋于分割还是整合:基于相对价格法的分析[M].世界经济,2006(2):20-30.

胡旭阳.民营企业家的政治身份与民营企业的融资便利——以浙江省民营百强企业为例[J].管理世界,2006(05):107-113.

胡旭阳,史晋川.民营企业的政治资源与民营企业多元化投资——以中国民营企业500强为例[J].中国工业经济:2008(4):5-14.

李善同,侯永志,刘云中,等.中国国内地方保护的调查报告——基于企业抽样调查的分析[J].经济研究参考,2004(11):78-84.

林毅夫,刘培林.地方保护和市场分割:从发展战略的角度考察[Z].北京大学中国经济研究中心工作论文,2004.

刘培林.地方保护和市场分割的损失[J].中国工业经济,2005(4):70-77.

陆铭,陈钊.中国区域经济发展中的市场整合与工业集聚[M].上海:上海人民出版社,2006.

陆铭,陈钊.市场分割的经济增长——为什么经济开放可能加剧地方保护?[J].经济研究,2009(3):42-52.

罗党论,刘晓龙.政治关系,进入壁垒与企业绩效——来自中国民营上市公司的经验证据[J].管理世界,2009(5):97-106.

巫景飞,何大军,林日韦,等.高层管理者政治网络与企业多元化战略:社会资本——基于我国上市公司面板数据的实证分析[J].管理世界,2008(8):107-118.

吴文锋,吴冲锋,芮萌.中国上市公司高管的政府背景与税收优惠[J].管理世界,2009(3):134-142.

余明桂,潘红波.政治关系,制度环境与民营企业银行贷款[J].管理世界,2008,(8):9-21.

张敏,黄继承.政治关联、多元化与企业风险——来自我国证券市场的经验证据[J].管理世界,2009(7):156-164.

郑毓盛,李崇高.中国地方分割的效率损失[J].中国社会科学,2003(1):64-72.

周黎安.晋升博弈中政府官员的激励与合作—兼论我国地方保护主义和重复建设问题长期存在的原因[J].经济研究,2004,39(06):33-40.

周黎安.中国地方官员的晋升锦标赛模式研究[J].经济研究,2007,42(07):36-50.

Adhikari A，Derashid C，Zhang H. Public policy，political connections，and effective tax rates：longitudinal evidence from Malaysia[J]. Journal of accounting and public policy，2006，25(5)：574 - 595.

Chaney P K，Faccio M，Parsley D. The quality of accounting information in politically connected firms[J]. Journal of accounting and economics，2011，51(1 - 2)：58 - 76.

Charumilind C，Kali R，Wiwattanakantang Y. Connected lending：Thailand before the financial crisis[J]. The journal of business，2006，79(1)：181 - 218.

Cingano F，Pinotti P. Politicians at work：The private returns and social costs of political connections[J]. Journal of the European economic association，2013，11(2)：433 - 465.

Claessens S，Feijen E，Laeven L. Political connections and preferential access to finance：the role of campaign contributions [J]. Journal of financial economics，2008，88 (3)：554 - 580.

Correia M M. Political connections，SEC enforcement and accounting quality [R]. Stanford University working paper，2012.

Faccio M. Politically connected firms[J]. American economic review，2006，96 (1)：369 - 386.

Faccio M，Parsley D C. Sudden deaths：Taking stock of geographic ties[J]. Journal of financial and quantitative analysis，2009，44(3)：683 - 718.

Faccio M，Masulis R W，McConnell J J. Political connections and corporate bailouts[J]. The journal of finance，2006，61(6)：2597 - 2635.

Fan J P H，Rui O M，Zhao M. Public governance and corporate finance：evidence from corruption cases[J]. Journal of comparative economics，2008，36(3)：343 - 364.

Fan J P H，Wiwattanakantang Y，Bunkanwanicha P. Why do shareholders value marriage? [J]. ECGI-finance working paper，2008 (227).

Fan J P H，Wong T J，Zhang T. Politically connected CEOs，corporate governance，and post-IPO performance of China's newly partially privatized firms[J]. Journal of financial economics，2007，84(2)：330 - 357.

Fan C S，Wei X. The law of one price：evidence from the transitional economy of China [J]. The review of economics and statistics，2006，88(4)：682 - 697.

Fisman R. Estimating the value of political connections[J]. American economic review，2001，91(4)：1095 - 1102.

Goldman E，Rocholl J，So J. Do politically connected boards affect firm value? [J]. The review of financial studies，2009，22(6)：2331 - 2360.

Goldman E，Rocholl J，So J. Politically connected boards of directors and the allocation of procurement contracts[J]. Review of finance，2013，17(5)：1617 - 1648.

Hung M，Wong T J，Zhang T. Political relations and overseas stock exchange listing：evidence from Chinese state-owned enterprises[R]. Working paper，2008.

Jenson M C，Meckling W H. Theory of the firm：managerial behavior，agency costs and ownership structure[J]. Journal of financial economics，1976，3(4)：305 – 360.

Johnson S，Mitton T. Cronyism and capital controls：evidence from Malaysia[J]. Journal of financial economics，2003，67(2)：351 – 382.

Khwaja A I，Mian A. Do lenders favor politically connected firms? Rent provision in an emerging financial market[J]. The quarterly journal of economics，2005，120(4)：1371 – 1411.

Li J，Qiu L D，Sun Q Y. Interregional protection：implications of fiscal decentralization and trade liberalization[J]. China economic review，2003，14(3)：227 – 245.

Lu Y. Political connections and trade expansion：evidence from Chinese private firms[J]. Economics of transition，2011，19(2)：231 – 254.

Naughton B. How much can regional integration do to unify China's markets? [R]. Standford：Standford University King Center on Global Development，2000.

Poncet S. 中国市场正在走向"非一体化"? ——中国国内和国际市场一体化程度的比较分析[J]. 世界经济文汇，2002，1(5)：3 – 17.

Poncet S. A fragmented China：measure and determinants of Chinese domestic market disintegration[J]. Review of international economics，2005，13(3)：409 – 430.

Ramanna K，Roychowdhury S. Elections and discretionary accruals：evidence from 2004 [J]. Journal of accounting research，2010，48(2)：445 – 475.

Riahi-Belkaoui A. Politically-connected firms：are they connected to earnings opacity? [J]. Research in accounting regulation，2004，17：25 – 38.

Wang Q，Wong T J，Xia L. State ownership，the institutional environment，and auditor choice：evidence from China[J]. Journal of accounting and economics，2008，46(1)：112 – 134.

Xu X. Have the Chinese provinces become integrated under reform? [J]. China economic review，2002，13(2 – 3)：116 – 133.

Young A. The razor's edge：distortions and incremental reform in the People's Republic of China[J]. The quarterly journal of economics，2000，115(4)：1091 – 1135.

▶夏立军感谢教育部"新世纪优秀人才支持计划"(NCET – 08 – 0802)、国家自然科学基金项目(70772101)和教育部重点研究基地重大项目(2009JJD790030)的资助；陆铭感谢"上海市领军人才计划"和上海市重点学科建设项目(B101)的资助。本文也是"复旦大学当代中国经济与社会工作室"的成果。感谢陈信元、陈钊、靳庆鲁、朱红军、朱凯及上海财经大学会计与财务研究院学术讨论会(2010)、复旦大学"发展经济学:历史、转型及结构变迁"学术研讨会(2011)上有关学者的宝贵意见。

Founder Control, Ownership Structure and Firm Value: Evidence from Entrepreneurial Listed Firms in China[*]

Abstract: In emerging markets, the deviation between the ultimate controlling shareholders' voting rights and their cash flow rights (hereafter "DVC") in the listed firms is quite prevalent. DVC could be introduced due to the ultimate controlling shareholders' opportunistic incentives, as well as by their incentives to improve firm efficiency. This study uses 229 listed firms ultimately controlled by individuals or families (hereafter "entrepreneurial firms") for 2004 in China, to investigate the effect of DVC on firm value and to determine whether it is different between founder and non-founder controlled firms. We find that DVC has a positive effect on firm value for founder controlled firms. This result implies that investors believe that their interests are better protected by founder controlled firms than by non-founder controlled firms.

Keywords: founder control; ownership structure; firm value, China, tunneling

1. Introduction

In recent years an increasing number of studies have examined the causes

---

* 本文选自：Xia L, Founder Control, Ownership Structure and Firm Value: Evidence from Entrepreneurial Listed Firms in China, *China Journal of Accounting Research*, 2008(1), 31 – 49。本文被香港上市公司商会(The Chamber of Hong Kong Listed Companies)杂志 *Momentum* 2008 年秋季刊"谈家族企业"栏目引用。

and consequences of corporate ownership structure. A seminal paper by La Porta et al. (1999) finds that many firms around the world have a concentrated ownership structure and a controlling shareholder, which usually is a family or state agency. Claessens et al. (2000) examined East Asia, Faccio and Lang (2002) and Barca and Becht (2001) examined Western Europe, Khanna (2000) examined emerging markets, and Morck et al. (2000) and Attig et al. (2003) examined Canada. Collectively they find that the controlling family uses a pyramidal ownership structure to control the firms in the business group. Recent research has examined the effect of family control and pyramidal ownership structure on corporate governance (Khanna and Palepu, 2000; Khanna and Rivkin, 2001; Bae et al., 2002; Bertrand et al., 2002; Claessens et al., 2002; Anderson and Reeb, 2003; Anderson et al., 2003; Attig et al., 2003; Lins, 2003; Lemmon and Lins, 2003; Villalonga and Armit, 2006). The causes of ownership structure, especially the pyramidal structure of family controlled firms have also been examined (Bertrand et al., 2005; Almeida and Wolfenzon, 2006). This research has added new theories and evidence about the corporate governance of family controlled firms in various countries. The findings are useful, not only to understand the corporate governance characteristics and behavior of family controlled firms, but also for evaluating corporate governance efficiency.

Since the founding of the Chinese stock market in the early 1990s, listed firms restructured from state-owned enterprises (SOEs) have been the majority of all listed firms. As a result, research on corporate governance issues of firms in China has mainly focused on corporate governance issues of state-controlled listed firms. There is little research on corporate governance issues of entrepreneurial listed firms.[1] However, in recent years, the number of entrepreneurial firms has increased notably as the result of reforms in IPO regulations and the privatization of state-controlled listed firms. By the end of 2004, about a quarter of listed firms were entrepreneurial firms (Kong and

---

[1] In this paper, state-controlled firms refer to the firms ultimately controlled by the government agencies, such as the finance bureau and the state asset supervisory and management committee, and entrepreneurial firms refer to the firms ultimately controlled by individuals or families.

Zhang, 2005). Subsequently, corporate governance issues of entrepreneurial firms have attracted the attention of researchers. Xia and Fang (2005) find that compared with the non-state-controlled listed firms, state-controlled listed firms, especially those controlled by the county or city level governments have lower firm value, especially in regions with weak institutional environments. Because the major part of the non-state-controlled listed firms are the entrepreneurial listed firms (the remainder are the firms controlled by towns and villages), their research implies that entrepreneur control is superior to government control.

To address the question of what determines firm value of entrepreneurial listed firms in China, Su and Zhu (2003) use a sample of 128 entrepreneurial listed firms in 2002 to investigate the effect of DVC on firm value. They find that DVC has a negative effect on firm value. However, their research can be improved in two ways. First, their sample year is before 2004 when listed firms were not required to disclose the ownership chain between their ultimate shareholders and the listed firms. This causes bias in calculating the DVC. Second, they performed univariate analysis on the effect of DVC on firm value but without controlling the effect of other variables. Fan et al. (2005) find that entrepreneurial listed firms demonstrate more layers between their ultimate controlling shareholders and them when the ultimate controlling shareholders' wealth is less. The finding indicates that setting up a pyramidal ownership structure is likely to help the ultimate controlling shareholders to mitigate the financial constraint. However, their research does not take into account the ultimate shareholders' opportunistic incentives to set up a pyramidal ownership structure[1]. Since tunneling behaviors are prevalent and investor protection is weak in the Chinese stock market, it is insufficient to analyze the causes of pyramidal ownership structure from the perspective of financial constraint alone.

---

[1] The term "pyramidal ownership structure" refers to a pyramidal-like organization structure that at the apex sits a controlling owner who controls a firm indirectly through layers of intermediate companies (La Porta et al., 1999; Claessens et al., 2000; Fan et al., 2005). The term "tunneling" refers to the expropriation of minority shareholders through the transfer of assets and profits of firms for the benefit of those in control (Johnson et al., 2000).

This research is based on the 229 entrepreneurial listed firms reported by the New Fortune "100 top entrepreneurs and 100 top capitalists" at the end of 2004. I investigate the economic consequences of pyramidal ownership structure by differentiating the firms into founder controlled and non-founder controlled. In China's transitional economy，firms cannot finance by debt or equity freely with low costs. Since investor protection is weak，a pyramidal ownership structure is not only a channel to mitigate financial constraint，but also a method of tunneling minority shareholders. However，the founders are more likely to care about the long term development of their firms and the image of themselves. The research findings are consistent with this argument. I find that DVC does not necessarily have a negative effect on firm value. The real effect is related to whether the firms are founder controlled or non-founder controlled. DVC is more likely to be a tunneling method in non-founder controlled firms than in founder controlled firms.

Compared with prior literature，the paper's main contribution is that it provides new evidence on understanding and evaluating the ownership structure and corporate governance efficiency of entrepreneurial firms in China. It differentiates entrepreneurial firms into founder controlled and non-founder controlled and combines the opportunistic view and the efficiency view of ultimate controlling shareholders' setting up the pyramidal ownership structure. The finding that investors believe that their interests are more likely to be protected by founder controlled firms also provides a useful perspective to examine market factors protecting investors in China's weak legal investor protection environment.

The remainder of the paper proceeds as follows. Section 2 theoretically analyzes the relationship among founder control，ownership structure and firm value. It then develops the hypothesis to be tested. Section 3 presents the research design，including sample selection，data sources，model and variables. Section 4 provides the empirical results and interpretations of the results. The final section concludes.

2. Theoretical Analysis and Hypothesis

The causes of the emergence of a pyramidal ownership structure of entrepreneurial listed firms can be explained either by the opportunistic view or by the efficiency view. The opportunistic view argues that the ultimate shareholders set up a pyramidal structure so as to tunnel the minority shareholders. The ultimate shareholders can separate their voting rights from cash flow rights through a pyramidal ownership structure so as to effectively control firms in the bottom of the pyramid. Under a pyramidal ownership structure the ultimate controlling shareholders have large voting rights but small cash flow rights. Hence, they have the incentive and ability to tunnel resources from the bottom level firms to the upper level firms in the pyramid, thereby tunneling the minority shareholders. The ultimate controlling shareholders' tunneling incentive and ability are even stronger in an environment of weak legal investor protection. This view is supported by Claessens et al. (2002) who examined 1301 listed firms in eight economies of East Asia and find that firm value increased with the increase of the ultimate controlling shareholders' cash flow rights, but decreased with the increase of their voting rights. Bertrand et al. (2002) examined India, Lins (2003) examined emerging markets and Lemmon and Lins (2003) examined East Asian firms during the financial crisis. All of these studies find similar evidence. With regard to research on Chinese listed firms, Zhou et al. (2003), He and Liu (2005), Li et al. (2005) also find evidence of large shareholder tunneling minority shareholders. Collectively, these research findings indicate that in the weak legal investor protection environment, ultimate controlling shareholders have an incentive and an ability to tunnel the minority shareholders. Furthermore, the pyramidal ownership structure separates the ultimate controlling shareholders' voting rights from cash flow rights and exacerbates the tunneling effect.[1]

The efficiency view argues that the pyramidal ownership structure can be used by the ultimate controlling shareholders to mitigate external financing difficulties, to establish an internal capital market, and to increase firm size and withstand risks so as to enhance firm value. Almeida and Wolfenzon (2006) show that through a pyramidal ownership structure, the ultimate controlling shareholders can use all the retained profits of the firms within the business group. Therefore, they have incentives to set up a pyramidal ownership structure when the cost of external financing is high. Because the cost of external financing *vis-à-vis* internal financing is normally higher in a weak investor protection environment, the ultimate controlling shareholders' incentive to set up a pyramidal ownership structure is even stronger. Fan et al. (2005) argue that when the ultimate controlling shareholders' wealth is less, they would face a tighter financing constraint. Their incentive would be stronger here to set up a pyramidal ownership structure. Fan et al. (2005) reveal that more layers exist between the ultimate controlling shareholders and the listed firms when the former owns less wealth. The result supports the view that a pyramidal ownership structure can be used by the ultimate controlling shareholders to mitigate financing constraints. In addition, the setting up of a pyramidal ownership structure also helps to increase firm size by realizing scale economies and improving the ultimate control of shareholders' political influence (Bertrand and Mullainathan, 2003; Morck et al., 2005). This is extremely important for the entrepreneurial firms facing political discrimination and government regulations in China's transitional economic

---

[1] A point against the opportunistic view is that if the controlling shareholders' tunneling behaviors are prevalent, why then would the minority shareholders seek to invest in these firms? Bertrand and Mullainathan (2003) propose three explanatory reasons. First, in some countries, information disclosure quality is quite low, so the minority shareholders may not be able to discover the controlling shareholders' tunneling behavior. Second, the pyramidal ownership structure may be useful to enhance firm value due to scale economies and more political connections, thereby counteracting the negative effect of the controlling shareholders' tunneling behaviors on firm value. Third, the minority shareholders may have no other choice, e.g., when the pyramidal ownership structure emerges due to mergers and acquisitions, the original minority shareholders cannot exit without bearing the loss of price falls even though they can successfully expect the tunneling behavior of the new controlling shareholders.

environment.

Taken together, the opportunistic view and the efficiency view on the causes of pyramidal ownership structure are both supported by theory and evidence. This research is concerned with whether ultimate controlling shareholders who are the founders or not determines the incentive (opportunistic or efficiency improving) to set up a pyramidal ownership structure. Here, the ultimate controlling shareholders refer to the current controlling shareholders who are the founders of the listed firms or their preexistences, while the non-founders are current controlling shareholders who are neither the founders of the listed firms nor of their preexistences.[1] I expect that difference in controlling shareholders to affect their incentives and behavior. As for the efficiency improving incentive, in China's transitional economy, due to underdevelopment of financial markets, it is difficult for the entrepreneurial firms to finance from the banks or stock market. The founder and non-founder controlled firms both face financial constraints. However, as for the opportunistic incentive, founders are usually more likely to focus on the businesses founded by themselves, to care about the development and the reputation of their firms and families (Anderson and Reeb, 2003; Anderson et al., 2003; Wang, 2005). Hence, the founders' incentive to set up a pyramidal ownership structure so as to tunnel the minority shareholders is weaker than that for non-founders.[2] Based on this discussion, the hypothesis is developed:

Hypothesis : The negative (positive) effect of DVC on firm value is smaller (larger) in founder controlled entrepreneurial listed firms than in non-founder controlled entrepreneurial listed firms.

---

[1] The ultimate controlling shareholders being the non-founders results from the cases that individuals or families acquire the controlling ownership of the listed firms or their preexistence (entrepreneurial firms or state-controlled firms) that were not founded by them and become the ultimate controlling shareholders of the listed firms.

[2] I find that in the sample firms, the age of the founder is significantly (both statistically and economically) larger than that of non-founder. Because the older is more likely the younger to be risk-averse and to have got reputation and the opportunistic behavior has the characteristics of high risk, high return and short-term, the difference in age between founder and non-founder is consistent with the difference in their opportunistic incentives.

3. Research Design

3.1 Sample Selection and Data Sources

Kong and Zhang (2005) report in *New Fortune* that by the end of 2004 there were 335 non-state-controlled listed firms in China's stock market. I selected 236 listed firms controlled by *New Fortune* "top 100 entrepreneurs and top 100 capitalists" at the end of 2004 as the original sample. Six firms are excluded because they disclosed no information on cash flow rights, and one firm is excluded because it was in the finance and insurance industry. The final sample of 229 firms represents about two thirds of all non-state-controlled firms and comprises a representative sample. These sample firms represent the relatively larger firms in the 335 non-state-controlled listed firms. In the 229 sample firms, the number of the founder and non-founder controlled firms are 81 and 148, respectively.

The differentiation between founder and non-founder is determined by whether the current ultimate controlling shareholders are the founders of the listed firm or their preexistences. These are differentiated according to disclosures about ultimate controlling shareholders in annual reports, and the firm history information in the IPO prospectus or listing announcements of listed firms. Data on financial variables, stock price, the ratio of tradable shares and industry category are from CSMAR (China Stock Market and Accounting Research) Database. The data on the marketization index of each region is taken from the 2000 index constructed by Fan et al. (2003). Voting rights, cash flow rights, and the wealth of the ultimate controlling shareholders are extracted directly from the statistics of *New Fortune*. To confirm data accuracy, data were cross checked on voting rights and cash flow rights with data in CCER (China Center for Economic Research) Database. Differences revealed between these two databases were reconciled from information obtained directly from the annual reports of listed firms. This process produced 229 sample firms where voting rights refer to the sum of the smallest percentage of ownership in each chain between the ultimate controlling shareholders and the listed firms. Cash flow rights refer to the product of percentage of ownership in each chain between the ultimate controlling shareholders and the listed firms. For example, if the ultimate controlling shareholder A owns 20% and 30% ownership of company B and company C, respectively, and company B and company C own 10% and 20% ownership of D respectively, then A, the ultimate controlling shareholder, has voting rights and cash flow rights in company D of 30% (10%+20%) and 8% (20% * 10%+30% * 20%) respectively. This calculation method is consistent with that of Claessens et al. (2000). In addition, in the sample firms, the ultimate controlling shareholders refer to the shareholders (individuals or families) that own the most voting rights and not less than 10% of the listed firms' voting rights. When the voting rights of different largest shareholders (individuals or families) differ at 10% or less than 10%, these largest shareholders usually have a close relationship with each other, so in this case, the ultimate controlling shareholders refer to these largest shareholders collectively. In the sample firms, less than 20 firms fall into this case with little expected impact on results.

3.2   Model and variables

I employ the following OLS regression model to test the hypothesis:

$$\text{Tobin Q} = \beta_0 + \beta_1 * \text{Founder} + \beta_2 * \text{DVC} + \beta_3 * \text{Founder} * \text{DVC} + \beta_4 * \text{CTLR} + \beta_5 * \text{Wealth} + \beta_6 * \text{SIZE} + \beta_7 * \text{Regulat} + \beta_8 * \text{ROA} + \beta_9 * \text{DR} + \beta_{10} * \text{TrdR} + \beta_{11} * \text{Index} + \varepsilon$$

Where, β_0 is the intercept, $\beta_1 \sim \beta_{11}$ are regression coefficients and ε is the residual term. The specifications of the variables are as follows.

3.2.1   Dependent Variable

Tobin Q represents firm value, i.e., the ratio of firm's year-end market value over its current acquisition value. Obtaining current acquisition value is difficult and hence book value is used as a proxy. Market value is the sum of the market value of the firm's liabilities, which includes short-term liabilities and long-term liabilities, and the market value of equity. Because listed firms in China have tradable and non-tradable shares, the market value of equity is the sum of the market value of tradable shares and non-tradable shares. However, because there is no market price for non-tradable shares and the non-tradable shares are usually transferred based on net assets per share, the market value of non-tradable shares was calculated as the product of the number of shares and net assets per share. Firm value is then calculated as: Tobin Q = firm's market value/current acquisition value = (stock price * number of tradable shares + net assets per share * number of non-tradable shares + book value of liability)/total book assets. All values in the formula are year end values. This method of calculating Tobin Q is consistent with that used by Su and Zhu (2003) and Xia and Fang (2005) for the China's listed firms. I denote the Tobin Q calculated by this method as Q1.

To mitigate the bias of calculating Tobin Q using net assets as the proxy of market value of non-tradable shares, the market value per share of non-tradable shares is calculated by 20%, 30% or 40% of stock price, and Tobin Q is denoted thereby as Q2, Q3 and Q4 respectively. Bai et al. (2004) adopt the method of calculating the market value of non-tradable shares by 20% and 30% of the stock price so as to calculate Tobin Q of China's listed firms. I followed their method here and take into account the method of calculating the market value of non-tradable shares by 40% of stock price as well so as to improve the robustness of the results.

3.2.2　Testing Variables

Founder is a dummy variable. Its value is 1 when the ultimate controlling shareholders are the founder of the listed firms or their preexistences, and 0 otherwise. DVC is the deviation of the ultimate controlling shareholders' voting rights from their cash flow rights in the listed firms, i.e., the ratio of voting rights over cash flow rights. For the calculation of voting rights and cash flow rights, refer to the subsection "Sample selection and data sources". Founder * DVC is the interaction term of Founder and DVC. The hypothesis predicts that this interaction term should be positively correlated with the dependent variable.

3.2.3 Control Variables

CTLR is the ultimate controlling shareholders' voting rights in the listed firms. Refer to the subsection "Sample selection and data sources" for its calculation. This variable is included because the larger the ultimate controlling shareholders' voting rights, the more ability they possess to tunnel the minority shareholders, this effect not being fully captured by the DVC variable.

Wealth is the natural logarithm of the wealth of the ultimate controlling shareholders. This variable is included because the more wealth possessed by the ultimate controlling shareholders, the higher can be expected regarding their managerial ability. Here, they would provide more support to the listed firms, to enhance reputation and be less concerned with tunneling minority shareholders. All of these aspects are likely to improve firm value.

SIZE is the natural logarithm of year-end total assets. *Regulat* is a dummy variable indicating the firm in regulated industry (value is 1) or not (value is 0). The following industries are classified as regulated based on the CSRC's industry category guide: Mining (B), Petroleum, Chemical and Plastics (C4), Metal and nonmetal (C6), Electric Power, Gas and Water Production and Supply (D), Transportation and Storage (F), and Information Technology (G).

Additionally, ROA, DR, TrdR and Index are included as control variables. ROA is the ratio of net income over total assets, DR is the ratio of total liability over total assets, and TrdR is the ratio of year-end number of tradable shares over that of non-tradable shares. These variables are used to control the effect of firm operation efficiency, liability ratio and tradable shares ratio on firm value. Index is the marketization index of the province level region in which the firm registers. This variable is to control the effect of a regional institutional environment on firm value. Data on this variable are from the 2000 index reported by Fan et al. (2003).

3.2.4 Summary Statistics

Table 1 presents the summary statistics of all variables in the regression model, and Panels A, B and C report the results on the total sample, founder controlled firms and non-founder controlled firms，respectively.

Table 1 Summary Statistics

Variables	N	Mean	S.D	Min	25%	Median	75%	Max
Panel A：Total Sample								
Q1	229	1.22	0.35	0.59	1.05	1.14	1.27	4.01
Q2	229	1.10	0.50	0.36	0.88	0.99	1.16	5.86
Q3	229	1.18	0.56	0.41	0.93	1.05	1.26	6.66
Q4	229	1.26	0.62	0.46	0.96	1.10	1.37	7.46
Founder	229	0.35	0.48	0.00	0.00	0.00	1.00	1.00
DVC	229	2.43	2.55	1.00	1.11	1.67	2.81	26.15
CTLR	229	0.38	0.15	0.09	0.28	0.30	0.49	0.75
Wealth	229	18.87	0.99	15.89	18.27	18.92	19.40	21.40
SIZE	229	21.01	0.77	18.56	20.54	21.00	21.51	23.15
Regulat	229	0.30	0.46	0.00	0.00	0.00	1.00	1.00
ROA	229	0.01	0.09	−0.68	0.01	0.03	0.05	0.20
DR	229	0.53	0.23	0.08	0.41	0.52	0.64	2.34
TrdR	229	0.37	0.12	0.06	0.29	0.35	0.43	1.00
Index	229	6.61	1.49	3.15	5.61	6.41	8.10	8.41
Panel B：Founder Controlled Firms								
Q1	81	1.19	0.25	0.59	1.05	1.15	1.28	2.20
Q2	81	1.02	0.32	0.36	0.85	0.93	1.10	2.57
Q3	81	1.11	0.38	0.41	0.92	1.00	1.18	2.87
Q4	81	1.20	0.43	0.46	0.96	1.07	1.29	3.17
DVC	81	1.76	1.29	1.00	1.01	1.25	1.95	9.59
CTLR	81	0.47	0.15	0.18	0.34	0.45	0.59	0.75
Wealth	81	19.25	0.85	17.18	18.83	19.23	19.62	21.40
SIZE	81	20.96	0.74	19.66	20.33	20.87	21.51	22.66
Regulat	81	0.33	0.47	0.00	0.00	0.00	1.00	1.00
ROA	81	0.04	0.06	−0.32	0.02	0.04	0.06	0.13

(continued)

Variables	N	Mean	S.D	Min	25%	Median	75%	Max
DR	81	0.42	0.19	0.08	0.29	0.42	0.55	0.93
TrdR	81	0.33	0.09	0.19	0.26	0.31	0.38	0.70
Index	81	7.01	1.53	3.15	5.70	7.90	8.32	8.41

Panel C: Non-founder Controlled Firms

Variables	N	Mean	S.D	Min	25%	Median	75%	Max
Q1	148	1.23	0.39	0.86	1.04	1.13	1.27	4.01
Q2	148	1.15	0.57	0.53	0.89	1.02	1.22	5.86
Q3	148	1.22	0.63	0.59	0.93	1.08	1.31	6.66
Q4	148	1.29	0.70	0.65	0.96	1.12	1.42	7.46
DVC	148	2.81	2.96	1.00	1.25	1.95	3.01	26.15
CTLR	148	0.32	0.12	0.09	0.26	0.29	0.37	0.68
Wealth	148	18.66	1.00	15.89	18.00	18.71	19.19	21.40
SIZE	148	21.04	0.79	18.56	20.59	21.02	21.53	23.15
Regulat	148	0.28	0.45	0.00	0.00	0.00	1.00	1.00
ROA	148	0.00	0.10	−0.68	0.01	0.02	0.04	0.20
DR	148	0.58	0.23	0.14	0.47	0.58	0.68	2.34
TrdR	148	0.40	0.13	0.06	0.31	0.38	0.46	1.00
Index	148	6.39	1.43	3.15	5.51	6.36	7.90	8.41

Panel A shows that for 229 sample firms, the mean of Q1 is 1.22, with minimum and maximum values of 0.59 and 4.01, respectively. Consistent with expectations, the mean of Q2 is smaller than that of Q3 and the mean of Q3 is smaller than that of Q4. The mean of DVC is 2.43, with the minimum and the maximum values 1.00 and 26.15, respectively, indicating that on average, voting rights are twice those of cash flow rights, the smallest DVC is no deviation between voting rights and cash flow rights, and the biggest DVC is 26.15. The mean of CTLR is 38%, and its minimum and maximum values are 10% and 75%, respectively, suggesting that the ultimate controlling shareholders have relatively large voting rights.

Panel B and Panel C show that the mean and median values of Q1 of the founder controlled firms are 1.19 and 1.15 respectively; those of the non-founder controlled firms are 1.23 and 1.13 respectively, thereby indicating that the two types of firms do not have obvious difference in firm values. However, the mean and median values of Q2, Q3 and Q4 of founder controlled firms are all slightly smaller than those of non-founder controlled firms. The mean and median values of DVC in non-founder controlled firms are both larger than those in founder controlled firms, and the mean and median values of CTLR in non-founder controlled firms are both smaller than those in founder controlled firms.[①] In addition, there are some differences between founder controlled firms and non-founder controlled firms in ultimate controlling shareholders' wealth, firm size, regulated industry category, operation efficiency, liability ratio and regional institutions index.

4. Empirical Results and Interpretations

4.1   Univariate Analysis

Table 2 reports the Pearson correlation coefficients among variables. It shows that the correlation coefficients among Q1, Q2, Q3 and Q4 all exceed 0.90, suggesting that the methods of calculating the market value of tradable shares has little affect on the calculation of Tobin's Q. Founder is negatively correlated with Q1, Q3 and Q4, but the correlation coefficients are insignificant, however, it is negatively correlated with Q2 and the correlation coefficient is significant at the 0.10 level, indicating that there is not much difference in Tobin Q between founder and non-founder controlled firms. DVC is positively correlated with Q1, Q2, Q3 and Q4, but the coefficients are not significant, suggesting that DVC does not necessarily harm firm value, and its effect on firm value is likely to be related to specific conditions. Founder is

---

① The maximum value of DVC in non-founder controlled firms is 26.15, which is much larger than its 75 percentile value, indicating that DVC is likely to have outliers. However, the 25 percentile value, median and 75 percentile value of DVC in non-founder controlled firms are all larger than those in founder controlled firms, indicating that the larger DVC in non-founder controlled firms relative to that in founder controlled firms is not due to outliers. The effect of outliers on DVC is further discussed in the subsection "Robustness checks".

negatively correlated with DVC, and positively correlated with CTLR, the coefficients of both significant at 0.01 level, indicating that founders have more voting rights in the listed firms and less DVC than non-founders. The column of Founder in Table 2 shows that in the founder controlled firms, the ultimate controlling shareholders' wealth is higher, operation efficiency is higher, liability ratio is lower, the ratio of tradable shares is lower and the degree of marketization of the region where the firm locates is higher than counterpart firms that are non-founder controlled. Since the univariate analysis shows only the relationship between two variables, I use a multivariate regression to further test the hypothesis.

Table 2   Pearson Correlation Coefficients

	Q1	Q2	Q3	Q4	Founder	DVC	CTLR	Wealth	SIZE	Regulat	ROA	DR	TrdR
Q2	0.965	1.000											
	0.000												
Q3	0.969	0.997	1.000										
	0.000	0.000											
Q4	0.967	0.990	0.998	1.000									
	0.000	0.000	0.000										
Founder	−0.060	−0.127	−0.095	−0.070	1.000								
	0.363	0.056	0.150	0.290									
DVC	0.063	0.087	0.069	0.053	−0.197	1.000							
	0.343	0.188	0.302	0.423	0.003								
CTRL	−0.063	−0.127	−0.097	−0.074	0.461	−0.260	1.000						
	0.345	0.055	0.142	0.268	0.000	0.000							
Wealth	0.004	−0.035	−0.015	0.002	0.287	−0.512	0.454	1.000					
	0.951	0.599	0.825	0.982	0.000	0.000	0.000						
SIZE	−0.474	−0.411	−0.440	−0.461	−0.050	0.013	−0.115	0.271	1.000				
	0.000	0.000	0.000	0.000	0.453	0.844	0.084	0.000					
Regulat	0.032	0.024	0.027	0.030	0.052	0.026	0.046	0.071	0.027	1.000			
	0.635	0.717	0.680	0.652	0.437	0.697	0.487	0.283	0.689				
ROA	0.087	−0.008	0.023	0.047	0.199	−0.074	0.145	0.219	0.002	−0.068	1.000		
	0.190	0.907	0.733	0.481	0.003	0.267	0.028	0.001	0.976	0.307			

(continued)

	Q1	Q2	Q3	Q4	Founder	DVC	CTLR	Wealth	SIZE	Regulat	ROA	DR	TrdR
DR	0.134	0.340	0.289	0.246	−0.340	0.176	−0.245	−0.180	0.186	0.003	−0.472	1.000	
	0.043	0.000	0.000	0.000	0.000	0.008	0.000	0.006	0.005	0.964	0.000		
TrdR	−0.022	0.003	−0.049	−0.091	−0.244	0.180	−0.391	−0.240	0.277	0.021	−0.130	0.122	1.000
	0.745	0.965	0.458	0.171	0.000	0.007	0.000	0.000	0.000	0.748	0.050	0.065	
Index	0.024	−0.004	0.015	0.030	0.197	−0.169	0.181	0.182	0.010	0.034	0.153	−0.140	−0.177
	0.719	0.952	0.824	0.656	0.003	0.010	0.006	0.006	0.879	0.614	0.020	0.034	0.007

Note: The number of observations is 229. Each variable has two rows of values, with the upper row presenting Pearson coefficients and the lower row presenting P values.

4.2 Multivariate Regression Analysis

4.2.1 Total Sample Analysis

Table 3 reports the regression results about the relation among founder control, ownership structure and firm value, with four sets of results corresponding to dependent variables Q1, Q2, Q3 and Q4 respectively.

Table 3 Founder Control, Ownership Structure and Firm Value (total sample)

Independent Variables	Predicted Sign	Q1 Coeff.	Q1 T Value	Q2 Coeff.	Q2 T Value	Q3 Coeff.	Q3 T Value	Q4 Coeff.	Q4 T Value
Intercept	?	4.991	8.95 ***	6.064	8.08 ***	7.008	8.19 ***	7.951	8.26 ***
Founder	+	−0.076	−1.18	−0.096	−1.11	−0.105	−1.07	−0.115	−1.03
DVC	?	0.019	2.28 **	0.024	2.05 **	0.026	1.99 **	0.028	1.93 *
Founder * DVC	+	0.044	1.76 *	0.061	1.84 *	0.071	1.87 *	0.081	1.89 *
CTLR	−	−0.403	−2.65 ***	−0.634	−3.09 ***	−0.727	−3.11 ***	−0.820	−3.12 ***
Wealth	+	0.148	5.82 ***	0.200	5.86 ***	0.227	5.83 ***	0.254	5.80 ***
SIZE	−	−0.336	−12.27 ***	−0.458	−12.43 ***	−0.523	−12.45 ***	−0.588	−12.45 ***
Regulat	+	0.027	0.70	0.032	0.61	0.042	0.70	0.051	0.77
ROA	+	0.931	3.85 ***	1.343	4.12 ***	1.540	4.14 ***	1.737	4.16 ***
DR	+	0.557	5.90 ***	1.236	9.72 ***	1.292	8.91 ***	1.348	8.27 ***
TrdR	+	0.518	3.14 ***	0.681	3.07 ***	0.577	2.28 **	0.473	1.66 *
Index	+	0.013	1.08	0.019	1.12	0.022	1.17	0.026	1.21
N		229		229		229		229	
F value		15.65		20.20		19.11		18.48	

(continued)

Independent Predicted		Q1		Q2		Q3		Q4	
Variables	Sign	Coeff.	T Value	Coeff.	T Value	Coeff.	T Value	Coeff.	T Value
Adj-R^2		0.41		0.48		0.47		0.46	

Note: * , ** and *** denote statistical significance at 0.10, 0.05 and 0.01 levels (two tailed).

In all results, DVC and Founder * DVC are both significantly positively correlated with the dependent variables, indicating that DVC is not necessarily harmful to firm value. In contrast, DVC is likely to enhance firm value, especially for the founder controlled firms. This is because in an emerging market, the ultimate controlling shareholders' incentive to form an internal capital market is likely to be stronger than their incentives to tunnel the minority shareholders. This is especially the case when the ultimately controlling shareholders are the founders. The above results support the hypothesis.

With regard to the control variables, in the four sets of results, CTLR is significantly negatively correlated with the dependent variable. This outcome suggests that voting rights have a negative effect on firm value because investors believe that the greater the voting rights of the ultimate controlling shareholders', the stronger their ability to tunnel the minority shareholders. Wealth is significantly positively correlated with the dependent variable, indicating that the ultimate controlling shareholders' wealth has a positive effect on firm value. SIZE is significantly negatively correlated with the dependent variable, suggesting that firm value decreases with the increase of firm size. This is consistent with Xia and Fang (2005) and might be explained by a lower propensity for growth opportunities experienced by large firms. ROA is significantly positively correlated with the dependent variable, indicating that better performing firms have higher firm values. DR is significantly positively correlated with the dependent variable, a result that is likely due to debt holders constraining firms' opportunistic behaviors. TrdR is significantly positively correlated with the dependent variable. This result is likely due to the monitoring role of tradable shareholders over non-tradable large shareholders. It may be due too to the method of calculating Tobin Q when there are non-tradable shares. For example, the market value of non-tradable shares is calculated based on net assets, or 20%, 30% or 40% of stock price, while the market value of tradable shares is calculated directly from stock prices, hence the firm value of the firms with high tradable shares ratio may be overestimated. Regulate and Index does not have a significant association with Tobin Q, indicating that industry regulation and regional environment do not have a significant effect on firm value. This result regarding regional environment is consistent with that of Xia and Fang (2005) for non-state-controlled firms.

4.2.2　Separate Analysis on Founder and Non-Founder Controlled Firms

I next analyze the founder and non-founder controlled firms separately so as to investigate the effect of DVC on firm value in these two types of firms. Table 4 and Table 5 report the results on these two types of firms, respectively.

Table 4　Ownership Structure and Firm Value (founder controlled firms)

Independent Variables	Predicted Sign	Q1		Q2		Q3		Q4	
		Coeff.	T Value	Coeff.	T Value	Coeff.	T Value	Coeff.	T Value
Intercept	?	3.045	4.10 ***	2.918	3.13 ***	3.373	3.12 ***	3.827	3.11 ***
DVC	?	0.086	4.47 ***	0.118	4.89 ***	0.138	4.93 ***	0.158	4.96 ***
CTLR	—	−0.593	−3.19 ***	−0.963	−4.14 ***	−1.119	−4.15 ***	−1.274	−4.15 ***
Wealth	+	0.271	5.95 ***	0.386	6.76 ***	0.449	6.79 ***	0.512	6.81 ***
SIZE	—	−0.354	−7.55 ***	−0.470	−8.00 ***	−0.544	−8.00 ***	−0.618	−7.98 ***
Regulat	+	0.031	0.70	0.013	0.23	0.017	0.27	0.021	0.29
ROA	+	0.071	0.16	−0.007	−0.01	0.005	0.01	0.017	0.02
DR	+	0.411	2.92 ***	0.921	5.22 ***	0.914	4.47 ***	0.907	3.90 ***
TrdR	+	0.530	1.80 *	0.788	2.13 **	0.748	1.75 *	0.709	1.46
Index	+	0.015	0.99	0.015	0.81	0.018	0.84	0.021	0.87
N		81		81		81		81	
F Value		8.84		9.79		9.96		10.26	

(continued)

Independent Variables	Predicted Sign	Q1		Q2		Q3		Q4	
		Coeff.	T Value	Coeff.	T Value	Coeff.	T Value	Coeff.	T Value
Adj-R²		0.47		0.50		0.50		0.51	

Note: *, ** and *** denote statistical significance at 0.10, 0.05 and 0.01 levels (two tailed).

Table 4 shows that in the four sets of results with Q1 to Q4 as dependent variables, DVC is significantly positively correlated with the dependent variable, indicating that DVC has a positive effect instead of a negative effect on firm value in founder controlled firms. This result is likely to be because in founder controlled firms, the efficiency improvement effect of DVC exceeds its tunneling effect on firm value. Table 5 shows that in four sets of results DVC is positively correlated with the dependent variable, but the correlation is insignificant, indicating that in non-founder controlled firms, DVC does not have a significant effect on firm value. This is likely to be because in non-founder controlled firms, the efficiency improvement effect of DVC is counteracted by its tunneling effect on firm value. The results of Table 4 and Table 5 together suggest that DVC is more likely to have a positive effect on firm value in founder controlled firms than in non-founder controlled firms, further supporting the hypothesis.

In addition, the results on control variables of Table 4 and Table 5 are similar to those of Table 3 with the exception that in Table 4, ROA does not have a significant relation with the dependent variable, a result possibly due to firm value being related more to factors other than accounting performance in founder controlled firms.

Table 5   Ownership Structure and Firm Value (Non-founder Controlled Firms)

Independent Variables	Predicted Sign	Q1		Q2		Q3		Q4	
		Coeff.	T Value	Coeff.	T Value	Coeff.	T Value	Coeff.	T Value
Intercept	?	5.804	7.60 ***	7.355	7.14 ***	8.482	7.26 ***	9.608	7.34 ***
DVC	?	0.012	1.19	0.013	0.93	0.013	0.85	0.014	0.78

(continued)

Independent Variables	Predicted Sign	Q1		Q2		Q3		Q4	
		Coeff.	T Value	Coeff.	T Value	Coeff.	T Value	Coeff.	T Value
CTLR	−	−0.514	−2.30 **	−0.763	−2.53 **	−0.878	−2.56 **	−0.993	−2.59 **
Wealth	+	0.110	3.40 ***	0.142	3.25 ***	0.158	3.19 ***	0.174	3.13 ***
SIZE	−	−0.343	−9.71 ***	−0.474	−9.93 ***	−0.539	−9.96 ***	−0.604	−9.96 ***
Regulat	+	0.033	0.59	0.061	0.81	0.076	0.90	0.092	0.96
ROA	+	1.067	3.57 ***	1.585	3.93 ***	1.816	3.97 ***	2.046	3.99 ***
DR	+	0.598	4.89 ***	1.319	7.99 ***	1.395	7.45 ***	1.470	7.01 ***
TrdR	+	0.554	2.71 ***	0.707	2.56 **	0.597	1.91 *	0.487	1.39
Index	+	0.023	1.31	0.038	1.60	0.046	1.68 *	0.053	1.73 *
N		148		148		148		148	
F Value		12.67		16.98		16.28		15.82	
Adj-R^2		0.42		0.49		0.48		0.48	

Note: *, ** and *** denote statistical significance at 0.10, 0.05 and 0.01 levels (two tailed).

4.3 Additional Analysis

The above analysis indicates that in founder controlled firms, the ultimate controlling shareholders' incentive is weak to set up a pyramidal ownership structure in order to tunnel minority shareholders. To provide additional evidence, I further examine the relation between founder control and the largest shareholders' behavior. Jiang et al. (2006) find that occupying assets of listed firms is an important way for the largest shareholders to tunnel minority shareholders. Using their approach, I adopt the ratio of year-end balance of "other accounts receivables" over total assets as the proxy of the degree of the largest shareholders' asset occupying behavior. This is denoted as Tunnel Proxy. Table 6 provides the effect of founder control and DVC on Tunnel Proxy, with the control variables the same as those in Table 4 and Table 5. Table 6 shows that Founder is significantly negatively correlated with Tunnel Proxy, while DVC does not have a significant relationship with Tunnel Proxy. The results indicate that founders are less likely to tunnel minority shareholders through asset occupying behavior than non-founders, and DVC does not have a significant effect on the largest shareholders' asset occupying behavior. These results further suggest that founders have weaker incentives to tunnel minority shareholders than do non-founders, and a pyramidal ownership structure may not result from the tunneling incentive of the ultimate controlling shareholders.

Table 6 Founder Control and Asset Occupying Behavior

Independent Variables	Predicted Sign	Dependent variable: Tunnel Proxy	
		Coeff.	T Value
Intercept	?	0.446	2.68 ***
Founder	—	−0.039	−2.96 ***
DVC	+	−0.002	−0.86
CTLR	+	0.020	0.43
Wealth	—	−0.010	−1.26
SIZE	+	−0.009	−1.07
Regulat	?	0.023	1.96 *
ROA	—	−0.505	−6.96 ***
DR	—	−0.015	−0.53
TrdR	+	0.058	1.18
Index	—	−0.003	−0.74
N		229	
F Value		10.77 ***	
Adj-R^2		0.30	

Note: *, ** and *** denote statistical significance at 0.10, 0.05 and 0.01 levels (two tailed).

4.4 Robustness Checks

The main results of this study have two alternative explanations, i.e., the diversification difference explanation and the acquisition explanation. First, founder controlled firms are likely to be more specialized (i.e., they focus on particular industries) and more likely to obtain listing directly. In contrast, non-founder controlled firms are likely to be more diversified (i.e., engaged in various industries) and more likely to be listed through the ultimate controlling shareholders' acquisition of some listed firms' controlling shares. As a result, the firm value difference between founder and non-founder controlled firms is likely to be caused by the difference in their degree of diversification or method of obtaining listing status. However, I argue that these alternative explanations are not of much importance because in China's emerging market and transitional economy, diversification may not harm firm value. Prior literature on Chinese firms also does not find evidence of a negative effect of diversification on firm value. The results of Table 3 to Table 5 show that DVC is more likely to have a positive effect on firm value in founder controlled firms than in non-founder controlled firms. The diversification difference explanation and the acquisition explanation do not easily explain why the founder's effect on firm value is related to DVC. Therefore, the results of this study are more likely to be explained by the combination of the opportunistic view and the efficiency view of the causes of pyramidal ownership structure. In addition, to examine the effect of outliers on the results, I exclude the observations beyond the three or five standard deviations on each variable mean, and redo the analyses in Table 3 to Table 5. The main results are unchanged.

5. Conclusions

Despite an increasing interest in corporate governance issues of family firms or entrepreneurial firms, little research has been undertaken on those of China's family firms or entrepreneurial firms. This study selects the 229 entrepreneurial listed firms reported by the *New Fortune* "top 100 entrepreneurs and top 100 capitalists" for 2004 as the research sample, and investigates the relation among founder control, ownership structure and firm value. I find that DVC is more likely to have a positive effect on firm value in founder controlled firms than in non-founder controlled firms. The result indicates that investors tend to believe that their interests are more likely to be protected by founder controlled firms.

The study contributes to the literature by providing new evidence to help us understand and evaluate the ownership structure and corporate governance efficiency of entrepreneurial firms in China. This is achieved by differentiating entrepreneurial firms into founder controlled and non-founder controlled, and by combining the opportunistic view and the efficiency view in explaining the ultimate controlling shareholders' purpose in establishing the pyramidal ownership structure. Moreover, the findings of this study also provide a useful attempt to identify the market forces protecting investors in China's weak legal investor protection environment.

The reader is reminded that, although this study investigates the difference in incentives and behavior of setting up a pyramidal ownership structure between founder and non-founder controlled firms, it is not designed to study factors which affect a founder's decision to control a firm. Information about this question would be useful to our understanding about corporate governance characteristics and behavior of entrepreneurial firms. Finally, this paper does not examine the effect of the degree of family involvement in corporate governance on firm value. These issues can be the focus of further research.

References

周勤业, 夏立军, 李莫愁. 大股东侵害与上市公司资产评估偏差[J]. 统计研究, 2003, 20 (10): 39 – 44.

孔鹏, 张炜迪. 2005 家族上市公司新财富 100 企业家[J]. 新财富, 2005 (8): 52 – 54.

Almeida H V, Wolfenzon D. A theory of pyramidal ownership and family business groups[J]. The journal of finance, 2006, 61(6): 2637 – 2680.

Anderson R C, Mansi S A, Reeb D M. Founding family ownership and the agency cost of debt[J]. Journal of financial economics, 2003, 68(2): 263 – 285.

Anderson R C, Reeb D M. Founding-family ownership and firm performance: evidence from the S&P 500[J]. The journal of finance, 2003, 58(3): 1301 – 1328.

Attig N, Fischer K, Gadhoum Y. On the determinants, costs, and benefits of pyramidal ownership[J]. Working paper, 2002.

Bae K H, Kang J K, Kim J M. Evidence from mergers by Korean business groups:

tunneling or value added? [J]. Journal of finance, 2002, 57(6): 2695 - 2740.

Barca F, Becht M. The control of corporate Europe[M]. Oxford: Oxford University Press, 2002.

Bertrand M, Johnson S, Samphantharak K, et al. Mixing family with business: a study of Thai business groups and the families behind them[J]. Journal of financial economics, 2008, 88(3): 466 - 498.

Bertrand M, Mehta P, Mullainathan S. Ferreting out tunneling: an application to Indian business groups[J]. The quarterly journal of economics, 2002, 117(1): 121 - 148.

Bertrand M, Mullainathan S. Pyramids [J]. Journal of the european economic association, 2003, 1(2 - 3): 478 - 483.

Claessens S, Djankov S, Fan J P H, et al. Disentangling the incentive and entrenchment effects of large shareholdings[J]. The journal of finance, 2002, 57(6): 2741 - 2771.

Claessens S, Djankov S, Lang L H P. The separation of ownership and control in East Asian corporations[J]. Journal of financial economics, 2000, 58(1 - 2): 81 - 112.

Fan G, Wang X L. China marketization index: report on the relative progress of marketization in various regions in 2001[M]. Beijing: Economic Science Press, 2003.

Faccio M, Lang L H P. The ultimate ownership of Western European corporations[J]. Journal of financial economics, 2002, 65(3): 365 - 395.

Fan J P H, Wong T J, Zhang T. The emergence of corporate pyramids in China[R]. Working paper, 2006.

He J G, Liu F. Large shareholder control, tunneling and investor protection: evidence from related party transactions in listed firms' acquisitions[J]. China accounting and finance review, 2005, 3: 25 - 35.

Jiang G H, Lee C M C, Yue H. Tunneling in China: the surprisingly pervasive use of corporate loans to extract funds from Chinese listed companies [J/OL]. Johnson school research paper series No. 31 - 06, 2005. http://papers.ssrn/com/sol3/paper.cfm? abstract_id =861445.

Li Z Q, Yu Q, Wang X K. Tunneling, propping M&A: evidence from Chinese listed companies[J]. Economic research journal, 2005, 40(1): 95 - 105.

Su Q L, Zhu W. Family control and firm value: evidence from China listed companies [J]. Economic research journal, 2003, 38(8): 36 - 45.

Xia L J, Fang Y Q. Government control, institutional environment and firm value: evidence from the Chinese securities market[J]. Economic research journal, 2005, 40(5): 40-51.

▶This paper was funded by the grants from the National Social Science Foundation of China (No. 06BJY016), the National Natural Science Foundation of China (No. 70772101) and the Major Project of Key Research Base on Humanities and Social Science of Ministry of Education of China (No. 07JJD630007). I appreciate helpful comments from an anonymous referee, Charles J. P. Chen, Zengquan Li, Feng Liu, Qifeng Zhang, Tianyu Zhang and the participants at International Conference on Accounting and Governance (2007, Guangzhou, China). All errors are my own.

企业家的"政由己出"

——民营 IPO 公司创始人管理、市场环境与公司业绩*

内容提要：本文以 1997 年至 2007 年期间中国民营 IPO 公司为对象，考察了创始人担任公司关键职务（董事长或总经理）对企业业绩的影响，以及这种影响如何因市场环境的不同而发生改变。研究发现，总体上，创始人担任公司关键职务有助于提升公司业绩以及公司业绩的稳定性，但是随着公司所在地区市场化程度改善，创始人的这一作用有所减弱。研究结果表明，对中国现阶段的民营企业而言，创始人亲自管理企业依然是公司治理的一个有效选择，尤其是在那些市场化程度较低的地区，创始人亲自管理企业的正面作用更为突出。

关 键 词：创始人管理；市场环境；公司业绩；民营企业

一、引言

在国家治理上，皇帝"政由己出"，则"明察善断"。如果在企业治理上，权威非常重要，那么，企业家"政由己出"则有利于提升企业绩效。本文基于中国民营上市公司，研究创始人担任公司关键职务（董事长或总经理）如何影响公司的业绩表现，以及这种影响如何因市场环境的不同而发生改变。

自 20 世纪 80 年代中期以来，随着政策管制的逐步放松，中国民营经济和民营企业取得了快速发展，已经越来越成为中国经济发展的重要推动力量。在快速发展的同时，民营企业的公司治理也面临着诸多挑战。其中一个重要的问题是创

---

* 本文选自：夏立军、郭建展、陆铭：企业家的"政由己出"——民营 IPO 公司创始人管理、市场环境与公司业绩，《管理世界》，2012 年第 9 期，第 132－141，155 页。本文被人大复印报刊资料《企业管理研究》2013 年第 1 期转载。

始人对企业的管理怎样才是适度的,或者换言之,创始人亲自管理企业对企业的发展是否有利。一方面,在长期的创业过程中,创始人积累了大量的经营管理经验、权威以及与政府部门的关系,因而创始人担任公司的关键管理职务可能有助于企业的发展;另一方面,随着时间的推移,创始人的知识、能力、视野等亦可能不再适应企业面临的、与创业初期所不同的经营环境,创始人继续担任企业关键职务可能成为企业的负担。那么,创始人是否需要像创业初期一样,继续担任企业的关键管理职务(董事长或总经理)?回答这一问题不仅有助于从理论上进一步理解创始人在民营企业公司治理中的作用,同时也将为民营企业有关的政策制定提供启发。

从现有文献来看,创始人管理企业的后果尚未有定论。一些文献发现,创始人担任公司总经理对公司治理和企业发展具有正面作用(Begley,1995;Certo et al.,2001;He,2008;Nelson,2003)。这种正面作用可能来自创始人的长期激励,即创始人更加关注企业的长期发展而不是短期表现,同时也可能来自创始人本身具有的经营管理企业的特殊资产(specific assets),如声誉、经验、能力及与外界的关系。然而,另一些文献发现创始人担任公司总经理对企业业绩没有影响甚至有负面影响(Daily and Dalton,1992)。例如,创始人可能缺乏管理上市公司的经验,公司上市之后需要面对更多外部竞争、财务、监管以及其他管理上的挑战,创始人本身具有的技能未必适合管理公众公司(Adams et al.,2009;Wasserman,2003)。对于中国转型经济环境中的民营企业而言,创始人管理对企业意味着什么,依然是一个有待研究的问题。

本文以 1997 年至 2007 年期间的 169 家中国民营 IPO(Initial Public Offering,初次公开发行股票)公司为对象,考察了创始人担任公司关键职务(董事长或总经理)对公司上市后业绩表现的影响。我们发现在控制了其他因素的影响后,相对创始人不担任公司关键职务的公司而言,创始人担任董事长或总经理的公司在上市后三年中的业绩表现(采用总资产收益率、主营业务收入净利润率度量)持续更优,并且公司业绩的稳定性更好。进一步分析还发现,创始人担任公司关键职务对公司业绩的正面作用随着公司所在地区市场化程度的提高而减弱。这些结果表明,对中国转型经济环境中的民营企业而言,创始人担任公司关键职务具有公司治理上的优势,尤其在那些市场化程度较低的地区,创始人的这一作用更为突出。

本文的贡献有以下几点。首先,本文从创始人的作用这一角度丰富了关于民营企业公司治理问题的研究。以往的公司治理研究着重分析公司所有权与控制权的分离对公司治理的影响以及大小股东之间的利益冲突（Jensen and Meckling，1976；La Porta et al.，1998）。虽然近年来一些文献开始重视创始家族股权在公司治理中的角色（Anderson and Reeb，2003；Jayaraman et al.，2000；Wang，2006；Xia，2008），但创始人自身在公司治理中的作用还有待更深入的理解。此外，本文所发现的创始人管理在市场化程度低的地区更为重要，对以往非正式制度如何缓解正式制度缺陷的文献（如 Allen，Qian，and Qian，2005）也是一个补充。在某种程度上，创始人担任公司关键管理职务，可以视为对正式的市场制度缺陷的反应。最后，本文的结果表明，中国民营上市公司的公司治理在很大程度上依赖创始人的作用，尤其是在那些市场化程度较低的地区。一旦创始人因年龄、健康状况、个人违法违规行为等原因不能亲自管理企业，企业的经营管理就可能面临极大的风险。因此，本文研究结果的政策启示是，加强正式的市场制度环境建设对中国民营企业和民营经济的发展尤为重要。

下文的安排如下：第二部分结合相关文献和中国的制度背景，对创始人管理与公司业绩的关系以及公司所处地区的市场环境对这一关系的影响进行分析，在此基础上提出研究假说；第三部分是研究设计，包括样本选择、数据来源、模型设定、变量说明等；第四部分报告并解释实证分析结果；最后一部分对全文进行总结。

二、理论分析和研究假说

（一）创始人管理与公司业绩

1. 创始人管理的正面效应

企业的发展离不开企业家。一个企业之所以存在是因为一个人或者一群人做出了创立一家企业的决定并且采取了行动，这个人或者这一群人是企业组织结构和战略最初的架构者以及企业文化的塑造者（Nelson，2003）。由此可以看出创始人对于企业组织的重要作用。企业的创始人为了企业的生存和发展付出了艰辛的努力，其对企业倾注的情感和归属感往往是职业经理人所不可比拟的。创始人本身的声誉与所创立企业的成功与否高度相关，因而可能付出更多的努力以维持声誉。创始人往往拥有所创立企业相当比例的所有权，而管理者拥有较高比例的所有权是减轻委托代理问题的有效机制（Fama and Jensen，1983；Nelson，2003），因而由创始人担任企业的管理者能够减少代理成本。Anderson and Reeb

(2003)对标准普尔 500 公司的研究发现,家族企业的业绩比非家族企业更好,尤其是创始人担任 CEO 的企业比外聘 CEO 的企业业绩更好。

以往研究表明,创始人与职业经理人无论是内在特质还是外在激励等方面都不相同,因而可能对公司的业绩产生正面的影响。相对于职业经理人,创始人更渴望成就一番事业、对公司有更强的心理归属感、在组织内具有更大权力和影响力、有更多的股权和经济激励、有更长投资视野,并且有更高的专业化于特定公司的技能(Begley,1995;Certo et al.,2001;He,2008;Nelson,2003)。因而,相比起职业经理人,创始人更愿意追求长期回报而避免过于重视短期利益,从而可能具有更稳定的业绩表现。在针对中国民营上市公司的研究中,Xia(2008)发现公司实际控制人拥有的控制权与现金流量权分离引起的代理问题,在那些创始人为公司实际控制人的企业中更弱。

2. 创始人管理的负面效应

然而,创始人管理也可能对企业价值产生负面影响。比如创始人(往往是大股东)与其他股东之间存在利益冲突,并且创始人股东可能过度地特权消费,从而导致公司业绩下降(Jensen and Meckling,1976)。创始人对于公司事务具有很强的控制欲,更加容易否决公司的现金分红政策,从而降低公司的价值(Shleifer and Vishny,1989)。创始人对公司强大的控制力可能使得权力过于集中,容易增加公司的决策风险。Adams,Almeida,and Ferreira(2005)的研究表明,强有力的 CEO 会增加公司业绩波动性,提高公司的风险。

此外,创始人可能缺乏管理上市公司的经验,公司上市之后需要面对更多外部竞争、财务、监管以及其他管理上的挑战,创始人本身具有的技能未必适合管理公众公司(Adams et al.,2009;Wasserman,2003)。组织生命周期理论认为,在公司发展的过程中存在某个规模临界点,超过这个临界点之后,创始人的管理技能和能力可能不足以很好地管理一个不断成长的公司,需要退位让贤(Gedajlovic et al.,2004;Hambrick and Crozier,1985)。在这种情况下,如果创始人仍然坚持对公司的控制和管理,会对公司的价值造成负面影响。

3. 创始人管理的综合作用

综上所述,对企业而言,创始人管理既有正面的作用,也有可能给企业带来成本和风险。在中国的背景下,民营企业往往在不同程度上与政府具有一定的政企纽带,具体的体现如企业家担任人大代表或政协委员,企业家与政府官员保持良好的私人关系,或者企业家本身就是"下海"的前任官员。这些政企纽带都是有利于企业经营的资源,而这些资源是难以传承或转移的,因此这会加强创始人管理企业的优势(陆铭、潘慧,2009)。此外,对于 IPO 公司而言,创始人的权威领导保证了经营管理的持续性和稳定性,减少了由于突然的战略变动而引起的风险。因此,新上市公司的声誉往往依赖于创始人的声誉(Aldrich,1979;Fischer and Pollock,2004)。

在中国的法律和市场机制相对不太完善的环境中,非正式制度(声誉、关系、权威等)能够在一定程度上缓解正式制度的缺陷,促进企业发展和经济增长(Allen,Qian,and Qian,2005)。同样,在公司层面上,基于创始人的声誉、关系和权威的非正式制度可能有助于公司业绩的提高,减轻企业经营管理面临的正式制度(产权保护、契约执行等)的缺陷。而在这方面,职业经理人或创始人的家族成员很难替代创始人的作用。另一方面,在一个市场制度(包括产权保护、契约执行、职业经理人市场等)不够完善的环境中,职业经理人或创始人新一代的家族成员的专业管理优势也很难体现出来。因此,在正式的市场和法律制度还非常欠缺的中国转型经济环境中,创始人管理的"人治"优势可能超过其给企业带来的负面影响。因此,我们提出了研究假说 1。

假说 1:在中国民营 IPO 公司中,相对创始人不担任关键管理职务的公司而言,创始人担任关键管理职务的公司具有更好的业绩表现。

(二)市场环境与创始人管理的后果

在公司治理理论中,外部治理机制或治理环境如公司控制权市场、产品竞争市场、法律保护等也会通过缓解委托代理问题而影响公司的业绩(Fama,1980;Hart,1983;Scharfstein,1988;La Porta et al.,1998;Holmström,1999)。中国各个地区由于地理位置、改革开放的先后、经济发展水平等原因,不同地区的市场化进程、政府干预程度、法治水平相差甚大,呈现东部好于中部,中部好于西部的状况(夏立军、方轶强,2005)。具有较低政府干预水平的地区,企业在应对政府干预上的支出就会减少;同样,法治水平比较高的地区,对于合约的履行以及保护股东方面做得更好,降低维护投资者和生产者权益的成本。市场化进程与政府干预和法治水平紧密联系在一起,因而公司所处的地区市场化进程的差异可能会影响创始人管理这种内部公司治理机制的效果。

根据樊纲、王小鲁、朱恒鹏(2010)的研究,市场化进程可以分为五个方面,分别是政府与市场的关系、非国有经济的发展、产品市场的发育程度、要素市场的发育程度以及市场中介和法律制度环境。那么这五个方面是如何影响创始人担任关键管理职务对于企业的作用呢？首先，从政府与市场的关系上看，随着市场程度的提高，政府由"干预型"向"服务型"转型加快，减少对市场的干预，使得市场机制发挥的作用更大，企业面临的市场竞争更加激烈，那么由创始人的"人治"所带来的收益可能就会减少，成本可能会上升，因而创始人管理对企业而言可能不是那么重要（Peng，2001），甚至产生负面影响。其次，在非国有经济发展越好和产品市场的发育程度越高的地区，产品价格和各种不同商品的上下游产业链由市场供求关系的决定程度越高，而政府的影响较小，那么创始人与政府的关系对于打开企业供销渠道的作用就会降低，个人权威的作用淡化（张军等，2006）。再次，从要素市场上看，如果经理人市场的发育相对更好，企业可以从外部市场聘请到很好的管理者，而研究表明家族外部的管理者的能力总体而言是更好的（Morck，Strangeland，and Yueng，2000），因而创始人担任关键管理职务的公司相对于其他公司的优势会缩小。总体而言，随着市场化进程的提高，企业面临的正式的市场和法律制度更加完善，导致创始人个人所拥有的关系网络、管理能力、个人权威等"人治"优势会降低。[①] 因此，我们提出研究假说 2。

假说 2：在中国民营 IPO 公司中，创始人担任公司关键管理职务对公司业绩表现的正面影响随着公司所在地区市场化程度的提高而减弱。

三、研究设计

（一）样本选择和数据来源

本文选取了 1997 年至 2007 年在 A 股市场进行首次公开发行股票（IPO）的民营上市公司作为研究样本，数据来源于国泰安公司 CSMAR 数据库中的民营企业研究数据。样本筛选程序如下：以 1997 年至 2007 年期间首次发行 A 股并且发行时为民营控股的 IPO 公司为初始样本，然后剔除数据缺失的样本。最后，我们得到 169 家以民营企业身份进行 IPO 的公司，样本的年度和行业分布如表 1 所示。为了满足计量方法的需要以及考虑时间序列上业绩波动性的测度问题，本文选取的样本公司在其 IPO 之后至少具有三个会计年度的数据，因此我们未考虑 2008 年 1 月 1 日后在 A 股市场上市的公司。

创始人的相关数据来自证券时报网（http://fundnotice.stcn.com/）"公告"栏

---

① 虽然我们尽可能从逻辑上分析并预测在中国的环境下创始人管理、市场环境与公司业绩之间的关系，但是这一关系依然是一个实证性的问题，有待后文经验证据的验证。

目中的各个上市公司的招股说明书和年报,我们手工整理样本公司的创始人名单。公司的财务和股票市场回报率数据、公司治理数据(包括董事长和总经理名单、董事会人数、独立董事比例、第一大股东持比例等)来自国泰安公司的CSMAR 数据库。市场化指数的数据来自樊纲、王小鲁、朱恒鹏(2010)所著的《中国市场化指数——各地区市场化相对进程 2009 年报告》。

表 1　样本公司 IPO 年度和所在行业分布

年度分布			行业分布			
上市年度	频率	占比(%)	行业名称	行业代码	频率	占比(%)
1997	5	3.0	农林副牧渔	A	5	3.0
1998	4	2.4	制造业	C	130	76.9
1999	4	2.4	建筑业	E	8	4.7
2000	11	6.5	交通运输、仓储业	F	2	1.2
2001	11	6.5	信息技术业	G	17	0.1
2002	8	4.7	批发和零售贸易	H	2	1.2
2003	17	10.1	房地产业	J	2	1.2
2004	37	21.9	社会服务业	K	1	0.6
2005	6	3.6	综合类	M	2	1.2
2006	28	16.6				
2007	38	22.5				
总计	169	100		总计	169	100

(二)变量说明和模型设定

1. 公司业绩及其波动性的度量

与以往文献一致,本文关于公司业绩的度量采用会计业绩(Adams et al.,2005;Cheng,2008;李琳、刘凤委、卢文彬,2009;权小峰、吴世农,2010 等)。会计业绩方面,使用总资产回报率(ROA)和主营业务收入利润率(ROS)来度量公司的业绩。由于本文考察创始人管理在公司上市之后的作用,因此对每个会计业绩指标都做了上市后三年、四年、五年的平均。经过平均的 ROA 和 ROS 分别标记为"ROA 均值"和"ROS 均值"。

本文测度公司业绩波动性主要从两方面展开。一是公司业绩的横向离散度。

横向离散度主要是测度公司业绩偏离正常业绩的幅度。业绩离散度主要是测度不同公司之间的波动性。二是公司业绩的纵向波动性。纵向波动性主要是测度同一公司在不同年度区间内业绩的波动性,也就是测度公司业绩在时间序列上的稳定性和持续性。

为了测度公司业绩的横向离散度,本文依据 Adams et al.(2005)和 Cheng(2008)的方法,将业绩指标 ROA、ROS 分别与影响业绩指标的各变量进行回归,预测业绩水平求得残差 u,用残差 u 的绝对值 $|u|$ 表示业绩的横向离散度,业绩离散度表示业绩偏离正常业绩水平的幅度。故 $|u|$ 越大,横向离散度越大。具体的横向离散度指标用"ROA 离散度""ROS 离散度"表示。

公司业绩纵向的波动性以公司在研究期间内的公司业绩指标 ROA、ROS 的标准差来表示。业绩的纵向波动性指标分别用"ROA 波动""ROS 波动"表示。

2. 创始人管理的度量

本文中的创始人是指企业最主要的创立者。我们根据各个样本公司的招股说明书中"发行人情况"这一部分的描述,查阅企业最初是由哪个人或者哪一群人发起设立的。对于由多人创立的公司,本文认为发挥最为重要作用(持有发行前股份最多,或者在企业最初创立过程中担任董事长或总经理等)的创立者为创始人。[①] 此外,由于民营上市公司上市之后披露的信息较多,也容易引起财经媒体的注意,与此相关的公司报道比较容易获取。我们通过百度和谷歌搜索每个公司的相关创业故事,从媒体的报道中验证企业的创始人是谁。

在确定了创始人之后,我们从 CSMAR 公司治理数据库中获得了该公司上市当时的董事长以及总经理(又称总裁、首席执行官等)的姓名,并与创始人姓名进行核对以确定创始人是否担任公司董事长或总经理。本文所关注的核心变量"创始人管理"是一个虚拟变量,如果创始人在上市当时担任公司董事长或者总经理,则创始人管理取值为 1,否则取 0。一般而言,公司董事、监事和高管的每一届任期为三年,并且可以连任,因此创始人担任公司董事长或总经理的情况在一个较长的期间内比较稳定,这有助于观察和识别创始人的作用。

3. 市场环境的度量

本文采用樊纲、王小鲁、朱恒鹏(2010)所著的《中国市场化指数——各地区市

---

① 以三一重工(股票代码 600031)为例。根据三一重工所发布的招股说明书第 34～38 页的"发行人历史沿革"部分,可以看到三一重工的控股公司三一控股有限公司是由梁稳根、唐修国、向文波、毛中吾、袁金华等九位自然人创立的,三一控股持有三一重工 96.56% 的股份。梁稳根持有三一控股公司 59% 的股份。此外,梁稳根担任三一重工的董事长以及法定代表人。由此可以判断出梁稳根为三一重工最主要的创立者,即创始人为梁稳根。

场化相对进程 2009 年报告》中所提供的市场化指数作为各地区市场环境的度量。该报告对我国省、自治区、直辖市的市场化相对进程做出一个基本的判断,建立了中国各地区市场化进程指标体系,从多个不同方面对各省、自治区、直辖市的市场化相对程度进行测量。测量的结果称为"中国各地区市场化进程相对指数"。该报告中市场化指由五个方面的指数构成:政府与市场的关系、非国有经济的发展、产品市场的发育程度、要素市场的发育程度、市场中介组织的发育和法律制度环境。该报告提供了 1997 年至 2007 年全国各省的市场化指数总得分。本文取各公司在 IPO 当年所在省份的市场化指数总得分作为市场环境的度量。

4. 控制变量

由于公司业绩波动性会受到其他因素的影响,因此本文在借鉴 Adams et al. (2005)、Cheng(2008)、李琳等(2009)文献的基础上,选取了以下变量作为控制变量:创始人的年龄及年龄的平方①、公司成立年限(企业年龄)、以公司总资产自然对数度量的公司规模、资产负债率、总资产周转率、董事会规模、独立董事所占比例、第一大股东持股比例(股权集中度),以及行业和 IPO 年度哑变量。其中,前三个控制变量为公司发行上市当时的情况,其余变量为上市当年末或当年度的情况。各变量具体定义见表 2,各变量的描述性统计见表 3。

表 2 变量定义

变量符号	变量定义与解释
ROA 均值	业绩指标,IPO 之后三、四、五年的 ROA(总资产报酬率)的均值
ROS 均值	业绩指标,IPO 之后三、四、五年的 ROS(主营业务收入净利润率)的均值
ROA 离散度	横向的业绩离散度指标,表示以 ROA 测度的离散度指标
ROS 离散度	横向的业绩离散度指标,表示以 ROS 测度的离散度指标
ROA 波动	纵向的业绩波动性指标,IPO 之后三年的 ROA 的标准差
ROS 波动	纵向的业绩波动性指标,IPO 之后三年的 ROS 的标准差
创始人管理	创始人担任董事长或者 CEO 取 1,否则取 0
市场化指数	代表该公司所在省份的市场化程度
年龄	创始人年龄

① 在模型中加入创始人年龄的平方项是考虑到创始人的年龄与企业业绩及其波动性之间可能呈现非线性关系。例如,创始人的经验和能力在中年时期可能比较强,而在青年和老年时期则可能相对较弱。当然,这是一个实证性的问题。

（续表）

变量符号	变量定义与解释
年龄平方	创始人年龄的平方
企业年龄	公司成立年限,等于 IPO 当年的年份减去公司注册登记年份数
企业规模	公司总资产（亿元）的自然对数
资产负债率	总负债/总资产
总资产周转率	总资产/营业收入
董事会规模	董事会人数的自然对数
独立董事比例	独立董事人数/董事会人数
股权集中度	第一大股东持股比例
行业	行业哑变量,以中国证监会公布的《上市公司行业指引》为依据
年份	年度哑变量,以公司上市当年的年度设定一个哑变量

表3　变量描述性统计结果

变量	N	均值	标准差	最小值	1/4 分位数	中位数	3/4 分位数	最大值
ROA	169	0.054	0.053	−0.366	0.034	0.057	0.079	0.190
ROS	169	0.065	0.566	−7.112	0.046	0.094	0.162	0.607
ROA 离散度	169	0.031	0.035	0.000	0.010	0.024	0.040	0.370
ROS 离散度	169	0.188	0.499	0.000	0.044	0.120	0.230	6.429
ROA 波动	169	0.025	0.056	0.001	0.009	0.015	0.023	0.675
ROS 波动	169	0.122	0.964	0.001	0.014	0.023	0.045	12.510
创始人管理	169	0.822	0.383	0.000	1.000	1.000	1.000	1.000
市场化指数	169	8.427	2.178	2.940	6.730	8.810	10.180	11.710
年龄	169	48.467	8.666	31.000	43.000	47.000	54.000	78.000
企业年龄	169	4.503	2.462	0.000	3.000	4.000	6.000	14.000
企业规模	169	2.053	0.607	0.881	1.603	1.959	2.358	4.223
资产负债率	169	0.339	0.153	0.028	0.208	0.343	0.431	0.747
总资产周转率	169	1.927	1.007	0.225	1.259	1.730	2.358	6.363
董事会规模	169	2.170	0.217	1.099	2.197	2.197	2.197	2.708
独立董事比例	169	0.295	0.141	0.000	0.333	0.333	0.364	0.667
股权集中度	169	0.374	0.141	0.061	0.263	0.370	0.475	0.724

5. 模型设定

(1)平均业绩模型。考察创始人管理与公司上市后平均业绩之间关系的 OLS 回归分析模型 1 如下:

$$
\begin{aligned}
\text{ROA 均值或 ROS 均值} =\ & \beta_0 + \beta_1 \text{创始人管理} + \beta_2 \text{市场化指数} + \\
& \beta_3 \text{创始人管理} * \text{市场化指数} + \beta_4 \text{年龄} + \\
& \beta_5 \text{年龄平方} + \beta_6 \text{企业年龄} + \beta_7 \text{企业规模} + \\
& \beta_8 \text{资产负债率} + \beta_9 \text{总资产周转率} + \\
& \beta_{10} \text{董事会规模} + \beta_{11} \text{独立董事比例} + \\
& \beta_{12} \text{股权集中度} + \text{行业} + \text{年份} + u
\end{aligned}
$$

其中,β_0 为截距项,$\beta_1 \sim \beta_{12}$ 为变量系数,u 为模型残差。

(2)横向离散度模型。为检验公司业绩横向离散程度,与 Cheng(2008)相似,本文采用了 Glejser(1969)的 Heteroskedasticity Tests 方法,分两阶段来检验创始人管理对公司业绩横向离散程度的影响。第一阶段通过将公司业绩水平指标(ROA 均值、ROS 均值)分别与影响业绩指标的各变量进行 OLS 回归(如模型(1)所示),预测业绩水平并得到残差 $\hat{u}$。第一步得到的残差表示"未预期"到的公司业绩,残差的绝对值 $|\hat{u}|$ 可以作为公司业绩波动性或者公司业绩的不可预测部分的代理变量。因此,Glejser(1969)的方法给我们提供了一种理解公司业绩波动性的可能途径。第二阶段中按照以下模型 2 进行 OLS 回归:

$$
\begin{aligned}
\text{ROA 离散度或 ROS 离散度} =\ & \beta_0 + \beta_1 \text{创始人管理} + \beta_2 \text{市场化指数} + \\
& \beta_3 \text{创始人管理} * \text{市场化指数} + \beta_4 \text{年龄} + \\
& \beta_5 \text{年龄平方} + \beta_6 \text{企业年龄} + \beta_7 \text{企业规模} + \\
& \beta_8 \text{资产负债率} + \beta_9 \text{总资产周转率} + \\
& \beta_{10} \text{董事会规模} + \beta_{11} \text{独立董事比例} + \\
& \beta_{12} \text{股权集中度} + \text{行业} + \text{年份} + e
\end{aligned}
$$

其中,β_0 为截距项,$\beta_1 \sim \beta_{12}$ 为变量系数,e 为模型残差。

(3)纵向波动性模型。公司业绩的纵向波动性以公司在 IPO 之后三年内的公司业绩指标(ROA、ROS)的标准差来表示。这样,每个公司形成一个标准差观测值,并以该标准差作为模型的因变量。回归模型 3 如下:

$$
\begin{aligned}
\text{ROA 波动或 ROS 波动} =\ & \beta_0 + \beta_1 \text{创始人管理} + \beta_2 \text{市场化指数} + \\
& \beta_3 \text{创始人管理} * \text{市场化指数} + \beta_4 \text{年龄} + \\
& \beta_5 \text{年龄平方} + \beta_6 \text{企业年龄} + \beta_7 \text{企业规模} + \\
& \beta_8 \text{资产负债率} + \beta_9 \text{总资产周转率} +
\end{aligned}
$$

$$\beta_{10}董事会规模 + \beta_{11}独立董事比例 +$$
$$\beta_{12}股权集中度 + 行业 + 年份 + e$$

其中，β_0 为截距项，$\beta_1 \sim \beta_{12}$ 为变量系数，e 为模型残差。

四、实证分析结果和解释

在这一部分，我们首先报告创始人管理与公司业绩及其稳定性之间的回归结果，然后进一步报告创始人管理的后果如何因市场环境的差异而改变，最后是稳健性检验的结果。

（一）创始人管理与公司业绩及其稳定性的关系

表 4 为创始人管理与公司业绩的回归结果。模型（1）、（2）、（3）分别表示为以 IPO 之后三年、四年、五年的 ROA 的平均值作为被解释变量；模型（4）、（5）、（6）表示 IPO 之后三年、四年、五年的 ROS 的平均值作为被解释变量。

由结果可见，无论是以 ROA 还是 ROS 作为公司业绩水平的度量，关键变量"创始人管理"的系数都显著为正，表示创始人管理可以显著地提高公司的业绩水平。此外，市场化指数的系数都为正，但是只有模型（3）、（5）、（6）的系数是显著的，表明良好的外部市场环境有利于公司业绩的提高，这个结论与国内的学者研究结果一致（孙早、刘庆岩，2006；夏立军、方轶强，2005）。其他的控制变量的符号显示，资产负债率越高，公司的会计业绩越差；总资产周转率越高，则公司经营业绩越低。但这两个控制变量上的结果仅在模型（1）中显著。其他控制变量与公司业绩之间没有显著的关系。

表 4　创始人管理与公司上市后业绩表现

变量及模型参数	ROA 均值			ROS 均值		
	（1）	（2）	（3）	（4）	（5）	（6）
创始人管理	0.0194 *	0.0677 **	0.0718 **	0.2979 **	0.4801 **	0.4927 **
	[0.0117]	[0.0317]	[0.0304]	[0.1335]	[0.2278]	[0.2256]
市场化指数	0.0043	0.0216	0.0171 *	0.0580	0.1418 **	0.1212 *
	[0.0033]	[0.0100]	[0.0093]	[0.0377]	[0.0720]	[0.0688]

（续表）

变量及 模型参数	ROA 均值			ROS 均值		
	（1）	（2）	（3）	（4）	（5）	（6）
年龄	0.0019	0.0103	0.0091	0.0341	0.0640	0.0684
	[0.0044]	[0.0122]	[0.0109]	[0.0506]	[0.0877]	[0.0806]
年龄平方	0.0000	−0.0001	−0.0001	−0.0002	−0.0004	−0.0005
	[0.0000]	[0.0001]	[0.0001]	[0.0005]	[0.0008]	[0.0008]
企业年龄	−0.0006	−0.0023	−0.0023	−0.0161	−0.0227	−0.0263
	[0.0019]	[0.0051]	[0.0057]	[0.0216]	[0.0366]	[0.0421]
企业规模	−0.0025	−0.0031	−0.0039	−0.0550	−0.0347	−0.0031
	[0.0100]	[0.0274]	[0.0271]	[0.1147]	[0.1966]	[0.2011]
资产负债率	−0.0763 *	−0.0335	0.0096	−0.1787	0.0179	0.1981
	[0.0401]	[0.1081]	[0.1030]	[0.4600]	[0.7756]	[0.7651]
总资产周转率	−0.0095 **	−0.0170	−0.0202	−0.0717	−0.0914	−0.1362
	[0.0048]	[0.0132]	[0.0131]	[0.0544]	[0.0945]	[0.0975]
董事会规模	−0.0226	−0.0229	−0.0308	−0.0331	−0.0430	−0.1551
	[0.0214]	[0.0674]	[0.0634]	[0.2448]	[0.4833]	[0.4709]
独立董事比例	−0.0379	0.0397	0.0283	0.0187	0.3709	0.1589
	[0.0614]	[0.1687]	[0.1460]	[0.7033]	[1.2104]	[1.0844]
股权集中度	−0.0202	−0.0411	−0.0443	−0.1382	−0.3559	−0.4762
	[0.0328]	[0.0936]	[0.0896]	[0.3757]	[0.6716]	[0.6656]
常数	0.0572	−0.5257	−0.1166	−1.0035	−3.8822	−1.6251
	[0.1359]	[0.4084]	[0.3393]	[1.5574]	[2.9300]	[2.5193]
行业	YES	YES	YES	YES	YES	YES
年份	YES	YES	YES	YES	YES	YES
观测值 N	169	122	92	169	122	92
R^2	0.2418	0.1751	0.2088	0.1228	0.1560	0.2059

注：*** , ** , * 分别表示在 1%、5%、10% 水平上显著，方括号内为系数的标准误。

　　严格说来，表 4 的发现可能并不能直接得出创始人管理能够提高企业效率的结论。如果创始人管理伴随着更高的企业绩效波动，那么这样的企业所获得的平均绩效更高可能只是对于"经营风险"的补偿。因此，我们认为必须结合对于企业绩效波动性的分析才能科学地评价创始人管理的作用。表 5 是创始人管理与公司业绩横向离散度的回归结果。

表 5　创始人管理与公司上市后业绩的横向离散度

变量及 模型参数	ROA 离散度			ROS 离散度		
	（1）	（2）	（3）	（4）	（5）	（6）
创始人管理	−0.0157 **	−0.0524 **	−0.0432 **	−0.3120 ***	−0.4579 **	−0.4230 **
	[0.0076]	[0.0243]	[0.0216]	[0.1117]	[0.1817]	[0.1693]
市场化指数	−0.0042 *	−0.0198 **	−0.0154 **	−0.0652 **	−0.1417 **	−0.1126 **
	[0.0022]	[0.0077]	[0.0066]	[0.0316]	[0.0575]	[0.0517]
年龄	−0.0056 *	−0.0125	−0.0101	−0.0375	−0.0412	−0.0359
	[0.0029]	[0.0094]	[0.0077]	[0.0424]	[0.0699]	[0.0605]
年龄平方	0.0001 *	0.0001	0.0001	0.0003	0.0002	0.0002
	[0.0000]	[0.0001]	[0.0001]	[0.0004]	[0.0007]	[0.0006]
企业年龄	−0.0009	−0.0002	−0.0013	0.0146	0.0143	0.0121
	[0.0012]	[0.0039]	[0.0040]	[0.0180]	[0.0292]	[0.0316]
企业规模	0.0074	0.0036	0.0063	0.0588	−0.0185	−0.0255
	[0.0066]	[0.0210]	[0.0192]	[0.0960]	[0.1569]	[0.1510]
资产负债率	−0.0452 *	−0.0343	−0.0401	−0.0383	−0.1425	−0.2689
	[0.0263]	[0.0829]	[0.0731]	[0.3849]	[0.6189]	[0.5743]
总资产周转率	0.0042	0.0136	0.0144	0.0966	0.1274 *	0.1414 *
	[0.0031]	[0.0101]	[0.0093]	[0.0456]	[0.0754]	[0.0732]
董事会规模	0.0051	0.0092	0.0111	0.0554	0.0674	0.1537
	[0.0140]	[0.0517]	[0.0450]	[0.2049]	[0.3856]	[0.3534]
独立董事比例	−0.0125	−0.0932	−0.0351	−0.2379	−0.6198	−0.2766
	[0.0402]	[0.1294]	[0.1036]	[0.5886]	[0.9658]	[0.8139]
股权集中度	−0.0006	0.0282	0.0015	0.1174	0.3747	0.2821
	[0.0215]	[0.0718]	[0.0636]	[0.3144]	[0.5359]	[0.4996]
常数	0.2011 **	0.6614 **	0.2286	1.5577	3.4790	0.8661
	[0.0890]	[0.3132]	[0.2408]	[1.3033]	[2.3380]	[1.8909]
行业	YES	YES	YES	YES	YES	YES
年份	YES	YES	YES	YES	YES	YES

（续表）

变量及	ROA 离散度			ROS 离散度		
模型参数	（1）	（2）	（3）	（4）	（5）	（6）
观测值 N	169	122	92	169	122	92
R^2	0.2296	0.2135	0.2656	0.1846	0.2272	0.2759

注：***，**，* 分别表示在 1%、5%、10% 水平上显著，方括号内为系数的标准误。

由结果可知，无论是以 ROA 离散度还是 ROS 离散度作为业绩横向离散度的度量指标，创始人管理的系数都显著为负，表示创始人管理可以显著地减低公司业绩的横向离散度。市场化指数的系数也显著为负，表明良好的市场环境可以减少公司业绩的波动性。

表 6 是创始人管理与公司业绩纵向波动性的回归结果，这部分主要是对创始人管理与同一企业不同时间序列上公司业绩的波动性之间的关系进行分析。被解释变量是 ROA、ROS 的三年、四年、五年的标准差，以此表示公司业绩的纵向波动性。

表 6   创始人管理与公司上市后业绩波动性

变量及	ROA 波动			ROS 波动		
模型参数	（1）	（2）	（3）	（4）	（5）	（6）
创始人管理	−0.0177	−0.0733 *	−0.1002 *	−0.4641 **	−0.5314 **	−0.7153 **
	[0.0129]	[0.0411]	[0.0541]	[0.2251]	[0.2661]	[0.3476]
市场化指数	−0.0066 *	−0.0254 *	−0.0328 *	−0.1127 *	−0.1766 **	−0.2117 **
	[0.0037]	[0.0130]	[0.0165]	[0.0636]	[0.0841]	[0.1060]
年龄	−0.0056	−0.0165	−0.0213	−0.0727	−0.0848	−0.1179
	[0.0049]	[0.0158]	[0.0193]	[0.0854]	[0.1024]	[0.1242]
年龄平方	0.0000	0.0001	0.0002	0.0005	0.0006	0.0009
	[0.0000]	[0.0002]	[0.0002]	[0.0008]	[0.0010]	[0.0012]
企业年龄	0.0014	0.0046	0.0055	0.0258	0.0265	0.0392
	[0.0021]	[0.0066]	[0.0101]	[0.0363]	[0.0427]	[0.0648]
企业规模	0.0054	0.0085	0.0014	0.0963	0.0448	−0.0099
	[0.0111]	[0.0355]	[0.0482]	[0.1934]	[0.2297]	[0.3098]

（续表）

变量及	ROA 波动			ROS 波动		
模型参数	（1）	（2）	（3）	（4）	（5）	（6）
资产负债率	−0.0687	−0.0851	−0.1163	−0.1800	−0.3891	−0.6471
	[0.0446]	[0.1401]	[0.1834]	[0.7755]	[0.9061]	[1.1786]
总资产周转率	0.0086	0.0194	0.0367	0.1876 **	0.1582	0.2632 *
	[0.0053]	[0.0171]	[0.0234]	[0.0918]	[0.1104]	[0.1502]
董事会规模	0.0200	0.0491	0.0799	0.0705	0.0976	0.3293
	[0.0237]	[0.0873]	[0.1129]	[0.4128]	[0.5646]	[0.7254]
独立董事比例	−0.0069	−0.1044	−0.0815	−0.1543	−0.5404	−0.4085
	[0.0682]	[0.2187]	[0.2600]	[1.1858]	[1.4139]	[1.6706]
股权集中度	0.0254	0.1166	0.1640	0.3589	0.5711	0.9293
	[0.0364]	[0.1213]	[0.1596]	[0.6335]	[0.7846]	[1.0254]
常数	0.1886	0.7546	0.4525	2.5765	4.8289	2.9860
	[0.1509]	[0.5293]	[0.6041]	[2.6258]	[3.4228]	[3.8810]
行业	YES	YES	YES	YES	YES	YES
年份	YES	YES	YES	YES	YES	YES
观测值 N	169	122	92	169	122	92
R^2	0.1656	0.1745	0.2293	0.1392	0.1785	0.2350

注：***、**、*分别表示在 1%、5%、10%水平上显著，方括号内为系数的标准误。

由结果可知，表 6 和表 5 的发现完全一致。换言之，创始人管理是有利于减少企业业绩波动的。此外，总体上来说，总资产周转率越高的企业，其公司经营业绩波动越大。

综合来看，表 4、表 5、表 6 的实证结果支持研究假说 1。这说明在中国民营 IPO 公司中，相对创始人不担任关键管理职务的公司而言，创始人担任关键管理职务的公司具有更好的业绩表现，并且公司业绩的稳定性更高。

（二）市场环境与创始人管理的后果

在上文分析的基础上，我们在回归方程中加入了创始人管理（创始人管理）与市场化指数的交互项（在表中表示为创始人管理 * 市场化指数），以考察创始人管理的作用与市场化进程之间的相互影响。

由结果可见,在表 7 中,无论是以 ROA 均值还是 ROS 均值作为公司业绩水平的度量,关键变量创始人管理的系数都显著为正,表示创始人管理可以显著地提高公司的业绩水平,与前文发现相同。此外,市场化指数的系数也显著为正,表明良好的外部市场环境有利于公司业绩的提高。而创始人管理与市场化指数的交互项系数显著为负,表明创始人管理对公司业绩的正面效应随着外部市场环境的改善而逐渐减少。我们可以看到市场化指数的系数和交互项的系数的大小差不多,且交互项系数略小一点,这说明当市场环境得以改善时,它非常强地削弱了创始人管理企业的正效应。同时,由于市场环境改善有益于提高企业业绩,因此市场环境改善对于企业业绩的净效应是正的。此外,由于创始人管理本身的系数除以市场化程度与创始人管理交互项的系数略小于 10,这说明只有极少数在市场化程度最高地区的企业,其采取创始人管理对企业业绩不利。这也再一次说明,不能简单地认为创始人管理对企业业绩的影响一定是好或坏,具体还要看市场环境。其他控制变量的系数与前面的分析基本相同,因此不再加以讨论。

表 7   创始人管理、市场环境与公司上市后业绩

变量及	ROA 均值			ROS 均值		
模型参数	(1)	(2)	(3)	(4)	(5)	(6)
创始人管理	0.1571 ***	0.5163 ***	0.6153 ***	2.4698 ***	3.9195 ***	4.7053 ***
	[0.0531]	[0.1472]	[0.1543]	[0.5944]	[1.0483]	[1.1358]
市场化指数	0.0180 ***	0.0657 ***	0.0726 ***	0.2740 ***	0.4798 ***	0.5512 ***
	[0.0061]	[0.0171]	[0.0177]	[0.0681]	[0.1218]	[0.1302]
创始人管理 * 市场化指数	−0.0160 ***	−0.0532 ***	−0.0651 ***	−0.2525 ***	−0.4078 ***	−0.5042 ***
	[0.006]	[0.0171]	[0.0181]	[0.0675]	[0.1216]	[0.1337]
年龄	0.000097	0.0049	0.0022	0.0050	0.0219	0.0154
	[0.0044]	[0.0118]	[0.0102]	[0.0490]	[0.0842]	[0.0749]
年龄平方	$6.79e-06$	−0.00003	−0.00001	0.00001	−0.0001	−0.00009
	[0.000042]	[0.00011]	[0.0001]	[0.0005]	[0.0008]	[0.0007]
企业年龄	−0.00006	−0.0004	0.0017	−0.0082	−0.0077	0.0049
	[0.0018]	[0.0049]	[0.0053]	[0.0207]	[0.0350]	[0.0393]
企业规模	−0.0035	−0.0035	−0.0142	−0.0705	−0.0371	−0.0838
	[0.0098]	[0.0262]	[0.0251]	[0.1097]	[0.1868]	[0.1848]

（续表）

变量及模型参数	ROA 均值			ROS 均值		
	（1）	（2）	（3）	（4）	（5）	（6）
资产负债率	−0.0689 *	−0.0432	0.0364	−0.0626	−0.0562	0.4058
	[.0394]	[0.1035]	[0.0952]	[0.4410]	[0.7372]	[0.7005]
总资产周转率	−0.0126 ***	−0.0273 **	−0.0323 **	−0.1212 **	−0.1703 *	−0.2302 **
	[0.0048]	[0.0130]	[0.0126]	0.0537	[0.0928]	[0.0924]
董事会规模	−0.0311	−0.0457	−0.0450	−0.1666	−0.2180	−0.2651
	[0.0211]	0.0649	[0.0585]	[0.2368]	[0.4621]	[0.4308]
独立董事比例	−0.0422	0.0338	−0.0029	−0.0496	0.3257	−0.0823
	[0.0601]	[0.1614]	[0.1348]	[0.6729]	[1.1500]	[0.9919]
股权集中度	−0.0243	−0.0489	−0.0455	−0.2036	−0.4142	−0.4856
	[0.0321]	[0.0896]	[0.0826]	[0.3597]	[0.6384]	[0.6076]
常数	0.0090	−0.9070 **	−0.1042	−1.2086	−6.8061 **	−1.5294
	[0.1214]	[0.4096]	[0.3124]	[1.3592]	[2.9171]	[2.2995]
行业	Yes	Yes	Yes	Yes	Yes	Yes
年份	Yes	Yes	Yes	Yes	Yes	Yes
观测值 N	169	122	92	169	122	92
R^2	0.2786	0.2523	0.3392	0.2036	0.2462	0.3485

注：***、**、* 分别表示在 1%、5%、10% 水平上显著，方括号内为系数的标准误。

对于市场环境和创始人管理的交互项的分析还有另一个重要的意义，它能够更好地说明创始人管理是企业经营绩效较好而绩效波动较小的原因，而非结果。表4～表6的分析表明，创始人管理的企业经营绩效较好而绩效波动较小，这完全可能是因为在这样的企业创始人没有被职业经理人替换的压力。如果是这样一个反向因果关系的话，当市场环境变得更好，企业绩效总体上得到提升之后，职业经理人的外部市场机会将更多。这时，就只有业绩更好的企业才会保留创始人管理者。于是我们应该看到，在市场化程度高的地方，创始人管理的企业应该绩效更好，两者的交互项应该为正才对。因此，表7的实际结果显示，表4～表6的结果更可能是因为创始人管理对公司业绩的影响，而不大可能是反向的因果关系。

表8是创始人管理、市场环境与公司业绩横向离散度之间关系的回归结果。

由结果可知,无论是以 ROA 离散度还是 ROS 离散度作为业绩横向离散度的度量指标,创始人管理和市场化指数各自的系数仍然显著为负,表明创始人管理和良好的市场环境可以减少公司业绩的波动性。创始人管理和市场化指数交互项的系数为正,表明创始人管理对于公司业绩的稳定作用会随着该地区市场化程度的提高而减弱。比较创始人管理和市场化指数的交互项系数与两者各自的系数,可以看到市场化程度提高所产生的稳定公司业绩的净效应是正的,而创始人管理的企业其业绩波动总体上较低,但在市场化程度最高的少数地区,创始人管理的企业业绩波动较大。

表 8　创始人管理、市场环境与公司上市后业绩的横向离散度

变量及	ROA 离散度			ROS 离散度		
模型参数	（1）	（2）	（3）	（4）	（5）	（6）
创始人管理	−0.1284 ***	−0.5642 ***	−0.4990 ***	−2.6324 ***	−4.4349 ***	−4.2302 ***
	[0.0318]	[0.0951]	[0.0850]	[0.4355]	[0.6871]	[0.6173]
市场化指数	−0.0154 ***	−0.0670 ***	−0.0618 ***	−0.2937 ***	−0.5165 ***	−0.4932 ***
	[0.0037]	[0.0111]	[0.0097]	[0.0499]	[0.0799]	[0.0708]
创始人管理 *	0.0128 ***	0.0585 ***	0.0543 ***	0.2658 ***	0.4605 ***	0.4462 ***
市场化指数	[0.0036]	[0.0110]	[0.0100]	[0.0495]	[0.0797]	[0.0727]
年龄	−0.0046 *	−0.0058	−0.0055	−0.0150	−0.0091	−0.0042
	[0.0026]	[0.0076]	[0.0056]	[0.0359]	[0.0552]	[0.0407]
年龄平方	0.00004 *	0.00004	0.00005	0.0001	$1.46e-06$	−0.00001
	[0.000025]	[0.00007]	[0.00005]	[0.0003]	[0.0005]	[0.0004]
企业年龄	−0.0005	−0.0006	−0.0037	0.0106	0.0085	−0.0177
	[0.0011]	[0.0031]	[0.0029]	[0.0152]	[0.0230]	[0.0213]
企业规模	0.0073	0.0036	0.0146	0.0701	−0.0014	0.0505
	[0.0058]	[0.0169]	[0.0138]	[0.0804]	[0.1224]	[0.1004]
资产负债率	−0.0583 **	−0.0540	−0.0751	−0.2963	−0.2697	−0.5797
	[0.0237]	[0.0668]	[0.0524]	[0.3231]	[0.4832]	[0.3806]
总资产周转率	0.0045	0.0188 **	0.0158 **	0.1132 ***	0.1652 ***	0.1360 ***
	[0.0029]	[0.0084]	[0.0069]	[0.0393]	[0.0608]	[0.0502]
董事会规模	0.0041	0.0217	0.0100	0.1450	0.1257	0.1977
	[0.0127]	[0.0419]	[0.0322]	[0.1735]	[0.3029]	[0.2341]

（续表）

变量及 模型参数	ROA 离散度			ROS 离散度		
	（1）	（2）	（3）	（4）	（5）	（6）
独立董事比例	−0.0106	−0.0788	−0.0475	−0.1222	−.3830	−0.1571
	[0.0361]	[0.1043]	[0.0743]	[0 4930]	[0.7537]	[0.5390]
股权集中度	−0.0103	0.0215	−0.0050	0 .1490	0.2932	0.2352
	[0.0193]	[0.0579]	[0.0454]	[0 .2636]	[0.4184]	[0.3302]
常数	0.2064 ***	1.1302 ***	0.3102 *	2.1434 **	7.6770 ***	1.5264
	[0.0729]	[0.2645]	[0.1721]	[0.9959]	[1.9119]	[1.2497]
行业	Yes	Yes	Yes	Yes	Yes	Yes
年份	Yes	Yes	Yes	Yes	Yes	Yes
观测值 N	169	122	92	169	122	92
R^2	0.3341	0.4193	0.5173	0.3470	0.4577	0.3380

注：*** 、** 、* 分别表示在 1%、5%、10% 水平上显著，方括号内为系数的标准误。

表 9 是创始人管理、市场环境与公司业绩纵向波动性的回归结果，这部分主要是对创始人管理与同一企业不同时间序列上公司业绩的波动性之间的关系进行分析。被解释变量是 ROA、ROS 的三年、四年、五年的标准差，以此表示公司业绩的纵向波动性。

表 9　创始人管理、市场环境与公司上市后业绩波动性

变量及 模型参数	ROA 均值			ROS 均值		
	（1）	（2）	（3）	（4）	（5）	（6）
创始人管理	−0.2057 ***	−0.6726 ***	−1.0974 ***	−4.1209 ***	−4.5573 ***	−7.1757 ***
	(0.0582]	[0.1902]	[0.2731]	[1.0024]	[1.2243]	[1.7515]
市场化指数	−0.0252 ***	−0.0843 ***	−0.1345 ***	−0.4762 ***	−0.5723 ***	−0.8713 ***
	[0.0067]	[0.0221]	[0.0313]	[0.1148]	[0.1423]	[0.2008]
创始人管理 * 市场化指数	0.0219 ***	0.0711 ***	0.1193 ***	0.4251 ***	0.4774 ***	0.7732 ***
	[0.0066]	[0.0221]	[0.0321]	[0.1138]	[0.1420]	[0.2062]
年龄	−.00030	−0.0092	−0.0087	−0.0237	−0.0356	−0.0367
	[0.0048]	[0.0153]	[0.0180]	[0.0827]	[0.0984]	[0.1155]

（续表）

变量及模型参数	ROA 均值			ROS 均值		
	（1）	（2）	（3）	（4）	（5）	（6）
年龄平方	0.00002	0.00006	.00007	0.0001	0.0002	0.0002
	[000005]	[0.0001]	[0.0002]	[0.0008]	[0.0009]	[0.0011]
企业年龄	0.0007	0.0020	−0.0019	[0.0125]	0.0090	−0.0085
	[0.0021]	[0.0064]	[0.0094]	[0.0349]	[0.0409]	[0.0605]
企业规模	0.0068	0.0089	0.0204	0.1223	0.0475	0.1130
	[0.0107]	[0.0339]	[0.0444]	[0.1851]	[0.2182]	[0.2850]
资产负债率	−0.0787 *	−0.0721	−0.1655	−0.3754	−0.3024	−0.9657
	[0.0431]	[0.1337]	[0.1684]	[0.7436]	[0.8610]	[1.0802]
总资产周转率	0.0128 **	0.0332 *	0.0589 ***	0.2708 ***	0.2507 **	0.4074 ***
	[0.0053]	[0.0168]	[0.0222]	[0.0906]	[0.1084]	[0.1425]
董事会规模	0.0316	0.0795	0.1059	0.2954	0.3025	0.4981
	[0.0232]	[0.0838]	[0.1035]	[0.3994]	[0.5397]	[0.6643]
独立董事比例	−0.001	−0.0964	−0.0244	−0.0394	−0.4875	−0.0387
	[0.0658]	[0.2086]	[0.2384]	[1.1345]	[1.3431]	[1.5295]
股权集中度	0.0310	0.1268	0.1663	0.4691	0.6393	0.9437
	[0.0352]	[0.1158]	[0.1461]	[0.6066]	[0.7456]	[0.9369]
常数	0.1759	1.2641 **	0.4298	2.5705	8.2516 **	2.8393
	[0.1330]	[0.5291]	[0.5529]	[2.2920]	[3.4070]	[3.5461]
行业	Yes	Yes	Yes	Yes	Yes	Yes
年份	Yes	Yes	Yes	Yes	Yes	Yes
观测值 N	169	122	92	169	122	92
R^2	0.2269	0.2566	0.3641	0.2183	0.2666	0.3711

注：*** 、** 、* 分别表示在 1%、5%、10% 水平上显著，方括号内为系数的标准误。

  由结果可知，表 9 和表 8 的发现完全一致。换言之，创始人管理在稳定公司业绩方面的作用随着该地区市场化进程的提高而减弱。

  综合表 7～表 9 的结果，从创始人管理与市场化指数的交互项来看，不管是业绩水平、业绩的横向离散度还是纵向波动性模型，交互项系数都与创始人管理和市场化指数本身的系数是符号相反的。市场化程度越高，创始人管理在改善企业业绩和稳定公司业绩的正面效应得到削弱,这支持研究假说 2。

(三)稳健性检验

上面的回归结果主要是考虑创始人担任 CEO 或者董事长的情况。在中国,民营企业的董事长既是企业真正的决策者同时也是企业的管理者,他们对企业很多事情都是亲力亲为。在我们的样本中,创始人担任董事长的比例要高过担任 CEO 的情况,且创始人担任公司总经理的情况较少。① 因此,本文选取了创始人只担任董事长的样本进行了稳健性检验。结果显示,表 3~表 9 的主要结论没有发生改变。此外,我们采用 ROE(净资产收益率)代替上文使用的 ROA(总资产收益率)指标,研究结论也不受影响。

五、全文总结

本文以 1997 年至 2007 年期间中国民营 IPO 公司为对象,考察了创始人担任公司关键管理职务对公司业绩及其波动性的影响。本文研究发现,在公司上市之后,创始人管理可以显著提升上市公司的业绩,同时起到降低公司业绩波动性的作用。企业所处省份的市场化水平也与公司业绩水平正相关,且具有降低公司业绩波动性的作用。更重要的是,本文发现在市场化水平较高的地区,创始人管理对公司业绩及其波动性的正面影响较小。在少数市场化水平最高的地区,创始人管理对公司业绩及其波动的作用将由正转负。

本文的发现揭示了创始人在中国民营企业经营管理中的重要作用,这也从侧面印证了民营企业"传承"的困难。同时,本文也对未来民营企业的顺利传承寄予乐观的预期,在更高市场化水平的地区,创始人管理的企业相对于其他企业的优势更小,因此创始人离职给企业造成的负面影响更小,那么企业的传承就相对容易实现。但是,在短期内也应看到在整体市场环境还不尽完善的时期,如果由于年龄或健康的原因导致民营企业的创始人必须离职,那么可能会对企业的业绩产生一定程度的负面冲击。因此,持续地完善正式的市场环境建设是保证企业基业长青的外部条件,当企业能够在更好的市场环境下摆脱创始人的"人治"影响时,企业才能将自己的发展寄希望于更加职业化的经理人管理。

---

① 创始人担任董事长的比例为 62%,担任 CEO 的不足 1%,还有 15.6%的兼任董事长和 CEO。

参考文献

樊纲,王小鲁,朱恒鹏.中国市场化指数——各地区市场化相对进程2009年报告[M].北京:经济科学出版社,2010.

李琳,刘凤委,卢文彬.基于公司业绩波动性的股权制衡治理效应研究[J].管理世界,2009(5):145-151.

陆铭,潘慧.政企纽带——民营企业家成长与企业发展[M].北京:北京大学出版社,2009.

权小峰,吴世农.CEO权力强度、信息披露质量与公司业绩的波动性——基于深交所上市公司的实证研究[J].南开管理评论,2010(4):142-153.

孙早,刘庆岩.市场环境,企业家能力与企业的绩效表现——转型期中国民营企业绩效表现影响因素的实证研究[J].南开经济研究,2006(2):92-104.

夏立军,方轶强.政府控制,治理环境与公司价值——来自中国证券市场的经验证据[J].经济研究,2005(05):40-51.

张军,等.转型,治理与中国私人企业的演进[M].上海:复旦大学出版社,2006.

Adams R B,Almeida H,Ferreira D. Powerful CEOs and their impact on corporate performance[J]. The review of financial studies,2005,18(4):1403-1432.

Adams R B,Almeida H,Ferreira D. Understanding the relationship between founder-CEOs and firm performance[J]. Journal of empirical finance,2009,16(1):136-150.

Aldrich H. Organizations and Environments[M]. Englewood Cliffs:Prentice Hall,1979.

Allen F,Qian J,Qian M. Law,finance,and economic growth in China[J]. Journal of financial economics,2005,77(1):57-116.

Anderson R C,Reeb D M. Founding-family ownership and firm performance:evidence from the S&P 500[J]. The journal of finance,2003,58(3):1301-1328.

Begley T M. Using founder status,age of firm,and company growth rate as the basis for distinguishing entrepreneurs from managers of smaller businesses[J]. Journal of business venturing,1995,10(3):249-263.

Certo S T,Covin J G,Daily C M,et al. Wealth and the effects of founder management among IPO-stage new ventures[J]. Strategic management journal,2001,22(6-7):641-658.

Cheng S J. Board size and the variability of corporate performance[J]. Journal of financial economics,2008,87(1):157-176.

Dalton D R,Daily C M. Financial performance of founder-managed versus professionally managed corporations[J]. Journal of small business economics,1992,30(2):25-34.

Fama E F. Agency problems and the theory of the firm[J]. Journal of political economy,

1980，88(2)：288 - 307.

Fama E F，Jensen M C. Separation of ownership and control[J]. The journal of law and economics，1983，26(2)：301 - 325.

Fischer H M，Pollock T G. Effects of social capital and power on surviving transformational change: the case of initial public offerings[J]. Academy of management journal，2004，47(4)：463 - 481.

Gedajlovic E，Lubatkin M H，Schulze W S. Crossing the threshold from founder management to professional management: a governance perspective [J]. Journal of management studies，2004，41(5)：899 - 912.

Glejser H. A new test for heteroskedasticity[J]. Journal of the American statistical association，1969，64(325)：316 - 323.

Hambrick D C，Crozier L M. Stumblers and stars in the management of rapid growth[J]. Journal of business venturing，1985，1(1)：31 - 45.

Hart O D. Optimal labour contracts under asymmetric information: an introduction[J]. The review of economic studies，1983，50(1)：3 - 35.

He L. Do founders matter? A study of executive compensation，governance structure and firm performance[J]. Journal of business venturing，2008，23(3)：257 - 279.

Holmström B. Managerial incentive problems: a dynamic perspective[J]. The review of economic studies，1999，66(1)：169 - 182.

Jayaraman N，Khorana A，Nelling E，et al. CEO founder status and firm financial performance[J]. Strategic management journal，2000，21(12)：1215 - 1224.

Jenson M C，Meckling W H. Theory of the firm: managerial behavior，agency costs and ownership structure[J]. Journal of financial economics，1976，3(4)：305 - 360.

La Porta R，Lopez-de-Silanes F，Shleifer A，et al. Law and finance[J]. Journal of political economy，1998，106(6)：1113 - 1155.

Morck R，Stangeland D，Yeung B. Inherited wealth，corporate control，and economic growth the canadian disease? [M]. Concentrated Corporate Ownership. Chicago: University of Chicago Press，2000：319 - 372.

Nelson T. The persistence of founder influence: management，ownership，and performance effects at initial public offering[J]. Strategic management journal，2003，24(8)：707 - 724.

Peng M W. How entrepreneurs create wealth in transition economies[J]. Academy of management perspectives，2001，15(1)：95 - 110.

Scharfstein D. Product-market competition and managerial slack[J]. The RAND journal of economics，1988：147 - 155.

Shleifer A，Vishny R W. Alternative mechanism for corporate control［J］. American economic review，1989，79：842－852.

Wang D. Founding family ownership and earnings quality［J］. Journal of accounting research，2006，44(3)：619－656.

Wasserman N. Founder-CEO succession and the paradox of entrepreneurial success［J］. Organization science，2003，14(2)：149－172.

Xia L J. Founder control，ownership structure and firm value：evidence from entrepreneurial listed firms in China［J］. China journal of accounting research，2008，1：31－49.

▶夏立军感谢教育部"新世纪优秀人才支持计划"（NCET－08－0802）和国家自然科学基金项目（70772101）的资助。陆铭感谢"上海市领军人才计划"和上海市重点学科建设项目（B101）的资助。本文也是"复旦大学当代中国经济与社会工作室"的成果。感谢金李、罗红、吴文锋的讨论。

下　篇
资本市场制度（会计/监管/司法）
与市场效率（政府与市场关系）

注册会计师对上市公司盈余管理的反应[*]

内容提要：上市公司的盈余管理以及注册会计师的审计质量是目前证券市场上备受关注的问题。本文以上市公司 2000 年度财务报告为研究对象，对上市公司审计意见和监管政策（股票特别处理、暂停交易以及配股的政策）诱导性盈余管理的关系进行了实证研究。研究结果表明，从整体上看，注册会计师并没有揭示出上市公司的这种盈余管理行为，注册会计师的审计质量令人担忧。

关 键 词：监管政策；盈余管理；审计意见；审计质量

一、研究背景

上市公司对外公布的财务报告，是投资者进行决策的重要依据，财务报告的信息质量，与投资者的经济利益息息相关。由于投资者和上市公司管理当局之间的信息不对称，以及由此引起的道德风险和逆向选择问题，客观上需要有一个独立的第三者对财务报告信息质量进行鉴证，以提高报告的可信赖程度，从而减轻代理成本。在证券市场上，这个独立的第三者的角色由注册会计师充当，注册会计师发表的审计意见则是鉴证的结果。注册会计师的审计质量越高，就越能减轻代理成本。正是由于注册会计师在减轻代理成本中的作用，使得注册会计师职业在经济发达国家备受重视，并已成为经济发达国家维护市场经济秩序的重要手段。

在我国，注册会计师审计的历史比发达国家要短得多，但是发展迅速，特别是 1995 年、1996 年和 1999 年分别颁布的三批独立审计准则以及 1998 年和 1999 年

---

* 本文选自：夏立军、杨海斌：注册会计师对上市公司盈余管理的反应，《审计研究》，2002 年第 4 期，第 28 - 34 页。

进行的脱钩改制,大大促进了我国注册会计师审计独立性的提高,注册会计师在社会公众中的地位与作用越来越高。然而,我们也看到在证券市场上,继原野、琼民源、红光实业、东方锅炉之后,近几年又爆出了郑百文、黎明股份、银广夏等涉及注册会计师责任的会计造假恶性事件,人们对我国注册会计师的能力和信誉产生了怀疑。目前,注册会计师有没有揭示出上市公司的盈余管理?[①] 上市公司审计的整体质量如何?[②] 这些问题并没有得到很好的回答。基于此,本文以上市公司2000年度财务报告为研究对象,对上市公司审计意见和监管政策(股票特别处理、暂停交易以及配股的政策)诱导性盈余管理的关系进行实证研究,并试图从这个角度回答上述问题。

二、文献回顾

在国外,盈余管理的主要动机是三大假设,即管理人员报酬计划、债务契约和政治成本。但是,在国内,情况有所不同。上市公司盈余管理的主要动机是为了应付证券市场特殊的监管政策,如发行上市政策、配股政策、特别处理政策以及暂停交易政策等。Aharony,Lee,and Wang(2000)发现中国的上市公司在初次发行股票时,存在做大盈余以提高发行价格的现象。Haw et al.(1998)以1994年至1997年的上市公司为研究对象,就中国上市公司针对监管政策的盈余管理进行了实证研究,结果发现在ROE(净资产收益率)10%下限的配股政策出台后,有边际ROE[③](ROE落在[10%,11%]中)的公司所占比例增加了三倍,并证实这些有边际ROE的公司运用线下项目和应计项目进行盈余管理,以达到配股下限。国内还有不少学者研究了盈余管理和监管政策之间的关系,同样表明盈余管理受到监管政策的很大影响(Chen and Yuan 2001;蒋义宏,1998;王跃堂,1999;陈小悦、肖星,2000)。

为了应付特殊的监管政策,上市公司普遍进行盈余管理。那么对上市公司进

---

① 关于盈余管理有不同的定义,我们将盈余管理定义为公司管理当局为了实现其自身或公司价值最大化,通过调节会计政策或公司业务等手段对公司财务报告进行操纵,以使公司对外披露的财务报告不能真实、公允地反映公司的实际经营成果。因此,依据中国注册会计师独立审计准则,注册会计师应该根据重要性原则对公司的盈余管理进行揭示,而重要性原则是以不误导财务报告使用者决策为标准。

② 注册会计师的审计质量是指注册会计师发现并且报告出被审计单位财务报告中的非真实、非公允性表达的概率。由于上市公司针对监管政策的盈余管理会误导投资者或监管部门的行为,因此可以从检验注册会计师对这种盈余管理的反应的角度来考察注册会计师的审计质量。

③ 所谓边际ROE是指公司的ROE超过特定的目标值,但是离特定的目标值很近。针对不同的配股政策,公司盈余管理的目标值也不一样。例如:对2000年的上市公司来说,配股要求每年ROE不小于6%,所以边际ROE可以定义为[6%,7%]。

行审计的注册会计师的反应如何呢？李树华(2000)就审计服务的需求、供给和会计师事务所的独立性进行研究,重点探寻政府管制和市场需求对转轨经济中注册会计师行业结构的深入影响。他在研究中发现,无论是在独立审计准则颁布实施前还是实施后,大事务所均比小事务所更具独立性,但是,国内"十大"事务所独立性提高后的市场份额却显著下降,由此说明国内证券市场还缺乏对高审计独立性的需求。Chen,Su,and Zhao(2000)以沪市 1995 年至 1997 年的上市公司为研究对象,对审计意见的市场反应进行了实证研究,研究结果表明审计意见具有信息含量,但是对于带解释说明段的无保留审计意见和其他非标准无保留审计意见[①],市场反应没有显著差异。

Chen,Chen,and Su(2001)以沪深股市 1995 年至 1997 年的上市公司为研究对象,专门研究了审计意见和盈余管理之间的关系,他们发现非标准无保留审计意见与具有边际 ROE(ROE 落在[10%,11%]或[0%,1%]中)的公司在统计上有显著的正相关关系,这一结果表明注册会计师揭示出了盈余管理。但他们的研究对象是 1995 年至 1997 年的上市公司,而 1997 年后上市公司和会计师事务所的监管环境发生了很大变化,例如:1999 年后配股政策进行了重大修改,而配股政策的修改会影响到上市公司的盈余管理行为;1998 年有证券审计资格的会计师事务所进行了脱钩改制,而这会大大改变注册会计师的风险和收益预期。因此,他们的研究结果不能反映监管环境变化后的情况。鉴于此,本文以上市公司2000 年度财务报告为研究对象,对上市公司审计意见和监管政策(股票特别处理、暂停交易以及配股的政策)诱导性盈余管理的关系进行进一步的研究。

三、研究假说

在西方发达国家,企业融资的顺序符合啄食顺序理论,即企业融资的顺序是先内部融资,再负债融资,最后是股权融资。但在我国,一方面,由于证券市场发展的时间比较短,各项法律法规还不完善,公司治理机制也没有很好地建立起来,使得企业股权融资的实际成本非常低;另一方面,由于企业经济效益欠佳,银行贷款偿还率低、呆账损失较多,致使银行不愿意向企业贷款,企业的负债融资受到限制。这两个因素导致企业对股权融资有着十分强烈的需求。在这种情况下,为了避免各

---

① 非标准无保留意见是指除了标准无保留意见即不带说明段的无保留意见之外的所有其他审计意见类型,包括带说明段的无保留意见、保留意见、否定意见和拒绝表示意见。

地区、各部门"一哄而上",最终使证券市场因"劣币驱逐良币"而陷入困境,证券监管部门只好对企业在证券市场上进行股权融资进行限制。对于上市公司来说,能否继续在证券市场上生存下来并进行股权融资,主要由股票特别处理政策、股票暂停交易政策和配股政策决定。在这些政策中,最主要的考察指标是公司是否盈利以及 ROE 是否达到配股下限,因此,可以预期上市公司为了避免股票被特别处理、被暂停交易或者为了获得配股资格,会有强烈的动机进行盈余管理,而盈余管理的结果是这些公司会具有边际 ROE(Haw et al., 1998;Chen and Yuan 2001)。

　　一般来说,上市公司和注册会计师都不希望公司年度报告被出具非标准无保留审计意见。因为,对上市公司来说,被出具非标准无保留审计意见会引起监管者的额外注意,还会对公司股价产生不利的市场反应,影响公司形象,增加融资成本。对注册会计师来说,出具非标准无保留审计意见可能会造成客户的不满,甚至会被客户解聘,从而失去审计公费的来源。但是,如果注册会计师没有揭示出公司财务报告中的盈余管理,那么注册会计师会面临被处罚或被起诉的风险。因此,注册会计师出具审计意见时面临着风险和收益的权衡。李树华(2000)和王跃堂、陈世敏(2001)的实证研究表明,独立审计准则的颁布,以及 1998 年有证券审计资格事务所脱钩改制的完成,大大提高了注册会计师审计的独立性。另外,由于财政部和中国证监会对有证券审计资格的事务所实行"许可证管理"制度,这也从另一方面促使事务所保持独立性,其原因是"许可证管理"制度实际上在现阶段建立了一项对事务所最行之有效的惩罚机制,增加了事务所违规的机会成本(李树华,2000)。事实上,"琼民源"一案中的北京中华会计师事务所、"红光实业"一案中的蜀都会计师事务所、"东方锅炉"一案中的四川会计师事务所,几乎都是因一家客户而被暂停数月乃至数年证券从业资格,进而使事务所的前途遭到毁灭性的打击。因此,我们预期整体来说注册会计师会揭示出上市公司的盈余管理,从而盈余管理可能性大的上市公司收到非标准无保留审计意见的可能性也更大。据此,我们提出如下假设:

　　研究假说:具有边际 ROE 的上市公司比不具有边际 ROE 的上市公司更容易收到非标准无保留审计意见。

四、研究方法

(一)样本选择和数据来源

为了能够准确地反映目前证券市场的审计质量,我们选取了截至 2000 年 12

月 31 日的沪深两市所有上市公司为研究对象。这样，共有 1 088 家上市公司作为研究样本，其中仅有 A 股的公司 955 家、仅有 B 股的公司 28 家、既有 A 股又有 B 股的公司 86 家、既有 A 股又有 H 股的公司 19 家。上市公司 2000 年度审计意见和主审事务所资料来自我们根据上市公司 2000 年度报告的逐一整理，上市公司 2000 年度报告来自中国证监会指定信息披露网站——巨潮咨讯网（www.cninfo.com.cn）。为了确保数据的准确性，我们将整理出的审计意见和事务所资料与中国证监会首会办编写的《谁审计中国证券市场——审计市场分析（2000）》中的数据进行了逐一核对，并纠正了其中的错误。

上市公司的行业类型来自中国证监会 2001 年颁布的《上市公司行业分类指引》，该指引以上市公司最近年度经审计后的营业收入为分类标准，具有较好的科学性和权威性，并与我们的研究对象吻合。上市公司的财务指标、上市时间等数据来自巨灵证券信息系统（2001），我们抽取了其中的部分数据与上市公司 2000 年度报告进行了核对，并补充了有关缺失的数据。本文数据的处理使用 SPSS 10.0 统计软件进行。

（二）样本特征描述性统计

截至 2000 年 12 月 31 日，上市公司总数为 1088 家，其中 15 家公司净资产为负数。由于净资产为负数的公司计算 ROE 没有意义，我们剔除了这 15 家公司以观察各 ROE 区间公司数量和非标准无保留审计意见的分布。图 1 分别列示了剩余的 1 073 家上市公司中公司数量和非标准无保留意见在各 ROE 区间的分布情况。上市公司分布的折线表示各 ROE 区间全部上市公司数，非标准无保留意见分布的折线表示各 ROE 区间被出具非标准无保留意见的上市公司数。

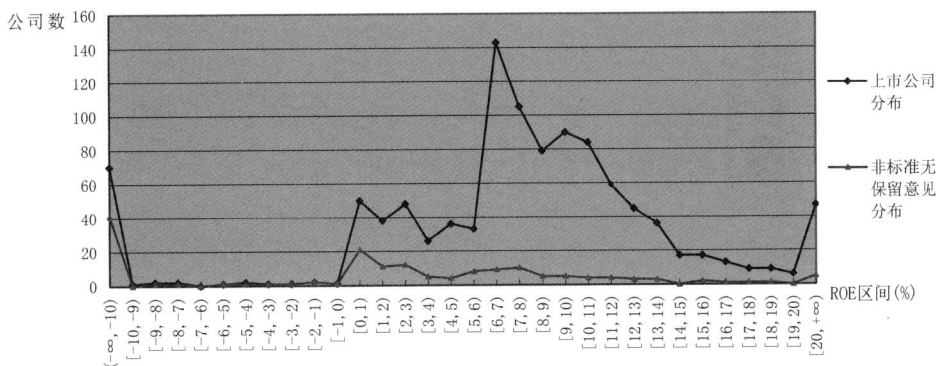

图 1　2000 年上市公司分布及非标准无保留意见分布

从图 1 我们可以看出：

（1）ROE 处于[0%，1%)和[6%，7%)之间的上市公司明显比其左右区域的上市公司要多，形成上市公司数分布的极值区。尤其是，ROE 处于[5%，6%)之间的上市公司只有 30 多家，而 ROE 处于[6%，7%)之间的上市公司则最多，达到 140 多家，显示了明显的盈余管理迹象。和以前年度相比，上市公司分布的"10% 现象"不再存在，却形成"6% 现象"，[1]我们认为这是和配股政策的变化分不开的。在 1999 年之前，上市公司配股政策要求 ROE 每年不低于 10%，而 1999 年后上市公司配股政策改为要求 ROE 每年不低于 6%。由此可见，上市公司的 ROE 分布受到配股政策的很大影响。[2]

（2）ROE 处于(−∞，−10%)之间的公司有一半以上被出具了非标准无保留意见，ROE 处于[0%，1%)之间的公司有 1/3 以上被出具了非标准无保留意见，而 ROE 处于[6%，7%)之间的公司只有不到 1/14 被出具了非标准无保留意见，可见盈利能力越差的公司被出具非标准无保留意见的可能性越大。另一方面，和上市公司数分布在 ROE[0%，1%)和[6%，7%)的区间形成极值区不同，非标准无保留意分布只在 ROE[0%，1%)的区间形成极值区，而在 ROE[6%，7%)的区间没有形成分布极值区。并且，ROE 处于[−4%，0%)之间的公司 100% 被出具了非标准无保留意见，而 ROE 处于[0%，1%)之间的公司这一比例为 42%。这大体可以说明，注册会计师没有揭示出 ROE[0%，1%)和[6%，7%)区间的盈余管理。

另外，我们考察了 15 家净资产为负数的上市公司的审计意见，发现被出具的都是非标准无保留意见，其中无保留意见加说明段 1 家，保留意见 4 家，拒绝表示意见 9 家，否定意见 1 家，可见净资产为负的公司审计意见普遍较差，这说明净资产为负数的上市公司问题较多，同时也表明注册会计师面对财务状况恶化的公司具有较强的风险意识。

（三）模型选择和变量说明

我们使用如下 Logistic 回归模型对研究假说进行检验：

---

[1] 10%现象和 6%现象分别指 ROE 处于 10% 和 6% 之间的上市公司异常地多于其他区域的现象。国内很多学者研究了"10%现象"（Haw et al.，1998;蒋义宏，1998;等等）。

[2] 值得一提的是，由于监管部门不断完善配股等监管政策，使得使用边际 ROE 方法来揭示盈余管理越来越不可靠。因此本文使用了截面修正的 Jones 模型对边际 ROE 方法进行了检验，检验结果证实本文定义的边际 ROE 区间有明显的盈余管理。由于篇幅关系，本文未列出检验过程及结果。

$$OP = \beta_0 + \beta_1\,De\text{-}list + \beta_2\,Rights + \beta_3\,AGE + \beta_5\,EPS + \beta_6\,\Delta EPS +$$
$$\beta_7\,NAPS + \beta_8\,CR + \beta_9\,DR + \beta_{10}\,FR + \beta_{11}\,Big10 + \varepsilon$$

其中：OP 代表审计意见类型，当公司被出具非标准无保留意见时取 1，被出具标准无保留意见时取 0。De-list 和 Rights 为测试变量，分别代表公司为避免被特别处理或被暂停交易和为获得配股资格的盈余管理动机。根据深沪两个交易所的规定，上市公司连续两年亏损将被特别处理；根据《中华人民共和国公司法》的规定，上市公司连续三年亏损将被暂停交易，如果没有在限期内消除，将会被中止股票上市。因此当公司的 ROE 处于[0%，1%]之中时，我们定义 De-list 为 1，ROE 为其他值时，De-list 为 0。① 对于 2000 年的上市公司，其配股政策是最近三年 ROE 平均不小于 10%，每年不小于 6%，因此当公司 ROE 处于[6%，7%]中时，我们定义 Rights 为 1，其他情况定义 Rights 为 0。

根据国内外有关审计意见影响因素的研究结果，我们选取了 9 个控制变量，以控制影响注册会计师出具审计意见的其他影响因素：AGE 代表公司的上市时间长短，用公司的上市日期距离 2000 年 12 月 31 日的天数除以 360 表示；EPS 为每股收益，代表公司当年的经营业绩；ΔEPS 为当年每股收益与上年每股收益的差额；NAPS 为每股净资产，代表公司财务状况和历年累计业绩；CR 为流动比率，代表公司短期偿债能力；DR 为资产负债率，代表公司长期偿债能力；FR 为公司 2000 年年末外资股股数和公司总股数的比例；Big10 为代表事务所类型的虚拟变量，如果公司的主审事务所为十大，则取 1，否则取 0，我们按事务所 2000 年年报审计的客户数来区分十大和非十大。

五、实证结果及解释

（一）单变量分析

我们先对检验模型中的各变量进行了单变量分析。表 1 列示了单变量分析的结果，其中 Panel A 是对所有数值变量均值差异性的 T 检验结果，Panel B 是对所有数值变量的 Mann-Whitney 非参数检验的结果，Panel C 是对虚拟变量的 x^2 检验的结果。从表中可以看出特征：①对于标准无保留意见和非标准无保留意见来说，除了 ΔEPS、FR 和 Big10 以外，其他所有变量均有显著差异。这表明标准

① 我们观察了 15 家净资产为负数公司的每股收益及其净资产收益率，发现它们的每股收益都小于 0，净资产收益率都不在本文定义的边际 ROE 区间中，因此本文定义的边际 ROE 区间不会引起样本混乱的问题。

无保留意见和非标准无保留意见的两类样本在很多变量特征上有明显的差异,因此注册会计师出具非标准无保留意见时可能受到这些因素的影响。②对于无保留加说明意见和保留、否定、拒绝意见来说,测试变量 De-list、Rights 和 AGE 均没有显著差异,说明注册会计师对于具有边际 ROE 的公司的盈余管理没能用不同性质的非标准无保留意见加以揭示。其原因可能是注册会计师为了达成与上市公司之间的妥协而使用无保留加说明的意见代替保留、否定或拒绝意见。

表 1 审计意见类型的单变量分析

Panel A:样本均值差异性的 T 检验

变量	标准无保留(909)	非标准无保留(179)	T 值	无保留加说明(107)	保留、否定、拒绝(72)	T 值
AGE	3.8883	5.3475	−8.285***	5.3453	5.3507	−0.017
EPS	0.2476	−0.1265	9.32***	0.0378	−0.3706	4.747***
ΔEPS	−0.0136	−0.0151	0.029	0.0115	−0.0546	0.542
NAPS	2.9456	1.4978	10.064***	1.9616	0.8086	3.717***
CR	1.9541	1.5058	2.373**	1.4623	1.5705	−0.242
DR	0.4074	0.6517	−7.262***	0.5362	0.8235	−3.88***
FR	0.0487	0.0576	−0.848	0.0505	0.0681	−0.865

Panel B:样本均值差异性的 Mann-Whitney 检验

变量	标准无保留(909)	非标准无保留(179)	Z 值	无保留加说明(107)	保留、否定、拒绝(72)	Z 值
AGE	511.99	709.61	−7.691***	89.21	91.18	−0.25
EPS	602.55	249.69	−13.733***	106.9	64.88	−5.32***
ΔEPS	549.88	517.18	−1.272	96.51	80.33	−2.049**
NAPS	594.34	291.41	−11.79***	101.02	73.62	−3.47***
CR	577.78	375.5	−7.873***	99.36	76.08	−2.948***
DR	504.69	746.65	−9.417***	79.1	106.19	−3.43***
FR	540.76	563.47	−1.375	87.93	93.07	−0.929

（续表）

Panel C：虚拟变量观察值为 1 的 x^2 检验（括号内为期望值）

变量	标准无保留（909）	非标准无保留（179）	Pearson x^2	无保留加说明（107）	保留、否定、拒绝（72）	Pearson x^2
Big10	298（295.8）	56（58.2）	0.153	34（33.5）	22（22.5）	0.03
De-list	29（42.6）	22（8.4）	27.72***	14（13.2）	8（8.8）	0.155
Rights	134（119.5）	9（23.5）	12.36***	6（5.4）	3（3.6）	0.187

注：*** ，** ，* 分别表示检验在 1%、5%、10%水平上统计显著（双尾检验）。审计意见类型下方括号内为样本数量（无 5 个标准差以外的异常值）。

（二）多变量分析

单变量分析没有控制变量之间的相互影响，因此我们再对检验模型进行多变量分析，以进一步考察各变量之间的相互关系。表 2 为检验模型的 Logistic 回归分析的结果，其中 A 列是对标准无保留意见和非标准无保留意见的分析结果，B 列是剔除了保留、否定和拒绝意见样本后对标准无保留意见和无保留加说明意见的分析结果，C 列是剔除了无保留加说明意见样本后的对标准无保留意见和保留、否定、拒绝意见的分析结果。三列模型的 Model x^2 值分别为 268.853、127.145、204.993，说明模型的拟合效果较好。另外经检查，模型没有严重的共线性和异方差问题。

表 2　审计意见类型的 Logistic 分析

模型：$OP = \beta_0 + \beta_1 De\text{-}list + \beta_2 Rights + \beta_3 AGE + \beta_5 EPS + \beta_6 \Delta EPS + \beta_7 NAPS + \beta_8 CR + \beta_9 DR + \beta_{10} FR + \beta_{11} Big10 + \varepsilon$

自变量	预测符号	A. 标准无保留与非标准无保留		B. 标准无保留与无保留加说明		C. 标准无保留与保留、否定、拒绝	
		系数	Wald x^2	系数	Wald x^2	系数	Wald x^2
截距	？	−1.554	3.897**	−1.320	1.794	−2.961	5.673**
De-list	＋	−1.011	9.912***	−0.976	6.959***	−1.298	7.733***

自变量	预测符号	A. 标准无保留与非标准无保留		B. 标准无保留与无保留加说明		C. 标准无保留与保留、否定、拒绝	
		系数	Wald x^2	系数	Wald x^2	系数	Wald x^2
Rights	+	0.440	1.380	0.464	1.074	0.249	0.155
AGE	+	0.102	5.059**	0.109	4.418**	0.046	0.377
EPS	−	−3.196	35.003***	−2.454	16.428***	−3.542	22.098***
∆EPS	+	1.155	7.375***	1.378	8.473***	0.653	1.293
NAPS	−	−0.343	6.303**	−0.433	7.084***	−0.324	2.152
CR	−	0.001	2.446	0.000	0.007	0.002	5.046**
DR	+	0.019	7.538***	0.012	1.885	0.028	7.039***
FR	−	−1.18	2.322	−1.889	3.810*	−0.143	0.017
Big10	+	0.304	1.961	0.187	0.576	0.576	2.44
N		1088=909+179		1016=909+107		981=909+72	
Model x^2		268.853***		127.145***		204.993***	

注:***、**、*分别表示检验在1%、5%、10%水平上统计显著(单尾检验)。N为样本数量(无5个标准差以外的异常值)。

从表中A列可以看出:①OP与De-list在0.01显著性水平上负相关,这说明ROE处于[0%,1%]区间的公司被出具非标准无保留意见的可能性反而更小,这与我们的研究假说不符。OP与Rights正相关,这说明ROE处于[6%,7%]的公司被出具非标准无保留意见的可能性更大,但是我们发现这种关系并不显著,同样说明我们的研究假说不能成立。这说明注册会计师并没有像我们预期的那样揭示出具有边际ROE的上市公司的盈余管理。②OP与AGE在0.05显著性水平上正相关,说明上市时间越长的公司获得非标准无保留意见的可能性越大。根据我们上面对监管政策与盈余管理关系检验中的结果,上市时间越长的公司进行盈余管理的可能性并不是更大。因此,上市时间越长的公司被出具非标准无保留意见的可能性更大,并不是因为其盈余管理的可能性更大,而更可能的原因是上市时间越长的公司其财务压力更大、积累的问题更多。这与Chen,Chen,and Su(2001)的解释不同,他们认为上市时间越长的公司被出具非标准无保留意见的可能性越大的原因是其盈余管理的可能性更大,但是他们没有对公司盈余管理和其上市时间长短的关系进行检验,因此他们的解释值得怀疑。③OP与EPS、NAPS显著负相关,与DR显著正相关,这说明公司盈利能力和财务状况越差的公司被出具非标准无保留意见的可能性越大;OP与∆EPS显著正相关,说明每股收益增长越快的公司被出具非标准无保留意见的可能性越大。可见,注册会计师在出具审计意见时具有较强的风险意识。④OP 与 CR、FR 的关系均不显著,公司流动比率和外资股比例对注册会计师出具审计意见的影响不大。OP 与 Big10 正相关,说明十大事务所出具的非标准无保留意见的比例更高,审计质量更好,但是这种关系并不显著,事务所规模还难以作为审计质量的替代指标。

表 2 的 B 列和 C 列主要用来考察注册会计师对各种不同审计意见类型的运用。从中我们可以看出:①无论是第 B 列还是 C 列,De-list 依然与 OP 显著负相关,而 Rights 与 OP 依然没有显著关系,说明注册会计师既没有用保留、否定、拒绝意见也没有用无保留意见加说明段揭示出具有边际 ROE 公司的盈余管理。由此可见,注册会计师并不认为这些具有边际 ROE 的公司具有更高的风险。②在 B 列中 OP 与 AGE 显著正相关,但在 C 列中 OP 与 AGE 的相关关系不显著,说明上市时间越长的公司被出具的非标准无保留意见的可能性越大,但主要是因为被出具的无保留意见加说明段的可能性更大了,而不是因为被出具保留、否定和拒绝意见的可能性更大了。③在 C 列中,除 De-list 外,只有 EPS、CR 和 DR 与 OP 显著相关,说明公司每股收益越差、流动比率越高、资产负债率越高,那么被注册会计师出具严厉的审计意见的可能性越大。流动比率越高被出具严厉的审计意见的可能性越大可能是因为有些经营不善的公司存货积压、资金闲置的缘故。④无论在 B 列还是 C 列,Big10 与 OP 都是正相关,但是相关关系都不显著,再次说明十大事务所和非十大事务所的审计质量并没有显著差异。另外,值得注意的是,在 B 列中 FR 与 OP 在 0.10 显著性水平上负相关,这表明外资股比例越多的公司获得无保留加说明段意见的可能性越小。

(三)敏感性测试

我们对边际 ROE 的定义进行了敏感性分析,分别测试了边际 ROE 为两个百分点、三个百分点时对检验模型的 Logistic 回归分析结果。另外我们还按照事务所客户总资产排名区分十大和非十大进行了敏感性分析。敏感性分析的结果不改变本文的研究结论,回归模型的检验结果具有较强的可靠性。

六、研究结论和局限

盈余管理是 20 世纪 80 年代中后期兴起的实证会计研究的一个重要研究领域。上市公司盈余管理的动机是什么? 注册会计师在抑制上市公司盈余管理中起到什么作用？研究这些问题可以从更深层次上理解会计盈余的有用性和会计行为的形成与作用机制，可以进一步验证会计行为的经济后果以及监管政策的有效性。本文以上市公司 2000 年度财务报告为研究对象，检验了注册会计师对上市公司针对监管政策的盈余管理的反应。我们的主要研究结论如下：①具有边际 ROE 的上市公司盈余管理迹象明显，表现为上市公司 ROE 分布的"6%"现象和"0%"现象。并且，ROE 处于[6%，7%]之间的上市公司比 ROE 处于[0%，1%]之间的上市公司盈余管理的可能性更大。②财务状况和盈利能力越差的公司被出具非标准无保留意见尤其是保留、否定和拒绝意见的可能性更大，说明注册会计师具有较强的风险意识。但是，具有边际 ROE 的公司被出具非标准无保留意见的可能性并不是更大，因此，从整体上说，注册会计师没有揭示出上市公司的这种盈余管理行为，注册会计师虽然有较强的风险意识，但是审计质量令人担忧。③上市时间越长的公司被出具非标准无保留意见的可能性越大，这不是因为上市时间越长的公司盈余管理的可能性越大，而是因为上市时间越长的公司其财务压力越大，积累的问题越多。④在控制了影响审计意见的其他因素后，十大事务所出具非标准无保留意见的可能性并不比非十大事务所出具非标准无保留意见的可能性更大。说明在国内，虽然近年来事务所间的联合兼并造就了不少大规模的事务所，但是这些大规模的事务所的审计质量和小规模的事务所并没有显著区别，事务所的规模还难以作为审计质量的替代衡量指标。

我们的研究结果表明，上市公司的盈余管理行为受到监管政策的很大影响，但是从整体上来说，注册会计师并没有揭示出上市公司的这种盈余管理。而 Chen and Yuan（2001）的研究表明，虽然 1996 年以来，中国证监会逐渐增加了对上市公司盈余管理的检查，但是由于这种检查是有限的，因此还有很多公司能够通过盈余管理获得配股资格，并且这些通过盈余管理获得配股资格的公司在以后年度的业绩显著地差于那些未进行盈余管理而获得配股资格的公司。在这种情况下，监管政策的有效性便失去保证，监管政策的资源配置效率也是值得怀疑的。我们认为证券市场的资源配置主要还是应该依靠市场的力量来进行，因此一方面需要继续完善监管政策尤其是配股政策，使其更加市场化；另一方面在监管政策的执行中应该更加重视注册会计师的审计意见，加强对注册会计师审计质量的监督，并尽快将民事诉讼制度引入证券市场审计责任问题解决的实践中，从而改变注册会计师的风险和收益预期。本文的主要局限是没有对审计意见和盈余管理的关系进行时间序列上的研究，但对比我们的研究结果和 Chen，Chen，and Su（2001）对 1995 年至 1997 年上市公司的研究结果可以发现，脱钩改制后，注册会计师的审计质量不仅没有上升,反而有所下降。这和王跃堂、陈世敏(2001)的研究结论一致,即独立性提高的同时,审计质量却下滑了。本文的另一局限是对上市公司盈余管理的计量和鉴别采用了边际 ROE 方法,而这种方法用于计量和鉴别公司的盈余管理不可避免地具有一定的主观成分。但本文使用了截面修正的 Jones 模型对此进行了检验,并且本文的研究结论经过敏感性测试后仍具有较强的可靠性,未来的研究可以进一步改进盈余管理的计量和鉴别方法。

参考文献

陈小悦,肖星,过晓艳.配股权和上市公司利润操纵[J].经济研究,2000(01):30-36.

陈信元,原红旗.上市公司资产重组财务会计问题研究[J].会计研究,1998(10):1-10.

蒋义宏.一个不容忽视的问题——上市公司利润操纵的实证研究[N].中国证券报,1998-3-19/20.

李树华.审计独立性的提高与审计市场的背离[M].上海:上海三联书店,2000.

王跃堂.对证券市场监管政策的经济后果的分析[J].经济科学,1999(5):82-87.

王跃堂,陈世敏.脱钩改制对审计独立性影响的实证研究[J].审计研究,2001(3):2-9.

原红旗.从中期报告看关联交易:现实问题与理性思考[J].会计研究,1998(4):1-6.

中国证券监督委员首席会计师办公室.谁审计中国证券市场——审计市场分析(2000)[M].北京:中国财政经济出版社,2001.

中国注册会计师协会.中国注册会计师独立审计准则汇编(1995—1999)[M].大连:东北财经大学出版社,1999.

Aharony J, Lee C W J, Wong T J. Financial packaging of IPO firms in China[J]. Journal of accounting research,2000,38(1):103-126.

Chen C J P, Chen S M, Su X J. Profitability regulation, earnings management, and modified audit opinions: evidence from China[J]. Auditing: a journal of practice & theory, 2001,20(2):9-30.

Chen C J P, Su X J, Zhao R. Market reaction to initial qualified audit opinions in an emerging market: evidence from the Shanghai Stock Exchange[J]. Contemporary accounting research,2000,17:281-301.

Chen K C W, Yuan H. Earnings management and capital resource allocation: evidence from China's accounting-based regulation of rights issues[J]. The accounting review, 2004,79(3):645-665.

Haw I M, Qi D, Wu W, et al. Earnings management of listed firms in response to security regulations in China's emerging capital market[R]. Working paper,1998.

转型经济中审计市场的需求特征研究[*]

内容提要：审计市场的需求在很大程度上决定了审计产品的供给，因此考察审计市场的需求特征对于理解审计市场具有重要意义。本文针对2001年和2002年的IPO审计市场，通过检验事务所特征与其IPO审计市场份额之间的关系，对我国IPO审计市场的需求特征进行了实证考察。研究发现，在样本期间的IPO审计市场上，存在着对管制便利、事务所规模和事务所地缘关系的需求，但依然缺乏对高质量审计的需求。研究结果表明，在我国转型经济中，政府管制对IPO公司选择事务所具有重要影响，而市场功能相对缺失。

关 键 词：审计市场；审计质量；管制便利；事务所规模；地缘关系；需求特征

一、问题的提出

随着我国从计划经济体制向市场经济体制的逐步转型以及证券市场的不断发展，注册会计师行业作为市场经济中的一个重要中介行业得到了充分发展。一批批独立审计准则的颁布、事务所的脱钩改制和联合兼并以及一次次的监管行动推动了我国注册会计师行业迅速发展。然而，近年来我国证券市场上发生了一连串"假账事件"，而注册会计师在这些"假账事件"中难辞其咎，说明我国注册会计师行业在发展过程中存在着不容忽视的问题。证券市场有效运转需要发挥会计信息的作用，而审计质量关系到会计信息的可靠性，因此审计质量对于证券市场的稳定和发展至关重要。在中国和美国证券市场分别发生了"银广夏事件"和"安

* 本文选自：朱红军、夏立军、陈信元：转型经济中审计市场的需求特征研究，《审计研究》，2004年第5期，第53-62页。本文被《经济观察报》2013年6月15日"发审委委员草根报告幕后玄机"一文引用。

然事件"以及其他一系列会计造假事件的背景下,探讨我国注册会计师行业存在的深层次问题尤为重要。

　　然而,已有文献似乎过多强调审计市场监管的作用,却忽视了对审计市场需求特征的深入分析。诚然,审计市场具有独特性,例如产品质量难以识别、不允许对产品进行广告宣传、审计产品的需求者与使用者不一致等。[①] 因此,监管之功不可或缺。但是,审计市场在本质上仍是一个买卖"审计服务"的产品市场。与一般的产品市场类似,审计市场需求特征对审计产品的供给具有重要的影响。如果市场上存在着对高质量审计的需求,那么事务所之间的竞争会促使提供高质量审计的事务所脱颖而出,从而提高整体的审计质量;相反,如果审计市场缺乏这种需求,甚至存在着对低质量审计的需求,那么竞争会导致"劣币驱逐良币",审计质量因此而降低。由此看来,创造和引导市场对高质量审计的需求可能比强调监管的作用更为重要。

　　李树华(2000)研究了审计产品的供求与事务所的独立性,并分析了政府管制和市场需求对转型经济中注册会计师行业结构的深入影响。他在研究中使用事务所出具的非标意见比例作为审计质量的衡量指标,研究发现:独立审计准则的颁布实施提高了审计质量(表现为非标意见比例的上升),但是在审计质量提高的同时,提供高质量审计的事务所其市场份额却显著下降,这表明在国内证券市场上还缺乏对高质量审计的需求。[②] 在我们所能检索到的文献范围内,这是迄今为止唯一一篇对国内审计市场需求特征进行实证研究的文献。但该文仅仅考察了审计市场需求特征的一个方面,而全面地分析市场对审计产品的需求特征还需要考察市场对管制便利、事务所规模、事务所所在地等方面的偏好。只有在清楚地了解审计市场的这些需求特征并找出其内在原因的基础上,监管者才能采取适当行动来引导或改变市场的需求偏好,从而充分利用市场力量来提高审计质量,优化市场资源配置。

　　同时,李树华(2000)一文的研究样本局限于我国早期的证券市场(其样本区间是 1993 年至 1996 年),而近几年来我国证券市场以及审计行业发生了很大变化。例如,不少事务所因为审计质量低下而被监管者处罚,监管者在新股发行审

---

① 在本文中,为了便于表述,我们将会计师事务所为上市公司提供的审计服务视为一种特殊产品。在证券市场上,上市公司是审计产品的需求者,但审计产品的使用者是广大的投资者以及监管机构。虽然审计产品使用者的偏好会影响上市公司对审计产品的需求,但审计产品需求者和使用者的偏好却不是完全一样的。

② 非标意见指注册会计师出具的除不带解释说明段的无保留意见以外的所有其他审计意见类型,具体包括带解释说明段的无保留意见、保留意见、否定意见和拒绝表示意见等四种审计意见类型。

核规则中对事务所进行区别对待,会计师事务所经历了脱钩改制和大规模的联合兼并,新股发行制度由审批制改为核准制,上市公司配股和增发股票的规则一再修改,会计准则和独立审计准则体系也更加完善,等等。在经历了这一系列制度变迁之后,公司选择事务所的动机是什么? 审计市场需求特征之现状如何? 这些问题还有待回答。

本文对我国审计市场需求特征进行更深入和全面的研究,以把握我国审计市场需求特征的现状和成因。我们以 2001 年和 2002 年的 IPO 审计市场①为研究对象,通过检验事务所特征与其 IPO 审计市场份额之间的关系,对 IPO 审计市场的需求特征进行了考察。研究发现,在本文的样本研究期间,IPO 审计市场依然缺乏对高质量审计的需求,却存在着对管制便利、事务所规模和事务所地缘关系的需求。和成熟资本市场上 IPO 公司对高质量审计的需求相比,这种需求特征体现了我国转型经济中政府管制对 IPO 公司选择事务所行为的影响。

本文以下部分安排如下:第二部分分析审计市场需求、事务所竞争优势与事务所 IPO 审计市场份额之间的关系,并提出本文的研究假说,第三部分是研究方法和数据描述,第四部分给出实证结果及解释,最后一节是研究结论和局限。

二、审计市场需求特征、事务所竞争优势与事务所市场份额

与一般的产品相比,审计服务这种“产品”至少具有以下两个特征:①法定审计由一系列审计准则所规范,因此审计产品的“生产工艺”基本是统一的;②审计产品表现为审计报告形式,而现代审计采用标准的简式审计报告格式,因此审计产品的形式也是统一的。虽然这两个特征使得审计产品几乎是标准化的,但审计产品也不是绝对无差异的。不同的事务所对同样的客户进行审计时,可能会在审计工作量、专业技能、审计价格、出具的审计意见类型以及为客户提供的衍生服务和管制便利等方面存在差异。在审计市场上,不同的审计产品供给者相互竞争以获取更多的市场份额。

审计服务的价值主要体现在:通过对会计信息的合法性和公允性提供鉴证,来减轻缔约双方之间的信息不对称,以使契约得以顺利签订和有效履行。对社会来说,理想的审计产品应具有“物美价廉”的特征,即以较低的审计成本提供较高

① IPO 审计指具有证券期货从业资格的会计师事务所对首次公开发行股票公司(IPO 公司)的上市审计,IPO 审计市场指 IPO 公司与会计师事务所之间互相选择的市场。

质量的审计产品。如果在审计市场上,存在着对高质量和低价格审计产品的需求,那么我们可以预期市场竞争会使提供"物美价廉"审计产品的事务所具有竞争优势,进而占取更多的市场份额,而社会福利由此增加。反之,则社会福利受损。因此,审计市场的需求特征是影响事务所竞争优势,并进而影响审计市场效率的一个重要因素。

考察审计市场的需求特征可以从两个方面展开:一是考察 IPO 公司对事务所的选择,二是考察事务所变更时上市公司如何选择后任事务所。本文之所以选择 IPO 审计市场为考察对象,第一个原因是事务所变更会给上市公司带来与新任事务所的熟悉和沟通成本,同时也会增加监管部门的关注,因此上市公司一旦选定事务所,则较少发生变更;第二个原因是 IPO 公司对事务所的选择通常代表着其对事务所的初次选择,因此体现了一般情况下公司对审计产品的需求,而事务所变更则反映了特定上市公司对审计产品需求的变化。

如上文所述,市场对审计产品的需求偏好是多方面的。本文将考察 IPO 公司对审计质量、管制便利、事务所规模、事务所地缘关系等四个方面的需求特征及其对事务所市场份额的影响。我们的研究框架是:IPO 审计市场的需求特征将使具有某些特征的事务所比其他事务所更具有竞争优势,从而能够获得更多的 IPO 审计市场份额。这种关系可以表示为图 1。举例来说,如果 IPO 审计市场存在着对高质量审计的需求,那么可以预期在其他条件相同的情况下,提供高质量审计产品的事务所更具有竞争优势,从而能够获得更多的市场份额。同样,如果 IPO 审计市场存在着对管制便利的需求,那么在其他条件相同的情况下,具有管制便利的事务所更具有竞争优势,从而可以获得更多的市场份额。

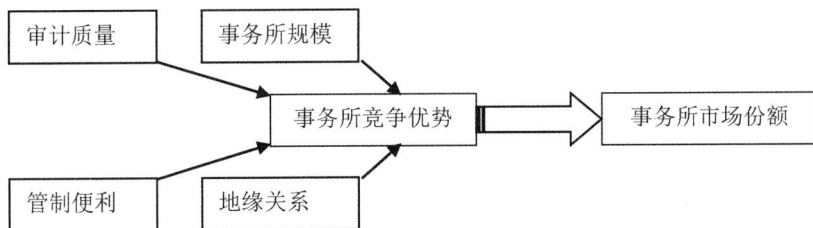

图 1 审计市场需求特征、事务所竞争优势与事务所市场份额

需要说明的是,和一般的产品市场类似,IPO 审计市场可能对产品价格也存在着特定需求偏好,即 IPO 公司可能倾向于选择审计价格高的或低的事务所。因此,全面考察 IPO 审计市场的需求特征也需要考察 IPO 审计市场对审计价格

的需求。但由于国内上市公司自 2001 年度起才开始披露支付给会计师事务所的
报酬,并且信息披露不太规范,违反相关信息披露规则的情况非常普遍(李爽、吴
溪,2004),因而我们很难获取有效数据对不同事务所的审计价格进行描述。同
时,IPO 公司更加看重的是其股票能否顺利发行以及发行定价是否能够达到目
标,而审计价格可能不是其选择事务所的主导因素。因此,本文不考察 IPO 公司
对审计价格的需求特征。

　　下面我们逐一考察 IPO 审计市场各个需求特征对事务所竞争优势进而对事
务所市场份额的影响,并提出相应的研究假说。

(一)审计质量与 IPO 审计市场份额

　　前已述及,独立审计的功能在于减轻缔约双方的信息不对称程度,从而使得
契约得以顺利签订和有效履行。对 IPO 审计来说,其价值在于减轻 IPO 公司与
潜在投资者之间的信息不对称,使投资者愿意将其资金投入公司,而拟 IPO 公司
可以获得其经营所需要的资金。如果审计质量较高,那么投资者就更信赖公司提
供的信息,从而有利于投资者对公司价值作出准确的评估,进而降低信息不对称
造成的成本,增加公司价值。国外的实证研究表明,选择高质量事务所的公司能
够获得更高的股票发行溢价(Balvers and McDonald,1988;Beatty,1989)。但
是,选择高质量事务所可能会增加公司的审计成本,同时高质量的审计也可能会
揭示出公司的不利情况从而降低公司的价值。因此,拟发行股票的公司对高质量
审计服务的需求取决于选择高质量事务所带来的收益与成本的比较。

　　在我国证券市场上,投资者投资渠道狭窄,监管部门控制股票供给(表现为对
公司发行股票的额度限制)。虽然在 2001 年股票发行方式由审批制改为核准制,
但是股票发行规模依然受到控制。因此,在很长一段时间内,公司股票处于一种
供不应求的局面,IPO 公司通常不用担心股票发行失败(李东平,2001)。与此同
时,股票发行定价也受监管部门的管制,在 1999 年之前,股票发行价格与公司过
去的业绩或盈利预测密切相关,因此很多公司为提高发行价格进行盈余管理
(Aharony,Lee and Wong,2000;林舒、魏明海,2000),从而降低了对高质量审计
的需求。1999 年后,股票发行定价向着市场化方向演变,这可能会在一定程度上
减轻 IPO 公司盈余管理的动机,并增加对高质量审计的需求。但是,由于事务所
发展时间尚短,市场公认的有声誉事务所还未形成,因此 IPO 公司选择高质量事
务所的收益还难以实现。另一方面,虽然已有研究显示,市场会对事务所出具的

非标意见产生不利反应(李增泉,1999;陈梅花,2002),但由于公司控股股东以及管理层持有的股票不流通,证券市场的股票价格机制对公司控股股东或管理层的影响较小,因此 IPO 公司选择高质量事务所来提高上市后股票价格的动机不足。根据以上讨论,我们预期在目前的证券市场上,IPO 公司选择高质量事务所的收益可能依然小于成本,从而高质量事务所不具有竞争优势。据此,我们提出如下研究假说1。

假说1:高质量事务所的 IPO 审计市场份额并不比低质量事务所高。

(二)管制便利与 IPO 审计市场份额

由于我国审计市场发展时间尚短,市场公认的有声誉的事务所还没有形成,因此为了提高审计质量,监管者总是试图对不同审计质量的事务所进行区分,并进而对低质量事务所设置市场进入壁垒。在证券市场上,早期的对事务所的区别对待表现在证券期货业务许可证上。从 1992 年开始,中国证券监督管理委员会和中华人民共和国财政部或中华人民共和国审计署根据事务所规模、经营情况等指标来决定哪些事务所具备证券期货业务审计资格,未获得资格的事务所不得从事证券期货相关审计业务(易琼,2003)。而对那些获得证券期货业务审计资格的事务所,证监会主要通过支持"信誉良好"的事务所和处罚"信誉不好"的事务所这两种手段对其进行激励和约束。对"信誉良好"的事务所的支持体现在补充审计业务资格和 IPO 专项复核业务资格的有关规定上。

证监会于 2001 年 12 月 31 日发布的《公开发行证券公司信息披露编报规则第 16 号—A 股公司实行补充审计的暂行规定》要求,"A 股公司在首次公开发行股票并上市,或在上市后在证券市场再融资时……应聘请获中国证监会和财政部特别许可的国际会计师事务所,按国际通行的审计准则,对其按国际通行的会计和信息披露准则编制的补充财务报告进行审计。"可见,证监会更加信赖国际会计师事务所。[①] 另外,中国证监会 2003 年 2 月 28 日发布的"股票发行审核标准备忘录第 16 号"规定,证监会发行监管部在审核 IPO 公司的申请文件时,如发现其申

[①]　在补充审计暂行规定发布后的答记者问中,证监会解释了出台补充审计暂行规定的背景、意图以及由国际著名会计师事务所进行补充审计的理由。根据证监会的解释,出台补充审计暂行规定是因为国内证券市场爆发了一系列上市公司提供虚假财务信息的案件,而注册会计师没有有效地进行揭示。为了有利于注册会计师顶住某些上市公司的压力、提高审计质量,证监会出台了此暂行规定。由国际著名会计师事务所进行补充审计的理由是这些事务所大多具有较长发展历史,并在全球形成公认的信誉,并且这些事务所出问题的概率比其他事务所要低。虽然补充审计暂行规定由于国内事务所的反对没有得到执行,但它已充分显示了证监会对国际著名会计师事务所的信赖。

报财务会计资料存在重大疑问,或其财务会计方面的内部控制制度有可能存在重大缺陷并由此导致申报资料存在重大问题时,可以要求其另行委托一家具备证券执业资格、信誉良好的会计师事务所对申报财务会计资料的特定项目进行专项复核。根据证监会会计部便函〔2002〕25 号规定,15 家事务所具备专项复核资格。① 可以预期,经过国际会计师事务所或这 15 家事务所审计的 IPO 公司将更容易通过发行审核,即这些事务所具备管制便利。

在对"信誉良好"的事务所进行界定并区别对待的同时,中国证监会还对那些违反执业规则的事务所进行处罚。从 1996 年开始至 2002 年期间,证监会对事务所的处罚共计有 33 家次,其中部分事务所被多次处罚。② 处罚的原因主要是这些事务所在为其客户进行验资、审计、资产评估或盈利预测审核中出具虚假报告或未能勤勉尽责。显然,对于证监会来说,被处罚过的事务所意味着"信誉不好"。可以预期,经过这些事务所审计的 IPO 公司的财务报告将被证监会认为可靠性较低,因此经过这些事务所审计的 IPO 公司将更难通过发行审核。为表述方便,本文将事务所遭受处罚带来的这种负面影响称之为"负管制便利"。

虽然监管者限于自身能力,对监管者事务所的上述区别对待并不一定准确无误,同时监管者是否完全按照审计质量对事务所进行区别对待也值得怀疑,但监管者做出的对事务所的区别对待措施将直接影响到 IPO 公司选择事务所的偏好。其原因是,在中国证券市场上,公司股票发行一直受到管制,为了顺利通过股票发行审核取得发行资格,IPO 公司具有迎合监管者偏好以选择事务所的动机。这样,具有管制便利的事务所将更具竞争优势,而具有负管制便利的事务所将处于竞争劣势。据此,我们提出如下研究假说。

假说 2a:如果事务所进入 IPO 专项复核名单或补充审计名单,那么其 IPO 审计市场份额更大。

假说 2b:如果事务所曾被证监会处罚,那么其 IPO 审计市场份额更小。

---

① 根据证监会会计部发布的《具备执行 A 股公司补充审计试点业务及首次发行证券过程中的专项复核业务资格的会计师事务所名单》(会计部便函〔2002〕25 号),15 家具备专项复核资格的事务所分别为:天健、北京京都、毕马威华振、信永中和、上海立信长江、上海众华沪银、安永大华、德勤华永、普华永道中天、江苏天衡、浙江天健、厦门天健、广东正中珠江、深圳大华天诚、深圳天健信德。同补充审计暂行规定一样,这份带有歧视小规模事务所性质的专项复核文件最终因为小规模事务所的反对而没有得到贯彻执行,但这份名单充分体现了证监会对这 15 家事务所的偏爱。

② 其中包含 2002 年根据对事务所 2000 年至 2001 年证券期货业务资格许可证年检结果进行的处罚。在此年检中,中天勤、深圳同人、深圳华鹏、华伦、中联信等五家事务所被吊销执业资格,中审和天一两家事务所被要求整改。

（三）事务所规模与 IPO 审计市场份额

针对成熟市场经济国家的研究表明,大规模事务所比小规模事务所具有更高的审计独立性,以及专业技能,因此大规模事务所的审计质量相对较高(DeAngelo,1981b;Dopuch and Simunic,1982;Nichols and Smith,1983;Simunic and Stein,1987;Davidson and Neu,1993)。在我国证券市场的早期,这样的结论也被李树华(2000)验证。然而,近期针对我国证券市场的研究却表明,事务所规模和审计质量并没有显著的相关关系(夏立军、杨海斌,2002;章永奎、刘峰,2002;原红旗、李海建,2003;李爽、吴溪,2003)。可能的原因是在早期的证券市场,大规模事务所审计质量高于小规模事务所,但由于市场缺乏对高质量审计的需求,因而 1995 年独立审计准则的颁布导致了大规模事务所的市场份额下降(李树华,2000)。于是,经过一定时间,那些低质量的小规模事务所规模逐渐变大,从而造成了事务所规模与审计质量的相关性不再显著。另一方面,由于在我国法律环境下审计失败的法律风险不高,因而大规模事务所和小规模事务所预期的审计失败损失可能没有显著差异。

虽然在我国目前的证券市场上,事务所规模与审计质量没有显著的相关关系,但 IPO 审计市场可能存在着对大规模事务所的需求。原因是:①大规模事务所审计经验更加丰富,而这可能会提高 IPO 公司财务报告通过发行审核的可能性;[①]②在投资者眼中,大规模事务所具备更高的担保能力,因而 IPO 公司选择大规模事务所可能能够提高其股票发行定价;③大规模事务所可以提供更好的非审计服务,例如管理咨询、财务顾问等。据此,我们提出研究假说 3。

假说 3:事务所规模越大,其 IPO 审计市场份额越高。

（四）地缘关系与 IPO 审计市场份额

在我国证券市场上,大量的上市公司选择了本地的事务所为其提供审计服务,审计市场存在着地区分割的现象。[②] 这一方面和我国转型经济中产品市场的

[①] Watts and Zimmerman(1986)认为,管制契约为事务所向其客户提供信息和游说服务创造了机会,潜在的客户在选择事务所时可能会考虑这些服务。显然,大规模事务所在提供这些服务时具有优势。美国国会(1976)甚至认为,证券交易委员会的管制和一些其他因素导致了八大事务对上市公司审计业务的有效垄断或卡特尔(Watts and Zimmerman,1986)。

[②] 根据中国证监会首会办公布的《谁审计中国证券市场——2002 年证券期货相关审计市场分析》,2002年度上市公司年报审计中,事务所异地客户有 285 家,本地客户有 951 家,即异地客户率平均为23.06%。在 71 家会计师事务所中,83%(59 家)的会计师事务所主要在本地或周边地区承揽业务(异地客户率低于 50%)。

地区分割有关,同时也和我国注册会计师行业原有的挂靠体制密不可分。由于审计服务与产品市场相联系,产品市场的地区分割会造成审计市场的地区分割,甚至审计产品的市场分割本身也是产品市场地区分割的一部分。而挂靠体制则使得事务所的执业范围受到限制,挂靠单位往往利用自己的影响力为其下属的事务所招揽业务提供便利,同时限制其他事务所在其影响力范围内执业,这进一步加剧了审计市场的地区分割。

正如产品市场的地区分割削弱了市场的竞争程度一样,审计市场的地区分割也造成了审计行业的地区垄断,从而阻碍了事务所规模的扩大和审计独立性的提高。虽然具有证券期货业务审计资格的事务所于 1998 年年底全部进行了脱钩改制,审计市场的地区分割开始被打破,但在大部分 IPO 公司中国有股占主导地位,尤其是地方政府控制着主要的股权,本着"肥水不流外人田"的原则,这些地方政府控制下的 IPO 公司更倾向于选择本地事务所。另一方面,选择本地事务所还有利于节约交通成本、沟通成本,以及"收买"审计意见。[①] 因此,我们预期 IPO 审计市场存在着对本地事务所的需求,本地事务所相对外地事务所具有更大的竞争优势。据此,我们提出假说 4。

假说 4:事务所所在地 IPO 公司数相对具有证券期货业务审计资格的事务所数越多,那么该事务所 IPO 审计市场份额越大。

(五)小结:IPO 公司选择事务所的动机

根据上文的分析可知,IPO 公司选择事务所的动机决定了 IPO 公司对不同事务所特征的需求。由于中国证券市场脱胎于中国转型经济中,并且发展证券市场的初衷是为国有企业改革服务,因此公司的股票发行一直受到政府的严格管制,即政府在资源配置中仍起主导作用。而对于 IPO 公司来说,选择事务所的主要目标是为其顺利获得证券市场资源服务。在这种情况下,IPO 公司会倾向于选择监管者眼中的"好"事务所以及那些 IPO 审计经验丰富的事务所,而回避监管者眼中的"坏"事务所。同时,由于 IPO 公司为了达到发行股票所要求的盈利指标往往进行财务包装(Aharony,Lee,and Wong,2001),为了掩盖其财务包装行为,IPO 公司会倾向于选择审计独立性较低的事务所。因此,IPO 公司可能倾向于选择具有管制便利的事务所、大规模事务所、本地事务所,而回避具有负管制便利的事务所和审计质量高的事务所。下文对上述研究假说进行检验。

---

① 本地事务所由于对当地政府和企业分别存在着政治和经济依赖,因此审计独立性可能相对较低。

三、研究方法和数据描述

(一)样本选择和数据来源

我们选择了具有证券期货业务资格,并且从事 2001 年和 2002 年 IPO 审计的事务所作为研究样本。之所以选择这一期间的事务所作为研究样本,是因为这一期间距离 1998 年事务所脱钩改制完成已经有两年以上时间,对此期间的 IPO 审计市场进行研究既可以考察事务所脱钩改制后审计市场的需求特征,又可以反映出 IPO 审计市场需求特征的现状。根据上文的分析,考察 IPO 审计市场的需求特征,需要考察事务所特征与其 IPO 审计市场份额的关系。对于事务所特征的刻画,我们根据事务所上年的上市公司年报审计情况来描述事务所特征。由于上年年报审计情况已为市场所观察到,因此我们认为根据上年年报审计情况来刻画事务所特征是合适的。

截至 2000 年年末和 2001 年年末,具有证券期货业务审计资格的事务所分别为 78 家和 72 家,即能够从事 2001 年 IPO 审计的事务所有 78 家,而能够从事 2002 年 IPO 审计的事务所有 72 家。在这些事务所中,江苏天华大彭和上海万隆众天未参加上市公司 2000 年年报审计,中审未参加上市公司 2001 年年报审计,因而无法按照上年年报审计情况来刻画事务所特征。我们剔除这 3 家事务所,这样 2001 年剩余样本为 76 家,2002 年剩余样本为 71 家,样本总数为 147 家。研究中使用到的数据来自 IPO 公司招股说明书、上市公司年报、中国证监会网站以及巨灵证券信息系统。数据的处理使用 SPSS 10.0 统计软件进行。

(二)检验模型和变量说明

根据上文的研究假说,我们构建如下多元回归模型以检验事务所特征与其 IPO 审计市场份额之间的关系:

$$MrktS_i = \beta_0 + \beta_1 Quality_i + \beta_2 Reputa_i + \beta_3 Penalty_i + \beta_4 SizeN_i +$$
$$\beta_5 LcoalN_i + \beta_6 Profit_i + \beta_7 DebtR_i + \beta_8 Year01_i + \varepsilon_i$$

其中,β_0 为截距,$\beta_1 \sim \beta_8$ 为系数,ε_i 为残差。模型中各变量的含义如下:

1. 因变量

$MrktS_i$ 表示按照客户个数衡量的事务所 i 的 IPO 审计市场份额,即事务所 i

当年 IPO 审计的客户数与当年 IPO 公司总数的比值。[①]

2. 测试变量

Quality$_i$代表审计质量,用事务所 i 上年年报审计中出具的非标意见比例衡量,这种衡量审计质量的方法和李树华(2000)一致。由于客户特征可能存在差异,因此使用事务所出具的非标意见比例来衡量审计质量可能会出现误差。但本文的研究目的是考察 IPO 公司对不同事务所的需求特征,而对于 IPO 公司来说,事务所出具的非标意见比例是一个比较容易观察到的审计质量指标。因此,本文使用事务所出具的非标意见比例来衡量审计质量。

Reputa$_i$和 Penalty$_i$分别代表管制便利和负管制便利。如果事务所进入补充审计业务资格或 IPO 专项复核业务资格名单,那么 Reputa$_i$取值为 1,否则 Reputa$_i$取值为 0。如果事务所 i 曾被中国证监会处罚,那么 Penalty$_i$取值为 1,否则 Penalty$_i$取值为 0。

SizeN$_i$代表事务所规模,用事务所 i 上年年报审计客户个数衡量。针对美国市场的研究通常使用六大和非六大的虚拟变量来衡量事务所规模(Becker et al.,1998)。[②] 针对国内市场的研究也借鉴了这一方法,例如李树华(2000)按事务所客户数多少将国内事务所分为十大和非十大。考虑到国内审计市场发展时间较短,尚没有形成明确的、与美国审计市场类似的大规模事务所群体,本文不采用虚拟变量而直接采用事务所客户数来衡量事务所规模。[③]

LcoalN$_i$代表事务所地缘关系,用事务所 i 所在地当年 IPO 公司个数与当地具有证券期货业务审计资格的事务所个数的比例来衡量。我们根据事务所所在地与上市公司注册地是否在同一省级行政区域(包括省、自治区、直辖市)作为划分当地和非当地的标志。如果事务所未发生合并,那么将事务所注册地作为事务

[①]   当年与非当年按照 IPO 公司上市时间确定。具体来说,如果某公司上市时间在 2001 年 1 月 1 日至 2001 年 12 月 31 日之间,那么认为此公司为 2001 年 IPO 公司。现有的国内外研究通常使用客户数或客户总资产之和来衡量事务所市场份额。由于本文的研究目的是考察 IPO 审计市场的需求特征,而使用客户数来衡量事务所市场份额可以免除客户规模的影响,从而更好地体现 IPO 公司对不同事务所的需求,因此本文使用客户数而不是客户总资产之和来衡量事务所市场份额。

[②]   在 1989 年的大型事务所合并前,是八大与非八大之分;在 1998 年的大型事务所合并后,是五大与非五大之分;安达信解体后,变为四大与非四大之分。

[③]   由于对于 IPO 公司来说,事务所上年年报审计的客户数而不是客户总资产更能反映事务所的审计经验,因此本文不使用事务所客户总资产来衡量事务所规模。我们对使用事务所客户总资产衡量事务所规模的情况进行了敏感性测试,研究结论基本不变。

所所在地；如果发生事务所合并，那么将合并前事务所注册地作为事务所所在地。①

3. 控制变量

Profit$_i$ 和 DebtR$_i$ 分别用来控制事务所客户的盈利能力和财务状况。Profit$_i$ 用事务所 i 上年年报审计所有客户的加权平均营业收入净利润率来衡量，DebtR$_i$ 用事务所 i 上年年报审计所有客户的加权平均资产负债率来衡量。由于我们用非标意见比例来衡量审计质量，而事务所出具的非标意见比例受到客户盈利能力和财务状况的影响（Chen，Chen，and Su，2001；夏立军、杨海斌，2002），因此需要控制这种影响。但由于 IPO 公司关注的是可观察的审计质量，因此不需要控制其他难以观察的因素对非标意见比例的影响。

Year01 是虚拟变量，用来控制不同年度样本间差异。对于 2001 年样本，Year01 取值为 1；对于 2002 年样本，Year01 取值为 0。

（三）样本特征描述性统计

表 1 给出了模型 1 和模型 2 中各变量的描述性统计结果。从表 1 可以看出，MrktS 的平均值和中位数分别为 0.0134 和 0.0132，两者比较接近，这说明模型中因变量的分布比较均衡。Quality 的平均值为 0.1324，说明事务所上年出具的非标意见比例平均数为 13.24%。Reputa 的平均值分别为 0.2313，说明在 147 家样本中，有 23.13% 的事务所进入补充审计业务资格和 IPO 专项复核业务资格名单。Penalty 的平均值分别为 0.2721，说明在 147 家样本中，有 27.21% 的事务所曾被中国证监会处罚。SizeN 的平均值为 15.2789，表明样本中事务所平均上年客户数为 152 789 个。LcoalN 的平均值为 0.7552，说明所有样本中，事务所所在地当年 IPO 公司个数与当地具有证券期货业务审计资格的事务所数比值的平均值为 0.7552。另外，从表 1 还可以看出，检验模型中各变量没有明显的异常值。

---

① 按事务所注册地确定事务所所在地的理由是：事务所机构主要在其注册地设立，人员主要在注册地居住和生活，因此主要受其注册地政治和经济的影响。由于行政力量的推动，2000 年以后，大量事务所发生合并，但合并后的事务所通常在原有地区的业务和机构通常还会继续，依然还会受到原有地区地方政府或上市公司的影响。我们对事务所发生合并情况下按合并后事务所注册地作为事务所所在地的情况进行了敏感性检验，研究结论不变。

表 1　变量描述性统计结果

	样本数	平均值	中位数	标准差	最小值	最大值
MrktS	147	0.0134	0.0132	0.0152	0.0000	0.0921
Quality	147	0.1324	0.0909	0.1531	0.0000	1.0000
Reputa	147	0.2313	0.0000	0.4231	0.0000	1.0000
Penalty	147	0.2721	0.0000	0.4466	0.0000	1.0000
SizeN	147	15.2789	13.0000	11.0378	1.0000	62.0000
LcoalN	147	0.7552	0.6000	0.6126	0.0000	3.5000
Profit	147	0.0556	0.0662	0.1090	-0.9987	0.3232
DebtR	147	0.4406	0.4292	0.1120	0.1516	0.8932
Year01	147	0.5170	1.0000	0.5014	0.0000	1.0000

四、实证检验结果及解释

在下文的实证检验结果中,我们首先对 2001 年和 2002 年混合样本进行单变量分析和多变量分析。在此基础上,我们再分别对 2001 年样本和 2002 年样本进行检验,以考察 IPO 审计市场需求特征在 2001 年和 2002 年之间的差异。

(一)混合样本分析

表 2 是混合样本情况下模型 1 和模型 2 中各变量的 Pearson 和 Spearman 相关分析结果。从表中可以看出:①在 Pearson 和 Spearman 相关分析中,MrktS 与 Reputa、SizeN 和 LcoalN 都显著正相关,而与 Quality 都没有显著相关关系;②在Pearson 相关分析中,MrktS 与 Penalty 显著负相关,并且在 Spearman 相关分析中,MrktS 与 Penalty 的相关性接近 0.10 显著性水平。这些单变量分析的结果基本上支持本文的四个研究假说,即 IPO 审计市场缺乏对高质量审计的需求,却存在着对管制便利、事务所规模和地缘关系的需求。我们接着进行多元回归分析以检验本文的研究假说。

表 3 给出了混合样本情况下对检验模型的多元回归分析结果。从表 3 可以看出,MrktS 与 Reputa 在 0.10 水平上显著正相关,与 SizeN 和 LcoalN 在 0.01 水平上显著正相关,与 Penalty 在 0.05 水平上显著负相关,而与 Quality 不具有显

著相关关系。这与单变量分析的结果基本一致,并支持本文的四个研究假说。表3 的结果说明,进入 IPO 专项复核名单或补充审计名单的事务所、大规模事务所和本地事务所更具竞争优势,从而能够获得更大的市场份额,而那些高质量事务所则不具有竞争优势。由此说明,在样本期间的 IPO 审计市场上,缺乏对可观察到的高质量审计的需求,而存在着对管制便利、事务所规模和地缘关系的需求。这种需求特征和成熟证券市场上 IPO 公司对高质量事务所的需求明显不同,体现了我国转型经济条件下政府管制对公司选择事务所偏好的影响。

表 2　有关变量的 Pearson 和 Spearman 相关分析(混合样本)

	MrktS	Quality	Reputa	Penalty	SizeN	LcoalN	Profit	DebtR	Year01
MrktS	1.000	0.013	0.227	−0.158	0.443	0.263	0.040	0.133	−0.042
	.	0.877	0.006	0.056	0.000	0.001	0.630	0.109	0.614
Quality	0.126	1.000	0.125	0.079	0.120	0.036	−0.025	0.174	0.049
	0.130	.	0.133	0.339	0.147	0.662	0.762	0.035	0.554
Reputa	0.250	0.126	1.000	−0.190	0.268	−0.204	0.017	0.159	−0.019
	0.002	0.128	.	0.021	0.001	0.013	0.836	0.054	0.822
Penalty	−0.133	0.122	−0.190	1.000	0.090	−0.037	−0.231	0.008	−0.021
	0.109	0.142	0.021	.	0.278	0.656	0.005	0.926	0.802
SizeN	0.506	0.367	0.247	0.143	1.000	0.052	0.002	0.395	−0.093
	0.000	0.000	0.003	0.085	.	0.531	0.983	0.000	0.262
LcoalN	0.181	0.037	−0.272	−0.027	−0.015	1.000	0.010	−0.074	0.062
	0.029	0.653	0.001	0.749	0.853	.	0.903	0.376	0.456
Profit	−0.070	−0.181	−0.054	−0.223	−0.224	0.108	1.000	−0.195	0.127
	0.397	0.028	0.519	0.007	0.006	0.193	.	0.018	0.127
DebtR	0.145	0.373	0.181	0.053	0.419	−0.169	−0.507	1.000	−0.138
	0.080	0.000	0.029	0.521	0.000	0.041	0.000	.	0.095
Year01	−0.159	0.073	−0.019	−0.021	−0.111	0.109	0.330	−0.128	1.000
	0.054	0.378	0.822	0.802	0.182	0.189	0.000	0.123	.

注:上三角形内为 Pearson 相关分析结果,下三角形内为括号内为 Spearman 相关分析结果。括号内为 P 值(双尾检验)。

表3   多元回归分析结果(混合样本)

自变量及 模型参数	预测 符号	系数	T 值	P 值	VIF 值
截距	?	0.0027	0.510	0.611	—
Quality	—	−0.0047	−0.648	0.518	1.065
Reputa	+	0.0054	1.917*	0.057	1.226
Penalty	—	−0.0053	−2.041**	0.043	1.155
SizeN	+	0.0006	5.148***	0.000	1.330
LcoalN	+	0.0066	3.624***	0.000	1.088
Profit	?	−0.0009	−0.089	0.929	1.130
DebtR	?	−0.0044	−0.398	0.691	1.303
Year01	?	−0.0006	−0.292	0.771	1.043
Model 参数			$N=147$,Adj-R^2=0.271,F 值=7.773***		

注:***、**和*分别表示在 0.01、0.05 和 0.10 水平上统计显著(单尾检验),N 为样本数。

(二)对分年度样本的分析

为了考察 IPO 审计市场的需求特征在不同样本年度的差异,我们对本文的研究样本进一步进行分年度分析,即分别对 2001 年样本和 2002 年样本进行单变量分析和多元回归分析。由于具有 IPO 专项复核和补充审计资格的事务所名单在 2002 年才为市场获知(证监会会计部便函[2002]),因此我们预期检验模型中 Reputa 与 MrktS 这两个变量在 2002 年样本中显著正相关,而在 2001 年样本中相关性不显著。

表 4 是对 2001 年样本的多元回归分析结果。从表 4 可以看出,MrktS 与 SizeN 和 LocalN 分别在 0.01 和 0.05 水平上显著正相关,与 Penalty 在 0.10 水平上显著正相关,而与 Quality 负相关但相关性不显著。这说明在 2001 年的 IPO 审计市场上,存在着对大规模事务所、本地事务所和管制便利的需求,而缺乏对高质量审计的需求。另外,MrktS 与 Reputa 正相关,但相关性不显著。这和我们的预期一致,说明证监会的 IPO 专项复核和补充审计资格事务所名单没有对 2001 年 IPO 审计市场产生显著影响。

表 5 是对 2002 年样本的多元回归分析结果。从表 5 可以看出,MrktS 与 SizeN 和 LocalN 分别在 0.10 和 0.01 水平上显著正相关,而与 Quality 在 0.10 水

平上负相关。这说明在 2002 年的 IPO 审计市场上,存在着对大规模事务所、本地事务所和低质量审计的需求。另外,MrktS 与 Reputa 在 0.05 水平上显著正相关。这和我们的预期一致,说明证监会的 IPO 专项复核和补充审计资格事务所名单对 2002 年 IPO 审计市场产生了显著影响。考察表 5 和表 4 的区别,可以发现:在对管制便利的需求上,2001 年 IPO 公司倾向于回避具有负管制便利的事务所,而 2002 年 IPO 公司倾向于选择具有管制便利的事务所;同时,2002 年 IPO 审计市场不仅缺乏对高质量审计的需求,而且甚至存在着对低质量审计的需求。这表明虽然监管制力图对事务所进行区别对待,却没有能够促使 IPO 公司选择高质量事务所。

表 4　多元回归分析结果(2001 年样本)

自变量及模型参数	预测符号	系数	T 值	P 值	VIF 值
截距	?	0.0083	1.048	0.298	—
Quality	—	0.0159	1.285	0.203	1.466
Reputa	+	0.0015	0.392	0.696	1.242
Penalty	—	−0.0063	−1.721*	0.090	1.242
SizeN	+	0.0008	5.463***	0.000	1.219
LcoalN	+	0.0051	2.136**	0.036	1.100
Profit	?	−0.0030	−0.261	0.795	1.137
DebtR	?	−0.0271	−1.394	0.168	1.501
Model 参数		N=76,Adj-R²=0.350,F 值=6.762***			

注:***、**和*分别表示在 0.01、0.05 和 0.10 水平上统计显著(单尾检验),N 为样本数。

表 5　多元回归分析结果(2002 年样本)

自变量及模型参数	预测符号	系数	T 值	P 值	VIF 值
截距	?	0.0017	0.227	0.821	—
Quality	—	−0.0161	−1.676*	0.099	1.010
Reputa	+	0.0097	2.372**	0.021	1.257
Penalty	—	−0.0053	−1.458	0.150	1.122

自变量及 模型参数	预测 符号	系数	T 值	P 值	VIF 值
SizeN	＋	0.0003	1.686*	0.097	1.473
LcoalN	＋	0.0082	2.867***	0.006	1.097
Profit	？	−0.0013	−0.051	0.959	1.203
DebtR	？	0.0065	0.438	0.663	1.502
Model 参数			$N=71$，Adj-$R^2=0.221$，F 值$=3.843$***		

注：***、**和*分别表示在 0.01、0.05 和 0.10 水平上统计显著（单尾检验），N 为样本数。

（三）敏感性分析

从上述表 3、表 4 和表 5 可以看出，所有自变量的 VIF 值均小于 2.0，说明检验模型不存在严重共线性问题。同时，在表 3、表 4 和表 5 中，模型 F 值均在0.01水平上显著，Adj-R^2 分别为 0.271、0.350 和 0.221，这说明模型拟合较好。我们分别在混合样本、2001 年样本和 2002 年样本三种情况下对检验模型进行了异方差怀特检验，结果表明模型没有严重异方差问题。

为了考察检验结果的可靠性，我们对表 3、表 4 和表 5 的结果进行了如下敏感性测试：①分别对剔除残差 5 倍标准差和 3 倍标准差以外异常值的情况进行敏感性检验，结果显示，异常值影响较小，研究结论不变；②对在检验模型中不纳入Profit 和 DebtR 这两个控制变量的情况进行敏感性检验，结果显示上述研究结论基本不受影响；③对 Penalty 变量分别按事务所最近一年、两年、三年以及三年以上遭受处罚的情况进行敏感性检验，结果显示在三年以内遭受处罚的事务所市场更小，而在三年以上遭受处罚的事务所市场份额不受影响；④利用上市公司披露的支付给事务所的报酬的有效信息，对在检验模型中纳入审计价格即单位资产审计收费这个变量进行敏感性检验，结果显示审计价格与事务所市场份额没有显著相关关系，研究结论基本不受影响。可见，本文的研究结果较为稳定和可靠。

五、研究结论与局限

在一个竞争的市场上，产品需求对产品供给会产生重要影响，审计市场也不例外。因此，考察审计市场的需求特征不仅有助于更好地理解审计市场，还有助于监管者改进监管,提高审计质量。在西方发达国家的证券市场上,IPO 公司或上市公司存在着对高质量审计的需求。然而,我国的证券市场根植于我国的转型经济中,其重要特征是政府在证券市场资源配置中起主导作用,同时上市公司大部分由国有企业改制而来,地方政府是大部分上市公司的控股股东。因此,我国审计市场的需求特征可能会体现出我国转型经济的特点。

本文以 2001 年和 2002 年的 IPO 审计市场为对象,在分析审计市场需求特征、事务所竞争优势与事务所 IPO 审计市场份额三者关系的基础上,对我国 IPO 审计市场的需求特征进行了实证考察。研究发现,在本文的样本期间,IPO 审计市场存在着对管制便利、事务所规模和事务所地缘关系的需求,却依然缺乏对高质量审计的需求,表现为具有管制便利的事务所、大规模事务所以及本地事务所更具竞争优势,从而能够获得更多市场份额,而提供高质量审计的事务所不具有竞争优势,从而没能获得更多市场份额。

上述研究结果表明,在我国证券市场上,IPO 选择事务所的动机主要是为了迎合政府管制以顺利获得股票发行资格,而不是为了向投资者传递公司经营情况的真实信号。我国 IPO 审计市场的上述需求特征体现了转型经济条件下政府管制对 IPO 公司选择事务所行为的影响,而市场功能相对缺失。虽然监管者力图对事务所进行区分并区别对待,但这种措施并没有能够促使 IPO 公司选择那些提供高质量审计的事务所。这说明我国 IPO 审计市场的需求结构还存在着缺陷,创造出对高审计质量的市场需求是未来证券市场监管改革的努力方向。

需要说明的是,本文还存在以下一些局限:①本文认为审计市场需求特征会导致具有这些特征的事务所更具竞争优势,从而能够获得更多市场份额,但出于规避审计风险考虑,这些能够获得更多市场份额的事务所并不一定会愿意获得更多市场份额。同时,事务所的竞争优势可能也不仅仅取决于审计市场的需求特征。这两个因素可能会导致本文使用事务所市场份额衡量事务所竞争优势并进而用以考察审计市场需求特征出现一定偏差。②本文仅仅考察了 IPO 审计市场的需求特征,而没有考察上市公司年报审计市场的需求特征。由于上市公司和 IPO 公司选择事务所的动机可能不同,因此 IPO 审计市场的需求特征可能不能反映审计市场需求特征的全貌。进一步考察不同类型审计市场的需求特征并进行时间序列分析是未来研究的方向。

参考文献

陈梅花.股票市场审计意见信息含量研究:来自 1995—1999 上市公司年报的实证证据[J].中国会计与财务研究,2002(1):62 - 105.

李东平.大股东控制、盈余管理与上市公司业绩滑坡[D].上海:上海财经大学,2001.

李树华.审计独立性的提高与审计市场的背离[M].上海:上海三联书店,2000.

李爽,吴溪.补充审计模式与审计独立性:中国 B 股市场的证据[J].中国会计与财务研究,2003(3):43 - 71.

李爽,吴溪.审计定价研究:中国证券市场的初步证据[M].北京:中国财政经济出版社,2004.

李增泉.实证分析:审计意见的信息含量[J].会计研究,1999(8):16 - 22.

林舒,魏明海.中国 A 股发行公司首次公开募股过程中的盈利管理[J].中国会计与财务研究,2000(2):87 - 107.

夏立军,杨海斌.注册会计师对上市公司盈余管理的反应[J].审计研究,2002(4):28 - 34.

易琮.中国会计师事务所产权制度的变迁及其绩效[J].中国会计与财务研究,2003,5(1):140 - 189.

原红旗,李海建.会计师事务所组织形式、规模与审计质量[J].审计研究,2003(1):32 - 37.

章永奎,刘峰.盈余管理与审计意见相关性实证研究[J].中国会计和财务研究,2002(1):1 - 13.

中国证监会首席会计师办公室.谁审计中国证券市场——2002 年证券期货相关审计市场分析[N].上海证券报,2003 - 12 - 30.

Aharony J,Lee C W J,Wong T J. Financial packaging of IPO firms in China[J]. Journal of accounting research,2000,38(1):103 - 126.

Balvers R J,McDonald B,Miller R E. Underpricing of new issues and the choice of auditor as a signal of investment banker reputation[J]. The accounting review,1988,63(4):605 - 622.

Beatty R P. Auditor reputation and the pricing of initial public offerings[J]. The accounting review,1989,64(4):693 - 709.

Becker C L,DeFond M L,Jiambalvo J,et al. The effect of audit quality on earnings management[J]. Contemporary accounting research,1998,15(1):1 - 24.

Chen C J P,Chen S,Su X. Profitability regulation,earnings management,and modified audit opinions:evidence from China[J]. Auditing:a journal of practice & theory,2001,20(2):9 - 30.

Davidson R A，Neu D. A note on the association between audit firm size and audit quality[J]. Contemporary accounting research，1993，9(2)：479 - 488.

DeAngelo L E. Auditor independence，"low balling"，and disclosure regulation [J]. Journal of accounting and economics，1981，3(2)：113 - 127.

DeAngelo L E. Auditor size and audit quality[J]. Journal of accounting and economics，1981，3(3)：183 - 199.

Dopuch N，Simunic D. Competition in auditing：an assessment[C]. Fourth symposium on auditing research. Urbana：University of Illinois，1982：401 - 405.

Nichols D R，Smith D B. Auditor credibility and auditor changes [J]. Journal of accounting research，1983：534 - 544.

Watts R L，Zimmerman J L. Positive accounting theory[M]. Upper Saddle River：Prentice Hall，Inc，1986.

Simunic D A，Stein M T. Product differentiation in auditing：auditor choice in the market for unseasoned new issues [R]. Vancouver：The Canadian Certified General Accountants' Research Foundation，1987.

独立审计为什么没能发挥公司治理功能?
——基于"盛润股份"连续十五年获得"非标"意见的案例分析①

内容提要：本文以"盛润股份"连续十五年获得非标准审计意见为例,分析这些"非标"意见没能发挥公司治理功能的原因。我们发现在这一案例中,独立审计之所以没能发挥公司治理功能,是因为审计师出具的"非标"意见未能给公司及其内部人带来显著的成本,而这又与市场价格机制和公司股权结构上的问题以及有效的监管和法律诉讼机制的缺失有关。本文的研究有助于深入了解中国证券市场上独立审计制度在公司治理中的功能及其存在的问题。

关 键 词：独立审计;非标意见;公司治理;盛润股份

一、引言

在成熟的证券市场上,上市公司独立审计制度是一项重要的公司治理外部机制。审计师的专业审计活动有助于监督上市公司行为及其财务报告信息质量,减轻投资者和公司内部人之间的信息不对称和代理问题,从而改进公司治理、提升公司价值。② 独立审计之所以能够发挥公司治理功能,主要是因为:①市场竞争和声誉机制以及监管和法律诉讼机制使得审计师的审计质量能够得到合理保证(Wallace,1980;Watts and Zimmerman,1983;Palmrose,1988;Carcello and Palmrose,1994;Krishnan and Krishnan,1997;Latham and Linville,1998;Shu,2000);②审计师出具非标准审计意见会给公司及其内部人带来融资条件的提高、更多的监管关注和投资者诉讼以及公司价值损失等方面的成本(Dodd et al.,

① 本文选自:陈信元、夏立军、林志伟:独立审计为什么没能发挥公司治理功能——基于"盛润股份"连续十五年获得"非标"意见的分析,《财经研究》,2009 年第 7 期,第 63－75 页。
② 本文中"审计师"是指为上市公司提供审计服务的注册会计师。

1984；Dopuch et al.，1986；Loudder et al.，1992）①，而公司聘任高质量审计师则可以降低融资成本、提升公司价值、减轻公司董事和高管的责任（Watts and Zimmerman，1983；Beatty，1989；Clarkson and Simunic，1994；Pitman and Fortin，2004；Eichenseher and Shields，1985）。换言之，在成熟的证券市场上，审计师具有提供高质量审计的激励，而公司具有聘任高质量审计师并改进公司治理的激励（Wallace，1980；Watts and Zimmerman，1983；夏立军，2005）。

借鉴成熟市场的经验，中国证券市场在设立不久也采用了独立审计制度。通过制定和执行独立审计准则、对事务所进行脱钩改制以及加强对审计师和事务所的监督、检查和处罚等措施，审计质量明显提高。例如，1995 年首批独立审计准则的颁布以及 1998 年事务所的脱钩改制均显著提高了审计师出具非标意见的比例（DeFond et al.，1999；王跃堂、陈世敏，2001；Yang et al.，2001）。② 然而，在审计师对大量上市公司出具非标准审计意见的同时，这些审计意见似乎没能促使公司吸取教训，改进公司治理。③ 一个突出的表现是，不少上市公司连续多个年度获得非标准审计意见，呈现出"屡教不改"的特征。由此，需要回答的问题是，为什么移植到中国证券市场的独立审计制度在发挥公司治理功能上却"南橘北枳"？其背后的原因是什么？

本文以广东盛润集团股份有限公司（股票代码 000030，以下简称"盛润股份"）为例，对上述问题进行分析。选取盛润股份进行案例分析的理由是，此公司自 1993 年上市之年起至 2007 年，连续十五年被审计师出具了"非标准无保留审计意见"（简称"非标意见"），堪称中国证券市场上连续多年被出具非标意见的典型。因此，通过对其进行仔细分析，可以在一定程度上回答上述问题。我们的分

---

① 根据中国独立审计准则的规定，审计意见分为四种类型，包括无保留意见、保留意见、否定意见和拒绝表示意见（无法表示意见）。其中无保留意见又分为标准无保留意见和无保留加说明（强调事项段）意见。无保留加说明（强调事项段）意见多用于强调那些不直接影响财务报告数据但对报告使用者来说具有重要性的交易或事项。本文将标准无保留意见以外的所有审计意见类型统称为"非标准审计意见"，这些意见意味着审计师认为客户财务报告中存在不公允陈述或需要引起投资者注意的事项。这也和中国证监会的分类方法一致。例如，中国证监会的年报内容和格式准则要求被出具非标准审计意见的上市公司在年度报告首页的"重要提示"中，对被出具的非标准审计意见类型（包括无保留加说明意见）进行说明。此外，在 2001 年 2 月中国证监会发布的《上市公司新股发行管理办法》以及 2001 年 11 月中国证监会颁布的《亏损上市公司暂停上市和终止上市实施办法（修订）》中，均将无保留加说明与保留、否定和拒绝表示意见一同作为"非标准审计意见"进行特别的监管考虑。

② 根据我们的统计，1995 年至 2007 年的年报审计中，中国上市公司被审计师出具非标意见的比例一直维持在 10% 左右，而 Lennox（2000）显示，英国 1988 年至 1994 年间上市公司被出具非标意见的比例约为 3%。这当然无法说明中国上市公司年报审计质量高于英国，但至少表明中国的审计师在一定程度上揭露了上市公司财务报告存在的问题。

③ 这可能也是 1995 年至 2007 年期间一直有 10% 左右的上市公司被出具非标意见的原因之一。换言之，很多上市公司可能并不在乎被出具非标意见。

析发现,在这一案例中,独立审计之所以没能发挥公司治理功能,是因为审计师出具的非标意见未能给公司及其内部人带来显著的成本,而这又与市场价格机制和上市公司股权结构上的问题以及有效的监管和法律诉讼机制的缺失有关。这一发现对于深入了解中国证券市场上独立审计制度在公司治理中的功能及其存在的问题具有理论和现实意义。

后文安排如下:第二部分介绍盛润股份的基本情况、财务状况以及历年的审计意见;第三部分从市场、监管和法律三个方面分析为什么盛润股份连续十五年被审计师出具非标意见而公司治理没有明显改进;最后一部分是对全文的总结。

二、盛润股份简介、财务状况及历年审计意见

(一)盛润股份简介

盛润公司在 2002 年之前名为深圳市莱英达集团股份有限公司(以下简称"莱英达"),其前身是 1984 年成立的深圳市轻工业公司,系深圳市属国营企业。1993年,深圳市轻工业公司获深圳市政府批准改组为公众股份有限公司,原公司净资产折合成国有股本 14 500 万股,占新成立公司股本的 66.36%,由深圳市投资管理公司持有。1993 年 6 月,公司发行 A 股 4350 万股(其中非流通 A 股1850 万股,流通 A 股2500 万股),B 股3000 万股,共募集资金 30 051 万元。同年 9 月,这些股份上市交易。

政府和投资者对莱英达公司曾寄予厚望。1994 年,莱英达是深圳市属重点企业,被评为深圳市优秀企业。1996 年更先后被确立为"全国重点扶持 1000 家国有大中型、广东省重点发展 70 家、深圳市重点发展的 30 家大型企业集团"之一。早期的莱英达拥有很多著名的产品,曾多年荣获深圳市三超企业第一名,有着良好的盈利能力。① 然而,好景不长,1998 年 6 月,连续两年亏损的莱英达成为中国 A 股市场上首批戴上 ST(特别处理)帽子的上市公司之一。② 此后,ST 的身

---

① 著名的中华牌自行车和金威啤酒就是莱英达旗下的产品。后来中华牌自行车由于欧美的反倾销和管理问题而日渐衰败。另外,莱英达在 1997 年将旗下深圳金威啤酒有限公司 20%的股权(仍保留 5%的股权)转让给香港港亮公司,失去了另一个重要的盈利产品。"三超"企业指销售收入、利税总额和出口创汇三项指标均符合认定标准的企业。

② 1998 年 4 月 22 日,沪深证券交易所宣布对财务状况或其他状况出现异常的上市公司的股票交易进行特别处理(special treatment,简称 ST)。财务状况或其他状况出现异常主要指两种情况,一是上市公司连续两个会计年度的经审计净利润均为负值,二是上市公司最近一个会计年度经审计的每股净资产低于股票面值。在被实行特别处理期间,上市公司的股票交易遵循以下规则:股票报价日涨跌幅限制为 5%,股票名称改为原股票名前加"ST",上市公司的中期报告必须审计。

份就一直伴随着莱英达。

2001 年,莱英达公司再次巨额亏损,亏损金额高达 99 538 万元。此时,莱英达已经处于资不抵债的境地。2001 年年底,莱英达持有的深圳新世纪饮水科技有限公司股权因诉讼被强制变卖,莱英达失去了最主要的收入和利润来源,基本失去了持续经营能力。2002 年,莱英达更名为广东盛润集团股份有限公司。2004 年,公司实际控制人由深圳市政府变更为深圳市莱英达集团有限责任公司工会。2005 年,盛润股份持有的深圳嘉年实业股份有限公司股权被法院强制查封拍卖,从而失去唯一的主营业务。此后,公司只能通过"清欠盘活"来维持日常经营。

(二)盛润股份财务状况

表 1 给出了盛润股份 1993 年至 2007 年间各年的主要财务指标。可以看出,除了上市当年的 1993 年度以及上市后第一年的 1994 年度公司每股收益较好以外,其他各个年度要么是微利,要么是亏损。尤其是 1998 年、2001 年、2002 年这三个年度发生巨额亏损。同时,自上市后,公司股东权益以及每股净资产呈现出不断下降的特征。2001 年年底,公司股东权益已是负数,这意味着公司上市时从市场上募集的 3 亿多元资金已经亏损殆尽。至 2007 年年末,公司股东权益为 -163 839 万元,即资不抵债金额高达 16 亿以上。这些财务状况指标反映出,公司上市后不久,经营管理上的各种问题就开始暴露,并且随着时间的推移,公司的经营管理不仅未能得到改进,反而问题越来越严重。此外,如图 1 所示,从上市月份的下月起,公司股票相对深圳 A 股等权平均市场回报率的累计异常回报率也呈现出总体上下降的特征,并且到 2006 年年底为止的累计异常回报率达到 -100% 左右。下面我们分析审计师是如何揭示这些问题的。

表 1　盛润公司历年主要财务指标

年度	每股收益(元)	净利润(万元)	每股净资产(元)	股东权益(万元)
1993	0.53	11 575	2.91	63 498
1994	0.45	11 731	2.53	66 237
1995	0.07	2013	2.45	70 685
1996	0.10	2858	2.55	73 497
1997	0.15	4334	1.74	50 229

（续表）

年度	每股收益（元）	净利润（万元）	每股净资产（元）	股东权益（万元）
1998	−1.42	−40 821	0.35	10 104
1999	0.17	5022	0.20	5769
2000	0.02	420	0.24	7009
2001	−3.45	−99 538	−3.37	−97 177
2002	−1.96	−56 649	−5.40	−155 640
2003	0.04	1139	−5.35	−154 447
2004	−0.17	−4794	−5.52	−159 199
2005	−0.20	−5718	−5.72	−164 917
2006	0.06	1866	−5.60	−161 632
2007	−0.08	−2208	−5.68	−163 839

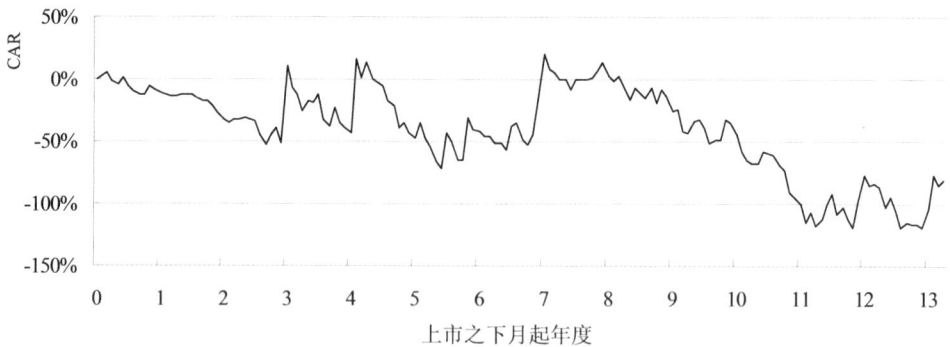

注：CAR＝（盛润股份月个股回报率－深圳 A 股市场等权平权月市场回报率）的累计加总。

图 1　盛润股份自上市下月开始的累计异常股票回报率（CAR）

（三）盛润股份历年审计意见

表 2 是盛润股份自 1993 年上市当年至 2007 年度的历年审计师、审计意见类型及审计意见主要内容。①

---

① 由于盛润股份不仅发行 A 股，还发行 B 股，因而根据证监会的有关规定，公司需要提供按中国会计准则和国际会计准则或境外主要募集行为发生地会计准则调整的两套财务报告，并分别由境内外会计师事务所审计。本文关注的焦点是 A 股市场的有关制度环境以及独立审计制度对公司治理的影响，因而我们只分析境内的审计情况。

表 2　盛润股份历年审计意见类型和内容

年度	事务所	意见类型	非标意见涉及事项	金　额
1993	深圳中华	无保留加说明	其他注册会计师工作	6 间联营公司由其他事务所审计
1994	深圳中华	保留	收入确认、审计范围受限	审计师不认同的销售收入 12 971 万元、销售成本 8 776 万元
1995	深圳中华	保留	将长期投资应计利息资本化、全资子公司未摊销利息	利息资本化 714 万元；应摊未摊利息 1049 万元。一家联营公司未审计
1996	深圳中诚	保留加说明	其他注册会计师工作、审计范围受限、利息摊销、长期投资利息资本化、评估后调增投资权益、存在不良资产	子公司未审计净利润2774万元；集团核算持股23%的子公司时由成本法转成权益法；1995 年应摊未摊利息剩 825 万元；上年利息资本化 714 万元的影响还未消除；多计投资收益 685 万元
1997	深圳中诚	保留	审计范围受限、子公司冲销已计提折旧和摊销、利息资本化、联营公司破产清算、存在巨额其他应收款、关联股权交易	子公司冲销折旧和摊销使公司多计投资收益计人民币 915 万元；自 1992 年至 1997 年利息资本化总额为 11 695 万元；联营公司破产对公司资产影响总额 5757 万元；可能无法收回的其他应收款 1460 万元
1998	深圳大华	保留	审计范围受限、会计政策及估计变更导致亏损	子公司"深中华"有境外应收款 10.89 亿元无法确定能否收回；会计政策及估计变更导致 1998 年记录亏损 12 909 万元
1999	深圳大华	保留	审计范围受限	持股 23.28%的子公司"深中华"存在巨额应收款无法收回问题

年度	事务所	意见类型	非标意见涉及事项	金　额
2000	深圳大华天诚	保留加说明	审计范围受限、股权转让	持股19.87%的子公司"深中华"存在巨额应收款可能无法收回；向关联方转让子公司股权，增加投资收益2670.81万元
2001	深圳大华天诚	无保留加说明	持续经营不确定性	净利润－99 538万元，年末股东权益－97 177万元。主要系核销应收款项、存货、长期投资等不良资产所致
2002	深圳大华天诚	保留	持续经营不确定性	净利润－56 649万元，年末股东权益－152 516.5万元
2003	深圳大华天诚	无保留加强调事项段	持续经营不确定性	未分配利润－233 764万元
2004	深圳大华天诚	无保留加强调事项段	持续经营不确定性	净利润－4794万元，未分配利润－238 558万元
2005	深圳大华天诚	无法表示意见	持续经营不确定性	净利润－5718万元，总资产3919.6万元，股东权益－164 917万元
2006	深圳大华天诚	无法表示意见	持续经营不确定性	主营业务收入为零，1866万元净利润来自坏账准备的转回；未分配利润－242 410万元
2007	深圳大华天诚	无法表示意见	持续经营不确定性	净利润－2207.5万元，未分配利润－244 618万元

可以看出，盛润股份1993年至1995年度聘任的会计师事务所为深圳中华会计师事务所，1996年至1997年度为深圳中城会计师事务所，1998年至1999年度为深圳大华会计师事务所，2000年至2007年度为深圳大华天诚会计师事务所。2000年深圳大华会计师事务所与广州天诚会计师事务所合并为深圳大华天诚会计师事务所，所以实际上2000年没有更换事务所。这样，在1993年至2007年度期间，公司共计更换了两次事务所。从审计意见来看，盛润股份自1993年上市后，连续十五个年度被审计师出具了非标意见，成为中国证券市场连续多年被审

计师出具非标意见的典型。并且,除了1993年、2001年、2003年、2004年度被出具无保留加说明(强调事项)意见以外,其他年度均被出具了保留意见或无法表示意见这些较为严厉的意见类型。

从非标意见涉及的事项来看,1993年是因为六家联营公司由其他事务所审计,1994年至2000年度主要涉及审计范围受限以及多计利润等问题,而2001年至2007年度都是涉及公司持续经营能力不确定。从非标意见揭示的金额来看,1994年度审计师不认同的收入确认12 971万元、销售成本确认8 776万元,两项合计多确认利润4 195万元。1995年度审计师不认同的利息资本化714万元,应摊未摊利息1 049万元,两项合计多确认利润1 763万元。1996年度子公司未审计的净利润2 774万元,并有其他几项多确认利润的情况。1997年度保留意见中则反映,自1992年以来公司累计利息资本化(即累计少计利息费用)金额达到11 695万元,并有其他多项少确认费用或损失的情况。1998年度保留意见中反映,子公司有108 900万元应收款无法确定能否收回,并且会计政策和估计变更导致公司记录亏损12 909万元。1999年和2000年度保留意见反映子公司存在巨额应收款无法收回问题。2001年至2007年度非标意见均反映公司持续经营能力存在不确定性。

以上审计意见内容表明,盛润股份从上市当时甚至上市之前起就已经是个"问题"公司。很难说审计师揭示出了公司财务报告中所有重大的不公允反映事项,但是审计师揭示出来的上述事项已经足以说明公司问题的严重性。并且,随着时间的推移,公司财务状况呈现出不断恶化的趋势。然而,审计师揭示出的这些问题引起了市场、监管者以及公司怎样的反应呢?下面对此进行分析。

三、为什么连续十五年非标意见没能发挥公司治理功能？

在成熟市场上,公司被出具非标意见的成本非常高,以至于仅有很小比例的公司被出具非标准意见,更不用说连续多个年度被出具非标准意见。非标意见带给公司的成本包括股价下跌引起的公司价值下降、更高的融资成本和更严格的融资条件、更多的监管关注和处罚、投资者对公司及其有关人员的民事赔偿诉讼等。但是,根据以上的分析,在盛润股份这一案例中,虽然公司连续十五个年度被审计师出具非标意见,非标意见中涉及的问题却不见改进。公司1993年上市时从市场募集的3亿元资金,到1998年就几乎亏损殆尽,且其后公司财务状况越发恶化。这意味着非标意见并未能发挥改善公司治理的功能。

接下来我们分别从非标意见的市场后果、监管后果以及法律后果三个角度分析其背后的原因。

（一）非标意见的市场后果

图 2 是年报各年年度报告公布当日公司股价相对深圳 A 股市场等权平均市场收益率的股价反应。若年报公布日为非交易日,则为年报公布日后下一个交易日的股价反应。可以看出,在 1993 年至 2005 年度共计十三个年度的年报公布市场反应中,仅有 1995 年、1996 年、2000 年、2004 年、2005 年这五个年度的市场反应为负,其他各个年度的市场反应均为正。而结合表 1 可见,在市场反应为正的八个年度中,仅有 1997 年、1999 年、2002 年、2003 年这四个年度的每股收益相对上年度增长,且 1997 年和 1999 年度非标意见均反映公司当年有大额虚计利润情况,而 2002 年和 2003 年度非标意见均反映公司持续经营存在不确定性。这说明,在市场反应为正的八个年度中,非标意见本身可能未引起市场显著的负面反应。[①]

在市场反应为负的五个年度里,1995 年度的负面反应较大,但 1995 年度相对上年的每股收益下降也比较大,因此很难说明负面反应是由非标意见本身引起的。1996 年度的每股收益相对上年有微小增加,但年报公布的市场反应为负数,考虑到 1996 年度非标意见中揭示出公司当年有虚计利润情况,负向的市场反应可能是市场一定程度上考虑了非标意见的结果。2000 年、2004 年及 2005 年年报公布的市场反应为负,但相应年度的每股收益相对上年下降也较大,难以说明负面反应是由非标意见引起的。因此,综合来看,市场对非标意见至多具有微弱的负面反应。这一点和以往大样本研究的发现也类似。Chen et al.(2000)对中国证券市场早期(1995 年至 1997 年度)的非标意见市场反应进行了大样本研究,结果发现非标意见在统计上具有显著的负面市场反应,但是在非标意见公布的前后对称的三个交易日内,累计的负面反应仅在 3% 左右。陈梅花(2002)研究了 1995 年到 1999 年间非标意见的市场反应,发现市场对非标意见没有显著负面反应,岳衡(2006)也发现了类似结果。

由此看来,非标意见本身并未引起公司股价的大幅下跌,这说明非标意见带给公司的价值损失成本比较小。这可能是非标意见揭示出的问题未能引起公司

---

① 审计意见表明 1997 年、1999 年、2002 年和 2003 年四个年度每股实际收益可能相对上年度是下降而非上升。如果投资者利用了审计意见所传达的信息,年报公告日的市场反应很可能为负而非为正。

重视的原因之一。而之所以非标意见本身的负面市场反应较小,可能是因为中国证券市场的"政策市"、"庄家"操纵、信息披露质量总体较低等特征使得投资者在投资决策时很少依靠会计信息。① 此外,即使非标意见有一定的负面市场反应,这些负面反应也难以转换为公司改善公司治理的动力。其原因是:①自上市年度的 1993 年起直到 2007 年度,盛润股份大股东和其他发起人股东所持股份一直不能在市场上流通(即"股权分置"),这使得大股东不太在意股票价格的波动,也不直接承受股价下跌的成本;②更重要的是,如果公司本身质量不高,上市融资成功只是被当作掠夺中小股东的一次性交易的话,大股东对股票价格的波动可能完全无动于衷;③盛润股份自上市开始直到 2007 年度,大股东所持股份比例一直在60% 以上,这使得以改进公司治理为目标的收购接管活动难以发生。概言之,市场价格机制以及公司股权结构上的问题使得非标意见带给公司及其大股东的市场后果较小,因而难以激励公司及其大股东改善公司治理。

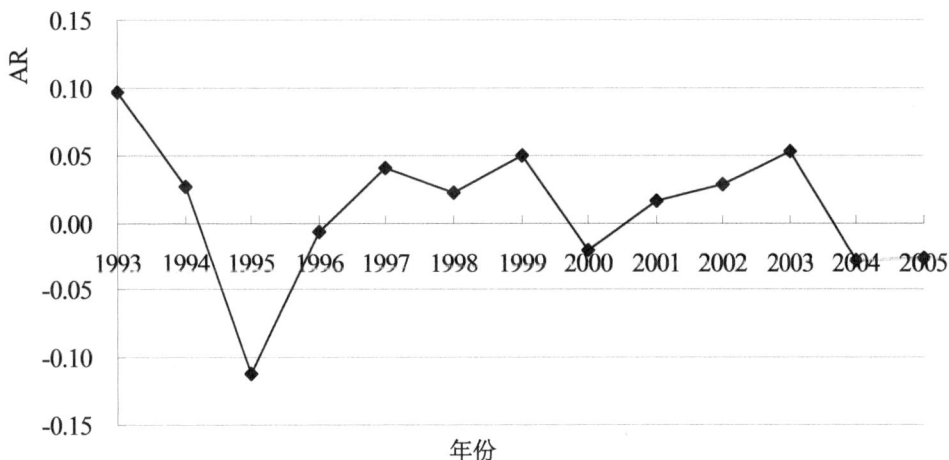

图 2　历年年报公布的市场反应

(二)非标意见的监管后果

公司被出具非标意见后,监管部门可以采取的监管措施主要包括三个方面,分别是:①再融资机会;②特别处理、暂停交易或摘牌;③行政处罚。从盛润股份来看,虽然公司 1993 年至 1997 年度的账面连续盈利,但自上市后从来没有获得

---

① 中国证券市场较弱的投资者保护导致投资者倾向于进行短期投资。在短期投资策略下,投资者更加关心政策信息和内幕信息,而非会计信息。

过配股、增发股票或发行债券资格。给定中国上市公司具有强烈再融资动机的事实,这说明监管部门在再融资决策上可能考虑了非标意见的影响。此外,根据公司 1998 年 6 月 12 日"关于股票交易实行特别处理的公告",由于公司近年财务审计报告连续存在保留意见,公司股票交易自 1998 年 6 月 15 日起实行特别处理(即股票简称前标记"ST")。这意味着,监管部门在特别处理上也考虑非标意见的影响。Chen et al.(2001)发现,1995 年至 1997 年度期间,上市公司为了达到配股盈利要求或避免亏损的盈余管理与非标意见正相关,而这是由于非标意见带给公司的成本小于公司盈余管理的收益所引起。夏立军、杨海斌(2002)对 2000 年度上市公司的类似研究则发现,公司为了达到配股盈利要求或避免亏损的盈余管理与非标意见没有显著关系,而这是由于监管部门从 1998 年开始在监管中考虑了非标意见的影响,从而导致非标意见带给公司的成本增加。根据这些文献,监管部门在再融资及特别处理上考虑非标意见的影响,应该是盛润股份所不愿意看到的。这可能也是其 1998 年更换会计师事务所的一个原因。

然而,在再融资机会以及特别处理监管导致非标意见给盛润股份带来成本的同时,监管部门在行政处罚上并没有使得非标意见带给公司显著成本。通过查阅盛润股份历年公告及证监会违法违规处罚情况可以发现,自上市之日起,盛润股份及其董事、监事和高管从未受到过证监会处罚。但无论从公司管理当局受托责任的履行还是从非标意见所揭示出的公司财务报告中违反会计准则的一些会计处理情况来看,公司及其董事、监事和高管从未受过监管部门处罚均是令人难以理解的。虽然再融资机会取消以及特别处理监管可以防止公司损害潜在投资者利益,但这两种措施难以保护公司既有中小股东的利益。可以想见,没有针对非标意见所揭示事项的监管处罚,非标意见难以带给公司监管后果上的成本以使其重视既有中小股东的利益。而之所以监管处罚不够有效,一方面可能和监管部门本身的监管能力有关,另一方面可能也和其独立性有关。由于各级地方政府具有保护下属国有控股上市公司甚至本地非国有上市公司的动机,作为国务院下属部级单位的证监会可能难以对这些具有各级政府背景或支持的上市公司实施有效处罚(刘鸿儒等,2003;夏立军,2005)。从盛润股份来看,如表 3 所示,其最终控制人在上市后直到 2003 年末一直为深圳市政府,2004 年由于大股东改制最终控制人变为原大股东的工会,2007 年最终控制人变更为自然人郭涛。这说明,在上市后的大部分时间里,盛润股份都是一家有很强地方政府背景的上市公司,这可能可以解释其从未受过行政处罚的原因。因此,非标意见并未带给公司及其董事、监事和高管人员监管处罚上的成本。这可能也是公司连续获得十五年非标意见而公司治理未见明显改善的原因之一。

表 3　盛润股份历年末股权结构

年末	第一股东名称	第一大股东 持股比例(%)	第一大股东 持股性质	最终控制人
1993	深圳市投资管理公司	66.36	非流通股	深圳市政府
1994	深圳市投资管理公司	66.36	非流通股	深圳市政府
1995	深圳市投资管理公司	66.36	非流通股	深圳市政府
1996	深圳市投资管理公司	66.36	非流通股	深圳市政府
1997	深圳市投资管理公司	66.36	非流通股	深圳市政府
1998	深圳市投资管理公司	66.36	非流通股	深圳市政府
1999	深圳市投资管理公司	66.36	非流通股	深圳市政府
2000	深圳市投资管理公司	66.36	非流通股	深圳市政府
2001	深圳市投资管理公司	66.36	非流通股	深圳市政府
2002	深圳市投资管理公司	66.36	非流通股	深圳市政府
2003	深圳市投资管理公司	66.36	非流通股	深圳市政府
2004	深圳市莱英达集团	66.36	非流通股	深圳市莱英达集团工会
2005	深圳市莱英达集团	66.36	非流通股	深圳市莱英达集团工会
2006	深圳市莱英达集团	66.36	非流通股	深圳市莱英达集团工会
2007	深圳市莱英达集团	66.36	非流通股	郭涛

注：表中"深圳市莱英达集团"全称为"深圳市莱英达集团有限责任公司"。

（三）非标意见的法律后果

　　从非标意见的法律后果来看，虽然公司连续十五年被审计师出具非标意见，并且其中揭示出公司经营管理以及会计处理上的诸多问题，但是公司及其董事、监事、高管上市后从未遭受投资者起诉。仅就 2001 年报中所反映的资产减值内容而言，2001 年度公司其他应收款余额为 31 730.19 万元，其中应收关联公司款占 70.43%，其他应收款对应的坏账准备为 20 520.79 万元，这意味着大量坏账损失是由关联公司拖欠款项引起。这表明，公司关联方可能存在从公司转移资源的行为。除此以外，非标意见揭示出公司多个年度会计处理存在违反会计准则现象，实质上是一种虚假陈述行为。从受托责任来看，无论是上市后的会计业绩还是股票业绩表现上,不仅公司上市时从市场上募集的资金很快被亏损殆尽,企业资不抵债金额也越积越大,这表明公司管理当局未能尽到应有的受托责任。

那么,为什么投资者没有要求公司及其管理当局承担相应的民事赔偿责任呢?这可能和我国证券市场上有效的民事诉讼和赔偿机制缺失有关。虽然我国证券市场自设立以来,投资者保护法律不断完善,但是包装上市、虚假陈述、利润操纵、大股东侵占、内幕交易等侵害中小股东利益的违法违规案件不断出现,呈现出一种法律法规不少但未能有效实施的局面(陈信元等,2007)。2001 年 9 月 21 日,"银广夏"事件后,最高人民法院发布《关于涉证券民事赔偿案件暂不予受理的通知》,规定"内幕交易、欺诈、操纵市场等行为引起的民事赔偿案件,暂不予受理",其理由是,"受目前立法及司法条件的局限,尚不具备受理及审理这类案件的条件"。2002 年 1 月 15 日,最高人民法院发布《关于受理证券市场因虚假陈述引发的民事侵权纠纷案件有关问题的通知》(简称"1/15 通知"),其中规定,"人民法院对证券市场因虚假陈述引发的民事侵权赔偿纠纷案件,凡符合《中华人民共和国民事诉讼法》规定受理条件的,自本通知下发之日起予以受理"。这是我国证券法律实施的一大进步,也是中国股票市场有史以来首次明确要求法院受理虚假陈述民事赔偿案件的司法解释。这一通知为虚假陈述民事赔偿诉讼打开了大门,通知发布后,各地法院陆续开始受理此类案件。2003 年 1 月 9 日,最高人民法院发布《关于审理证券市场因虚假陈述引发的民事赔偿案件的若干规定》,在"1/15 通知"的基础上,对审理虚假陈述民事赔偿案件做出了更为详细的规定。然而,根据活跃在虚假陈述民事赔偿诉讼一线的维权律师宣伟华的统计,自虚假陈述民事赔偿开闸以来的 20 例上市公司因虚假陈述而遭到投资者的起诉中,多个案件经历了"起诉不受理""受理不开庭""开庭不判决"或"判决不执行"的遭遇。陈信元等(2007)利用 2002 年 1 月 15 日最高人民法院颁布《关于受理证券市场因虚假陈述引发的民事侵权纠纷案件有关问题的通知》这一事件,以那些存在虚假陈述或有虚假陈述嫌疑的上市公司为样本,采用事件研究法,实证考察了司法独立性对投资者保护法律实施的影响。他们发现,投资者倾向于认为,"1/15 通知"及与其相关的民事诉讼法律能够得到一定程度的实施,但地方政府对当地法院的影响降低了这些投资者保护法律得到实施的可能性。种种事实说明,我国证券市场还缺乏有效的民事诉讼和赔偿机制,非标意见难以给公司及其管理当局带来显著的法律后果。

（四）非标意见对公司治理的影响

从以上的分析可见，虽然盛润股份连续十五年被审计是出具了非标意见，但这些非标意见并未带给公司及其管理当局显著的市场后果、监管后果以及法律后果。从盛润股份公司治理的实际情况来看，虽然公司在 1993 年至 2007 年度期间曾五次更换总经理、三次更换董事长，在 2004 年最终控制人变更为母公司工会并于 2007 年变更为自然人，但无论是表 1 的企业会计绩效还是图 1 的股票收益都显示，这些公司治理结构上的改变并未对公司治理效果有实质性的改善。其背后的原因不难理解，连续十五年的非标意见不断地揭示出公司经营管理上的问题，但由于非标意见未能带给公司及其管理当局显著的市场后果、监管后果及法律后果，因而也就难以促使企业改进公司治理、保护中小股东利益。

这一分析结论看起来与近年来关于独立审计公司治理功能的大样本研究有所矛盾，但实质上是对这些研究的补充和扩展。例如，Chen et al.(2001)发现，市场对公司获得非标意见具有负面反应，进而推测独立审计在中国证券市场具有公司治理功能。我们认为，他们的研究仅仅代表了公司治理上保护潜在投资者的一面，而未能考虑保护既有股东的一面，非标意见引起的股价下跌未必能够带给公司显著的市场后果以改进公司治理。Fan and Wong(2005)对东亚八国(不包括中国)公司的研究发现，股权结构上代理问题严重的公司更倾向于选择国际五大会计师事务所为其审计，这一结果在那些经常需要融资的公司中尤为明显；并且，代理问题严重的公司在选择国际五大会计师事务所其审计后，其股价折价更低，而国际五大会计师事务所对于代理问题严重的公司收取了更高的审计收费，出具了更多的非标意见。他们据此认为，国际五大的审计在东亚新兴市场上具有公司治理功能。Choi and Wong(2007)以 39 个国家的公司为样本，考察了投资者法律保护环境与独立审计的公司治理功能的关系，他们发现独立审计是对弱投资者法律保护环境的一个替代而不是补充。换言之，在投资者法律保护环境较弱的国家，独立审计更能够发挥公司治理功能。实际上，Fan and Wong(2005)、Choi and Wong(2007)这两项研究都是通过考察公司的会计师事务所选择以及审计师的审计收费和审计意见行为对独立审计的公司治理功能进行间接检验，更为直接的检验是考察审计师出具非标意见后企业公司治理上的反应，而间接检验的结论未必一定和直接检验的结论相同。同时，中国证券市场的市场机制、监管效率和法治情况可能与他们样本中东亚八国的情况也有所不同。

四、总结

本文通过对盛润股份连续十五年获得非标意见进行案例分析,考察了独立审计未能发挥公司治理功能的原因。研究发现,在这一案例中,独立审计之所以没能发挥公司治理功能,是因为非标意见未能带给公司显著的市场成本、监管成本和法律成本以促使其改进公司治理。本文的研究表明,独立审计发挥公司治理功能,不仅需要"上市公司→事务所选择"以及"事务所选择→审计意见"环节上的有效性,更需要"审计意见→公司治理改进"环节上的有效性,而这依赖于有效的市场机制、监管机制和法律机制。如果仅有前两个环节上的有效性而没有后一环节上的有效性,仅能保证公司选择高质量的会计师事务所以及审计师揭露出公司财务报告中的问题,而不能保证非标意见所揭示出的问题能够引起公司的重视进而促使其改进公司治理,这样最终由公司股东所负担的审计成本对整个证券市场来说将可能小于其收益。在这一点上,本文是对 Chen et al.(2001)、Fan and Wong(2005)、Choi and Wong(2007)等以往大样本研究的一个补充和扩展,也对证券市场有关制度安排的改革形成启发。未来研究可以借鉴本文的分析框架,对中国证券市场上独立审计制度发挥公司治理功能的约束条件进行更严格的大样本检验。

参考文献

陈梅花.股票市场审计意见信息含量研究:来自 1995 - 1999 上市公司年报的实证证据[J].中国会计与财务研究,2002(1):62 - 105.

陈信元,李莫愁,芮萌,等.司法独立性与投资者保护法律的实施[R].上海:上海财经大学会计与财务研究院工作论文,2007.

刘鸿儒,等.探索中国资本市场发展之路——理论创新推动制度创新[M].北京:中国金融出版社,2003.

王跃堂,陈世敏.脱钩改制对审计独立性影响的实证研究[J].审计研究,2001(3):2 - 9.

夏立军.政府干预与市场失灵——上市公司之会计师事务所选择研究[D].上海:上海财经大学,2005.

夏立军,杨海斌.注册会计师对上市公司盈余管理的反应[J].审计研究,2002(4):28 - 34.

岳衡.大股东资金占用与审计师的监督[J].中国会计评论,2006(1):59 - 68.

Beatty R P. Auditor reputation and the pricing of initial public offerings[J]. Accounting review，1989，64(4)：693 - 709.

Carcello J V，Palmrose Z V. Auditor litigation and modified reporting on bankrupt clients[J]. Journal of accounting research，1994，32：1 - 30.

Chen C J P，Chen S，Su X. Profitability regulation，earnings management，and modified audit opinions：evidence from China[J]. Auditing：a journal of practice & theory，2001，20 (2)：9 - 30.

Chen C J P，Su X，Zhao R. An emerging market's reaction to initial modified audit opinions：evidence from the Shanghai Stock Exchange [J]. Contemporary accounting research，2000，17(3)：429 - 455.

Choi J H，Wong T J. Auditors' governance functions and legal environments：an international investigation[J]. Contemporary accounting research，2007，24(1)：13 - 46.

Clarkson P M，Simunic D A. The association between audit quality，retained ownership， and firm-specific risk in US vs. Canadian IPO markets[J]. Journal of accounting and economics，1994，17(1 - 2)：207 - 228.

DeFond M L，Wong T J，Li S. The impact of improved auditor independence on audit market concentration in China[J]. Journal of accounting and economics，1999，28 (3)： 269 - 305.

Dodd P，Dopuch N，Holthausen R，et al. Qualified audit opinions and stock prices： Information content，announcement dates，and concurrent disclosures[J]. Journal of accounting and economics，1984，6(1)：3 - 38.

Dopuch N，Holthausen R W，Leftwich R W. Abnormal stock returns associated with media disclosures of "subject to" qualified audit opinions[J]. Journal of accounting and economics，1986，8(2)：93 - 117.

Eichenseher J W，Shields D. Corporate director liability and monitoring preferences[J]. Journal of accounting and public policy，1985，4(1)：13 - 31.

Fan J P H，Wong T J. Do external auditors perform a corporate governance role in emerging markets? Evidence from East Asia[J]. Journal of accounting research，2005，43(1)： 35 - 72.

Krishnan J，Krishnan J. Litigation risk and auditor resignations[J]. Accounting review， 1997：539 - 560.

Latham C，Linville M. A review of the literature in audit litigation[J]. Journal of accounting literature，1998，17：175 - 213.

Lennox C. Do companies successfully engage in opinion-shopping? Evidence from the UK [J]. Journal of accounting and economics，2000，29(3)：321 - 337.

Loudder M L，Khurana I K，Sawyers R B，et al. The information content of audit qualifications[J]. Auditing, 1992, 11(1): 69 - 82.

Pittman J A, Fortin S. Auditor choice and the cost of debt capital for newly public firms [J]. Journal of accounting and economics, 2004, 37(1): 113 - 136.

Shu S Z. Auditor resignations: Clientele effects and legal liability[J]. Journal of accounting and economics, 2000, 29(2): 173 - 205.

Wallace W A. The economic role of the audit in free and regulated markets: a look back and a look forward[J/OL]. Research in accounting regulation, 2004, 17: 267 - 298. https://doi.org/10.1016/s1052-0457(04)17012-4.

Watts R L, Zimmerman J L. Agency problems, auditing, and the theory of the firm: some evidence[J]. The journal of law and economics, 1983, 26(3): 613 - 633.

Yang L, Tang Q, Kilgore A, et al. Auditor-government associations and auditor independence in China[J]. The British accounting review, 2001, 33(2): 175 - 189.

Zoe-Vonna P. An analysis of auditor litigation and audit service quality[J]. The accounting review, 1988, 63(1): 55 - 73.

▶作者感谢教育部人文社会科学重点研究基地重大项目"政府管制、公司治理与企业价值"(项目批准号:05JJD630028)以及上海财经大学"'十五''211工程'重点学科建设项目"对本项研究的资助。

大股东侵害与上市公司资产评估偏差 *

内容提要：本文以沪市上市公司 2001 年至 2002 年期间披露的资产评估报告书摘要为研究对象，考察了上市公司大股东侵害动机与资产评估增值率偏差的关系。研究发现：在上市公司接受被评估资产情形中，与大股东交易型的资产评估增值率显著高于其他类型的资产评估增值率，说明上市公司大股东利用资产评估侵害中小股东的情况比较普遍，其手段主要是过高评估大股东向上市公司注入的资产。

关　键　词：上市公司；大股东侵害；评估质量

一、问题的提出

上市公司与投资者之间的信息不对称是影响证券市场有效运转的重要因素，中介制度是减轻这种信息不对称的最重要的制度安排之一。在我国，随着证券市场的不断发展，中介制度也不断发展和完善，经过 10 年左右的时间，不仅建立了较为完善的独立审计制度，还初步建立了资产评估制度。在证券市场上设置这两项制度的目的主要是为了减轻上市公司与投资者之间的信息不对称，维护证券市场公开、公平、公正运转。然而，琼民源、红光实业、郑百文、银广夏、蓝田股份等案件的相继爆发，表明证券市场上中介制度依然存在着比较严重的问题。①

大量的文献对中国证券市场上独立审计的质量和作用进行了研究。研究结

---

* 本文选自：周勤业、夏立军、李莫愁：大股东侵害与上市公司资产评估偏差，《统计研究》，2003 年第 10 期，第 39－44 页。

① 这些案件不仅涉及低质量的独立审计，还涉及低质量的资产评估，例如琼民源和红光实业两案都涉及虚假资产评估问题。

果大体表明，独立审计准则的颁布、事务所的脱钩改制等措施提高了审计独立性（李树华，2000；王跃堂、陈世敏，2002；易琼，2002；等等），但证券市场上还存在着"收买"审计意见、审计意见变通、对盈余管理关注不够等情况，这说明审计质量依然不高（李东平、黄德华、王振林，2001；李爽、吴溪，2002；夏立军、杨海斌，2002；等等）。另外，对于审计意见市场反应的研究发现审计意见信息含量不高，审计意见的作用有限（李增泉，1999；陈梅花，2002；等等）。

相对于证券市场上对独立审计问题的研究，对资产评估问题的理论和实证研究非常缺乏。陆德民（1998）以1992年至1996年沪深两市262家公司为样本，最早尝试对公司上市前资产评估结果及其影响进行分析，研究发现公司资产结构、资本结构、证券承销方式、行业等因素对资产评估增值率具有一定的影响。肖时庆（2001）则通过考察资产评估结果与公司未来一定期间的经营性收益的关系，试图对公司上市前资产评估的准确性做出判断，文章的分析结果没有发现公司资产评估存在整体上的高估或低估行为。

上述两项研究都是以公司上市前的资产评估为研究对象，没能考察公司上市后的资产评估行为。1997年以来，证券市场上出现了大量的资产重组活动（陈信元、叶鹏飞、陈冬华，2003），由于资产评估是资产重组中的一个重要环节，而资产评估结果也是重组各方对资产进行定价的主要依据，因此资产评估的重要性得以显现。[①] 在我国公司治理存在缺陷的环境下，公司上市后的资产评估质量如何？上市公司大股东是否利用资产评估来侵害中小股东？本文首次对公司上市后的资产评估进行系统的实证研究，考察上市公司资产评估中的增值率偏差，试图回答这两个问题。

本文的研究至少具有两个方面的作用：①为我国正在进行的资产评估行业改革和资产评估准则制定提供借鉴；②为研究上市公司大股东侵害行为[②]提供新的视角和证据。本文的以下部分作如下安排：第二部分对资产评估中的机会主义行为进行分析，讨论证监会和财政部有关管制规定的影响，并提出本文的研究假说；第三部分是样本选择和数据来源，第四部分是实证结果和解释，最后一部分给出研究结论和政策建议。

[①]　从媒体的报道来看，根据我们的检索，《中国证券报》2000年、2001年、2002年关于资产评估行业的报道分别达到6、10、13篇，可见资产评估行业已经逐渐受到市场关注。

[②]　本文中大股东侵害行为是指上市公司大股东利用其控股地位通过非公允交易等手段侵害中小股东利益的行为。

二、资产评估中的机会主义行为及其管制

(一)盈余管理观与大股东侵害观

根据已有的研究文献,上市公司的机会主义行为主要是盈余管理和大股东侵害。蒋义宏(1998),陈小悦、肖星(2000)等发现,上市公司为了达到证监会的配股要求,存在普遍性的盈余管理行为。唐宗明、蒋位(2002)以沪深两市 88 家上市公司共 90 项大宗国有股和法人股转让事件作为样本的研究表明,中国证券市场上存在着严重的大股东侵害中小股东的情况,并且这种侵害程度远高于英、美等国。由于资产评估结果是资产重组中资产定价的主要依据,而资产定价的高低会影响到上市公司的盈余和大股东的利益,因此,可以预期上市公司具有操纵资产评估结果的动机。

那么上市公司是否具有操纵资产评估结果的可能呢?考察资产评估行业的现状可以发现,相对于独立审计行业来说,我国的资产评估行业的发展显得落后。这主要体现在资产评估行业缺乏一套完整的法律法规和执业准则体系①,同时资产评估行业还存在着较为严重的多头管理现象②,而独立审计行业不仅有完善的法规和准则体系,而且行业管理权也已经统一到中注协和财政部。因此,相对注册会计师来说,注册资产评估师在执业过程中拥有更多的"自由裁量权"和职业判断的空间。这种情况使得注册资产评估师选择低评估质量的成本较低,从而为上市公司操纵资产评估结果提供了可能。

在上市公司具有操纵资产评估结果的动机和可能的情况下,盈余管理动机和大股东侵害动机对资产评估结果的影响是怎么样的呢?首先,有理由认为操纵资产评估结果的现象主要发生在关联交易中,因为在非关联方交易中交易双方是独立的,交易双方的自利动机会使得资产评估结果相对公正,而在上市公司与关联方尤其是大股东进行交易时,交易的不独立性使得资产评估结果容易受到操纵。其次,上市公司盈余管理动机和大股东侵害动机对资产评估结果的影响是不同

---

① 针对实践中无形资产评估存在的问题,财政部于 2001 年 7 月 23 日发布了《资产评估准则——无形资产》,并从 2001 年 9 月 1 日起施行,这是我国第一个资产评估准则,标志着我国资产评估准则建设工作已走上了正轨。但是,全面规范资产评估行业的法律如《资产评估法》《注册资产评估师法》至今尚未出台,这使得资产评估准则的制订缺乏依据。《资产评估法》已于 2016 年 7 月 2 日发布,自 2016 年 12 月 1 日起实施;于 2014 年 8 月 12 日取消注册资产评估师资格许可和认定,鉴于本文发表时间较早,有些信息已有更新,但考虑到全书的连贯性,文章不做改动。更名为资产评估师。

② 目前我国资产评估行业除了有注册资产评估师资格外,还有房地产估价师、二手车评估师、价格鉴定师等多种执业资格,它们分别隶属不同的政府部门管辖。

的。如果某项资产重组活动涉及的是上市公司给出被评估资产的情形,那么,比资产实际价值更高的资产定价会有利于上市公司实现更多的盈余,而比资产实际价值更低的资产定价会有利于侵害中小股东的利益,因此,在上市公司给出资产的情形中,上市公司的盈余管理动机会使得资产评估增值率偏高,大股东侵害动机会使得资产评估增值率偏低,而在上市公司接受资产的情形中,情况则相反。①

(二)证监会和财政部的有关管制规定

中国证监会于 2001 年 3 月 15 日发布了"关于做好上市公司新股发行工作的通知"(证监发〔2001〕43 号,以下简称"证监会 43 号文")并于当日开始实施。此规定修订了上市公司配股和增发条件,将配股规定对上市公司净资产收益率的要求改为"公司最近 3 个会计年度加权平均净资产收益率平均不低于 6%,扣除非经常性损益后的净利润与扣除前的净利润相比,以低者作为加权平均净资产收益率的计算依据"。同时,增发的要求改为原则上和配股要求一致。由于资产重组损益一般为非经常性损益,而已有的研究表明上市公司盈余管理的主要目的是获得配股和增发资格,因此证监会修订后的配股规定是从会计指标使用角度对利用资产重组进行盈余管理的抑制。

另外,财政部于 2001 年 12 月 21 日发布了《关联方之间出售资产等有关会计处理问题暂行规定》(财会〔2001〕64 号,以下简称"财政部 64 号文"),对上市公司与关联方之间的非公允交易会计处理进行规范,并于发布当日起执行。其主要内容是:如果没有确凿证据表明上市公司与关联方之间交易价格是公允的,那么对显失公允的交易价格部分,一律不得确认为当期利润,应当作为资本公积处理。根据此规定,关联交易非公允部分不能计入当期损益,因此财政部 64 号文是从会计收益计量角度对上市公司利用关联交易进行盈余管理的抑制。

综上,证监会和财政部的这两个规定使得上市公司利用资产重组和关联交易进行盈余管理变得困难,表 1 是两份文件的比较。由于资产评估一般发生于资产重组活动中,因此,证监会 43 号文会使得具有配股、增发盈余管理动机的上市公司操纵资产评估结果的动机减弱。同时,由于操纵资产评估结果的现象主要存在于关联交易中,因此,财政部 64 号文会使得具有盈余管理动机的上市公司操纵资

---

① 如果资产评估涉及的交易导致被评估资产流入上市公司,那么将对应资产评估归类为"上市公司接受资产";如果资产评估涉及的交易导致被评估资产从上市公司流出,那么将对应资产评估归类为"上市公司给出资产";不能划分为这两种类型的归类为"其他类型",例如上市公司与其他公司共同投资设立新的公司,而对其他公司投入新设公司的实物资产进行评估,那么这样的资产评估归类为"其他类型"。

产评估结果的动机减弱。这样我们可以认为,在本文的研究样本中,资产评估中的机会主义行为将主要表现为上市公司大股东侵害中小股东利益,而不是上市公司的盈余管理。

表 1　证监会 43 号文和财政部 64 号文的比较

管制项目	证监会 43 号文	财政部 64 号文
执行日期	2001 年 3 月 15 日	2001 年 12 月 21 日
管制的角度	会计指标使用	会计收益计量
抑制的盈余管理动机	配股、增发	所有盈余管理动机
抑制的盈余管理手段	操纵非经常性损益	关联交易中非公允部分
对资产评估的影响	重组收益计入非经常性损益	关联方交易资产评估中非公允部分

(三)研究假说

根据本节第(一)部分和第(二)部分的讨论,有理由认为,在本文的研究区间,上市公司资产评估的机会主义行为主要是大股东侵害行为。据此,我们提出如下研究假说。

假说 1:在上市公司给出资产情形中,上市公司与大股东交易时资产评估的增值率低于上市公司与非大股东交易时资产评估的增值率。

假说 2:在上市公司接受资产情形中,上市公司与大股东交易时资产评估的增值率高于上市公司与非大股东交易时资产评估的增值率。

假说 3:由于在上市公司接受资产情形中,上市公司大股东利用资产评估侵害中小股东利益比在上市公司给出资产情形中更为容易,因此,假说 2 中的关系比假说 1 中的关系更为显著。

三、样本选择与数据来源

我们以沪市上市公司 2001 年 1 月 1 日至 2002 年 12 月 31 日期间披露的资产评估报告书摘要为研究对象。资产评估报告书摘要一般包括评估目的、评估对象、评估方法、评估基准日、账面价值、调整后账面价值、评估价值、评估增减值、评估增减率、评估结论有效期、评估机构、评估报告提交日等内容。通过检索中国证监会"中国金融证券期货类报刊信息检索系统",我们获得沪市上市公司公开披露的资产评估报告书摘要 382 份,其中 2001 年披露 242 份,2002 年披露 140 份。[①]

　　本文以这 382 份资产评估报告书摘要为研究样本。之所以选择 2001 年至 2002 年之间披露的资产评估报告书摘要作为研究样本,是因为根据上文的分析, 上市公司在此期间利用资产评估进行盈余管理的可能性较小,这样我们可以集中考察上市公司资产评估中的大股东侵害行为。同时,通过比较 2001 年与 2002 年披露的评估报告增值率的差异,还可以考察财政部 64 号文的影响。

四、实证结果及解释

(一)样本特征描述性统计

1. 样本类型年度间分布

　　表 2 是样本总体的分布情况。我们通过检索上市公司有关的公告、独立财务顾问报告等公开信息来判断资产评估涉及交易是否为关联交易,并进一步将关联交易分为与大股东交易和一般关联交易两种类型,以考察一般关联交易和与大股东交易是否损害资产评估的独立性并进而影响资产评估的质量。

表 2　样本类型年度间分布

样本类型		2001 年	2002 年	增长比例	合计报告数
上市公司给出资产	与大股东交易	41	14	−65.85%	55
	一般关联交易	10	5	−50.00%	15
	非关联方交易	8	10	25.00%	18
	小计	59	29	−50.85%	88
上市公司接受资产	与大股东交易	135	70	−48.15%	205
	一般关联交易	17	7	−58.82%	24
	非关联方交易	20	27	35.00%	47
	小计	172	104	−39.53%	276

[①]　"中国金融证券期货类报刊信息检索系统"包含国内知名的专业证券报刊、综合报刊、权威研究报刊及重要的研究刊物,包括上市公司指定信息披露报刊《中国证券报》《上海证券报》《证券时报》的所有内容,因此,本文的研究样本基本上包括了 2001 年 1 月 1 日至 2002 年 12 月 31 日期间沪市上市公司披露的所有资产评估报告书摘要。

（续表）

样本类型		2001 年	2002 年	增长比例	合计报告数
其他类型	与大股东交易	5	1	−80.00%	6
	一般关联交易	2	5	150.00%	7
	非关联方交易	4	1	−75.00%	5
	小计	11	7	−36.36%	18
合　计		242	140	−42.15%	382

从表 2 可以看出：①无论是 2001 年还是 2002 年，接受资产的资产评估报告份数大大多于给出资产类型的评估报告份数，而其他类型最少，这说明大部分资产重组采用的是向上市公司注入资产方式；②在接受或给出资产类型中，无论是在 2001 年还是在 2002 年，与大股东交易资产评估数量远多于一般关联交易和非关联交易资产评估数量，这说明上市公司资产重组主要在上市公司与大股东之间进行；③比较 2001 年和 2002 年资产评估报告书数量，可以发现评估报告数量大大减少，由 242 份下降到 140 份，具体考察减少的资产报告涉及交易类型，发现减少的主要是关联交易中与大股东交易类型，而非关联交易资产评估数量基本没有减少，这说明财政部 64 号文可能对上市公司的资产重组活动数量产生了影响。表 2 的这些特征说明，资产评估中机会主义行为较为明显。

2. 评估增值率描述性统计

由于"其他类型"资产评估数量较少，因此我们剔除其他类型资产评估的样本，以集中考察上市公司给出和接受资产类型的资产评估增值率情况，在下文的所有分析中，我们都进行这样的处理。在增值率描述性统计中，我们剔除了调整后账面价值为零无法计算增值率的样本 6 个，并剔除了增值率 3 倍标准差以外异常值样本 2 个。表 3 是进行上述处理后评估增值率的描述性统计表。图 1 和图 2 分别是表 3 中增值率平均值和中位数的折线图。

从表 3 和图 1、图 2 可以看出，上市公司接受资产型的资产评估增值率平均值普遍高于上市公司给出资产型的资产评估增值率平均值，并且两类合计的增值率平均值和中位数分布折线更趋近于上市公司接受资产情形的增值率平均值和中位数分布折线，其原因主要是上市公司接受资产情形的样本远多于上市公司给出资产情形的样本。

表 3 评估增值率描述性统计

分类		样本数	平均值（%）	中位数（%）	最小值（%）	最大值（%）	标准差（%）
						指标	
上市公司给出资产	与大股东交易	55	10.61	0.19	−184.51	337.57	64.18
	一般关联交易	15	13.33	1.51	−5.26	119.91	30.92
	非关联方交易	18	21.54	2.19	−14.78	135.22	43.96
	小计	88	13.31	0.94	−184.51	337.57	55.74
上市公司接受资产	与大股东交易	201	54.10	13.76	−368.16	1934.75	180.02
	一般关联交易	24	41.26	1.24	−258.67	1108.45	235.69
	非关联方交易	43	40.34	0.98	−263.03	442.46	124.18
	小计	268	50.74	9.89	−368.16	1934.75	177.54
两类合计	与大股东交易	256	44.75	9.17	−368.16	1934.75	163.12
	一般关联交易	39	30.52	1.51	−258.67	1108.45	184.83
	非关联方交易	61	34.79	1.11	−263.03	442.46	106.85
	小计	356	41.49	5.24	−368.16	1934.75	157.25

注：两类合计样本数（356 个）为全样本（382 个）剔除其他类型交易样本（18 个）、调整后账面价值为零无法计算增值率的样本（6 个）和增值率 3 倍标准差以外异常值样本（2 个）后的样本个数。

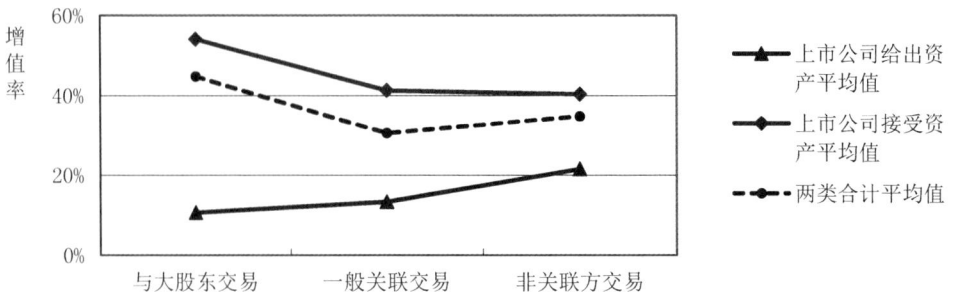

图 1 资产评估增值率平均值

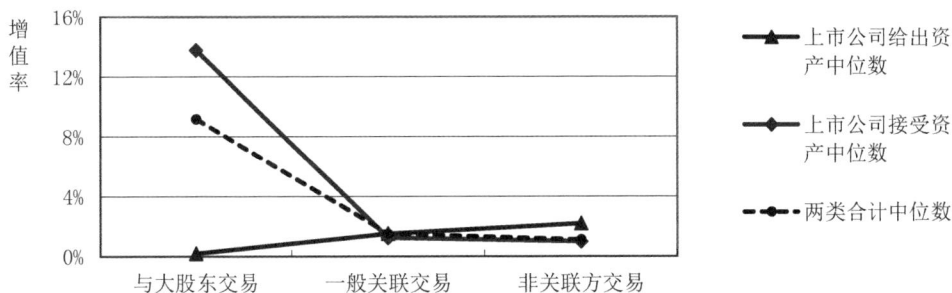

图 2　资产评估增值率中位数

同时,在上市公司给出资产情形中,非关联方交易资产评估增值率的平均值和中位数最大,一般关联交易增值率的平均值和中位数其次,与大股东交易增值率的平均值和中位数最小,这与本文的研究假说 1 相符。而在上市公司接受资产情形中情况正好相反,即与大股东交易增值率的平均值和中位数最大,一般关联交易增值率的平均值和中位数其次,非关联方交易增值率的平均值和中位数最小,这与研究假说 2 相符。下文我们进行进一步的统计检验。

(二)样本均值差异非参数检验

我们首先对样本的增值率进行了正态分布假设检验,检验结果显示研究样本增值率不服从正态分布。因此,我们采用非参数检验对有关变量的增值率均值差异进行分析。表 4 是变量说明,分别检验与大股东交易资产评估、关联交易资产评估、评估报告披露日、评估机构规模对增值率的影响。表 5 是增值率均值差异 Mann-Whitney 检验的结果。

从表 5 可以看出,在上市公司给出资产情形中,与大股东交易资产评估增值率低于其他交易类型资产评估增值率,关联方交易资产评估增值率低于非关联方交易资产评估增值率,这符合研究假说 1。但是,这种关系统计上不显著,说明低评上市公司给出的资产不是大股东或关联方侵害中小股东的主要手段。在上市公司接受资产情形中,与大股东交易资产评估增值率高于其他交易资产评估增值率,并且在 0.01 水平上统计显著,这符合研究假说 2 和假设 3。而关联方交易资产评估增值率虽然高于非关联方交易资产评估增值率,但统计上不显著,这说明侵害中小股东行为主要发生在大股东(而不是上市公司的一般关联方)向上市公司注入资产情形中。

表 4　变量说明

变量名	说　明	变量名	说　明
BigHolder	上市公司与大股东交易取 1,其他情况取 0	Year01	评估报告披露日在 01 年取 1,在 02 年取 0
Related	上市公司与关联方交易取 1,其他情况取 0	Big8N	按完成评估报告数排名前 8 大评估机构取 1,其他情况取 0

表 5　增值率均值差异 Mann-Whitney 检验

分类变量		上市公司给出资产			上市公司接受资产		
变量名	取值	样本数	均值排列	Z 值	样本数	均值排列	Z 值
BigHolder	0	33	49.39	−1.392	68	112.80	−2.771***
	1	55	41.56		202	143.14	
Related	0	18	50.33	−1.086	44	118.41	−1.587
	1	70	43.00		226	138.83	

注:表中上市公司接受资产类型样本(共 270 个)系剔除调整后账面价值为零无法计算增值率的样本(6 个)后的样本数。 *** 表示在 0.01 水平上统计显著(双尾检验)。

　　由于根据上文,资产评估中机会主义行为主要发生在与大股东交易时,因此我们接着专门分析与大股东交易的样本资产评估增值率的特征,我们选取 Year01 和 Big8N 两个变量以分别考察财政部 64 号文和评估机构规模对资产评估增值率的影响。① 从表 6 可以看出,无论是在上市公司给出资产还是上市公司接受资产情形中,Year01 都不显著,这说明财政部 64 号文对资产评估增值率没有显著影响。

　　在上市公司给出资产情形中,Big8N 与评估增值率负相关,但统计上不显著,而在上市公司接受资产情形中,Big8N 与评估增值率正相关,并且在 0.01 水平上统计显著。这说明,大规模评估机构的评估质量可能比小规模评估机构的评估质量更低,表现在大规模评估机构比小规模评估机构更倾向于高评大股东向上市公司注入的资产。

① 按完成 382 个样本中评估报告多少排名的前八大评估机构依次为:上海东洲资产评估有限公司、东方资产评估事务所有限公司、北京六合正旭资产评估有限责任公司、上海立信资产评估有限公司、青岛天和资产评估有限责任公司、湖北众联咨询评估有限公司、北京德威评估有限公司、北京中企华资产评估有限责任公司。我们对按评估后资产净价值总额排名的前八大评估机构进行了敏感性测试,文中结论不变。

表 6　与大股东交易时增值率均值差异 Mann-Whitney 检验

分类变量		上市公司给出资产			上市公司接受资产		
变量名	取值	样本数	均值排列	Z 值	样本数	均值排列	Z 值
Year01	0	14	28.54	−0.145	69	92.81	−1.522
	1	41	27.82		133	106.01	
Big8N	0	30	29.07	−0.541	141	93.72	−2.875 ***
	1	25	26.72		61	119.48	

注：*** 表示在 0.01 水平上统计显著（双尾检验）。

五、研究结论与政策建议

本文考察了上市公司大股东侵害动机与资产评估增值率偏差之间的关系，主要发现如下：

（1）在上市公司接受资产情形中，与大股东交易的资产评估增值率显著高于其他交易类型的资产评估增值率；而在上市公司给出资产情形中，与大股东交易的资产评估增值率低于其他交易类型的资产评估增值率，但统计上不显著。这说明在上市公司资产评估中，存在着大股东操纵评估结果以侵害中小股东利益的情况，并且其手段主要是高评上市公司接受来自大股东的资产，而不是低评上市公司给出到大股东的资产。

（2）由于我们的研究样本限于证监会 43 号文和财政部 64 号文颁布施行之时和之后，而这两个文件是对上市公司以盈余管理为目的资产重组和关联交易活动的抑制，因此在本文的研究期间之前，上市公司资产评估中的机会主义行为可能还包括上市公司的盈余管理行为。如果研究样本向前扩展，那么研究结论可能会有一定差异。

（3）对大规模评估机构和小规模评估机构评估增值率差异的检验表明，大规模评估结构的评估质量可能比小规模评估机构的评估质量更低。可能的原因是，在我国证券市场上还缺乏对高评估质量的市场需求，相反却存在着对低评估质量的需求，因此低质量的评估机构容易获得更多的市场份额而成为大规模评估机构。

需要说明的是,由于资产评估不仅依赖于一系列的经济、政策、法律假定,同时资产评估的活动领域本身就是那些资产价值具有高度不确定性的领域,因此资产评估的质量是一个难以判断的问题。本文的结果不是对上市公司资产评估质量的精确判断,但是,在中国证券市场上公司治理存在缺陷的情况下,上市公司大股东往往具有侵害中小股东的动机,并实际拥有资产评估机构的聘任权,因此在上市公司接受大股东资产情形中,资产评估出现系统性的高评估增值率,足以表明上市公司资产评估质量有待提高。根据研究结论,我们提出如下政策建议:

(1) 加强上市公司资产评估信息披露,对上市公司资产评估信息披露做出具体和明确的要求。在可能的情况下,应当要求上市公司披露资产评估报告书全文。同时,应当要求上市公司在资产评估报告书摘要中清晰地披露上市公司与评估各方的关系、资产评估是否涉及关联交易尤其是与大股东交易等情况。

(2) 对上市公司涉及关联交易尤其是与大股东交易的资产评估以及增值率绝对值特别大的资产评估进行特别规定,实行更严格的信息披露要求,并要求上市公司和评估机构对增值率绝对值特别大的原因进行特别说明,以利于市场对资产评估质量进行判断。

(3) 进一步改革我国资产评估行业管理体制,实行政府统一监管和行业自律相结合的管理体制,尽快统一资产评估行业的监管权限,充分发挥中注协在行业管理方面的作用。同时,应当加快行业法规和准则建设,尽快出台《资产评估法》《注册资产评估师法》以及有关的资产评估准则,营造对高质量资产评估的市场需求和对低质量资产评估的有效惩罚环境。

参考文献

陈梅花.股票市场审计意见信息含量研究:来自 1995－1999 上市公司年报的实证证据[J].中国会计与财务研究,2002(1):62－105.

陈小悦,肖星,过晓艳.配股权和上市公司利润操纵[J].经济研究,2000(01):30－36.

陈信元,叶鹏飞,陈冬华.机会主义资产重组与刚性管制[J].经济研究,2003(05):13－22＋91.

蒋义宏.一个不容忽视的问题——上市公司利润操纵的实证研究[N].中国证券报,1998－3－19/20.

李东平,黄德华,王振林."不清洁"审计意见,盈余管理与会计师事务所变更[J].会计研究,2001(6):51－82.

李树华.审计独立性的提高与审计市场的背离[M].上海:上海三联书店,2000.

李爽,吴溪.审计意见变通及其监管:经验证据[J].中国会计与财务研究,2002(4):1-57.

李增泉.实证分析:审计意见的信息含量[J].会计研究,1999(8):16-22.

陆德民.上市改组过程中的资产评估:一项实证研究[J].会计研究,1998(5):9-16.

唐宗明,蒋位.中国上市公司大股东侵害度实证分析[J].经济研究,2002(04):44-50+94.

王跃堂,陈世敏.脱钩改制对审计独立性影响的实证研究[J].审计研究,2001(3):2-9.

夏立军,杨海斌.注册会计师对上市公司盈余管理的反应[J].审计研究,2002(4):28-34.

肖时庆.证券市场资产评估问题研究[D].厦门:厦门大学,2001.

易琮.中国会计事务所产权制度的变迁与绩效[J].中国会计与财务研究,2003,5(1):140-189.

IFRS Adoption in China and Foreign Institutional Investments[①]

Abstract: We examine the effectiveness of China's IFRS adoption from the perspective of an important set of financial report users, foreign institutional investors. We find that foreign institutional investment does not increase after China's IFRS adoption, and some evidence shows that it actually declines, particularly among firms with weaker incentives to credibly implement IFRS, or with greater ability to manipulate IFRS's fair value provisions. We also find that the association between earnings and returns generally declines after IFRS adoption, consistent with reduced earnings quality. In addition, we find that foreign institutional investors' returns decrease after China's IFRS adoption. Finally, the decline in foreign institutional investment is greater among investors from countries with weak institutions that have also adopted IFRS. Taken together, our evidence suggests that the weak institutional infrastructure in China's transitional economy impairs IFRS's intended goal of attracting institutional investment through improved financial reporting quality. Further, financial information users' home country institutions and IFRS adoption experience affect the effectiveness of IFRS adoption.

Keywords: IFRS; foreign institutional investment; institutions; China

---

① 本文选自: DeFond M, Gao X, Li O Z and and Xia L. IFRS Adoption in China and Foreign Institutional Investments. China Journal of Accounting Research, 2019(12)(1): 1-32.

1. Introduction

In an effort to improve financial reporting quality and attract foreign investment, China's domestic capital markets now use International Financial Reporting Standards (IFRS).[1] Advocates of IFRS claim that it reduces information acquisition costs, thereby increasing investors' willingness to invest across borders (e.g., SEC, 2008). IFRS, however, is modeled on developed economies with strong institutions, and little is known about the effects of IFRS adoption in large transitional economies such as China, where institutions are weak. Further, foreign institutional investors' home country institutions and IFRS adoption experience may affect the ability of IFRS to attract foreign investment. The purpose of our study is to test whether China's IFRS adoption has achieved its intended goal of attracting foreign institutional investment and whether foreign investors' home country institutions and IFRS adoption experience influence the association between IFRS adoption and foreign institutional investment.

The stated goal of the International Accounting Standards Board (IASB) in formulating IFRS is to create a single set of high quality accounting standards that take into account the financial reporting needs of emerging economies. As a result, many developing countries have adopted or are planning to adopt IFRS in the near future. Consistent with this trend, China mandated IFRS adoption for all publicly traded firms beginning in 2007. A primary goal of China's IFRS adoption is to attract greater foreign investment.

Prior research has generally found positive capital market consequences following mandatory IFRS adoption (Daske et al., 2008; Li, 2010; Tan et al.,

---

[1] As with many IFRS adopters, China's new accounting standards contain modifications to IFRS designed to reflect its unique environment (as discussed in detail later). However, for ease of exposition, we follow prior literature (e.g., He et al., 2012) and refer to the adoption of these new standards simply as IFRS adoption.

2011; DeFond et al., 2011). Much of this research, however, is based on evidence from the European Union (EU), where economic and legal institutions tend to be stronger than those in China. In settings where IFRS is unlikely to be credibly implemented, the benefits of IFRS adoption tend to be weak or non-existent, consistent with the notion that the effectiveness of high quality accounting standards depends critically on managers' reporting incentives (Fan and Wong, 2002; Ball 2006; Ball, Robin, and Wu, 2003; Leuz, 2003). Characterized by poor investor protection, weak rule of law, and poor audit quality, China's institutional setting creates weak incentives for managers to produce high quality financial statements (DeFond et al., 2000; Chen and Yuan, 2004; Wang et al., 2008; He at al., 2012). In addition, IFRS's principles-based standards and a greater use of fair value accounting provide more opportunities for Chinese managers to misreport (He et al., 2012). Therefore, we predict that IFRS adoption in China is unlikely to result in increased financial reporting quality that will attract greater foreign investment.

We perform our primary analysis using Chinese domestically listed public firms during 2005 through 2008. During the period of our analysis, foreign investors in China's domestic market consist of 50 Qualified Foreign Institutional Investors (QFIIs) from 13 countries and districts.[1] Our primary analysis uses panel data to compare the change in firm-level QFII ownership in each Chinese listed firm from the pre-adoption period (2005 and 2006) to the post adoption period (2007 and 2008).[2] Following Bradshaw et al. (2004), we measure foreign investment using three firm-level measures — a binary variable indicating whether a QFII holds stock in a Chinese listed firm, the number of QFIIs holding stock in a firm, and the percentage of a firm's shares owned by QFIIs. In addition, our multivariate tests control for a number of firm-level characteristics that are potentially associated with changes in foreign investment, including stock returns, return volatility, return on equity, analyst coverage, cross-listings, dividend yield, growth, and others.

---

[1]   Our sample includes Hong Kong, which is a special administrative region of China.

[2]   The term "foreign investors" and QFIIs are used interchangeably throughout the text.

We find no evidence of an increase in foreign institutional investment in Chinese domestically listed firms after IFRS adoption. Further, we find a modest but statistically significant decline in foreign investment, using all three measures of foreign institutional investment. We also continue to find these results after limiting our analysis to 2006 – 2007, suggesting that our results are not driven by the global financial crisis that began in 2008. We then perform cross-sectional tests designed to further identify channels through which IFRS adoption affects foreign investment. As expected, we find that the decline is larger among firms with weaker incentives to credibly implement IFRS and a greater ability to manipulate IFRS's fair value provisions. This is consistent with foreign investors reducing their investment in Chinese firms after IFRS adoption due to concerns over declining financial reporting quality, including increased earnings manipulation. Predictable cross-sectional differences in the reduction in foreign institutional investment due to incentives and opportunities presented by IFRS directly links our results to China's IFRS adoption. This provides comfort that our results are not driven by changes in other macroeconomic factors.

To explore why foreign investment declined following IFRS adoption, we investigate whether IFRS adoption impairs financial reporting quality in China. We find that the association between reported earnings and stock returns declines after IFRS adoption, consistent with IFRS' reducing earnings quality. In addition, we find a decline in foreign investors' returns following IFRS adoption, consistent with IFRS' making it more difficult for foreign investors to pick high performing stocks.

Finally, we investigate whether foreign investors' home country institutions affect their reaction to IFRS adoption in China. We find that foreign investors from countries with weak legal and economic institutions, similar to those in China, reduce their investment by a greater amount than foreign investors from countries with strong institutions. We also find that home country adoption of IFRS exacerbates the decline in investment from countries with weak institutions, while it attenuates the decline in investment from countries with strong institutions. These findings are consistent with investors from countries with weak institutions having relatively low confidence in IFRS's credible implementation in China and with IFRS adoption being relatively less successful in countries with weak institutions when compared with countries with strong institutions.

Our study contributes to the literature in several ways. First, our evidence suggests that China's weak institutions impair IFRS's ability to attract foreign institutional investment. Prior research primarily studies developed economies and generally finds that IFRS has positive capital market consequences, particularly in countries with strong legal and economic institutions (Covrig et al., 2007; DeFond et al., 2011). We add to the literature by identifying capital market consequences of IFRS adoption in a developing economy with weak institutions. These findings complement and extend He et al. (2012), who find increased earnings management among firms with trading securities and debt restructuring following mandatory IFRS adoption in China.

Second, examining IFRS adoption in China is useful in evaluating whether IFRS achieves its stated objective of fulfilling the financial reporting needs of emerging economies, which include attracting foreign investment. This potentially has implications for other developing economies that have more recently adopted IFRS, such as Brazil, India and Russia.

Third, we enhance our understanding of the interplay between IFRS and international institutional investors or cross-border investments. De George et al. (2016) suggest that international institutional investors care about IFRS adoption because it helps them familiarize investees at a lower cost, improve the accounting information quality of investees or increase the visibility of long distance investees. While Yu and Wahid (2014) show evidence that familiarity with investees' accounting standards can improve cross-order investments, Florou and Pope (2010) cannot conclude whether investors care about information quality or familiarity. We provide evidence that institutional investors care about the information quality when investing in emerging markets such as China.

Finally, we contribute to the examination of investor background and home country institutions. Florou and Pope (2010) provide evidence that different type of investors, active versus passive, react differently to the IFRS adoption. Yu and Wahid (2014) show that accounting distance between investors' and investees' countries affect global investment decisions. Prior studies also find that economic and legal institutions affect IFRS's impact on financial reporting quality and foreign investment (Armstrong et al., 2010; DeFond et al., 2011), these studies focus primarily on the adopting countries' institutions. We provide new insights into the role of foreign investors' home country institutions on IFRS adoption. We find that foreign investors' home country institutions, and whether they are IFRS adopters, also have consequences.

The remainder of the paper proceeds as follows. Section 2 is the literature review. Section 3 introduces China's institutional settings. Section 4 develops our hypotheses. Section 5 discusses empirical results on foreign institutional investment after China's IFRS adoption. Section 6 explores firm-level cross-sectional variation of the main results. Section 7 examines the effect of foreign investors' home country institutions on their investment in China after IFRS adoption. Section 8 conducts robustness tests. Section 9 is the conclusion.

2. Literature Review

2.1   Research on Mandatory IFRS Adoption

Following widespread mandatory IFRS adoption in 2005, researchers have investigated numerous capital market consequences associated with mandatory IFRS adoption.[①] Landsman et al. (2012) find greater abnormal return volatility and abnormal trading volume around earnings announcements after mandatory IFRS adoption relative to firms that use domestic accounting standards. This suggests that IFRS-based earnings have greater information content than earnings based on local standards. Kim and Li (2010) show evidence of a stronger stock market reaction by IFRS firms to earnings releases of other IFRS firms in the same industry after 2005, consistent with greater

---

① There is also a stream of research that examines firms that voluntarily adopt IFRS (Covrig et al., 2007). However, issues such as self-selection make it difficult to generalize the findings from those studies to mandatory IFRS adoption, such as in China. Thus, we restrict our literature review to mandatory IFRS adoption studies.

information transfer and externality gains from mandatory IFRS adoption. Daske et al. (2008) provide weak evidence of a decline in the cost of capital, as well as a decline in market liquidity after IFRS adoption. Using a longer post-adoption period, Li (2010) finds evidence that the cost of capital declines after IFRS adoption in the EU. Byard et al. (2011) demonstrate that analyst forecast errors and variance decline after IFRS adoption in the EU, suggesting that IFRS earnings are more predictable than earnings under local GAAP. Armstrong et al. (2010) find an incrementally positive market reaction to 16 events associated with IFRS adoption in the EU for firms with lower quality pre-adoption information and with higher pre-adoption information asymmetry, consistent with investors' expecting net information quality benefits from IFRS adoption. They also find that the market reaction is incrementally negative for firms domiciled in code law countries, consistent with investors' concerns over the implementation of IFRS in those countries. As far as we are aware, this is the only study that finds a negative capital market consequence of IFRS adoption. Finally, and perhaps the most relevant to our study, DeFond et al. (2011) show that foreign mutual fund ownership increases following mandatory IFRS adoption in the EU.[①]

A common finding in the above studies is that the benefits of IFRS adoption accrue primarily to firms where IFRS is likely to be credibly implemented, such as those in countries where legal enforcement is strong. In the settings where local institutions are unlikely to result in a credible implementation, IFRS adoption tends to have little or no economic consequences.

2.2　Research on IFRS Adoption in China

Research on the economic consequences of China's IFRS adoption is limited, but provides some insight into whether IFRS can successfully attract foreign investment. Prior to IFRS adoption, Chinese firms with A-shares must report using Chinese Accounting Standards (CAS), while Chinese firms with B-shares must report using the international standards. This means that firms

---

[①]　See Bruggemann, Hitz, and Sellhorn (2013) for a detailed literature review.

with both A and B shares issue financial reports using both CAS and international standards. Using data from 1990 through 2001, Eccher and Healy (2000) and Lin and Chen (2005) exploit this setting by comparing the value relevance of CAS with the value relevance of the International Accounting Standards (IAS), which is the predecessor to IFRS. These studies find that accounting numbers reported using CAS tend to be more value relevant than those reported using IAS. While IAS differs from IFRS in many important respects, these findings are interesting because they suggest that CAS can be better suited to capturing the value of Chinese firms than international standards. More recently, He et al. (2012) examine Chinese firms that adopt IFRS in 2007 and examine the effect of the fair value provisions under IFRS. They find that IFRS results in increased earnings manipulation among Chinese firms with large portfolios of trading securities and debt restructuring. Overall, prior research generally suggests that IFRS adoption in China may not necessarily improve financial reporting quality.

3. Institutional Background

3.1 Adoption of IFRS in China

China's Ministry of Finance (MOF) declared its intention to converge CAS with IFRS in 2005 (Peng and Smith, 2010). The new standards were released in 2006 with mandatory implementation by public companies as of January 1, 2007. The new standards are designed to converge CAS with IFRS, where "converge" refers to the elimination of current differences between IFRS and CAS, and preventing future differences from arising (Hussey and Ong, 2005). With the exception of a few modifications designed to accommodate the local Chinese environment, there is a general agreement that the new standards are substantially equivalent to IFRS (Peng and Simth, 2010).①

---

① The modifications include the inability to upwardly revalue fixed assets after they have been written down for impairment, and the inability to use the equity method or proportional consolidation for joint ventures. In addition, related party transaction disclosures are modified to take into account the large government holdings in many public firms.

3.2   China's QFII System

While China's stock market is one of the largest in the Asia-Pacific region, foreign institutional investors' share of the market is far below that of more developed foreign stock markets. The Chinese government believes that this limits China's capital market development and as a result has taken measures to boost foreign investment. One such measure is the "Provisional Regulations on Investment from Qualified Foreign Institutional Investors in the Domestic Securities Market" in 2002. This was followed by the formal "Regulations on Investment from QFIIs in the Domestic Securities Market" in 2006. Contents of these two documents are consistent and similar. The QFII system is designed to facilitate and regulate foreign institutional investment in China's domestic securities markets. Among other things, the QFII system uses a strict approval process to vet new entrants, and as a result the QFIIs tend to be well capitalized, with medium or long-term investment philosophies. As of December 31, 2008, 74 QFIIs from 16 countries were approved to buy shares in China's A-share (domestic) market, of which 66 were granted investment quotas allowing them to invest.[①] Fifty of these 66 QFIIs invest in Chinese A-shares during the period of our analysis, while 16 have yet to invest. Eight of these 50 liquidated their investment by the end of 2008, leaving 42 QFIIs from 13 countries at the end of our sample period. Appendix A presents detailed information on these QFIIs, their home countries, approval time, investment quotas and quota approval time.

4. Hypothesis Development

4.1   Main Hypothesis

Ball (2001) argues that an economically efficient financial reporting and disclosure system requires strong fundamental institutions. This is consistent with prior research which finds that the capital market benefits of IFRS

[①]   These quotas are determined by initial contributed capital and can be exceeded if market values increase.

adoption are essentially non-existent in settings where IFRS is unlikely to be credibly implemented (Daske et al., 2008; Li, 2010; Tan et al., 2011; DeFond et al., 2011). China's weak legal and economic institutions provide managers with weak incentives to produce high quality financial statements (DeFond et al., 2000; Chen and Yuan, 2004; Wang et al., 2008; Piotroski and Srinivasan, 2008). Without major changes in its institutional infrastructure, there is probably no credible implementation of IFRS. If QFIIs understand this, IFRS adoption may not increase foreign investment.

Compared with IFRS, CAS can also potentially be better suited to curtailing the earnings management incentives engendered by China's weak institutions. While CAS has evolved to place a strong emphasis on reliability, IFRS is more investor-oriented, with a greater emphasis on value relevance. In the presence of weak institutions, a reduced emphasis on reliability potentially erodes financial reporting quality by creating greater opportunities for earnings manipulation. Further, while CAS tends to be rule-based, IFRS is decidedly principle-based. A shift from CAS to IFRS can further exacerbate managers' ability to report opportunistically. IFRS is also much more fair value-oriented, which provides several new opportunities for earnings management. For example, while trading securities are valued at historical cost under CAS, IFRS values them at fair value, with the corresponding change included in earnings. This allows managers to selectively classify trading securities for the purpose of maximizing reported gains. Another example is gains from debt restructuring, which are credited to equity under CAS (and thus have no effect on earnings), but which flow through the income statement under IFRS. Finally, while investment in real estate is recorded at historical cost under CAS, managers are able to record them at fair value under IFRS, with the change in their market value flowing through the income statement. If QFIIs understand these new opportunities for earnings management under IFRS, they are not likely to respond positively to China's IFRS adoption. Based on the above argument, we propose the following hypothesis.

Hypothesis 1: Foreign institutional investment in China's domestic stock market does not increase after China's mandatory IFRS adoption.

Note that we are not arguing that IFRS is necessarily inferior to CAS，but rather that CAS may better fit China's current stage of economic and institutional development than IFRS. While reporting quality is poor under CAS，it may be even poorer after IFRS adoption if managers have an increased ability to manipulate accounting information.

4.2   Firm-Level Cross-Sectional Hypotheses

4.2.1   Management Incentives

There is variation across Chinese listed firms in terms of their incentives to credibly implement IFRS. Jiang et al. (2010) argue that the major agency problem for Chinese listed firms is not between shareholders and managers，but between minority shareholders and controlling shareholders. They support this argument by finding pervasive evidence that controlling shareholders of Chinese listed firms tunnel resources from listed firms through intercorporate loans. This is consistent with a large body of literature that suggests that firms with high ownership concentration and entrenched controlling shareholders have incentives to increase financial reporting opacity in order to obfuscate their self-serving behavior (Leuz，Nanda，and Wysocki，2003). Obfuscation can occur，for example，by controlling shareholders withholding or selectively disclosing unfavorable information，or opportunistically timing the release of value-relevant information. In addition，when the controlling shareholder is Chinese government (i.e.，state-owned enterprises)，managers are more likely to have goals that are not profit maximizing，and as a result are prone to communicating financial information through private information channels and engaging in related party transactions (Wang et al.，2008；Piotroski and Wong，2010；He et al.，2012).

Because firms with high ownership concentration or large government ownership lack incentives to supply quality financial information，we expect that they are less likely to credibly implement IFRS. If foreign investors realize this，we expect to find the decline in foreign institutional investment to be more pronounced in firms with high ownership concentration or with large state ownership. We predict the following hypothesis.

Hypothesis 2a: The decline in foreign institutional investment due to China's mandatory IFRS adoption is greater in firms with high ownership concentration and large state ownership.

4.2.2 Firms Prone to Fair Value Manipulation

We also expect the fair value accounting provisions of IFRS to provide managers with greater opportunities for earnings manipulation. While fair value adjustment can go to the income statement, firms can also manage the timing of securities trading to boost earnings. Both trading and available-for-sale securities can provide opportunities for firms to manipulate earnings. This is consistent with He et al. (2012), who find that Chinese firms manage earnings through fair value accounting by selling available-for-sale securities. If QFIIs understand this, we expect the decline in foreign institutional investment to be more pronounced among firms with greater opportunities to manipulate earnings through fair value accounting. We propose the following hypothesis.

Hypothesis 2b: The decline in foreign institutional investment due to China's mandatory IFRS adoption is greater in firms with opportunities to manipulate earnings through fair value accounting.

4.3 Country-Level Cross-Sectional Hypothesis

A potential source of cross-sectional variation in foreign investors' response to IFRS adoption in China is the heterogeneous nature of QFIIs. While prior research finds that IFRS adopters' institutional environment affects whether IFRS is credibly implemented (Daske et al., 2008; Li, 2010; Tan et al., 2011; DeFond et al., 2011), we are unaware of research that indicates investor heterogeneity affects investment in IFRS adopters, though we know that institutional investors are not uniform and they differ in style, sophistication and horizon (Bushee, 1998). By the end of 2008, QFIIs investing in China come from thirteen different countries, with large variation in legal origins, investor protection institutions, and accounting systems. Since IFRS implementation tends to be less credible in countries with relationship-based institutions, investors from such countries are likely to be more aware of and familiar with this fact, and thus are more skeptical of IFRS's ability to improve China's financial reporting environment. Further, investors from countries with relationship-based institutions, being used to investing under a weaker institutional environment, have their unique investment styles and methods of processing information. They are more apt to process information based on relationships, and historical cost, but not on fair market value. They are also more likely to doubt the effectiveness of market based information due to their past investment experience in their own countries. In sum, culture and institutions influence institutional investors' decisions. Therefore, we expect a larger decline in QFII investment from countries with relationship-based institutions. We propose the following hypothesis.

Hypothesis 3: The decline in foreign institutional investment due to China's mandatory IFRS adoption is greater for institutional investors from countries with relationship-based institutions.

Specifically, countries with relationship-based institutions tend to have code law origin (La Porta et al., 1997), low anti-director rights (La Porta et al., 1997), government only sources of accounting standards (Alford et al., 1993), continental accounting cluster (Mueller et al., 1994; Hung, 2001), high book-tax conformity (Coopers and Lybrand, 1993; Hung, 2001).

5. Empirical Tests

5.1 Data and Sample

We test our hypothesis over the period 2005 – 2008, with period 2005 – 2006 pre-IFRS adoption and period 2007 – 2008 as post-adoption. Panel A in Table 1 presents the sample selection process, which begins with all A-share companies on the Shanghai and Shenzhen stock exchanges. We focus on A-share market for it is the main investment channel through which foreign institutional investors invest in China, and for its total market capitalization is twenty times larger than that of the B-share market.[①] We exclude firm-year observations with missing data on monthly return volatility, yearly returns or year-end prices, and delete observations with negative book values. Our final sample contains 5 518 firm-year observations. Panel B in Table 1 shows the industry distribution of firm-year observations in our sample. Firms are present in 22 major industries and tend to cluster in petrochemical and machinery industries.

Information on QFIIs' approval years, investment quotas and other details are obtained from the websites of the China Securities Regulatory Commission and China's Foreign Exchange Control Bureau. Information on QFIIs' shareholdings and the number of QFIIs per firm is based on the top 10 shareholders of firms' tradable shares obtained from the WIND Info database (provided by Wind Information Co., Ltd.). Firm-level accounting and market numbers are obtained from the WIND Info and CSMAR databases.

Table 1   Sample Selection and Distribution

Panel A: Sample Selection Process

	2005	2006	2007	2008	Total
Number of Year-End Chinese A-Share Listed Firms	1324	1384	1516	1593	5817
Exclude:					
Firms with Negative Book Value of Equity	48	58	54	52	212
Firms Missing Data for Monthly Stock Return Volatility, Yearly Stock Return or Year-End Stock Price	0	31	39	17	87
Final Sample	1276	1295	1423	1524	5518

---

①   Individual QFIIs cannot own more than 10% of a firm's shares and all QFIIs collectively cannot own more than 20%. Actual QFII holdings are far below these numbers (CSRC fund regulation 2006 No. 176). Therefore, the restrictions are not binding. The B-share market was originally created for foreign investors only. H-shares are shares listed in the Hong Kong Stock Exchange.

(continued)

Panel B: Sample Distribution by Industry

CSRC Code	CSRC Industry Name	SIC equivalent	# of Obs.	Percentage (%)
A	Agriculture, Forestry & Fishery	01,02,07,08,09	132	2.39
B	Mining	10,12,13,14	100	1.81
C0	Food & Beverage	20	233	4.22
C1	Textiles & Apparel	22,23	260	4.71
C2	Wood & Furnishing	25	15	0.27
C3	Paper & Printing	26,27	112	2.03
C4	Petrochemicals	28,29,30	576	10.44
C5	Electronics	36	223	4.04
C6	Metals & Non-metals	32,33,34	508	9.20
C7	Machinery	35,36,37	870	15.76
C8	Pharmaceuticals	38	352	6.38
C9	Other Manufacturing	39	72	1.30
D	Utilities	49	250	4.53
E	Construction	15,16,17	120	2.17
F	Transportation	40,41,42,44,45,46,47	233	4.22
G	IT	48	332	6.02
H	Wholesale & Retail Trade	50,51,52,53,54,55, 56,57,58,59	347	6.29
I	Finance	60,61,62,63,64,67	73	1.34
J	Real Estate	65	225	4.08
K	Social Services	43,70,80,82,83	168	3.04
L	Broadcasting & Culture	78,79,84	35	0.63
M	Conglomerate		282	5.11
Total			5518	100

This table presents the sample selection process by calendar year in Panel A and sample distribution by industry membership in Panel B. # of obs. refers to the number of observations from each industry through the entire sample period.

5.2　Empirical Model

We test our hypothesis by estimating the following regression model:

$$D\_QFII_{it}, N\_QFII_{it}, P\_QFII_{it} = \beta_0 + \beta_1 POST_{it} + \beta_2 SIZE_{it} + \beta_3 LEV_{it} + \\ \beta_4 TOP1_{it} + \beta_5 ROE_{it} + \beta_6 DIV_{it} + \\ \beta_7 STDRET_{it} + \beta_8 BTM_{it} + \beta_9 RETURN_{it} + \\ \beta_{10} XLIST_{it} + \beta_{11} DOWJ_{it} + \beta_{12} XSALE_{it} + \\ \beta_{13} ANALYST_{it} + \beta_{14} BIG4_{it} + \\ \text{Industry Dummy} + \varepsilon_{it}. \qquad (1)$$

Following prior research (Bradshaw et al., 2004; DeFond et al., 2012), we sequentially test three dependent measures of QFII investment, each of which captures a different aspect of QFII ownership: ① D_QFII, an indicator variable capturing whether any QFII owns stock in the firm at year end; ② N_QFII, the logarithm transformation of one plus the number of QFIIs that own stock in each sample firm at year end; ③ P_QFII, the cumulative percentage of QFII ownership in each sample firm at year end. Our independent variable of interest in Equation (1) is POST, which is coded 1 for years 2007 and 2008, and 0 for years 2005 and 2006. POST captures the effect of IFRS adoption on QFII investment. To correct standard errors for possible serial correlation and heteroskedasticity, we employ Huber-White standard errors clustered by firm throughout our regression analyses. Following Covrig et al. (2007) and DeFond et al. (2011), we include control variables that are defined in Appendix B. All continuous variables are winsorized at the top and bottom one percentile of their distributions.

5.3　Univariate Hypothesis Tests

Descriptive statistics on QFII ownership, by QFII country and year, are presented in Table 2. Panel A in Table 2 indicates that the US has the largest number of QFIIs, with 9 to 14 per year. Australia and Norway have the smallest number of QFIIs, with 0 to 1 per year. The middle four columns in Table 2 report the average percentage ownership of total shares for each country-year, across all Chinese listed firms. However, many Chinese listed firms have a large block of essentially non-tradable shares owned by government entities. Thus, the right four columns of Panel A report the average percentage ownership based on tradable shares. These columns show that the US has the highest percentage ownership of tradable shares, with 0.057% to 0.199%, and that Australia and Norway have the lowest average percentage ownership, both with 0.000% to 0.001%. While the percentage of tradable shares is larger, the pattern is similar to that computed using the total number of shares.[1]

Panel B in Table 2 compares three measures of QFII ownership before and after mandatory IFRS adoption. Consistent with our hypothesis, Panel B shows that the mean and median value of each of our QFII ownership measures declines significantly after IFRS adoption. One potential issue in this comparison, however, is that some Chinese listed firms may not be in the feasible investment set for foreign investors. Thus, Panel C repeats the analysis in Panel B after restricting the sample to the 1 466 A-share firm years with at least one QFII investor. This panel also shows that the mean and median values of each QFII ownership measure declines significantly after IFRS adoption. Thus, our univariate tests support our first hypothesis. However, as many firm-specific factors affect foreign investment, we rely on multivariate analysis to formally test our predictions.

Table 3 presents descriptive statistics of control variables in Equation (1), partitioned based on D_QFII, which indicates whether a QFII owns shares in the firm, and on POST, which indicates whether the firm has adopted IFRS. Financial statement variables indicate that QFIIs tend to invest in firms that are larger, more highly leveraged, that have high ROE, higher dividend yields, higher growth (low book-to-market ratio), and lower stock return volatility. Corporate governance variables show that QFIIs tend to invest in firms with larger ownership by the largest shareholder. Variables capturing the information environment indicate that QFIIs tend to invest in firms included in important market indices, firms with more analysts following, and firms with Big-4 auditors.

---

[1] The total market capitalization of stock owned by all the QFIIs ranges from the equivalent of US $ 1.5 billion to US $ 5.3 billion during the period analyzed.

Table 2 Number of QFIIs and Their Shareholdings by Home Country and Year

Panel A: QFII Shareholdings

Home Country	Number of QFIIs				Average Percentage Ownership of Total Shares Outstanding (%)				Average Percentage Ownership of Total Tradable A-Shares (%)			
	2005	2006	2007	2008	2005	2006	2007	2008	2005	2006	2007	2008
Australia	0	0	1	1	0.000	0.000	0.001	0.001	0.000	0.000	0.001	0.001
Belgium	1	2	1	1	0.020	0.033	0.009	0.007	0.060	0.073	0.021	0.015
Canada	0	1	2	2	0.000	0.000	0.002	0.002	0.000	0.002	0.003	0.003
France	3	4	4	4	0.003	0.008	0.006	0.013	0.005	0.020	0.013	0.021
Germany	1	1	1	1	0.013	0.020	0.005	0.003	0.041	0.044	0.010	0.006
Hong Kong	2	3	3	3	0.012	0.022	0.016	0.009	0.029	0.047	0.032	0.014
Japan	2	2	3	3	0.013	0.017	0.003	0.004	0.032	0.051	0.007	0.008
Netherlands	1	2	2	2	0.005	0.023	0.023	0.004	0.017	0.060	0.042	0.007
Norway	0	0	0	1	0.000	0.000	0.000	0.001	0.000	0.000	0.000	0.001
Singapore	0	2	3	3	0.000	0.004	0.003	0.004	0.000	0.011	0.007	0.006
Switzerland	2	2	3	3	0.030	0.041	0.038	0.018	0.091	0.099	0.073	0.035
UK	2	2	3	4	0.001	0.019	0.018	0.014	0.004	0.038	0.037	0.024
US	9	12	13	14	0.036	0.077	0.059	0.030	0.112	0.199	0.118	0.057

Panel B: Descriptive Statistics on QFII Investments as Captured by the Three Dependent Variables Measuring QFII Investment

Dep. Variable		MEAN	STD	MIN	MEDIAN	MAX	Diff.	POST = 1 vs. POST = 0
D_QFII	POST = 0	0.128	0.334	0.000	0.000	1.000	MEAN	−0.031 ***
	POST = 1	0.097	0.296	0.000	0.000	1.000	MEDIAN	−0.000 ***
N_QFII	POST = 0	0.124	0.353	0.000	0.000	2.079	MEAN	−0.040 ***
	POST = 1	0.084	0.275	0.000	0.000	1.946	MEDIAN	−0.000 ***
P_QFII	POST = 0	0.005	0.019	0.000	0.000	0.273	MEAN	−0.002 ***
	POST = 1	0.003	0.012	0.000	0.000	0.200	MEDIAN	−0.000 ***

Panel C: Descriptive Statistics of QFII Investment in Firms with QFII Investment in Any Year of the Sample Period

Dep. Variable		MEAN	STD	MIN	MEDIAN	MAX	Diff.	POST=1 vs. POST=0
D_QFII	POST=0	0.467	0.499	0.000	0.000	1.000	MEAN	−0.093 ***
	POST=1	0.374	0.484	0.000	0.000	1.000	MEDIAN	−0.000 ***
N_QFII	POST=0	0.454	0.553	0.000	0.000	2.079	MEAN	−0.129 ***
	POST=1	0.325	0.462	0.000	0.000	1.946	MEDIAN	−0.000 ***
P_QFII	POST=0	0.019	0.032	0.000	0.000	0.273	MEAN	−0.008 ***
	POST=1	0.011	0.023	0.000	0.000	0.200	MEDIAN	−0.000 ***

Variable definitions are presented in Appendix B. P-values in Panels B and C are from t-tests of mean differences or Wilcoxon-tests when POST = 1 minus POST = 0. $N = 5,518$ for Panels A and B, and $N = 1466$ for Panel C. *** $p<0.01$, ** $p<0.05$, * $p<0.10$.

Table 4 presents Pearson correlation coefficients. Whether QFII investment is measured as the existence of at least one QFII investor (D_QFII), the number of QFII investors (N_QFII), or the percentage of QFII investors (P_QFII), it is positively correlated with firm size (SIZE), dividend yield (DIV), shareholding of the largest shareholder (TOP1), firm visibility (XLIST, DOWJ), analyst following (ANALYST), and Big 4 audit (BIG4). D

_QFII, N_QFII and P_QFII are negatively correlated with financial leverage (LEV), book-to-market ratio (BTM), and return volatility (STDRET). These results are consistent with Table 3. D_QFII, N_QFII and P_QFII are also positively correlated with ROE, suggesting that QFIIs tend to invest in profitable firms. D_QFII, N_QFII and P_QFII are negatively correlated with POST, suggesting that QFIIs reduce investments in Chinese listed firms after IFRS adoption, consistent with our univariate results in Panels B and C, Table 2.

Table 3   Descriptive Statistics on Control Variables Partitioned on the Indicator Dependent Variable D_QFII

Variables	IFRS Adoption	D_QFII = 0 (N = 4905)		D_QFII = 1 (N = 613)		D_QFII = 0 vs. D_QFII = 1	
		Mean	Median	Mean	Median	t-test p-values	Wilcoxon p-values
SIZE	POST=0	21.212	21.137	22.219	21.977	0.000	0.000
	POST=1	21.520	21.359	22.085	21.864	0.000	0.000
LEV	POST=0	0.518	0.538	0.481	0.488	0.001	0.000
	POST=1	0.502	0.512	0.491	0.485	0.334	0.219
TOP1	POST=0	0.378	0.350	0.419	0.427	0.000	0.000
	POST=1	0.361	0.344	0.386	0.379	0.008	0.005
ROE	POST=0	−0.005	0.043	0.098	0.102	0.000	0.000
	POST=1	0.051	0.073	0.111	0.109	0.000	0.000
DIV	POST=0	0.009	0.000	0.019	0.015	0.000	0.000
	POST=1	0.006	0.001	0.008	0.006	0.000	0.000
BTM	POST=0	0.745	0.763	0.657	0.647	0.000	0.000
	POST=1	0.538	0.505	0.497	0.445	0.011	0.009
RETURN	POST=0	−0.240	−0.215	0.024	−0.022	0.000	0.000
	POST=1	0.316	0.077	0.401	0.103	0.141	0.205
STDRET	POST=0	0.126	0.116	0.118	0.110	0.010	0.003
	POST=1	0.204	0.196	0.191	0.187	0.000	0.000

(continued)

Variables	IFRS Adoption	D_QFII = 0 (N = 4905)		D_QFII = 1 (N = 613)		D_QFII = 0 vs. D_QFII = 1	
		Mean	Median	Mean	Median	t-test p-values	Wilcoxon p-values
XLIST	POST=0	0.080	0.000	0.146	0.000	0.000	0.000
	POST=1	0.087	0.000	0.112	0.000	0.151	0.151
DOWJ	POST=0	0.399	0.000	0.823	1.000	0.000	0.000
	POST=1	0.376	0.000	0.639	1.000	0.000	0.000
ANALYST	POST=0	2.141	0.000	7.802	7.000	0.000	0.000
	POST=1	6.310	2.000	11.561	8.000	0.000	0.000
BIG4	POST=0	0.049	0.000	0.216	0.000	0.000	0.000
	POST=1	0.065	0.000	0.140	0.000	0.000	0.000

Variable definitions are presented in Appendix B. P-values are from t-test of mean difference or Wilcoxon-tests of D_QFII = 0 minus D_QFII = 1. *** $p < 0.01$, ** $p < 0.05$, * $p < 0.10$.

Table 4 Pearson Correlations

	D_QFII	N_OFII	P_QFII	POST	ROE	SIZE	LEV	TOP1	DIV	BTM	RETURN	STDRET	XLIST	DOWJ	ANALYST
N_QFII	0.926														
	(0.00)														
P_QFII	0.693	0.828													
	(0.00)	(0.00)													
POST	−0.049	−0.063	−0.076												
	(0.00)	(0.00)	(0.00)												
ROE	0.107	0.100	0.076	0.106											
	(0.00)	(0.00)	(0.00)	(0.00)											
SIZE	0.206	0.200	0.129	0.099	0.170										
	(0.00)	(0.00)	(0.00)	(0.00)	(0.00)										
LEV	−0.040	−0.037	−0.035	−0.032	−0.253	0.295									
	(0.00)	(0.01)	(0.01)	(0.02)	(0.00)	(0.00)									
TOP1	0.072	0.069	0.061	−0.066	0.088	0.203	−0.055								
	(0.00)	(0.00)	(0.00)	(0.00)	(0.00)	(0.00)	(0.00)								
DIV	0.160	0.168	0.130	−0.154	0.231	0.265	−0.167	0.219							
	(0.00)	(0.00)	(0.00)	(0.00)	(0.00)	(0.00)	(0.00)	(0.00)							

(continued)

	D_QFII	N_QFII	P_QFII	POST	ROE	SIZE	LEV	TOP1	DIV	BTM	RETURN	STDRET	XLIST	DOWJ	ANALYST
BTM	-0.059	-0.046	-0.054	-0.373	-0.113	0.308	0.213	0.046	0.211						
	(0.00)	(0.02)	(0.00)	(0.00)	(0.00)	(0.00)	(0.00)	(0.00)	(0.00)						
RETURN	0.051	0.034	0.028	0.311	0.144	0.106	0.063	-0.006	-0.084	-0.358					
	(0.00)	(0.17)	(0.04)	(0.00)	(0.00)	(0.00)	(0.00)	(0.68)	(0.00)	(0.00)					
STDRET	-0.075	-0.084	-0.083	0.577	0.010	-0.047	0.054	-0.085	-0.244	-0.400	0.490				
	(0.00)	(0.00)	(0.00)	(0.00)	(0.44)	(0.00)	(0.00)	(0.00)	(0.00)	(0.00)	(0.00)				
XLIST	0.052	0.048	0.054	0.002	0.016	0.281	0.049	0.039	0.046	0.035	-0.010	-0.008			
	(0.00)	(0.00)	(0.00)	(0.90)	(0.22)	(0.00)	(0.00)	(0.00)	(0.00)	(0.01)	(0.45)	(0.54)			
DOWJ	0.223	0.208	0.141	-0.052	0.196	0.603	-0.003	0.060	0.245	0.015	0.155	-0.093	0.074		
	(0.00)	(0.00)	(0.00)	(0.00)	(0.00)	(0.00)	(0.85)	(0.00)	(0.00)	(0.27)	(0.00)	(0.00)	(0.00)		
ANALYST	0.185	0.170	0.125	0.226	0.225	0.502	-0.016	0.091	0.240	-0.064	0.055	0.005	0.144	0.372	
	(0.00)	(0.00)	(0.00)	(0.00)	(0.00)	(0.00)	(0.25)	(0.00)	(0.00)	(0.00)	(0.00)	(0.70)	(0.00)	(0.00)	
BIG4	0.151	0.150	0.120	0.004	0.063	0.436	0.023	0.097	0.160	0.061	-0.011	-0.070	0.428	0.215	0.302
	(0.00)	(0.00)	(0.00)	(0.79)	(0.00)	(0.00)	(0.09)	(0.00)	(0.00)	(0.00)	(0.43)	(0.00)	(0.00)	(0.00)	(0.00)

Variable definitions are presented in Appendix B. $N = 5518$. P-values are in parentheses.

5.4 Multivariate Hypothesis Tests

Multivariate tests are reported in Panel A, Table 5. The coefficients on POST are negative and significant for all QFII investment measures (-0.7535, Z-statistic $= -5.66$ using D_QFII; -0.0808, t-statistic $= -7.36$ using N_QFII; -0.0040, t-statistic $= -7.55$ using P_QFII). Thus, consistent with univariate tests, our multivariate results support our first hypothesis.

A potential concern in Panel A, Table 5 is that the feasible set of Chinese firms suitable for foreign investment is likely limited. Thus, we repeat our analysis in Panel A after restricting the sample to the 1 466 A-share firm year observations with at least one QFII investor at the end of the year. The results, reported in Panel B, Table 5, also show that the coefficients on POST are negative and significant for all QFII measures (-0.6699, z-statistic $= -4.11$ using D_QFII; -0.1888 t-statistic $= -5.39$ using N_QFII; -0.0100, t-statistic $= -5.88$ using P_QFII). Thus, Panel B, Table 5 suggests that Panel A results are not driven by firms not in QFIIs' feasible investment set.

Another potential concern is that our results may be explained by an overall decline in investment following the global financial crisis in 2008. We investigate this issue by repeating the analysis in Panel A, Table 5 after restricting the sample to 2006 – 2007, where POST equals 0 for 2006 and 1 for 2007. Panel C again reports that QFII investment significantly declines based on all three ownership measures (-0.8534, Z-statistics $= -4.62$ for D_QFII; -0.1148, t-statistics $= -5.74$ for N_QFII; -0.0053, t-statistics $= -5.60$ for P_QFII). Thus, results in Panel C, Table 5 are consistent with the decline in foreign investment being due to China's IFRS adoption, and not to an investment downturn following the financial crisis.

Overall, results in Table 5 support our first hypothesis by showing that China's IFRS adoption is actually followed by reduced foreign institutional investment. We acknowledge, however, that QFIIs' percentage ownership of the China's A-share market is very low, suggesting that the overall capital market consequences of the decline are somewhat limited. Specifically, Panel

B in Table 2 indicates that among the top 10 shareholders，the mean percentage of QFII ownership was 0.005% pre-IFRS adoption，and 0.003% post-IFRS adoption. Nonetheless，the important implication of our finding is that IFRS adoption in China did not achieve the government's intended goal of increasing foreign institutional investment，and in fact resulted in a modest reduction in foreign investment.

Table 5　IFRS Adoption and Foreign Institutional Investment

Panel A：IFRS Adoption and QFII Investment for Total Sample

	D_QFII	N_QFII	P_QFII
POST	-0.7535 ***	-0.0808 ***	-0.0040 ***
	(-5.66)	(-7.36)	(-7.55)
SIZE	0.4525 ***	0.0545 ***	0.0018 ***
	(5.39)	(6.33)	(4.04)
LEV	-0.5226	-0.0564 **	-0.0019
	(-1.48)	(-2.03)	(-1.40)
TOP1	-0.6516 *	-0.0493	-0.0012
	(-1.77)	(-1.42)	(-0.70)
ROE	0.7022 **	0.0166	0.0007
	(1.98)	(1.52)	(0.89)
DIV	13.7498 ***	1.9882 ***	0.0811 ***
	(3.29)	(3.89)	(3.29)
STDRET	-2.6272 ***	-0.2231 ***	-0.0147 ***
	(-2.62)	(-2.87)	(-3.73)
BTM	-2.0655 ***	-0.2166 ***	-0.0100 ***
	(-7.82)	(-9.68)	(-8.88)
RETURN	0.0496	0.0036	0.0004
	(0.81)	(0.58)	(1.20)
XLIST	-0.4539 **	-0.0461 **	-0.0006
	(-2.32)	(-2.50)	(-0.58)

(continued)

	D_QFII	N_QFII	P_QFII
DOWJ	0.5085 ***	0.0181	0.0002
	(3.16)	(1.30)	(0.23)
XSALE	0.1152	0.0066	0.0003
	(0.89)	(0.62)	(0.55)
ANALYST	0.0143 **	0.0018 **	0.0001 **
	(2.40)	(2.37)	(2.22)
BIG4	0.3542 *	0.0666 **	0.0029 *
	(1.77)	(2.28)	(1.85)
Constant	−10.1080 ***	−0.8203 ***	−0.0225 **
	(−6.01)	(−4.84)	(−2.58)
Industry Indicators	yes	yes	yes
Pesudo/Adj-R^2	0.151	0.103	0.064

Panel B: IFRS Adoption and QFII Investment in Firms Where the Indicator Dependent Variable D_QFII = 1 in at Least One Year

	D_QFII	N_QFII	P_QFII
POST	−0.6699 ***	−0.1888 ***	−0.0100 ***
	(−4.11)	(−5.39)	(−5.88)
SIZE	0.0686	0.0398 *	0.0003
	(0.81)	(1.84)	(0.24)
LEV	0.1631	0.0269	0.0020
	(0.45)	(0.30)	(0.38)
TOP1	−0.6811 **	−0.1815 *	−0.0015
	(−2.05)	(−1.83)	(−0.25)
ROE	−0.1164	−0.0073	−0.0032
	(−0.28)	(−0.08)	(−0.49)
DIV	11.7385 **	3.4629 ***	0.1319 **
	(2.45)	(2.92)	(2.04)
STDRET	0.2090	0.0444	−0.0233 *
	(0.18)	(0.17)	(−1.72)

（continued）

	D_QFII	N_QFII	P_QFII
BTM	−1.7179 ***	−0.4108 ***	−0.0224 ***
	（−6.05）	（−6.32）	（−6.52）
RETURN	0.0171	−0.0118	0.0003
	（0.21）	（−0.60）	（0.23）
XLIST	0.0127	−0.0352	0.0041
	（0.07）	（−0.73）	（1.35）
DOWJ	0.1060	−0.0074	−0.0023
	（0.69）	（−0.20）	（−1.05）
XSALE	0.0627	0.0217	0.0004
	（0.49）	（0.68）	（0.21）
ANALYST	0.0006	−0.0004	0.0001
	（0.10）	（−0.28）	（0.70）
BIG4	0.2464	0.0648	0.0029
	（1.31）	（1.30）	（1.08）
Constant	−0.7772	−0.1361	0.0297
	（−0.47）	（−0.32）	（1.17）
Industry Indicators	yes	yes	yes
Pesudo/Adj-R^2	0.0486	0.052	0.055

Panel C: IFRS Adoption and QFII Investment after Restricting Analysis to 2006 （Pre-adoption Year） and 2007 （Post-Adoption Year）

	D_QFII	N_QFII	P_QFII
POST	−0.8534 ***	−0.1148 ***	−0.0053 ***
	（−4.62）	（−5.74）	（−5.60）
SIZE	0.3941 ***	0.0522 ***	0.0016 **
	（3.45）	（3.90）	（2.53）
LEV	−0.1366	−0.0212	−0.0003
	（−0.32）	（−0.56）	（−0.18）
TOP1	−0.7707	−0.0709	−0.0009
	（−1.61）	（−1.31）	（−0.34）

(continued)

	D_QFII	N_QFII	P_QFII
ROE	0.4992	0.0212	0.0004
	(1.39)	(1.25)	(0.48)
DIV	21.3428 ***	3.6509 ***	0.1810 ***
	(3.56)	(3.76)	(3.65)
STDRET	−3.3750 ***	−0.2225 **	−0.0168 ***
	(−2.61)	(−2.00)	(−2.77)
BTM	−2.3116 ***	−0.2729 ***	−0.0130 ***
	(−4.59)	(−5.19)	(−4.98)
RETURN	0.0687	0.0045	0.0006
	(0.96)	(0.58)	(1.23)
XLIST	−0.6705 ***	−0.0855 ***	−0.0027 **
	(−2.85)	(−3.47)	(−2.14)
DOWJ	0.3805 *	0.0074	−0.0008
	(1.96)	(0.36)	(−0.75)
XSALE	0.0804	−0.0025	−0.0003
	(0.54)	(−0.17)	(−0.45)
ANALYST	0.0226	0.0053 **	0.0003 ***
	(1.54)	(2.48)	(2.77)
BIG4	0.5613 **	0.0919 **	0.0039 *
	(2.32)	(2.16)	(1.82)
Constant	−8.8522 ***	−0.7499 ***	−0.0182
	(−4.06)	(−3.02)	(−1.50)
Industry Indicators	yes	yes	yes
Pesudo/Adj-R^2	0.148	0.112	0.076

Variable definitions are presented in Appendix B. This table reports regressions of D_QFII (existence of QFIIs), N_QFII (log of one plus the number of QFIIs) and P_QFII (investment scale of QFIIs) on all independent variables. We estimate the regression using a logistic specification in Column 1 and OLS in Columns 2 and 3. Z-statistics (reported in parentheses in Column 1) and t-statistics (reported in parentheses in Columns 2 and 3) are corrected for heteroskedasticity and based standard errors clustered by firm. For all variables, we use observation for a given firm over the entire sample period. $N = 5\,518$ for Panel A, $N = 1\,466$

for Panel B and $N = 2\,718$ for Panel C. *** $p < 0.01$，** $p < 0.05$，* $p < 0.10$.

6. Firm-Level Cross-Section Analyses

6.1 Management Incentives

We test Hypothesis 2a by estimating the following regression：

$$
\begin{aligned}
D\_QFII_{it}，N\_QFII_{it}，P\_QFII_{it} = {} & \beta_0 + \beta_1 POST_{it} + \beta_2 INCENTIVE_{it} + \\
& \beta_3 POST_{it} * INCENTIVE_{it} + \beta_4 SIZE_{it} + \\
& \beta_5 LEV_{it} + \beta_6 TOP1_{it} + \beta_7 ROE_{it} + \\
& \beta_8 DIV_{it} + \beta_9 STDRET_{it} + \beta_{10} BTM_{it} + \\
& \beta_{11} RETURN_{it} + \beta_{12} XLIST_{it} + \\
& \beta_{13} DOWJ_{it} + \beta_{14} XSALE_{it} + \\
& \beta_{15} ANALYST_{it} + \beta_{16} BIG4_{it} + \\
& \text{Industry Dummy} + \varepsilon_{it}. \quad\quad (2)
\end{aligned}
$$

To examine the effect of ownership concentration，INCENTIVE equals 1 if the largest shareholder owns more than 50% of a firm's total shares and 0 otherwise. To examine the effect of state ownership，INCENTIVE equals 1 if a firm is ultimately controlled by the government and 0 otherwise. Table 6 presents the results of this analysis. When we define INCENTIVE based on ownership concentration，all three of the coefficients on POST * INCENTIVE are negative and significant （-0.4883，Z-statistic $= -2.13$ for D_QFII；-0.0656，t-statistic $= -3.13$ for N_QFII；-0.0033，t-statistic $= -2.77$ for P_QFII）. When we define INCENTIVE based on state ownership，the coefficients on POST * INCENTIVE are negative and significant for N_QFII （-0.0280，t-statistics $= -2.31$） and P_QFII （-0.0015，t-statistics $= -2.36$）. Thus，Table 6 suggests that QFIIs are more likely to reduce their investment in Chinese firms that have low incentives to credibly implement IFRS. Importantly，Table 6 finds that the decline in QFII investment is related to IFRS adoption，as opposed to merely a time-trend in foreign investment during the period of our analysis.

Table 6   IFRS Adoption, Firm Incentives, and Foreign Institutional Investment

	Ownership Concentration			State Ownership		
	D_QFII	N_QFII	P_QFII	D_QFII	N_QFII	P_QFII
POST	−0.6367 ***	−0.0667 ***	−0.0033 ***	−0.5555 ***	−0.0563 ***	−0.0027 ***
	(−4.48)	(−5.85)	(−6.35)	(−3.00)	(−4.00)	(−3.72)
INCENTIVE	−0.0583	0.0087	0.0006	0.1431	0.0191 *	0.0007
	(−0.39)	(0.50)	(0.57)	(1.33)	(1.75)	(1.17)
POST * INCENTIVE	−0.4883 **	−0.0656 ***	−0.0033 ***	−0.2018	−0.0280 **	−0.0015 **
	(−2.13)	(−3.13)	(−2.77)	(−1.46)	(−2.31)	(−2.36)
SIZE	0.4580 ***	0.0556 ***	0.0019 ***	0.4515 ***	0.0546 ***	0.0018 ***
	(5.48)	(6.47)	(4.19)	(5.29)	(6.22)	(4.04)
LEV	−0.5423	−0.0577 **	−0.0021	−0.5084	−0.0539 *	−0.0018
	(−1.53)	(−2.08)	(−1.49)	(−1.43)	(−1.94)	(−1.34)
TOP1				−0.7007 *	−0.0557	−0.0013
				(−1.83)	(−1.52)	(−0.70)
ROE	0.7112 *	0.0162	0.0006	0.7053 **	0.0164	0.0006
	(1.95)	(1.47)	(0.87)	(1.97)	(1.49)	(0.82)
DIV	12.8335 ***	1.8916 ***	0.0779 ***	13.4228 ***	1.9475 ***	0.0782 ***
	(3.07)	(3.73)	(3.20)	(3.20)	(3.82)	(3.18)
STDRET	−2.6370 ***	−0.2216 ***	−0.0147 ***	−2.7353 ***	−0.2322 ***	−0.0151 ***
	(−2.65)	(−2.85)	(−3.71)	(−2.74)	(−3.01)	(−3.84)

(continued)

	Ownership Concentration			State Ownership		
	D_QFII	N_QFII	P_QFII	D_QFII	N_QFII	P_QFII
BTM	−2.0700 ***	−0.2190 ***	−0.0102 ***	−2.0541 ***	−0.2159 ***	−0.0099 ***
	(−7.81)	(−9.77)	(−8.92)	(−7.76)	(−9.66)	(−8.86)
RETURN	0.0504	0.0031	0.0004	0.0526	0.0037	0.0004
	(0.82)	(0.50)	(1.13)	(0.86)	(0.60)	(1.22)
XLIST	−0.4593 **	−0.0452 **	−0.0006	−0.4575 **	−0.0466 **	−0.0006
	(−2.34)	(−2.47)	(−0.57)	(−2.31)	(−2.53)	(−0.55)
DOWJ	0.5086 ***	0.0173	0.0001	0.5005 ***	0.0173	0.0001
	(3.17)	(1.25)	(0.07)	(3.09)	(1.24)	(0.19)
XSALE	0.1073	0.0059	0.0003	0.1143	0.0063	0.0003
	(0.83)	(0.56)	(0.50)	(0.88)	(0.59)	(0.53)
ANALYST	0.0154 ***	0.0020 **	0.0001 **	0.0147 **	0.0019 **	0.0001 **
	(2.60)	(2.56)	(2.42)	(2.46)	(2.43)	(2.27)
BIG4	0.3582 *	0.0656 **	0.0028 *	0.3529 *	0.0661 **	0.0029 *
	(1.79)	(2.25)	(1.83)	(1.75)	(2.26)	(1.84)
Constant	−10.4569 ***	−0.8601 ***	−0.0251 ***	−10.2034 ***	−0.8367 ***	−0.0242 ***
	(−6.20)	(−5.04)	(−2.80)	(−5.98)	(−4.84)	(−2.69)
Industry Indicators	yes	yes	yes	yes	yes	yes
Adjusted/Pseudo R^2	0.153	0.106	0.066	0.152	0.104	0.065

This table reports regressions of D_QFII (existence of QFIIs), N_QFII (log of one plus the number of QFIIs) and P_QFII (investment scale of QFIIs) on all independent variables. We estimate the regression using a logistic specification in Column 1 and OLS in Columns 2 and 3. Z-statistics (reported in parentheses in Column 1) and t-statistics (reported in parentheses in Columns 2 and 3) are corrected for heteroskedasticity and based on error terms clustered by firm. For all variables, we use observations for a given firm over the entire sample period. $N = 5\,518$. INCENTIVE $= 1$ if the largest shareholder owns more than 50% for the "ownership concentration" columns, or if the firm is ultimately controlled by the government for the "state ownership" columns, and 0 otherwise. The definitions of other variables are presented in Appendix B. *** $p < 0.01$, ** $p < 0.05$, * $p < 0.10$.

6.2　Firms Prone to Fair Value Manipulation

We test Hypothesis 2b by estimating the following regression:

$$
\begin{aligned}
\text{D\_QFII}_{it}, \text{N\_QFII}_{it}, \text{P\_QFII}_{it} = {} & \beta_0 + \beta_1 \text{POST}_{it} + \beta_2 \text{SMALL\_FA}_{it} + \\
& \beta_3 \text{POST}_{it} * \text{SMALL\_FA}_{it} + \\
& \beta_4 \text{LARGE\_FA}_{it} + \\
& \beta_5 \text{POST}_{it} * \text{LARGE\_FA}_{it} + \beta_6 \text{SIZE}_{it} + \\
& \beta_7 \text{LEV}_{it} + \beta_8 \text{TOP1}_{it} + \beta_9 \text{ROE}_{it} + \\
& \beta_{10} \text{DIV}_{it} + \beta_{11} \text{STDRET}_{it} + \beta_{12} \text{BTM}_{it} + \\
& \beta_{13} \text{RETURN}_{it} + \beta_{14} \text{XLIST}_{it} + \\
& \beta_{15} \text{DOWJ}_{it} + \beta_{16} \text{XSALE}_{it} + \\
& \beta_{17} \text{ANALYST}_{it} + \beta_{18} \text{BIG4}_{it} + \\
& \text{Industry Dummy} + \varepsilon_{it}.
\end{aligned}
\tag{3}
$$

We assume that firms with a high level of financial assets, which include trading securities and available-for-sale securities, have a greater ability to manipulate earnings through fair value accounting after IFRS adoption. Thus, we create two indicator variables to capture the size of financial assets: SMALL_FA equals 1 if the ratio of financial assets scaled by total assets is below the sample median of firms with non-zero financial assets and 0 otherwise; LARGE_FA equals 1 if the ratio of financial assets scaled by total assets is above the sample median of firms with non-zero financial assets and 0 otherwise. We interact SMALL_FA and LARGE_FA with POST and expect the coefficient on POST * LARGE_FA to be negative if our conjecture is correct.

Panel A in Table 7 shows that the coefficients on POST * SMALL_FA are always insignificant, and that the coefficients on POST * LARGE_FA are negative and significant for N_QFII (-0.0444, t-statistics $= -2.04$) and P_QFII (-0.0024, t-statistics $= -1.96$), indicating that QFIIs reduce their investment in firms with large financial assets both in terms of the number of firms and percentage ownership. Overall, these findings are consistent with our expectations.

We further explore this issue by examining whether the decline in investment is larger for firms that report gains from fair value adjustments. This analysis is motivated by the observation that the incentive to manage earnings upward is likely stronger than the incentive to manage downward. Thus, firms reporting fair value gains are more likely to be manipulating earnings than firms reporting fair value losses. If QFIIs understand this, we expect the decline in foreign institutional investment to be more pronounced in firms reporting gains under the fair value provisions of IFRS than firms reporting losses. We test this conjecture by estimating the following regression:

$$D\_QFII_{it}, N\_QFII_{it}, P\_QFII_{it} = \beta_0 + \beta_1 POST_{it} + \beta_2 FAIR\_LOSS_{it} +$$
$$\beta_3 POST_{it} * FAIR\_LOSS_{it} +$$
$$\beta_4 FAIR\_GAIN_{it} +$$
$$\beta_5 POST_{it} * FAIR\_GAIN_{it} +$$
$$\beta_6 SIZE_{it} + \beta_7 LEV_{it} + \beta_8 TOP1_{it} +$$
$$\beta_9 ROE_{it} + \beta_{10} DIV_{it} +$$
$$\beta_{11} STDRET_{it} + \beta_{12} BTM_{it} +$$
$$\beta_{13} RETURN_{it} + \beta_{14} XLIST_{it} +$$
$$\beta_{15} DOWJ_{it} + \beta_{16} XSALE_{it} +$$
$$\beta_{17} ANALYST_{it} + \beta_{18} BIG4_{it} +$$
$$Industry\ Dummy + \varepsilon_{it}. \qquad (4)$$

We define two indicator variables to capture expected fair value manipulation. FAIR_LOSS equals 1 if the fair value adjustment results in a loss in the income statement and 0 otherwise. FAIR_GAIN equals 1 if the fair value adjustment results in a gain in the income statement and 0 otherwise. We interact FAIR_LOSS and FAIR_GAIN with POST and expect the coefficient on POST * FAIR_GAIN to be negative.

Panel B in Table 7 shows that while the coefficients on POST * FAIR_LOSS are all insignificant, the coefficients on POST * FAIR_GAIN are negative and significant for N_QFII (-0.0471, t-statistics $= -1.78$) and P_QFII (-0.0019, t-statistics $= -1.73$). This further supports our conjecture that the decline in investment is more pronounced in firms with greater opportunities to manipulate earnings through fair value accounting. It also provides cross-sectional evidence that the decline in QFIIs' investment is not merely due to a time trend as fair value accounting is associated with IFRS adoption.

Table 7   IFRS Adoption and Fair Value Accounting

Panel A: IFRS Adoption, Financial Assets and QFII Investment

	D_QFII	N_QFII	P_QFII
POST	−0.6488 ***	−0.0708 ***	−0.0036 ***
	(−4.23)	(−5.69)	(−5.38)
SMA_FA	−0.1524	−0.0164	−0.0011
	(−0.89)	(−0.99)	(−1.42)
POST * SMALL_FA	−0.1455	0.0030	0.0009
	(−0.56)	(0.14)	(0.87)
LARGE_FA	−0.0437	0.0183	0.0013
	(−0.25)	(0.93)	(1.04)
POST * LARGE_FA	−0.3476	−0.0444 **	−0.0024 **
	(−1.41)	(−2.04)	(−1.96)
SIZE	0.4726 ***	0.0555 ***	0.0018 ***
	(5.58)	(6.46)	(4.03)
LEV	−0.5509	−0.0540 *	−0.0018
	(−1.53)	(−1.94)	(−1.25)
TOP1	−0.7069 *	−0.0521	−0.0013
	(−1.92)	(−1.51)	(−0.79)
ROE	0.6909 *	0.0172	0.0007
	(1.95)	(1.57)	(0.99)
DIV	13.7228 ***	1.9668 ***	0.0798 ***
	(3.27)	(3.86)	(3.25)
STDRET	−2.5706 **	−0.2253 ***	−0.0148 ***
	(−2.57)	(−2.91)	(−3.76)
BTM	−2.0439 ***	−0.2148 ***	−0.0099 ***
	(−7.76)	(−9.61)	(−8.84)

(continued)

	D_QFII	N_QFII	P_QFII
RETURN	0.0560	0.0039	0.0005
	(0.92)	(0.64)	(1.25)
XLIST	−0.4178 **	−0.0445 **	−0.0006
	(−2.10)	(−2.38)	(−0.54)
DOWJ	0.5178 ***	0.0186	0.0002
	(3.20)	(1.33)	(0.27)
XSALE	0.1369	0.0072	0.0003
	(1.05)	(0.68)	(0.58)
ANALYST	0.0135 **	0.0018 **	0.0001 **
	(2.27)	(2.27)	(2.16)
BIG4	0.3685 *	0.0674 **	0.0029 *
	(1.84)	(2.30)	(1.88)
Constant	−10.4812 ***	−0.8404 ***	−0.0230 ***
	(−6.19)	(−4.96)	(−2.60)
Industry Indicators	yes	yes	yes
Adjusted/Pseudo R^2	0.153	0.104	0.065

Panel B: IFRS Adoption, Fair Value Accounting and QFII Investment

	D_QFII	N_QFII	P_QFII
POST	−0.6567 ***	−0.0744 ***	−0.0040 ***
	(−4.69)	(−6.33)	(−6.22)
FAIR_LOSS	−0.0243	−0.0149	−0.0015 *
	(−0.13)	(−0.75)	(−1.74)
POST * FAIR_LOSS	−0.1504	0.0113	0.0013
	(−0.56)	(0.46)	(1.26)
FAIR_GAIN	−0.1989	−0.0036	−0.0001
	(−1.00)	(−0.16)	(−0.10)
POST * FAIR_GAIN	−0.4567	−0.0471 *	−0.0019 *
	(−1.55)	(−1.78)	(−1.73)

(continued)

	D_QFII	N_QFII	P_QFII
SIZE	0.4876 ***	0.0568 ***	0.0019 ***
	(5.73)	(6.59)	(4.31)
LEV	−0.5592	−0.0599 **	−0.0021
	(−1.56)	(−2.15)	(−1.50)
TOP1	−0.7524 **	−0.0557	−0.0016
	(−2.05)	(−1.61)	(−0.92)
ROE	0.7108 **	0.0168	0.0007
	(1.97)	(1.53)	(0.93)
DIV	13.5471 ***	1.9774 ***	0.0813 ***
	(3.19)	(3.87)	(3.30)
STDRET	−2.5950 ***	−0.2268 ***	−0.0149 ***
	(−2.58)	(−2.92)	(−3.78)
BTM	−2.0638 ***	−0.2161 ***	−0.0099 ***
	(−7.80)	(−9.69)	(−8.88)
RETURN	0.0620	0.0046	0.0005
	(1.01)	(0.75)	(1.36)
XLIST	−0.3844 **	−0.0418 **	−0.0004
	(−1.97)	(−2.27)	(−0.38)
DOWJ	0.4904 ***	0.0179	0.0001
	(3.05)	(1.28)	(0.20)
XSALE	0.1377	0.0083	0.0004
	(1.06)	(0.77)	(0.72)
ANALYST	0.0144 **	0.0017 **	0.0001 **
	(2.38)	(2.22)	(2.04)
BIG4	0.3665 *	0.0681 **	0.0030 *
	(1.82)	(2.32)	(1.89)
Constant	−10.7150 ***	−0.8572 ***	−0.0241 ***
	(−6.31)	(−5.07)	(−2.79)

(continued)

	D_QFII	N_QFII	P_QFII
Industry Indicators	yes	yes	yes
Pesudo/Adj-R^2	0.157	0.105	0.066

This table reports regressions of D_QFII (existence of QFIIs), N_QFII (log of one plus the number of QFIIs) and P_QFII (investment scale of QFIIs) on all independent variables. We estimate the regression using a logistic specification in Column 1 and OLS in Columns 2 and 3. Z-statistics (reported in parentheses in Column 1) and t-statistics (reported in parentheses in Columns 2 and 3) are corrected for heteroskedasticity and based on error terms clustered by firm. For all variables, we use observations for a given firm over the entire sample period. N = 5 518. In Panel A, SMALL_FA=1 if the firm's financial assets (trading securities and available-for-sale securities) scaled by total assets are among the bottom 50% percentile of sample firms whose average of financial assets at the end of year 2007 and 2008 are non-zero; LARGE_FA = 1 if the firms' financial assets (trading securities and available-for-sale securities) scaled by total assets are among the top 50% percentile of sample firms whose average of financial assets at the end of year 2007 and 2008 are non-zero. In Panel B, FAIR_GAIN= 1 if a firm has fair value gains in its income statement during 2007 or 2008; FAIR_LOSS= 1 if a firm has fair value losses in its income statement during 2007 or 2008. Other variable definitions are presented in Appendix B. *** $p<0.01$, ** $p<0.05$, * $p<0.10$.

6.3 Further Corroborative Analyses

6.3.1 Usefulness of Accounting Earnings

We test our conjecture that IFRS is likely to impair financial reporting quality in China by comparing the earnings-return association under IFRS versus CAS. This test exploits the fact that the initial 2007 financial reports under IFRS must include restated 2006 financials under IFRS. We estimate the following equation:

$$CAR_{it} = \beta_0 + \beta_1 X_{it}/P_{it} + \beta_2 (X_{it} - X_{it-1})/P_{it-1} + \beta_3 IFRS_{it} + \beta_4 IFRS_{it} * X_{it}/P_{it-1} + \beta_5 IFRS_{it} * (X_{it} - X_{it-1})/P_{it-1} +$$

$$\text{Industry Dummy} + e_{it}, \tag{5}$$

Where CAR is the fifteen-month (from the first month of the fiscal year to the third month after the end of the fiscal year) cumulative abnormal monthly return for year 2006 using the market model; X_{it} is earnings for 2006 under CAS or earnings for year 2006 restated under IFRS; X_{it-1} is earnings for 2005 computed under CAS; IFRS equals 1 for 2006 earnings restated under IFRS and 0 otherwise.[①] If IFRS impairs financial reporting quality, we expect the association between CAR_{it} and unexpected earnings $(X_{it}-X_{it-1})/P_{it-1}$ to be lower for IFRS restated earnings when compared to CAS earnings, consistent with a negative coefficient on $IFRS_{it} * (X_{it}-X_{it-1})/P_{it-1}(\beta_5 < 0)$.

Table 8 reports that while the coefficients on X_{it}/P_{it-1} and $(X_{it}-X_{it-1})/P_{it-1}$ are significantly positive, the coefficient on $IFRS_{it} * X_{it}/P_{it-1}$ is insignificant and the coefficient on $IFRS_{it} * (X_{it}-X_{it-1})/P_{it-1}$ is significantly negative (-0.1213, t-statistic $= -2.02$). This suggests that the association between stock returns and earnings is lower under IFRS than under CAS. A limitation of this analysis, however, is that IFRS restated earnings for 2006 are announced in 2007, while stock returns are measured in 2006. Thus, we also perform a test that compares the earnings-return association before and after IFRS adoption using earnings reported in the income statement (i.e., without regards to the restatement of IFRS earnings in 2006). This analysis is based on estimating the following equation:

$$CAR_{it} = \beta_0 + \beta_1 X_{it}/P_{it} + \beta_2(X_{it}-X_{it-1})/P_{it-1} + \beta_3 POST_{it} +$$
$$\beta_4 POST_{it} * X_{it}/P_{it-1} + \beta_5 POST_{it} * (X_{it}-X_{it-1})/P_{it-1} +$$
$$Industry\ Dummy + \varepsilon_{it}, \qquad\qquad (6)$$

Where all variables are as defined earlier, and POST equals 1 for years 2007 and 2008, and zero for years 2005 and 2006. If IFRS impairs financial reporting quality subsequent to its adoption in 2007, we expect the association between CAR_{it} and unexpected earnings $(X_{it}-X_{it-1})/P_{it-1}$ to be lower during the two years after IFRS adoption, consistent with a negative coefficient on $POST_{it} * (X_{it}-X_{it-1})/P_{it-1}(\beta_5 < 0)$.

Table 8 reports that while the coefficients on X_{it}/P_{it-1} and $(X_{it}-X_{it-1})/P_{it-1}$ are significantly positive, the coefficient on $POST_{it} * X_{it}/P_{it-1}$ is

---

① X_{it-1} is 2005CAS and $(X_{it}-X_{it-1})$ is [2006CAS—2005CAS]. IFRS $*$ X_{it} indicates 2006IFRS and IFRS $*$ $(X_{it}-X_{it-1})$ indicates [2006IFRS—2005CAS] where 2006IFRS is 2006CAS restated based on IFRS.

insignificant and the coefficient on $POST_{it} * (X_{it} - X_{it-1})/P_{it-1}$ is significantly negative (-1.6607, t-statistic $= -5.31$). This again suggests that the association between stock returns and earnings is lower under IFRS than under CAS.

In conclusion, results in Table 8 are consistent with deteriorating earnings quality after IFRS adoption, as reflected in a decline in the association between abnormal earnings and stock returns.

Table 8   IFRS Adoption and the Usefulness of Accounting Earnings

	CAR_{2006}	$CAR_{2005, 2006}$ versus $CAR_{2007, 2008}$
X_t/P_{t-1}	0.4696 ***	0.2084 *
	(2.76)	(1.71)
$(X_t - X_{t-1})/P_{t-1}$	0.4288 ***	0.5351 ***
	(4.31)	(5.28)
$IFRS_t$	-0.0321 ***	
	(-3.90)	
$IFRS_t * X_t/P_{t-1}$	-0.0092	
	(-0.07)	
$IFRS_t * (X_t - X_{t-1})/P_{t-1}$	-0.1213 **	
	(-2.02)	
$POST_t$		0.2354 ***
		(16.30)
$POST_t * X_t/P_{t-1}$		0.3605
		(1.57)
$POST_t * (X_t - X_{t-1})/P_{t-1}$		-1.6607 ***
		(-5.31)
Constant	-0.0620	-0.0188
	(-1.04)	(-0.73)
Industry indicators	yes	yes
Observations	2 445	5 098
Adjusted R-squared	0.140	0.107

We estimate the regression using OLS. t-statistics (reported in parentheses) are corrected for heteroskedasticity and are based on error terms clustered by firm. CAR is the cumulative abnormal return of firm i in year t over the 15 months extending from the first month of a fiscal year to 3 months after the fiscal-year end, calculated using residuals from a monthly market model $R_{jt} = b_{0t} + b_{1t}R_{mt} + e$, where R_{mt} is the value-weighted market return for month t. This model is estimated over the 36 months prior to the beginning of the fiscal year (Brown et al., 1987; Easton and Harris, 1991). X_t is the earnings per share, P_{t-1} is the beginning-of-period share price. In the first column, the dependent variable CAR is the fifteen-month cumulative abnormal monthly return for year 2006, IFRS$_t$ equals 1 for year 2006 earnings restated under IFRS and 0 otherwise. In the second column, CAR$_t$ is the annual fifteen-month cumulative abnormal monthly return of firm i in year t, and POST$_t$ equals 1 for years 2007 and 2008 and 0 for years 2005 and 2006. *** $p < 0.01$, ** $p < 0.05$, * $p < 0.10$.

6.3.2　Foreign Investors' Ability to Identify Profitable Investments

If IFRS provides more opportunities for earnings management (He, Wong and Young 2012), it will diminish the reliability of accounting information. Poor information quality will hamper the decision usefulness of financial reporting, causing investment efficiency to decline for QFIIs. This can be reflected in an increase in difficulty for QFIIs to identify profitable investments after IFRS adoption. We test this possibility by examining whether QFIIs' ability to identify profitable investments declines after IFRS adoption using the following model:

$$
\begin{aligned}
ADJRET_{it+1} = {} & \beta_0 + \beta_1 POST_{it} + \beta_2 D\_QFII_{it}(\text{or } N\_QFII_{it}, P\_QFII_{it}) + \\
& \beta_3 POST_{it} * D\_QFII_{it}(\text{or } N\_QFII_{it}, P\_QFII_{it}) + \\
& \beta_4 LEV_{it} + \beta_5 TOP1_{it} + \beta_6 ROE_{it} + \beta_7 DIV_{it} + \\
& \beta_8 STDRET_{it} + \beta_9 BTM_{it} + \beta_{10} RETURN_{it} + \\
& \beta_{11} XLIST_{it} + \beta_{12} DOWJ_{it} + \beta_{13} XSALE_{it} + \\
& \beta_{14} ANALYST_{it} + \beta_{15} BIG4_{it} + \\
& \text{Industry Dummy} + \varepsilon_{it}.
\end{aligned}
\tag{7}
$$

Our dependent variable is the one-year ahead market-adjusted stock return, an *ex post* measure of profitable investment. If it becomes more difficult for QFIIs to identify profitable investments after IFRS adoption, we expect the coefficients on POST * D_QFII, POST * N_QFII and POST * P_QFII to be negative. Table 9 reports that the coefficients on POST * D_QFII (−0.3201, t-statistics = −4.58), POST * N_QFII (−0.2926, t-statistics = −4.33) and *POST * P_QFII* (−4.0576, t-statistics = −3.07) are all significantly negative. Thus, as expected, China's IFRS adoption appears to compromise QFII's stock picking ability.

Table 9   IFRS Adoption and Foreign Institutional Investors' Ability to Identify Good Investments

	Dependent Variable: Firm's Future One Year Market-Adjusted Stock Return		
POST	0.1204 ***	0.1140 ***	0.0971 ***
	(3.42)	(3.24)	(2.79)
D_QFII	0.2235 ***		
	(3.31)		
D_QFII * POST	−0.3201 ***		
	(−4.58)		
N_QFII		0.1938 ***	
		(2.90)	
N_QFII * POST		−0.2926 ***	
		(−4.33)	
P_QFII			2.6156 **
			(2.00)
P_QFII * POST			−4.0576 ***
			(−3.07)
SIZE	−0.0209	−0.0198	−0.0165
	(−1.09)	(−1.04)	(−0.87)
LEV	0.2914 ***	0.2897 ***	0.2845 ***
	(3.83)	(3.81)	(3.74)
TOP1	−0.2023 **	−0.2029 **	−0.2063 ***
	(−2.54)	(−2.55)	(−2.59)

(continued)

	Dependent Variable：Firm's Future One Year Market-Adjusted Stock Return		
ROE	0.1998 ***	0.2000 ***	0.2006 ***
	(3.32)	(3.32)	(3.33)
DIV	0.8429	0.8410	1.1359
	(0.70)	(0.70)	(0.96)
STDRET	0.9779 ***	0.9688 ***	0.9811 ***
	(4.08)	(4.04)	(4.08)
BTM	0.3709 ***	0.3659 ***	0.3556 ***
	(6.36)	(6.28)	(6.13)
RETURN	−0.1548 ***	−0.1538 ***	−0.1542 ***
	(−9.93)	(−9.83)	(−9.84)
XLIST	−0.0480	−0.0478	−0.0527
	(−1.04)	(−1.04)	(−1.14)
DOWJ	−0.0049	−0.0046	−0.0044
	(−0.15)	(−0.14)	(−0.13)
XSALE	0.0107	0.0103	0.0099
	(0.40)	(0.39)	(0.37)
ANALYST	−0.0032 **	−0.0032 **	−0.0034 ***
	(−2.41)	(−2.44)	(−2.59)
BIG4	−0.1392 ***	−0.1399 ***	−0.1388 ***
	(−3.03)	(−3.04)	(−2.98)
Constant	0.1214	0.1103	0.0560
	(0.33)	(0.30)	(0.15)
Industry Indicators	yes	yes	yes
Adj-R^2	0.049	0.049	0.047

Variable definitions are presented in Appendix B. We estimate the regression using OLS. t-statistics (reported in parentheses) are corrected for heteroskedasticity and are based on error terms clustered by firm. For all variables we use observations for a given firm over the entire sample period. Ten observations are dropped due to missing data on future one year market-adjusted returns. $N=5508$. *** $p<0.01$, ** $p<0.05$, * $p<0.10$.

7. Effects of Foreign Investors' Home Country Institutions and IFRS Experience

To investigate whether foreign institutional investors' home country institutions affect the association between IFRS adoption and QFII investment, we partition our sample based on whether a QFII is from a country where the legal and financial reporting institutions are market-based or relationship-based, using: legal origins (code law versus common law); anti-director rights (based on the median level of anti-director rights from La Porta et al., 1997); government versus private standard setters (from Ali and Hwang, 2000), accounting clusters (from Mueller et al., 1994; Hung, 2001); and book-tax conformity (from Coopers and Lybrand, 1993; Hung, 2001). Appendix C reports the classifications for each QFII country. Information on QFIIs' home country IFRS adoption experience is from Armstrong et al. (2010) and Daske et al. (2008).

Panel A in Table 10 presents results incorporating QFIIs' home country institutions using D_QFII as our dependent variable in regression Equation (1). For brevity, we only report the coefficients on POST. After IFRS adoption, QFII investment significantly declines for QFIIs from both market-based and relationship-based countries. The coefficients on POST are negative and significant based on all five measures of market-based or relationship-based orientation. However, the decline is larger for QFIIs from relationship-based countries than for QFIIs from market-based countries in four of the five measures. The difference in the coefficients on POST between these two groups is 0.3229 (Chi-squared value = 3.84) based on legal origin; 0.3888 (Chi-squared value = 5.95) based on source of standards; 0.3978 (Chi-squared value = 6.30) based on accounting cluster; or 0.4047 (Chi-squared value = 6.56) based on financial tax alignment. This same pattern exists and tends to be statistically stronger when we use N_QFII (Panel B) or P_QFII (Panel C) as the dependent variable. Specifically, in Panels B and C the decline is larger in magnitude for QFIIs from relationship-based countries than for QFIIs from market-based countries for all five measures (at $p \leqslant 0.05$). Thus, results in Table 10 support our second hypothesis that the decline in QFII investment after IFRS adoption is stronger among QFIIs from countries with relationship-based institutions.

QFIIs' expectations regarding IFRS are also likely to be a function of whether their home countries have adopted IFRS. IFRS adoption is more likely to have positive consequences in countries with market-based institutions, but not in countries with relationship-based institutions. If QFIIs are from countries with primarily market-based institutions, they are more likely to view IFRS adoption favorably. In contrast, if the QFIIs are from countries with primarily relationship-based institutions, they are less likely to view IFRS adoption favorably. Thus, we expect the decline in investment to be relatively small for QFIIs from countries with market-based institutions that have adopted IFRS, as compared with QFIIs from countries with relationship-based institutions that have adopted IFRS.

Table 11 incorporates a partitioning variable that captures whether a QFII's home country has adopted IFRS. Again, we only report coefficients on POST. Panel A uses D_QFII as the dependent variable and finds that among QFIIs with market-based home countries, QFII investment declines less after IFRS adoption for those with IFRS experience than for those without IFRS experience.[①] The difference in the coefficients on POST is significantly positive (0.9608, Chi-squared value = 17.83 based on legal origin; 0.7401, Chi-squared value = 10.51 based on anti-director rights; 0.7074, Chi-squared value = 12.50 based on the source of standards; 0.7223, Chi-squared value = 13.25 based on accounting cluster; and 0.7387, Chi-squared value = 14.04 based on book-tax alignment). This suggests that home country IFRS experience attenuates the decline in investment for QFIIs from market-based countries. However, Panel A in Table 11 also shows that, among QFIIs with relationship-based home

---

①　We note that the coefficients are identical across some partitions. For example, the coefficients on legal origin and anti-director rights for countries without IFRS experience are identical in Panel A. This is because the legal origin partition and the anti-director rights partition for countries without IFRS experience capture the identical set of countries.

countries, there is no significant difference in the decline in QFII investment for QFIIs with and without IFRS experience.

In Panel B, we use the number of QFIIs, N_QFII, as the dependent variable. For QFIIs from market-based countries, we find results similar to those in Panel A. For QFIIs from relationship-based countries, we find that QFIIs investment declines more after IFRS adoption for those from countries with IFRS experience than for those from countries without IFRS experience. The difference in the coefficients on POST between QFIIs from countries with and without IFRS experience is significantly negative (-0.0022, F-value $=$ 8.18 based on legal origin; -0.0017, F-value $=$ 5.86 based on anti-director rights; -0.0028, F-value $=$ 11.26 based on source of standards; -0.0026, F-value $=$ 8.77 based on accounting cluster; and -0.0024, F-value $=$ 7.30 based on book-tax alignment). This suggests that home country IFRS experience exacerbates the decline in investment for QFIIs from relationship-based countries.

Panel C uses the percentage ownership as the dependent variable, P_QFII, with qualitatively similar results to those in Panel B. Therefore, results in Table 11 support our conjecture that the decline in foreign institutional investment is smaller for QFIIs from countries with market-based institutions that have adopted IFRS; and greater for QFIIs from countries with relationship-based institutions that have adopted IFRS.

Table 10 IFRS Adoption and Foreign Institutional Investors' Home Country Institutions

Panel A: IFRS Adoption and QFII Indicator (D_QFII) Partitioned on QFIIs' Home Country Institutions

Specific Institution of QFII's Home Country	Market-Based Institutions		Relationship-Based Institutions		Diff. in coeffs. on POST
	POST	Pseudo R^2	POST	Pseudo R^2	
Legal Origin	-0.5874 ***	0.144	-0.9103 ***	0.144	0.3229
	(-3.57)		(-5.85)		(3.84) **
Anti-director Rights	-0.6769 ***	0.142	-0.7901 ***	0.144	0.1132
	(-4.08)		(-5.12)		(0.47)

(continued)

Specific Institution of QFII's Home Country	Market-Based Institutions		Relationship-Based Institutions		Diff. in coeffs. on POST
	POST	Pseudo R^2	POST	Pseudo R^2	
Source of Standards	−0.5929 ***	0.150	−0.9817 ***	0.137	0.3888
	(−3.72)		(−5.94)		(5.95) **
Accounting Cluster	−0.5892 ***	0.150	−0.9870 ***	0.137	0.3978
	(−3.72)		(−5.93)		(6.30) **
Book-Tax Alignment	−0.5862 ***	0.151	−0.9909 ***	0.136	0.4047
	(−3.71)		(−5.94)		(6.56) **

Panel B: IFRS Adoption and Number of QFIIs (N_QFII) Partitioned on QFIIs' Home Country Institutions

Specific Institution of QFII's Home Country	Market-Based Institutions		Relationship-Based Institutions		Diff. in coeffs. on POST
	POST	Adj-R^2	POST	Adj-R^2	
Legal Origin	−0.0029 ***	0.074	−0.0050 ***	0.080	0.0021
	(−6.83)		(−7.89)		(26.96) ***
Anti-director Rights	−0.0031 ***	0.073	−0.0046 ***	0.082	0.0015
	(−6.99)		(−7.93)		(10.88) ***
Source of Standards	−0.0028 ***	0.070	−0.0055 ***	0.085	0.0027
	(−6.96)		(−7.98)		(42.50) ***
Accounting Cluster	−0.0029 ***	0.071	−0.0053 ***	0.083	0.0024
	(−7.13)		(−7.61)		(35.34) ***
Book-Tax Alignment	−0.0029 ***	0.071	−0.0052 ***	0.082	0.0023
	(−7.19)		(−7.37)		(31.79) ***

Panel C: IFRS Adoption and Percentage Ownership of QFII (P_QFII) Partitioned on QFIIs' Home Country Institutions

Specific Institution of QFII's Home Country	Market-Based Institutions		Relationship-Based Institutions		Diff. in coeffs. on POST
	POST	Adj-R^2	POST	Adj-R^2	
Legal Origin	−0.0013 ***	0.039	−0.0027 ***	0.055	0.0014
	(−4.35)		(−7.12)		(19.66) ***

(continued)

Specific Institution of QFII's Home Country	Market-Based Institutions		Relationship-Based Institutions		Diff. in coeffs. on POST
	POST	Adj-R^2	POST	Adj-R^2	
Anti-director Rights	−0.0013 ***	0.037	−0.0027 ***	0.056	0.0014
	(−4.52)		(−6.99)		(20.75) ***
Source of Standards	−0.0016 ***	0.038	−0.0024 ***	0.057	0.0008
	(−4.81)		(−6.84)		(4.99) **
Accounting Cluster	−0.0016 ***	0.038	−0.0024 ***	0.056	0.0008
	(−4.79)		(−6.86)		(5.11) **
Book-Tax Alignment	−0.0016 ***	0.037	−0.0024 ***	0.057	0.0008
	(−4.78)		(−6.88)		(5.23) **

Variable definitions are presented in Appendix B. This table reports regressions of the QFII indicator variable (D_QFII), log of one plus the number of QFIIs (N_QFII), and percentage investment of QFIIs (P_QFII) after partitioning on QFIIs' country level institutions. We estimate the regression using a logistic specification in Panel A and OLS in Panels B and C. Z-statistics (reported in parentheses in Panel A except for the last volume) and t-statistics (reported in parentheses in Panels B and C except for the last column) are corrected for heteroskedasticity and are based on error terms clustered by firm. For all variables we use observations for a given firm over the entire sample period. For the last column, Chi-squared values are reported in parentheses of Panel A and F-values are reported in parentheses of Panels B and C. $N = 5518$. *** $p<0.01$, ** $p<0.05$, * $p<0.10$.

Table 11 IFRS Adoption and Foreign Institutional Investors' Home Country Experience with IFRS

Panel A: IFRS Adoption and QFII Indicator (D_QFII) Partitioned on QFIIs' Home Country Institutions and IFRS Experience

Specific Institution of QFII's Home Country	Market-Based Institutions			Relationship-Based Institutions		
	IFRS Experience	No-IFRS Experience	Diff. in Coeffs. on POST	IFRS Experience	No-IFRS Experience	Diff. in Coeffs. on POST
Legal Origin	0.0528	−0.9080 ***	0.9608	−0.9273 ***	−1.0411 **	0.1138
	(0.23)	(−4.62)	(17.83) ***	(−5.70)	(−2.42)	(0.49)
Anti-director Rights	−0.1679	−0.9080 ***	0.7401	−0.7873 ***	−1.0411 **	0.2538
	(−0.74)	(−4.62)	(10.51) ***	(−4.86)	(−2.42)	(2.46)
Source of Standards	−0.2006	−0.9080 ***	0.7074	−0.9945 ***	−1.0411 **	0.0466
	(−1.00)	(−4.62)	(12.50) ***	(−5.67)	(−2.42)	(0.07)
Accounting Cluster	−0.1857	−0.9080 ***	0.7223	−1.0007 ***	−1.0411 **	0.0404
	(−0.94)	(−4.62)	(13.25) ***	(−5.67)	(−2.42)	(0.05)
Book-Tax Alignment	−0.1693	−0.9080 ***	0.7387	−1.0049 ***	−1.0411 **	0.0362
	(−0.86)	(−4.62)	(14.04) ***	(−5.67)	(−2.42)	(0.04)

Panel B: IFRS Adoption and Number of QFIIs (N_QFII) Partitioned on QFIIs' Home Country Institutions and IFRS Experience

Specific Institution of QFII's Home Country	Market-Based Institutions			Relationship-Based Institutions		
	IFRS Experience	No-IFRS Experience	Diff. in Coeffs. on POST	IFRS Experience	No-IFRS Experience	Diff. in Coeffs. on POST
Legal Origin	−0.0016 ***	−0.0039 ***	0.0023	−0.0055 ***	−0.0033 ***	−0.0022
	(−2.86)	(−6.91)	(15.93) ***	(−7.34)	(−2.90)	(8.18) ***
Anti-director Rights	−0.0022 ***	−0.0039 ***	0.0017	−0.0050 ***	−0.0033 ***	−0.0017
	(−3.17)	(−6.91)	(6.13) **	(−7.46)	(−2.90)	(5.86) **
Source of Standards	−0.0021 ***	−0.0039 ***	0.0018	−0.0061 ***	−0.0033 ***	−0.0028
	(−3.69)	(−6.91)	(10.02) ***	(−7.38)	(−2.90)	(11.26) ***
Accounting Cluster	−0.0023 ***	−0.0039 ***	0.0016	−0.0059 ***	−0.0033 ***	−0.0026
	(−4.05)	(−6.91)	(8.45) ***	(−6.92)	(−2.90)	(8.77) ***
Book-Tax Alignment	−0.0023 ***	−0.0039 ***	0.0016	−0.0057 ***	−0.0033 ***	−0.0024
	(−4.17)	(−6.91)	(8.03) ***	(−6.60)	(−2.90)	(7.30) ***

Panel C: IFRS Adoption and Percentage Ownership of QFII (P_QFII) Partitioned on QFIIs' Home Country Institutions and IFRS Experience

Specific Institution of QFII's Home Country	Market-Based Institutions			Relationship-Based Institutions		
	IFRS Experience	No-IFRS Experience	Diff. in Coeffs. on POST	IFRS Experience	No-IFRS Experience	Diff. in Coeffs. on POST
Legal Origin	-0.0001	-0.0012 ***	0.0011	-0.0022 ***	-0.0004 ***	-0.0018
	(-0.74)	(-4.98)	(53.17) ***	(-6.53)	(-2.99)	(27.59) ***
Anti-director Rights	-0.0001	-0.0012 ***	0.0011	-0.0022 ***	-0.0004 ***	-0.0018
	(-0.86)	(-4.98)	(65.05) ***	(-6.39)	(-2.99)	(26.38) ***
Source of Standards	-0.0004 **	-0.0012 ***	0.0008	-0.0019 ***	-0.0004 ***	-0.0015
	(-2.14)	(-4.98)	(17.37) ***	(-6.13)	(-2.99)	(22.52) ***
Accounting Cluster	-0.0004 **	-0.0012 ***	0.0008	-0.0019 ***	-0.0004 ***	-0.0015
	(-2.11)	(-4.98)	(17.53) ***	(-6.15)	(-2.99)	(22.75) ***
Book-Tax Alignment	-0.0004 **	-0.0012 ***	0.0008	-0.0019 ***	-0.0004 ***	-0.0015
	(-2.08)	(-4.98)	(17.72) ***	(-6.17)	(-2.99)	(22.89) ***

Variable definitions are presented in Appendix B. This table reports regressions of the QFII indicator variable (D_QFII), log of one plus the number of QFIIs (N_QFII), and percentage investment of QFIIs (P_QFII) after partitioning on QFIIs' country level institutions and IFRS experience. We estimate the regression using a logistic specification in Panel A and OLS in Panels B and C. Z-statistics (reported in parentheses in Panel A except for the last column) and t-statistics (reported in parentheses in Panels B and C except for the last volume) are corrected for heteroskedasticity and are based on error terms clustered by firm. For all variables, we use observation for a given firm over the entire sample period. For the column "Diff. in Coeffs. on POST", Chi-squared values are reported in parentheses in Panel A and F-values are reported in parentheses of Panel B and Panel C. N = 5 518. *** $p<0.01$, ** $p<0.05$, * $p<0.10$. We note that in some columns, the coefficients are identical across different partitions. This is because the partitioned countries are identical across some of the partitioning variables.

8. Robustness Tests

8.1 Investigating Whether QFIIs Spread Their Investments More Thinly after IFRS Adoption

Our data on QFII investors is necessarily restricted to those among the top 10 shareholders of tradable shares, since this is the only information available on QFII ownership.[①] If IFRS actually improves reporting quality in China, QFIIs may spread their investment across more firms, with relatively less invested in each firm. If so, they may end up not being the top 10 shareholders for a specific stock even though they have actually maintained or increased their overall investment in Chinese firms. We emphasize, however, that this seems unlikely given that our analysis in Tables 8 and 9 shows that accounting quality appears to decline after IFRS adoption. Specifically, we find that: ① the association between earnings and returns is larger under CAS than under IFRS; ② the association between earnings and returns declines after IFRS adoption; and ③ QFII's investment returns decline following IFRS adoption. These findings are consistent with He et al. (2012), who also find that accounting quality declines after China's IFRS adoption.

Nevertheless, we conduct two additional analyses to determine whether restricting the data on QFIIs to those among the top 10 largest shareholders is likely to bias our results. Our first test is based on the notion that if this restriction results in a bias, the bias will likely become larger as the restriction becomes narrower. For example, if a bias exists, we would expect it to be greater if our data are restricted to QFII investors among the top 5 shareholders. Thus, we repeat our tests in Panel A, Table 5 after limiting ownership data to the top 9, top 8, top 7, top 6 and top 5 shareholders. We continue to find negatively significant coefficients on POST ($p < 0.01$) with all successive restrictions. More importantly, we find no evidence that the

---

① Similar reporting threshold issues exist in the US setting. SEC 13Γ filing is required only for institutional investors with total investment discretion above USD 100 million and for specific investment above USD 200 000.

magnitude of the negative coefficient on POST declines as we move from restricting the analysis to the top 5, top 6, 7, 8, 9 and 10 shareholders, which would be the case if the bias is larger when QFII data is restricted to be fewer than the top 10 shareholders. In fact, when our dependent variables are N_QFII and P_QFII, the negative coefficient on POST is significantly larger in magnitude when QFIIs are restricted to the top 8, 9, and 10, when compared to the top 5 shareholders. Thus, the results of this analysis are not consistent with a bias resulting from restricting the QFIIs to those among the top 10 shareholders.

Our second analysis repeats our tests in Panel A, Table 5 using P_QFII as the dependent variable, after limiting the sample to firms with the same QFIIs among the top 10 shareholders both before and after adoption. By limiting the analysis to firms where a QFII is a top 10 shareholder both before and after IFRS adoption, we are certain that the QFII's investment in those firms did not decline due to the QFII ceasing to be among the top 10 shareholders. We find that the coefficient on POST remains significantly negative ($p < 0.01$). Thus, the results of this analysis are not consistent with a bias resulting from restricting our analysis to QFIIs among the top 10 shareholders.

8.2　Dropping US QFIIs

As the US has the largest number of QFIIs, we repeat our tests in Panel A, Table 5 after dropping US QFIIs. The coefficients on POST remain significantly negative ($p < 0.01$), suggesting that our results are not driven by US QFIIs.[①]

8.3　Effects of IPOs and SEOs

Since new equity issues may affect our results for the percentage of QFII ownership (P_QFII), we repeat our tests in Panel A, Table 5 after dropping the 463 observations with IPOs or SEOs in 2007 or 2008. The coefficients on

---

① Results here and in subsequent analyses are not tabulated for brevity.

POST remain significantly negative ($p < 0.01$), suggesting that our results are not driven by of SEOs or IPOs.

8.4 Alternative Distribution Density Functions Underlying the Regression Model

We repeat our tests in Panel A, Table 5 using the raw number of QFIIs instead of the logarithm of one plus the number of QFIIs as a measure of our dependent variable N_QFII. The raw number of QFIIs range from 0 to 7. Using a Tobit or a Poisson regression model, we find that the coefficients on POST remain significantly negative ($p < 0.01$).

8.5 Other Data Issues

The number of approved QFIIs increased during our sample period, with 22 QFIIs newly granted quotas in 2007 or 2008. When we repeat our tests in Panel A, Table 5 after excluding these newly approved QFIIs, the coefficients on POST remains significantly negative ($p < 0.01$) for all three measures of the dependent variable. Also, our tests are performed using annual data. When we use quarterly data, we obtain qualitatively similar results.

9. Conclusion

We examine the effect of China's mandatory IFRS adoption on foreign institutional investment in China's domestic stock market. We hypothesize that due to China's institutional setting, foreign investment is unlikely to increase after IFRS adoption. We also hypothesize that the association between IFRS adoption and foreign institutional investment should vary with investors' home country institutions and IFRS adoption experience.

Our analysis supports our predictions by finding: ① foreign institutional investment declines after China's IFRS adoption; ② the decline is more pronounced for firms with weak incentives to credibly implement IFRS, and for firms with greater opportunities to manipulate earnings through the fair value provisions of IFRS; ③ the association between earnings and returns declines for QFIIs after IFRS adoption; ④ IFRS adoption compromises QFIIs' ability to identify profitable investments; ⑤ the decline in investment after IFRS adoption is more pronounced for QFIIs from countries with relationship-based institutions than for QFIIs from countries with market-based institutions; and ⑥ home country IFRS experience attenuates the decline in investment from QFIIs from market-based countries while it exacerbates the decline in investment from QFIIs from relationship-based countries.

Although we likely cannot fully rule out the 2008 financial crisis effect or some other confounding effects on QFII investment, we conclude that mandatory IFRS adoption does not help China achieve its goal of attracting more foreign investments. Further, the effect of IFRS adoption on foreign institutional investment is a function of investors', and therefore financial information users', home country institutions and IFRS adoption experience.

Appendix A
QFIIs' Profiles

QFII Name	Home Country	Qualification Date	Total Quota (100 million USD)	Date of Initial Quota	Initial Quota (100 million USD)
AMP Capital Investors Ltd.	Australia	2006.04.10	3.00	2006.08.01	2.00
Platinum Investment Company Ltd.	Australia	2008.06.02	1.50	2008.09.10	1.50
First State Investment Management (UK) Ltd.	Australia	2008.09.11	0.00	2009.06.16	1.20
Fortis Bank SA/NV	Belgium	2004.09.29	5.00	2004.11.21	1.00
KBC Asset Management NV	Belgium	2008.06.02	1.50	2008.07.31	1.50
KBC Financial Products UK Ltd.	Belgium	2006.04.10	1.00	2006.06.09	1.00
Caisse de Depot et Placement du Quebec	Canada	2008.08.22	2.00	2008.11.03	2.00
Power Corporation of Canada	Canada	2004.10.15	0.50	2004.11.21	0.50
The Bank of Nova Scotia	Canada	2006.04.10	1.50	2006.06.09	1.50
BNP Paribas	France	2004.09.29	2.00	2004.10.27	0.75
Calyon S. A.	France	2004.10.15	0.75	2005.01.10	0.75
La CompagnieFinancierr Edmond de Rothschild Banque	France	2006.04.10	1.00	2006.07.19	1.00
SocieteGenerale	France	2004.09.02	0.50	2004.09.17	0.50
Allianz Global Investors Luxembourg SA	Germany	2008.12.16	0.00	2009.03.04	1.00
Deutsche Bank Aktiengesellschaft	Germany	2003.07.30	4.00	2003.08.26	0.50

(continued)

QFII Name	Home Country	Qualification Date	Total Quota (100 million USD)	Date of Initial Quota	Initial Quota (100 million USD)
Dresdner Bank Aktiengesellschaft	Germany	2004.09.27	0.75	2004.11.08	0.75
Hang Seng Bank Ltd.	China *	2004.05.10	1.00	2004.06.22	0.50
HSBC Global Asset Management (Hong Kong) Ltd.	China *	2006.09.05	2.00	2007.02.13	2.00
JF Asset Management Ltd.	China *	2005.12.28	1.50	2006.04.12	1.50
The Hong Kong and Shanghai Banking Corporation Ltd.	China *	2003.08.04	4.00	2003.08.26	0.50
DAIWA Asset Management Co.	Japan	2008.09.11	1.00	2008.12.26	1.00
Daiwa Securities SMBC Co., Ltd.	Japan	2004.05.10	0.50	2004.07.05	0.50
Mitsubishi UFJ Securities Co., Ltd.	Japan	2008.12.29	0.00	2009.03.25	1.00
Mizuho Securities Co., Ltd	Japan	2006.09.05	0.50	2007.02.13	0.50
Nikko Asset Management Co., Ltd.	Japan	2003.12.11	4.50	2004.02.09	0.50
Nomura Securities Co., Ltd.	Japan	2003.05.23	3.50	2003.06.04	0.50
Sumitomo Mitsui Asset Management Company, Ltd.	Japan	2006.09.25	3.00	2007.02.13	2.00
The Dai-ichi Mutual Life Insurance Company	Japan	2005.12.28	2.00	2006.02.22	1.00

* 此处指香港特别行政区。

(continued)

QFII Name	Home Country	Qualification Date	Total Quota (100 million USD)	Date of Initial Quota	Initial Quota (100 million USD)
ABN AMRO Bank NV	Netherland	2004.09.02	1.75	2004.09.17	0.75
ING Bank NV	Netherland	2003.09.10	4.00	2003.10.16	1.00
Robeco Institutional Asset management BV	Netherland	2008.05.05	1.50	2008.06.20	1.50
Shell Asset Management Company BV	Netherland	2008.09.12	0.00	2009.12.08	1.00
Norges Bank	Norway	2006.10.24	5.00	2008.01.24	2.00
DBS Bank Ltd.	Singapore	2006.02.13	1.00	2006.04.12	1.00
Government of Singapore Investment Corporation Pte Ltd.	Singapore	2005.10.25	3.00	2005.11.16	1.00
Oversea-Chinese Banking Corporation Ltd.	Singapore	2008.08.28	1.50	2008.11.12	1.50
Temasek Fullerton Alpha Investments Pte Ltd.	Singapore	2005.11.15	1.00	2005.12.12	1.00
United Overseas Bank Ltd.	Singapore	2006.08.05	0.50	2006.11.07	0.50
UOB Asset Management Ltd.	Singapore	2008.11.28	0.00	2009.08.25	0.50
Mirae Asset Global Investments Co., Ltd.	South Korea	2008.07.25	1.50	2008.09.02	1.50
Samsung Investment Trust Management Co., Ltd.	South Korea	2008.08.25	1.50	2008.11.07	1.50
ACE INA International Holdings, Ltd.	Switzerland	2008.08.05	1.50	2008.11.13	1.50

(continued)

QFII Name	Home Country	Qualification Date	Total Quota (100 million USD)	Date of Initial Quota	Initial Quota (100 million USD)
Credit Suisse (Hong Kong) Ltd.	Switzerland	2003.10.24	5.00	2003.11.28	0.50
Pictet Asset Management Ltd.	Switzerland	2006.10.25	1.00	2008.04.01	1.00
UBS Global Asset Management (Singapore) Ltd.	Switzerland	2006.09.25	2.00	2007.01.11	2.00
Credit Suisse	Switzerland	2008.10.14	0.00	2009.05.22	2.00
UBS AG	Switzerland	2003.05.23	8.00	2003.06.04	3.00
ABU Dhabi Investment Authority	UAE	2008.12.03	0.00	2009.01.17	2.00
Barclays Bank PLC	UK	2004.09.15	2.00	2004.10.15	0.75
Martin Currie Investment Management Ltd.	UK	2005.10.25	1.20	2005.11.24	1.20
Prudential Asset Management Co., Ltd.	UK	2008.04.07	0.75	2008.05.04	0.75
Prudential Asset Management (Hong Kong) Ltd.	UK	2006.07.07	3.00	2006.10.12	2.00
Schroder Investment Management Ltd.	UK	2006.08.29	2.00	2006.12.11	2.00
Standard Chartered Bank (Hong Kong) Ltd.	UK	2003.12.11	0.75	2004.05.19	0.75

(continued)

QFII Name	Home Country	Qualification Date	Total Quota (100 million USD)	Date of Initial Quota	Initial Quota (100 million USD)
Alliance Bernstein Ltd.	US	2008.08.28	0.50	2008.11.12	0.50
INVESCO Asset Management Ltd.	US	2004.08.04	2.50	2005.03.08	0.50
Lehman Brothers International (Europe)	US	2004.07.06	2.00	2004.08.16	0.75
Merrill Lynch International	US	2004.04.30	3.00	2004.07.16	0.75
State Street Global Advisors Asia Ltd.	US	2008.05.16	0.50	2008.11.03	0.50
Citigroup Global Markets Ltd.	US	2003.06.05	5.50	2003.06.18	0.75
Goldman Sachs Asset Management International	US	2005.05.09	2.00	2005.11.16	2.00
Morgan Stanley & Co. International Ltd.	US	2003.06.05	4.00	2003.07.01	3.00
AIG Global Investment Corp.	US	2005.11.14	0.50	2005.12.12	0.50
Bill & Melinda Gates Foundation	US	2004.07.19	1.00	2004.08.28	1.00
Capital International, Inc.	US	2008.12.18	0.00	2009.03.31	1.00
GE Asset Management Incorporated	US	2006.08.05	1.88	2007.01.11	2.00
Goldman, Sachs & Co.	US	2003.07.04	3.00	2003.07.24	0.50
JPMorgan Chase Bank, National Association	US	2003.09.30	1.50	2003.11.04	0.50
Morgan Stanley Investment Management Inc.	US	2006.07.07	2.00	2006.09.05	2.00
President and Fellows of Harvard College	US	2008.08.22	2.00	2008.11.14	2.00
Stanford University	US	2006.08.05	1.00	2006.11.07	0.50
T. Rowe Price International, Inc.	US	2008.09.12	1.10	2008.12.03	1.10
The Trustees of Columbia University in New York	US	2008.03.12	1.00	2008.04.07	1.00
Yale University	US	2006.04.14	1.50	2006.08.01	0.50

Appendix B

Variable Definitions

Variable	Definition
Dependent Variables	
D_QFII	Indicator variable equals to 1 if a firm has at least one QFII in the top 10 shareholders of tradable A-shares at the end of each year, and 0 otherwise
N_QFII	Log of one plus the number of QFIIs among the top 10 shareholders who own tradable A-shares at the end of each year
P_QFII	The percentage of a firm's A-shares held by the QFIIs among the top 10 shareholders who own tradable shares, divided by the firm's total tradable A-shares at the end of each year
Experimental Variables	
POST	Indicator, 1 for years 2007 and 2008 (post-adoption), and 0 for years 2005 and 2006 (pre-adoption)
Control Variables	
SIZE	Firm size, computed as the natural logarithm of year-end total assets
LEV	Financial leverage, computed as the ratio between year-end total liabilities and total assets
TOP1	Year-end percentage shareholdings of the largest shareholder
ROE	Return on equity computed as net income scaled by year-end shareholders' equity
DIV	Dividend yields, computed as dividend per share scaled by stock price at the end of each year
STDRET	Standard deviation of a firm's monthly stock returns for each year
BTM	The ratio between a firm's book value and market value of total assets
RETURN	Market-adjusted annual stock return of a firm for each year
XLIST	Indicator variable equals to 1 if a firm issues B-shares or H-shares, and 0 otherwise

(continued)

Variable	Definition
DOWJ	Indicator variable equals to 1 if a firm is included in the Dow-Jones 600 index and 0 otherwise
XSALE	Indicator variable equals to 1 if a firm discloses sales from foreign subsidiaries and 0 otherwise
ANALYST	The number of analysts following a firm
BIG4	Indicator variable equals to 1 if a firm is audited by a BIG 4 auditor and 0 otherwise

Appendix C

Institutions of QFIIs' Home Countries

Institutions by QFIIs' home countries

	Legal System		Accounting System			IFRS Adoption
	Legal Origin	Anti-director Rights	Source of Standards	Accounting Cluster	Financial Tax Alignment	
Australia	1	4	Government-only	British-American	0	1
Belgium	0	0	Government-only	Continental	1	1
Canada	1	4	Government & Private	British-American	0	0
France	0	2	Government-only	Continental	1	1
Germany	0	1	Government-only	Continental	1	1
Hong Kong	1	4	Government & Private	British-American	0	1
Japan	0	3	Government-only	Continental	1	0
Netherlands	0	2	Government & Private	British-American	0	1
Norway	0	3	Government-only	Continental	0	1
Singapore	1	3	Government & Private	British-American	0	1
Switzerland	0	1	Government-only	Continental	1	1
UK	1	4	Government & Private	British-American	0	1
US	1	5	Government & Private	British-American	0	0

(continued)

	Legal System		Accounting System			IFRS Adoption
	Legal Origin	Anti-director Rights	Source of Standards	Accounting Cluster	Financial Tax Alignment	

Classification of Institutions of QFIIs' Home Countries

	Legal Origin	Anti-director Rights	Source of Standards	Accounting Cluster	Financial Tax Alignment	IFRS Adoption
Market-Based	1	>3	Government & Private	British-American	0	NA
Relationship-Based	0	≤3	Government-Only	Continental	1	NA

Legal origin: 1 for common law countries and 0 for code law countries (La Porta et al., 1997).

Anti-director rights: an index aggregating the shareholder rights, where the index ranges from 0 to 5 (La Porta et al., 1997).

Source of standards: accounting standards set by governmental bodies only or in conjunction with private-sector bodies (Alford et al., 1993).

Accounting cluster: cluster classification according to the country's accounting practices (Mueller et al., 1994; Hung, 2001).

Tax-book conformity: equals 1 for countries with high tax-book conformity, and 0 for countries with low conformity (Coopers and Lybrand, 1993; Hung, 2001).

IFRS adoption: from Daske et al. (2008) and Armstrong et al. (2010), equals 1 for countries where IFRS is permitted or required, and 0 otherwise.

References

Ali A, Hwang L S. Country-specific factors related to financial reporting and the value relevance of accounting data[J]. Journal of accounting research, 2000, 38(1): 1 - 21.

Armstrong C S, Barth M E, Jagolinzer A D, et al. Market reaction to the adoption of IFRS in Europe[J]. The accounting review, 2010, 85(1): 31 - 61.

Ball R. Infrastructure requirements for an economically efficient system of public financial reporting and disclosure[J]. Brookings-Wharton papers on financial services, 2001 (1): 127 - 169.

Ball R. International Financial Reporting Standards (IFRS): pros and cons for investors[J]. Accounting and business research, 2006, 36(1): 5 - 27.

Ball R, Robin A, Wu J S. Incentives versus standards: properties of accounting income in four East Asian countries[J]. Journal of accounting and economics, 2003, 36 (1 - 3): 235 - 270.

Bradshaw M T, Bushee B J, Miller G S. Accounting choice, home bias, and US investment in non-US firms[J]. Journal of accounting research, 2004, 42(5): 795 - 841.

Brown L D, Hagerman R L, Griffin P A, et al. An evaluation of alternative proxies for the market's assessment of unexpected earnings[J]. Journal of accounting and economics, 1987, 9(2): 159 - 193.

Brüggemann U, Hitz J M, Sellhorn T. Intended and unintended consequences of mandatory IFRS adoption: a review of extant evidence and suggestions for future research[J]. European accounting review, 2013, 22(1): 1 - 37.

Bushee B J. The influence of institutional investors on myopic R&D investment behavior [J]. Accounting review, 1998: 305 - 333.

Byard D, Li Y, Yu Y. The effect of mandatory IFRS adoption on financial analysts' information environment[J]. Journal of accounting research, 2011, 49(1): 69 - 96.

Chen K C W, Yuan H. Earnings management and capital resource allocation: evidence from China's accounting-based regulation of rights issues[J]. The accounting review, 2004, 79 (3): 645 - 665.

Cooper L. International accounting summaries: a guide for interpretation and comparison [M]. New York: Wiley, 1993.

Covrig V M, Defond M L, Hung M. Home bias, foreign mutual fund holdings, and the voluntary adoption of international accounting standards[J]. Journal of accounting research,

2007, 45(1): 41 - 70.

Daske H, Hail L, Leuz C, et al. Mandatory IFRS reporting around the world: early evidence on the economic consequences[J]. Journal of accounting research, 2008, 46(5): 1085 - 1142.

DeFond M, Hu X, Hung M, et al. Has the widespread adoption of IFRS harmed US firms' ability to attract foreign capital[J]. Journal of international accounting research, 2012, 11(2): 27 - 55.

DeFond M, Hu X, Hung M, et al. The impact of mandatory IFRS adoption on foreign mutual fund ownership: the role of comparability[J]. Journal of accounting and economics, 2011, 51(3): 240 - 258.

DeFond M L, Wong T J, Li S. The impact of improved auditor independence on audit market concentration in China[J]. Journal of accounting and economics, 1999, 28(3): 269 - 305.

De George E T, Li X, Shivakumar L. A review of the IFRS adoption literature[J]. Review of accounting studies, 2016, 21(3): 898 - 1004.

Eccher E A, Healy P M. The role of international accounting standards in transitional economies: a study of the People's Republic of China[J/OL]. SSRN electronic journal, 2000 [2019 - 03 - 06]. http://dx.doi.org/10.2139/ssrn.233598.

Easton P D, Harris T S. Earnings as an explanatory variable for returns[J]. Journal of accounting research, 1991, 29(1): 19 - 36.

Fan J P H, Wong T J. Corporate ownership structure and the informativeness of accounting earnings in East Asia[J]. Journal of accounting and economics, 2002, 33(3): 401 - 425.

Florou A, Pope P F. Mandatory IFRS adoption and institutional investment decisions[J]. The accounting review, 2012, 87(6): 1993 - 2025.

Yu G, Wahid A S. Accounting standards and international portfolio holdings[J]. The accounting review, 2014, 89(5): 1895 - 1930.

He X, Wong T J, Young D. Challenges for implementation of fair value accounting in emerging markets: evidence from China[J]. Contemporary accounting research, 2012, 29 (2): 538 - 562.

Hung M. Accounting standards and value relevance of financial statements: an international analysis[J]. Journal of accounting and economics, 2000, 30(3): 401 - 420.

Hussey R, Ong A. International financial reporting standards desk reference: overview, guide, and dictionary[M]. Hoboken: John Wiley & Sons, Inc., 2005.

Jiang G, Lee CM C, Yue H. Tunneling through intercorporate loans: the China experience[J]. Journal of financial economics, 2010, 98(1): 1 - 20.

Kim, Y, Li, S Q. Mandatory IFRS adoption and intra-industry information transfer[R/

OL]. Working paper，2010［2019 － 04 － 06］. https://www. mendeley. com/catalogue/1e2377f2-2a27-36f8-a2d0-15d0976cd119/.

La Porta R，Lopez-de-Silanes F，Shleifer A，et al. Legal determinants of external finance[J]. The journal of finance，1997，52(3)：1131－1150.

Porta R L，Lopez-de-Silanes F，Shleifer A，et al. Law and finance[J]. Journal of political economy，1998，106(6)：1113－1155.

Landsman W R，Maydew E L，Thornock JR. The information content of annual earnings announcements and mandatory adoption of IFRS[J]. Journal of accounting and economics，2012，53(1－2)：34－54.

Leuz C. IAS versus US GAAP：information asymmetry-based evidence from Germany's new market[J]. Journal of accounting research，2003，41(3)：445－472.

Leuz C，Nanda D，Wysocki P. Investor protection and earnings management：an international comparison[J]. Journal of financial economics，2003，69(3)：505－527.

Li S. Does mandatory adoption of international financial reporting standards in the European Union reduce the cost of equity capital？ [J]. The accounting review，2010，85(2)：607－636.

Lin Z J，Chen F. Value relevance of international accounting standards harmonization：evidence from A-and B-share markets in China[J]. Journal of international accounting，auditing and taxation，2005，14(2)：79－103.

Mueller G G，Gernon H. Accounting：an international perspective[M]. Chicago：Irwin Professional Publishing，1997.

Peng S，van der Laan Smith J. Chinese GAAP and IFRS：an analysis of the convergence process[J]. Journal of international accounting，auditing and taxation，2010，19(1)：16－34.

Piotroski J D，Srinivasan S. Regulation and bonding：the Sarbanes-Oxley Act and the flow of international listings[J]. Journal of accounting research，2008，46(2)：383－425.

Piotroski J D，Wong T J. Institutions and information environment of Chinese listed firms［M］//Fan J P H，Morck R. Capitalizing China. Chicago：University of Chicago Press，2012.

Tan H，Wang S，Welker M. Analyst following and forecast accuracy after mandated IFRS adoptions[J]. Journal of accounting research，2011，49(5)：1307－1357.

Wang Q，Wong T J，Xia L J. State ownership，the institutional environment，and auditor choice：evidence from China[J]. Journal of accounting and economics，2008，46(1)：112－134.

▶ This study is funded by grants from the National Natural Science Foundation of China (No. 71172142, 71372103) and Shanghai University of Finance and Economics. We appreciate helpful comments from Mingyi Hung and from workshop participants at Chongqing University, Fudan University, Nanjing University, Shanghai Jiao Tong University, University of Washington, the 2010 China Accounting and Finance Review International Symposium, and the 2012 American Accounting Association International Accounting Section Meetings.

股票市场发展与有限政府、有效政府行为*

内容提要：本文对我国股票市场上政府与市场的关系进行了探讨，分析表明，我国股票市场“失灵”的根本原因可能在于政府过多地干预了市场。这种干预主要包括政府控股和政府管制两大方面，即各级政府作为大部分上市公司的最终控股股东直接参与市场，同时政府监管部门为股票市场设定了大量的限制市场竞争和价格机制的管制规则。据此，本文提出，要建设一个“好的股票市场”，防止出现“坏的股票市场”，政府在股票市场上应当是一个“有限并且有效的政府”。

关 键 词：有限政府；有效政府；股票市场

一、我国股票市场上政府与市场的关系

在《国富论》中，亚当·斯密（1776）指出，一国的财富来自其国民所从事的生产性劳动，但劳动需要资本去推动和维持，而资本又来自其国民每年劳动生产物的节省，即储蓄。因此，储蓄能够在多大程度上有效地转化为资本，是影响一国财富创造的重要因素。在现代经济中，储蓄转化为资本通常有两种渠道，一是通过银行系统，二是通过股票市场。相对银行系统来说，股票市场更具备“扩展秩序”的特征（哈耶克，2000），它直接将社会上闲散的储蓄资金转化为生产性投资，并在此过程中调动起市场上分散的知识和信息，由此产生激励和约束，使分工和协作

---

* 本文选自：夏立军、陈信元：股票市场发展与有限政府、有效政府行为，《改革》，2006 年第 7 期，第 97 - 103 页。

不断深化,从而增进国民财富。但另一方面,股票市场并不能自发地运转良好,它需要政府的适当监管以及有效的法治作为支撑,因此股票市场的设立并不必然会促进经济发展,增进国民财富。在很多国家,尤其是新兴市场国家,股票市场并没有充分发挥其增进国民财富的潜在作用。实际上,政府监管不当、干预过多或者投资者法律保护不力等因素均可能使股票市场丧失其资源配置功能,产生市场失灵,甚至可能使股票市场沦为"寻租"和"掠夺"[①]的场所,严重时还可能导致金融危机和社会动荡。正是由于股票市场的这种两面性,政府与市场的关系在股票市场上面临着巨大的考验。

自 20 世纪 90 年代初设立以来,我国股票市场已经越来越牵动着国人的神经。这不仅因为其与成千上万名投资者的利益密切相关,更因为其对国民经济的广泛影响。如朱镕基所说,十多年来,我国股票市场发展很快,成绩很大,但是很不规范。[②] 这种"很不规范"已经使我国股票市场远离一个"好的股票市场",却使其面临着成为"坏的股票市场"的危险。种种证据表明,我国股票市场资源配置效率低下,显示出"市场失灵"的迹象。与股票市场设立前一样,股票市场设立后,我国经济继续保持快速增长。随着经济增长,城乡居民储蓄不断增加。[③] 但是,如表 1 所示,在我国股票市场设立后的十多年中,股票市场每年的筹资额占当年GDP 或当年居民储蓄余额的比例仅有 1% 左右。如图 1 所示,沪深股市股票价格指数的走势与我国 GDP 增长趋势也不同步,在 2000 年后两者还出现明显背离。如表 2 和表 3 所示,上市公司每股营业利润和净资产营业利润率呈现出一年不如一年的趋势,并且在单个年度中呈现出上市时间越长经营业绩越差的趋势。这表明我国股票市场未能成为将储蓄有效地转化为投资的场所。

---

① 所谓"掠夺",包括私人掠夺和政府掠夺,前者可以是私人掠夺私人,也可以是私人掠夺国家,主要是因为私人行为未能受到有效约束;后者包括政府作为一种组织如地方政府、政府部门或政府整体的掠夺,政府的一些官员利用政府权力为自己的掠夺,以及私人通过政府权力的掠夺,主要是因为政府权力未能受到有效约束(钱颖一,2004)。在某种程度上,"寻租"也是一种私人通过政府权力的掠夺。

② 见"九届人大三次会议举行记者招待会朱镕基总理会见中外记者回答记者提问",2002 – 3 – 15.

③ 这与日常生活中经常听到的企业融资难,尤其是民营企业和中小企业融资难,形成鲜明对照。其原因应该在于我国银行系统和股票市场的低效率,即银行系统和股票市场都未能有效地将居民储蓄转化为企业投资。

表 1　我国 GDP、城乡居民储蓄、股票市场筹资及股价指数情况（1993—2003）

年度	GDP（亿元）	城乡居民储蓄存款年末余额（亿元）	股票市场筹资总额（亿元）	股票市场筹资总额占当年 GDP 的比例	股票市场筹资总额占城乡居民储蓄的比例	上证指数	深证指数
	（1）	（2）	（3）	（4）	（5）	（6）	（7）
1993	34 634	15 204	315	0.91%	2.07%	834	238
1994	46 759	21 519	138	0.30%	0.64%	648	141
1995	58 478	29 662	119	0.20%	0.40%	555	113
1996	67 885	38 521	342	0.50%	0.89%	917	327
1997	74 463	46 280	934	1.25%	2.02%	1194	381
1998	78 345	53 408	795	1.01%	1.49%	1147	344
1999	82 068	59 622	883	1.08%	1.48%	1367	402
2000	89 468	64 332	1511	1.69%	2.35%	2074	636
2001	97 315	73 762	1182	1.21%	1.60%	1646	476
2002	105 172	86 911	737	0.70%	0.85%	1358	389
2003	117 252	103 618	661	0.56%	0.64%	1497	379

注:表中数据根据《中国统计年鉴》和《中国证券期货统计年鉴》整理,均为按当年价格计算。其中:(4)=(3)/(1);(5)=(3)/(2)。"股票市场筹资总额"为股票市场 A、B 股首次发行以及再发行筹资总额。各年的上证和深证指数分别为当年末上证 A 股综合指数和深证 A 股综合指数的收盘价。

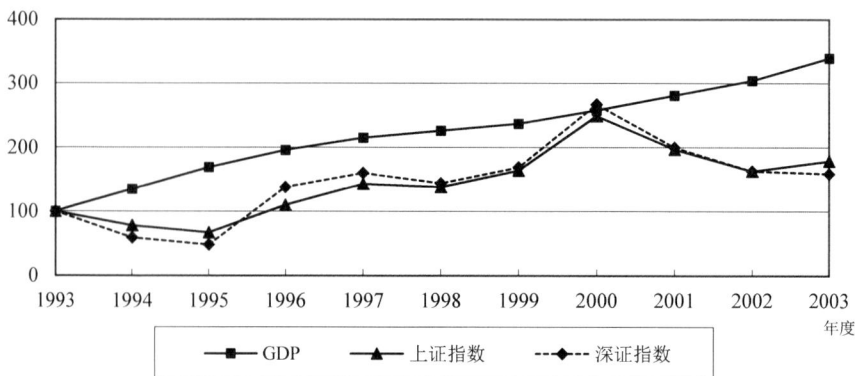

注:图中数据=(各年 GDP、上证指数或深证指数的实际值/1993 年相应的实际值)×100。各年的上证和深证指数的实际值分别为当年末上证 A 股综合指数和深证 A 股综合指数的收盘价。

图 1　我国 GDP 以及股票市场走势（1993—2003）

表2　上市公司加权平均每股营业利润比较（1993—2003）

单位：人民币元

上市时间 ＼ 年度	1993	1994	1995	1996	1997	1998	1999	2000	2001	2002	2003
≤1992	0.421	0.261	0.147	0.089	0.072	−0.045	0.079	0.046	−0.180	0.049	0.127
1993	0.317	0.318	0.263	0.185	0.169	0.084	0.123	0.150	0.138	0.138	0.249
1994		0.310	0.239	0.232	0.241	0.176	0.107	0.124	0.056	0.095	0.196
1995			0.319	0.102	0.068	−0.032	0.096	0.111	0.033	0.038	0.074
1996				0.335	0.282	0.200	0.172	0.169	0.084	0.119	0.111
1997					0.375	0.292	0.264	0.246	0.180	0.202	0.202
1998						0.362	0.341	0.330	0.240	0.234	0.297
1999							0.324	0.302	0.201	0.213	0.214
2000								0.336	0.286	0.351	0.470
2001									0.304	0.306	0.436
2002										0.298	0.361
2003											0.265
全体平均	0.348	0.305	0.240	0.239	0.259	0.199	0.206	0.219	0.155	0.194	0.251

注：表中数据根据香港理工大学中国会计与金融研究中心和深圳国泰安信息技术有限公司联合开发的"CSMAR中国股票市场研究数据库"中的有关数据计算而得。由于金融保险行业上市公司以及仅发行B股的上市公司数据不全，参与表中指标计算的公司为各年末所有上市公司剔除这些数据不全的公司之后的上市公司。

表3　上市公司加权平均净资产营业利润率比较（1993—2003）

单位：%

上市时间 ＼ 年度	1993	1994	1995	1996	1997	1998	1999	2000	2001	2002	2003
≤1992	14.54	9.68	5.97	3.58	2.94	−2.11	3.75	2.17	−10.22	2.78	6.83
1993	14.30	13.87	11.79	8.00	7.20	3.59	5.43	6.49	5.94	6.01	10.12
1994		12.93	10.40	9.63	9.87	7.14	4.22	4.82	2.32	3.83	7.61
1995			14.39	4.63	3.07	−1.43	4.53	4.88	1.40	1.69	3.64
1996				12.95	11.76	8.10	7.39	6.78	3.56	4.97	4.61
1997					13.23	10.88	9.68	8.56	6.37	7.03	7.08

（续表）

上市时间 ＼ 年度	1993	1994	1995	1996	1997	1998	1999	2000	2001	2002	2003
1998						13.35	13.43	11.88	8.33	8.20	9.69
1999							11.45	10.35	7.20	7.55	7.51
2000								10.85	9.32	11.52	14.14
2001									14.29	13.81	17.66
2002										12.94	14.70
2003											8.56
全体平均	14.37	12.76	10.54	9.65	10.13	7.66	8.09	7.96	5.69	7.42	9.14

注：表中数据根据香港理工大学中国会计与金融研究中心和深圳国泰安信息技术有限公司联合开发的"CSMAR 中国股票市场研究数据库"中的有关数据计算而得。由于金融保险行业上市公司以及仅发行 B 股的上市公司数据不全，参与表中指标计算的公司为各年末所有上市公司剔除这些数据不全的公司之后的上市公司。

　　不仅如此，在我国股票市场上，市场机制未能有效地发挥作用，以激励和约束市场主体。例如，DeFond，Wong，and Li(1999)以及李树华(2000)的研究发现，我国 1995 年首批独立审计准则的颁布实施提高了审计独立性，却导致了高质量会计师事务所(十大事务所)的市场份额下降，即出现审计独立性的提高与审计市场份额的背离，说明上市公司缺乏对高质量审计的需求。可见，在我国股票市场上，上市公司聘任会计师事务所对其进行审计在很大程度上只是因为监管或法律的强制，而非因为市场本身的自发需求。实际上，在我国股票市场上，除了会计师事务所聘任以外，上市公司的独立董事聘任、股东大会运作、董事会运作、信息披露行为等，莫不如此。在这些方面，上市公司往往只会满足监管或法律的最低要求，而不会主动地"弃恶从善"。这说明我国股票市场缺乏一种自发的激励和约束公司行为的力量，显示出"市场失灵"①迹象。

　　那么，我国股票市场"失灵"的原因何在？为回答这一问题，理论和实务界已作了不懈的探索和努力，然而对于此问题的回答依然众说纷纭，莫衷一是。将其归结为投资者素质低下的有之，将其归结为监管不力的有之，将其归结为公司治

---

① 所谓"市场失灵"，是指市场竞争和价格机制不能有效地激励和约束市场主体，以优化资源配置。它可能源自垄断、外部性、公共品或信息不对称问题，也可能源自政府对产权的保护不力或对市场的干预过多等问题。在我国股票市场设立后的十多年中，公司欺诈和舞弊、大股东侵害中小股东、庄家操纵市场等行为屡屡发生，同样说明市场机制未能有效地激励和约束市场主体。

理不善的亦有之,而实务界的一些人士则把其归结为"股权分置"①,甚至把"股权分置"上升到前所未有的高度,似乎它是股票市场一切问题的根源。当然,也有研究者认识到,要回答上述问题,必须从我国股票市场的特殊制度背景出发,对股票市场上的政府行为进行分析。近年来,一些研究在此方面进行了探索。例如,李东平(2001)研究了公司改制上市过程中的资产重组以及政府行为在其中所起的作用;陈小悦、肖星(2000)对配股权管制与上市公司盈余管理之间的关系进行了分析;陈晓、李静(2001)研究了地方政府财政行为在提升上市公司会计业绩中的作用;陈冬华(2002)从上市公司董事会中具有政府工作背景的董事这一角度考察了地方政府对公司治理以及企业绩效的影响;李增泉(2002)考察了国家控股对公司治理有效性的影响;陈信元、叶鹏飞、陈冬华(2003)研究了配股权刚性管制与公司机会主义重组之间的关系;Chen and Yuan(2004)研究了配股权管制、盈余管理与资源配置的关系;曾庆生(2004)考察了政府作为公司最终控制人对企业雇佣行为以及公司价值的影响;陈冬华、陈信元、万华林(2005)对国有控股上市公司中的高管薪酬管制与在职消费进行了研究;夏立军、方轶强(2005)研究了各级政府作为公司最终控制人以及公司所处地区的制度环境对公司价值的影响;孙铮、刘凤委、李增泉(2005)考察了地区市场化程度、政府干预与上市公司债务期限结构的关系;Fan,Wong,and Zhang(2006)考察了公司高管的政府任职背景对公司治理和企业绩效的影响;Fan,Wong,and Zhang(2005)研究了政府干预对公司"金字塔"形组织结构的影响。

总体上,这些研究可以分为两类,一类考察政府作为最终股东对公司行为的影响,另一类考察政府管制政策对公司行为的影响。实质上,这些研究考察的是股票市场上的两类政府干预活动对公司行为的影响。研究结果多发现,政府干预对公司治理以及企业绩效具有不利影响,并且还导致了公司的机会主义行为。随着研究积累,问题已逐渐变得清晰,现象与本质的混淆也有望厘清。但是,现有研究仍局限于考察政府干预对企业行为的影响,虽然已触及政府与市场的关系,但始终未能对其进行深入分析。而更重要的问题是,为什么市场机制没有在激励和约束市场主体以及优化资源配置上发挥应有的作用? 在股票市场这样的政府与市场关系面临较大考验的领域,政府大量地干预市场将会对市场产生什么影响? 本文拟对此进行分析。

---

① 所谓"股权分置",是指上市公司的一部分股份上市流通,一部分股份暂不上市流通,这一情况为我国股市所独有(尚福林,2005)。

二、政府控股、政府管制与我国股票市场失灵

从世界范围来看,股票市场的产生是市场经济高度发展的产物。但与自由市场经济中自发产生的股票市场不同,我国股票市场产生于我国转型经济的土壤中。虽然其最初的产生并非是政府有意安排的结果,但其后来的发展却受到政府的高度干预(胡继之,1999)。在股票市场设立初期,政府干预的动机更多地在于培育市场、维护秩序以及纠正市场失灵。但是,随着股票市场的发展,各级政府很快意识到股票市场为国企改革和脱困服务的巨大潜力。于是,政府开始深度介入股票市场。在这种情况下,我国股票市场逐渐演变成一个"多重目标下的股票市场",既要优化资源配置,更要为国企改革和脱困服务。[①] 总体上,我国股票市场上的政府干预有两大类型:一类是政府作为上市公司的最终控股股东直接参与市场;另一类是政府为股票市场设定大量的限制市场竞争和价格机制的管制规则。[②] 这两类政府干预的产生既与计划经济的惯性以及公有制的意识形态有关,同时也与股票市场为国企改革和脱困服务的目标有关。无疑,政府大量干预市场将会对市场主体的动机和行为并最终对市场运行产生影响。

为了更好地理解我国股票市场上政府与市场的关系,不妨先来看日常生活中最普通的市场——菜市场是如何运转的。在菜市场上,买者和卖者可以自由地进出市场,并且买者和卖者之间的交易多为现货交易和人格化交易,即一手交钱一手交货,并且买者和卖者仅限于较小的社区中。这种交易的实现主要依赖隐性合约,即它的执行主要靠卖者的信誉。如果卖者诚信经营,那么其信誉就会逐渐形成,从而可以获得更多销量和更高价格;相反,如果卖者欺骗买者,那么由于市场上有很多卖者,买者可以在下次选择其他卖者。这样,在隐性合约的作用下,卖者的行为受到适当的激励和约束。在这样的场合,政府的作用主要是协助隐性合约的执行,它所要提供的只是较少的监管和法治(显性合约),以防止强买强卖、欺行

[①] 除此之外,我国股票市场在特定时期还有一些政治目标。例如,1997 年是我国政治生活中极其重要的一年,面临着香港回归和党的"十五大"召开两件具有历史意义的大事,因此保持社会和经济的稳定显得尤为迫切。为了控制股票市场可能引起的风险,在这一年政府采取了一系列平抑股市的措施,主要有:宣布 1997 年为风险教育年,控制舆论导向;严禁国有企业和上市公司炒作股票;禁止银行资金违规流入股市;严厉查处证券市场违规机构;追加 1996 年新股发行额度 50 亿元,并宣布 1997 年新股发行额度为 300 亿元;提高股票交易印花税(胡继之,1999)。

[②] 在本文中,"政府干预"是指政府在保护产权、执行合同以及维护市场竞争秩序这些基本职能以外的其他活动和行为,如政府直接参与市场或对市场实行限制竞争和价格机制的管制。在我国股票市场发展的某些阶段,政府干预市场还包括政府作为证券公司、会计师事务所的控股股东直接参与市场,政府利用媒体(如发表《人民日报》评论员文章)直接影响股票价格,等等。

霸市、操纵菜价等不正当行为,从而维持正常的市场秩序。

与菜市场相比,股票市场的运转要复杂得多。其一,"非人格化交易"成为主要的交易方式。在这种交易中,买卖双方互不熟悉,也不认识。其二,交易的对象是股票,即股票发行公司未来的经营收益,而不再是现货交易。与菜市场的菜不同,股票的质量不容易识别,买者和卖者之间存在着严重的信息不对称。其三,买者(投资者)投入资金与取得回报之间有很大的时间差,这就给卖者(股票发行公司)很大的机会从事不利于买者的活动,即道德风险问题。其四,购买同一公司股票的买者人数众多而且分散,由于免费搭车问题,他们很难集体行动,结果他们的利益容易受到侵犯。鉴于这些特征,在股票市场上,仅靠双方信任而完成交易往往是行不通的,这就需要第三方(通常是政府)提供比菜市场更多的监管和法治,如强制信息披露、强制财务报告审计、对关联交易的限制、对公司治理的要求、对股东权益特别是中小股东权益的法律保护,等等。

但是,从本质上来看,自由股票市场与菜市场的运转机制是类似的。① 如图 2 左图所示,在自由股票市场上,激励和约束市场主体行为的力量主要是市场竞争和价格机制以及监管和法律机制。前者是一种隐性合约,代表市场"看不见的手"的作用;而后者是一种显性合约,代表政府"看得见的手"的作用。与监管和法律机制相比,市场竞争和价格机制的优势在于其自动执行以及分散决策的特点。当某个市场主体的"善"行或"恶"行被发现时,市场上现有的和潜在的签约主体会利用市场上已有的信息,并根据各自的判断自动做出反应;并且,从根本上来讲,市场上其他主体(主要是投资者)是此市场主体行为的裁判者,这使得更大量、更广泛的信息可以被利用。因此,与监管和法律系统中经常需要采用硬性指标不同,市场的这种自动执行的"准法官"机制可以更准确地判断市场主体行为的善恶程度,从而更恰当地对其进行激励和约束。鉴于市场竞争和价格机制的优势,在自由股票市场上,市场竞争和价格机制是比监管和法律机制更为基础、更为重要的力量,监管和法律机制主要是起协助市场竞争和价格机制、纠正市场失灵的作用。换言之,市场本身在激励和约束市场主体、优化资源配置中发挥着基础性作用,政府主要提供适当的监管和法治,以保护产权,执行合同,维持市场秩序,即政府主要起一个"守夜人"的作用。

---

① 在现实中,完全自由的、不受政府干预的股票市场并不存在,因此这里的"自由股票市场"是一种相对意义上的自由市场,指市场本身在资源配置中起基础性作用,而政府主要提供适当的监管和法治,以确保合同执行,保护个人不受市场上其他人的侵害和压迫,即政府主要承担"守夜人"的职责。按照这样的定义,英国的股票市场在其证券管理法律《公司法》(Company Act)实施前后,美国的股票市场在其《1933 年证券法》(Securities Act of 1933)实施前后,均可称为自由市场。

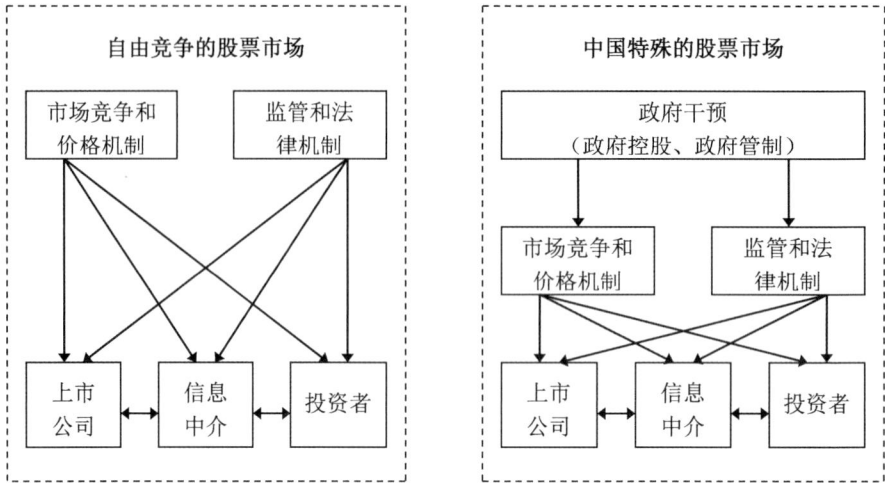

图2　自由竞争的股票市场与中国股票市场比较图

与自由股票市场不同，我国股票市场产生和发展于我国从计划经济体制向市场经济体制转型的过程中。因此，自其诞生之日起，便不可避免地带有很多"中国特色"。如图2右图所示，在我国股票市场上，决定市场主体行为的主要力量并非是市场竞争和价格机制以及监管和法律机制，而是政府干预，并且市场竞争和价格机制以及监管和法律机制均受政府干预影响。政府干预的产生不仅与计划经济的惯性和公有制的意识形态有关，更与股票市场为国企改革和脱困服务的目标有关。从内容来看，这些干预主要包括两大方面，一是政府作为大部分上市公司的最终控股股东直接参与市场，二是政府作为监管者为股票市场设定大量的限制市场竞争和价格机制的管制规则。在这两种政府干预的影响下，市场竞争和价格机制以及监管和法律机制均难以有效地发挥作用，以激励和约束市场主体、优化资源配置。以下分别考察之。

（一）政府控股与股票市场失灵

在政府作为大部分上市公司的最终控股股东直接参与股票市场的情况下，其利用自身权力支持和保护下属上市公司几乎不可避免。在我国转型过程中，政府权力配置经历了从集权到分权的过程，在此过程中，地方政府发展经济的积极性被调动起来，但其竞争资源的动机也由此产生（Qian and Weingast，1996；Cao，Qian and Weingast，1999；Poncet，2005）。正如吸引外资一样，从股票市场获取资源同样有利于解决就业问题,发展地方经济,改善当地形象,并最终给政府官员带来利益。虽然地方政府通过支持当地的非国有企业上市融资也可以从股票市场获取资源,但支持国有企业上市融资不仅符合国家宏观政策,还可以缓解其困境,减轻财政负担,促进社会稳定,并增加政府官员直接控制下的资源。因此,作为"理性人"的地方政府,自然会充分利用其权力支持当地的国有企业从股票市场获取资源。当各地政府均采用这一策略时,其结果便是股票市场上企业之间的正常竞争受到限制。

在支持国有企业从股票市场获取资源的同时,政府对其控股的上市公司还存在着隐性担保。其一,政府控股的公司往往承担了政府的政策性负担,如经济发展战略、就业、税收、社会稳定等。于是,在公司出现困难或陷入困境时,政府难以分清责任,预算软约束问题产生(Lin,Cai,and Li,1998)。其二,由于政府具有维护社会稳定的目标,在上市公司发生重大丑闻时,作为控股股东的政府通常会对其实施救助,并对遭受损失的投资者作出一定补偿。[①] 其三,在我国股票市场上,企业上市资格受到管制,"壳"资源稀缺,为了维持上市资格,避免公司被摘牌或退市,在上市公司发生亏损时,作为控股股东的政府通常也采用各种办法对其进行支持和保护(李树华,2000;李东平,2001)。因此,对于投资者来说,政府控股的公司实际上受到隐性担保。当大部分上市公司均为各级政府所控股时,整个股票市场在某种程度上也受到政府隐性担保,并由此产生严重的预算软约束问题。[②] 这将导致股票价格扭曲,难以充分反映公司本身的质量。

在我国股票市场上,上市公司股份还被分为流通股和非流通股,即所谓的"股权分置"。设置非流通股的做法因防止国有资产流失的目的而产生,因其可以人为地减少股票供给,抬高股票价格,为国企改革和脱困服务而得以保留(李茂生,2002 年;刘鸿儒等,2003)。换言之,这种独特的设计也是政府干预市场的结果。在股权分置的情况下,大部分股票不流通,人为地造成了股票供求关系的非均衡,导致股票价格扭曲。并且,由于非流通股股东(通常是大股东)在上市公司中处于控股地位,潜在的购并者对上市公司控制权的竞争难以实现,流通股股东(通常是中小股东)也很难通过"用脚投票"即价格机制来激励和约束上市公司。

---

① 典型的案例是琼民源。该公司在 1996 年年报中虚列收入 5.66 亿元,虚构利润 5.4 亿元,虚增资本公积 6.57 亿元。案件暴露后,琼民源股价严重缩水,投资者损失惨重,涉及 10 万余名投资者。由于该案社会影响十分严重,为了维护社会稳定,琼民源的最终控股股东——北京市政府通过实施一系列重组,将琼民源与中关村进行股票置换,最终使投资者的损失得到补偿,甚至使一部分投资者获利。

② 政府对股票市场的这种隐性担保的表现之一是政府将股票价格作为监管目标,因而在股票价格指数"过高"或"过低"时,利用政策、媒体(如发表《人民日报》评论员文章)等手段直接影响股票价格。

政府作为上市公司的最终控股股东直接参与股票市场也会对监管和法律机制产生负面影响。在大部分上市公司最终为各级政府控股的情况下,监管和法治的目标很难集中在维护市场秩序、优化资源配置上,却常常要为维护国有股权利益、配合国企改革和脱困服务。同时,在我国讲究行政级别的社会环境中,作为部级单位的证监会要对各级政府控股的上市公司实施监管,实属困难;在司法体系不够独立、各级政府对辖区内的司法部门具有实质性影响的情况下,法治力量也难以对政府控股的公司发挥作用。实际上,地方政府帮助和纵容上市公司弄虚作假、违法违规,利用自身特殊地位干扰监管部门和司法部门的调查和处罚行为的情形屡见不鲜(刘鸿儒等,2003)。[①]

(二) 政府管制与股票市场失灵

政府作为监管者为股票市场设定大量的管制规则,同样会限制市场竞争、扭曲股票价格以及市场主体的行为。与菜市场和自由股票市场不同,在我国股票市场上,股票需求方可以自由进出市场,但股票供应方不然。无论是公司首次股票发行,还是上市公司再融资以及特别处理、暂停上市和终止上市,均受到政府严格管制(剧锦文,2003;李树华,2000;李东平,2001)。在这些管制规则下,股票市场资源被中央政府采用"计划管理、规模控制"的办法分配到全国,并在各地区、各部门之间进行利益平衡。同时,国有企业在此过程中享受特别优待。自然,不同类型的企业之间正常的融资竞争受到了限制,代之而来的是地区之间、部门之间和企业之间为获取融资资格而进行的"寻租"竞争。

而股票发行中的"规模控制"做法,与公司大部分股票不流通的设计一起,则人为地造成了股票市场长期的"供需瓶颈",股票长期供不应求,从而导致股票价格成为某种程度上的"垄断价格"。在这种情况下,股票价格脱离公司真实价值,并且股票供求关系难以根据股票价格自发调整。即便如此,如果股票发行价格采用市场化价格,那么股票发行公司虽可以获得"垄断价格",但至少还会部分地考虑市场反应,以获得更高的发行价格,并防止发行失败。然而,为了配合计划式分配资源的办法,在很长时期内,公司首次股票发行价格也受到管制,并且管制后的发行价格往往与二级市场价格相差甚远。这样,公司股票发行失败的可能性非常低,公司只需要满足政府的管制要求,即可将股票发行出去,而不太需要关注市场

---

① 陈信元、陈冬华、万华林(2005)的研究也支持这一判断。他们通过对比分析地方法院对"大庆联谊"和"ST 渤海"这两个证券民事赔偿案的审判情况,发现地方保护对当地法院的审判行为具有重要影响。

的反应。

不仅如此,股票发行价格长期采用固定市盈率与每股税后利润(已实现数或预测数)乘积决定的办法。为了提高股票发行价格,获取更多资源,股票发行公司普遍进行盈利操纵(Aharony,Lee,and Wong,2000;林舒、魏明海,2000)。同时,由于公司获得首次发行上市资格和再融资资格均需要满足严格的盈利要求,并且上市公司连续亏损将被特别处理、暂停上市或终止上市,为了规避这些管制,公司也具有很强的盈利操纵和机会主义重组动机(蒋义宏,1998;陆建桥,1999;陈小悦、肖星,2000;陈信元、叶鹏飞、陈冬华,2003;Chen and Yuan,2004;Haw et al.,2005)。如果管制者能够有效地识别和限制公司的盈利操纵或机会主义重组,采用能够反映公司未来前景的指标实施管制,那么管制可能会在优化资源配置中发挥一定作用。但是,在现实中,这一假定并不成立,管制者既不是大公无私的,也不是全知全能的。表4给出了中国证监会1992年至2004年的落马官员情况,从中可见,管制者并不是大公无私、谋求公众利益最大化的,其本身也是追求私利的"理性人"。

表 4　中国证监会落马官员一览表(1992—2004)

官员姓名	案发时间	案发前任职	案由和处理情况
鲁晓龙	1995	中国证监会上市部副主任	收受泰山石油(000554)20多万元贿赂。因受贿罪被判处有期徒刑13年
钟志伟	1995	中国证监会上市部副处长	接受湖北一家企业大约4万股原始股。因受贿罪被判处有期徒刑3年
高良玉	1995	中国证监会发行部副处长	受贿。由于情节较轻,最终检察机关同意中国证监会自行处理此案,但提出要求:高良玉绝不能在中国证监会继续工作。但中国证监会最终没有按检察机关提出的意见进行处理。高良玉继续在证监会工作,直至后来进入南方基金
刘明	1999	上海证券交易所专员办主任,曾任中国证监会发行部副主任	两名亲属受贿。2000年,中纪委给中国证监会的处理意见是:建议刘明离开证监会,留党察看。中国证监会经讨论,最后给出结论:"解除公职,开除党籍。"

（续表）

官员姓名	案发时间	案发前任职	案由和处理情况
段素珍	2001	中国证监会期货处副处长、太原证券监管特派员	为他人乱批营业执照,收受好处费52.7万元。2001年7月被逮捕
高勇	2004	中国证监会贵阳特派办党委书记、主任,兼中国证监会成都稽查局副局长	索贿120万元。2004年8月被逮捕
王小石	2004	中国证监会发行监管部发审委工作处副处长	在2003年凤竹纺织(600493)"过会"(即通过发审会审核)的过程中出卖发审委员名单,并在深圳某上市公司发行可转债的过程中参与公关、介绍受贿。2004年11月被逮捕

注:参见李箐:《证监会落马官员盘点》,《财经》2005年1月10日。

同时,管制者也不是先知先觉、无所不能的,管制者的行为往往与亚当·斯密(1759)在《道德情操论》中的描述类似,"在政府中掌权的人,容易自以为非常聪明……他似乎认为他能够像用手摆布一副棋盘中的各个棋子那样非常容易地摆布偌大一个社会中的各个成员;他并没有考虑到:棋盘上的棋子除了手摆布时的作用之外,不存在别的行动原则;但是,在人类社会这个大棋盘上每个棋子都有它自己的行动原则,它完全不同于政府机关可能选用来指导它的那种行动原则"。我国股票市场大量发生的盈利操纵行为和机会主义重组以及公司上市或配股后业绩"变脸"(陈文斌,2005)的现象,印证了亚当·斯密的这一论断。

三、有限政府、有效政府与"好"的股票市场

上文的分析显示,政府对股票市场的过多干预可能是导致我国股票市场"失灵"的根本原因。那么,在股票市场上,政府与市场的关系应当是怎样的呢?要回答这一问题,有必要回顾一下经济学家对于政府与市场关系的认识过程。在《国富论》中,亚当·斯密(1776)认为,在一个自由竞争的市场上,每个人追求自己利益的同时,也不知不觉地促进了社会的整体利益,"确实,他通常既不打算促进公共的利益,也不知道他自己是在什么程度上促进那种利益……在这场合,像在其他许多场合一样,他受着一只看不见的手的指导,去尽力达到一个并非他本意想

要达到的目的。也并不因为事非出于本意，就对社会有害。他追求自己的利益，往往使他能比在真正出于本意的情况下更有效地促进社会的利益"。按照亚当·斯密"看不见的手"原理，市场竞争以及价格机制是实现资源有效配置的最佳工具，政府所要做的仅仅是提供国防以保卫人民，公正司法以保护个人不受社会上其他人的侵害和压迫，以及建设并维持某些公共事业和公共设施，即政府只起一个"守夜人"的作用。

以后的经济学家认识到，虽然市场经济是人类迄今为止最具效率和活力的经济运行机制和资源配置手段，它具有任何其他机制和手段不可替代的功能优势，但市场本身也存在着局限。例如，市场竞争可能会导致垄断，并进而限制竞争；在公共品和存在外部性的领域，市场并不能充分和有效地发挥作用；由于信息不对称，市场配置资源的功能可能受到限制；市场并不能自动实现宏观经济的稳定和平衡，也不能克服社会"两极分化"的趋势。总体来看，在垄断、公共品、外部性以及信息不对称等领域，市场并不能有效地配置资源，达至社会福利的最大化，即存在"市场失灵"。诺贝尔经济学奖获得者萨缪尔森认为，"当今没有什么东西可以取代市场来组织一个复杂的大型经济。问题是，市场既无心脏，也无头脑，它没有良心，也不会思考，没有什么顾忌"。因此，政府不能只起一个"守夜人"的作用，还要在某些特定领域积极地干预经济，纠正"市场失灵"。

然而，"市场失灵"并不必然意味着政府干预的成功，政府同样会"失灵"，并且有时候"政府失灵"比"市场失灵"更为严重。首先，政府难以获得分散的个体所拥有的知识和信息，亦难以根据个人的偏好对其进行激励和约束，因此政府干预很容易产生干预过多、干预过少、干预不当或者干预无效的问题。其次，政府由政府官员组成，而政府官员和普通民众一样，也会追求其个人私利，因此政府并不总是会为社会大众的利益服务。政府这只"看得见的手"既可能是一只"帮助之手"，亦可能是一只"掠夺之手"(Shleifer and Vishny，1998)。最后，由于政府具有垄断性权力，政府官员可能追求个人私利，政府也可能被某些利益集团"俘获"，并且政府干预的成本由社会承担，而效果难以计量，因此政府干预具有自我膨胀的倾向。在现实社会中，政府干预的上述缺陷都会有所体现。近年来，经济学家越来越认识到，要建设一个好的市场经济，政府应当是一个"有限并且有效的政府"，即政府首先必须受到法治约束，以防止其滥用权力，在此基础上，政府还必须保护产权，执行合同,维持市场秩序。①

从我国来看,对政府与市场关系的认识也在不断变化。新中国成立后,百废待兴,新生政权面临着帝国主义威胁,因此实行赶超战略成为合理的选择。而实行赶超战略必然要求政府代替市场进行资源配置,以迅速集中社会资源发展重工业。于是,为了推行重工业优先发展的赶超战略,我国逐步走上了计划经济之路(林毅夫、蔡昉、李周,2002)。② 然而,政府高度干预经济活动,甚至代替市场进行资源配置,并没有达到预期的效果,30 年的计划经济试验最终走入困境。其根本原因在于,由于缺乏竞争和价格机制,计划经济无法解决资源配置上的信息和激励问题。认识到计划经济的这种致命缺陷,自 1978 年起,我国开始实行市场化取向的改革,并进而走上从计划经济向市场经济转型的道路。20 多年来,我国经济发展成就巨大,以至林毅夫、蔡昉、李周(2002)称之为"中国的奇迹"。但是,20 多年的转型实践表明,转型之路并不平坦。仅是在政府与市场关系的认识上,从改革之初的"计划经济为主、市场调节为辅"到认识到应当充分发挥市场在资源配置中的基础性作用,便经历了 20 多年的时间。更不用说,在很多领域,改革实践还远远落后于思想认识。

从我国股票市场来看,如上文分析所显示的,在政府大量地干预市场的情况下,市场竞争和价格机制以及监管和法律机制难以发挥作用,以激励和约束市场主体、优化资源配置。一方面,当股票市场上大量的上市公司都是政府控股时,股票市场的目标便难以集中在优化资源配置上,政府亦难以为股票市场提供有效的监管和法治环境。另一方面,当股票市场具有多重目标,甚至股票市场的主要目标偏离优化资源配置而变为服务于国企改革和脱困时,股票市场便难以在增进国民财富中发挥作用,其为国企改革和脱困服务的目标亦难以为继。因此,减少政府对市场的过多干预,使市场在资源配置中发挥基础性作用是我国股票市场进一

---

① 从历史上看,经济学家对政府与市场关系的认识总是受到社会经济形势的影响。20 世纪 30 年代以前,大部分经济学家接受亚当·斯密的"看不见的手"的原理,但其后发生的美国经济危机为政府干预经济提供了强大的理由。此后,"市场失灵"学说盛行,政府干预主义渐占上风,"凯恩斯主义"开始大行其道。在一些国家,甚至政府干预的极端形式——计划经济也得到实践。但围绕"政府与市场关系"的争论一直没有停止过,在"凯恩斯主义"大行其道的年代里,哈耶克始终强调自由市场的优越性,呼吁人们警惕政府干预带来的危险,甚至认为计划经济是一条"通往奴役之路"。20 世纪 70 年代美国经济出现的"滞胀"以及苏联和中国计划经济的困境,促使经济学家认识到政府干预的局限性,并促使他们重新思考政府与市场的关系。近年来,经济学家尤其是从事比较经济学研究的经济学家认识到,市场经济既有"好的市场经济"也有"坏的市场经济",要建设一个"好的市场经济",必须要有一个"有限并且有效的政府"(钱颖一,2003,2004)。

② 当然,建国时马列主义在中国的指导地位以及当时苏联计划经济的良好发展也是影响中国走上计划经济之路的重要因素。

步改革的关键。唯如此,股票市场才能恢复其本色,亦才能在增进国民财富中发挥其应有的作用。

　　需要指出的是,虽然我国股票市场"失灵"的根本原因可能在于政府过多地干预了市场,但并不能就此否定政府在股票市场的积极作用。其原因是,市场竞争和价格机制发挥作用需要以政府有效地保护产权、执行合同和维持市场秩序为前提条件。政府应当为股票市场提供适当的监管和法治,以有利于市场竞争和价格机制在资源配置中发挥主导作用,而不是作为上市公司的最终控股股东直接参与股票市场,或者作为监管者为股票市场设定大量的限制市场竞争和价格机制的管制规则。换言之,要建设一个"好的股票市场",防止出现"坏的股票市场",政府在股票市场上亦应当是一个"有限并且有效的政府",即政府在股票市场的行为首先必须受到法治约束,而不能任意地干预市场,同时政府必须有效地保护产权、执行合同、维护股票市场竞争秩序。如果说我国股票市场初期的"很不规范"可以归结为思想认识的落后或特定的政治经济条件的限制,那么在我国经济体制转型已经二十多年、股票市场发展已经十多年后的今天,这种"很不规范"理应得到重视和解决。

参考文献

陈冬华.地方政府、公司治理与企业绩效[D].上海:上海财经大学,2002.

陈冬华,陈信元,万华林.国有企业中的薪酬管制与在职消费[J].经济研究,2005(2):92-101.

陈文斌.上市公司IPO之后财务业绩变脸研究[J].改革,2005(5):104-108.

陈晓,李静.地方政府财政行为在提升上市公司业绩中的作用探析[J].会计研究,2001(12):20-28.

陈小悦,肖星.配股权和上市公司利润操纵.经济研究,2000(01):30-36.

陈信元,陈冬华,万华林.投资者保护和地方保护[Z].上海财经大学会计与财务研究院工作稿,2005.

陈信元,叶鹏飞,陈冬华.机会主义资产重组与刚性管制[J].经济研究,2003(05):13-22+91.

哈耶克.致命的自负——社会主义的谬误[M].冯克利,等,译.北京:中国社会科学出版社,2000.

胡继之.中国股市的演进与制度变迁[M].北京:经济科学出版社,1999.

蒋义宏.一个不容忽视的问题——上市公司盈利操纵的实证研究[N].中国证券报,1998-

3-19/20.

剧锦文.资本市场对国有企业产权改革影响的实证分析[Z].中国社会科学院经济研究所工作稿,2003.

李东平.大股东控制,盈余管理与上市公司业绩滑坡[D].上海:上海财经大学,2001.

李茂生.中国证券市场透析[M].北京:中国社会科学出版社,2002.

李箐.证监会落马官员盘点[J].财经,2005(1):78-79.

李树华.审计独立性的提高与审计市场的背离[M].上海:上海三联书店,2000.

李增泉.国家控股与公司治理的有效性——一项基于中国证券市场的实证研究[D].上海:上海财经大学,2002.

林舒,魏明海.中国A股发行公司首次公开募股过程中的盈利管理[J].中国会计与财务研究,2000(2):87-107.

林毅夫,蔡昉,李周.中国的奇迹:发展战略与经济改革[M].上海:格致出版社,2002.

刘鸿儒,等.探索中国资本市场发展之路——理论创新推动制度创新[M].北京:中国金融出版社,2003.

陆建桥.中国亏损上市公司盈余管理实证研究[J].会计研究,1999(9):25-35.

钱颖一.现代经济学与中国经济改革[M].北京:中国人民大学出版社,2003.

钱颖一.走向好的市场经济,避免坏的市场经济[N].经济观察报,2004-12-5.

尚福林.积极稳妥地解决股权分置问题——中国证监会负责人就启动股权分置改革试点问题发表谈话[N].证券时报,2005-4-30.

孙铮,刘凤委,李增泉.市场化程度,政府干预与企业债务期限结构——来自我国上市公司的经验证据[J].经济研究,2005(05):52-63.

夏立军.政府干预与市场失灵——上市公司之会计师事务所选择研究[D].上海:上海财经大学,2005.

夏立军,方轶强.政府控制,治理环境与公司价值——来自中国证券市场的经验证据[J].经济研究,2005(05):40-51.

斯密.道德情操论[M].蒋自强,钦北愚,朱钟棣,等,译.北京:商务印书馆,1997.

斯密.国民财富的性质和原因的研究(简称"国富论")[M].郭大力,王亚南,译.北京:商务印书馆,1974.

曾庆生.国家控股,超额雇员与公司价值——一项基于中国证券市场的实证研究[D].上海:上海财经大学,2004.

李箐.证监会落马官员盘点[J].财经,2005(1):78-79.

Aharony J,Lee C W J,Wong T J. Financial packaging of IPO firms in China[J]. Journal of accounting research,2000,38(1):103-126.

Cao Y,Qian Y Y,Weingast B R. From federalism,Chinese style to privatization,Chinese style[J]. Economics of transition,1999,7(1):103-131.

Chen K C W，Yuan H. Earnings management and capital resource allocation：evidence from China's accounting-based regulation of rights issues[J]. The accounting review，2004，79 (3)：645 - 665.

DeFond M L，Wong T J，Li S. The impact of improved auditor independence on audit market concentration in China[J]. Journal of accounting and economics，1999，28(3)：269 - 305.

Fan J P H，Wong T J，Zhang T. Politically connected CEOs，corporate governance，and post-IPO performance of China's newly partially privatized firms[J]. Journal of financial economics，2007，84(2)：330 - 357.

Fan J P H，Wong T J，Zhang T. The emergence of corporate pyramids in China[R]. Working paper，2006.

Haw I N M U，Qi D，Wu D，et al. Market consequences of earnings management in response to security regulations in China[J]. Contemporary accounting research，2005，22 (1)：95 - 140.

Lin J Y，Cai F，Li Z. Competition，policy burdens，and state-owned enterprise reform [J]. The American economic review，1998，88(2)：422 - 427.

Poncet S. A fragmented China：measure and determinants of Chinese domestic market disintegration[J]. Review of international economics，2005，13(3)：409 - 430.

Qian Y Y，Weingast B R. China's transition to markets：market-preserving federalism，Chinese style[J]. The journal of policy reform，1996，1(2)：149 - 185.

Shleifer A，Vishny R W. The grabbing hand：government pathologies and their cures [M]. Cambridge：Harvard University Press，2002.

司法独立性与投资者保护法律实施
——最高人民法院"1/15 通知"的市场反应[*]

内容提要：以往大量文献强调了投资者法律保护对公司治理和金融市场发展的重要性，但少有研究考察投资者法律保护受什么因素影响。本文利用 2002 年 1 月 15 日最高人民法院颁布《关于受理证券市场因虚假陈述引发的民事侵权纠纷案件有关问题的通知》(简称"1/15 通知")这一事件，以那些存在虚假陈述或有虚假陈述嫌疑的上市公司为样本，采用事件研究法，实证考察了司法独立性对投资者保护法律实施的影响。我们预期，当公司最终控制人为地方政府并且该地方政府是公司虚假陈述案件管辖法院的本地同级政府时，法院的司法独立性可能受到干扰。据此，我们将样本公司分为司法相对独立和相对不独立的两组公司。我们发现，在"1/15 通知"颁布日前后几个交易日内，样本公司的市场反应显著为负；并且与司法相对独立组公司相比，司法相对不独立组公司的负向市场反应程度更小。这说明，投资者倾向于认为"1/15 通知"及与其相关的民事诉讼法律能够得到一定程度的实施，但地方政府对当地法院的影响降低了这些投资者保护法律得到实施的可能性。

关　键　词：司法独立性；投资者保护；法律实施；虚假陈述

＊ 本文选自：陈信元、李莫愁、芮萌、夏立军：司法独立性与投资者保护法律实施——最高人民法院"1/15 通知"的市场反应，《经济学(季刊)》，2009 年第 9 卷第 1 期，第 1 - 28 页。作者按姓氏拼音排序，通讯作者，本期首篇。本文揭示了"全国性资本市场与地方化司法"之间的矛盾，基于研究结论提出了设立专门的证券法院的改革建议，这一建议已被后来的司法改革如中央深改委 2018 年决定设立的全国首家专门金融法院——上海金融法院所验证。

一、引言

近年来,国际上"法与金融"学派逐渐兴起,以 La Porta et al.(1997,1998, 1999,2000a,2000b,2002)为代表的一系列研究强调了法律制度对公司治理、投资者保护以及金融市场发展的重要性。例如,La Porta et al.(1998)发现,一国法律渊源对其投资者法律保护程度具有重要影响,表现为普通法系国家的投资者法律保护程度最高,德国和斯堪的纳维亚大陆法系国家的投资者法律保护程度次之,法国大陆法系国家的投资者法律保护程度最低。并且,一国的投资者法律保护程度与其上市公司数量、规模、股利支付比率及公司价值正相关(La Porta et al., 1997,2000b,2002;Kumar et al.,1999;Claessens et al.,2002),与其上市公司股权集中度和控制权私人收益负相关(La Porta et al.,1998,1999;Claessens et al., 2000;Zingales,1994;Nenova,2003)。随后的研究还发现,在投资者法律保护越强的国家,投资机会与实际投资之间的相关度越高(Wurgler,2000),应计制会计信息的有用性更高(Ali and Hwang,2000;Hung,2001;Leuz et al.,2003;Haw et al.,2004;DeFond et al.,2007),在上市公司业绩下滑时总经理更可能被更换(DeFond and Hung,2004),国际四大会计师事务所相对其他事务所的公司治理重要性越低(Choi and Wong,2007)。这些研究表明,一个国家的投资者法律保护程度在很大程度上决定了其公司治理特征和金融市场发展程度,良好的投资者法律保护是公司治理和金融市场发展的基础。

但现有研究还集中于考察投资者法律保护(立法或司法层面)的经济后果,少有研究关注什么因素影响投资者法律保护程度,尤其是关于什么因素影响投资者保护法律实施的研究还非常缺乏。虽然 La Porta et al.(1998,2008)发现,一国法律渊源(普通法系还是大陆法系)是其投资者法律保护程度的重要影响因素,但法律渊源已植入一国整个的法律意识形态和传统之中,殊难改变。此外,多数国家(包括中国)已制定了投资者保护的有关法律,但遗憾的是,这些法律未能得到有效实施。因此,对那些投资者法律保护比较弱的国家和新兴市场来说,更重要的是找出现实中影响投资者保护法律实施的关键因素,并加以改进。在研究方法上,现有文献多采用跨国截面研究方法,但投资者法律保护与公司治理、企业价值、资本市场发展程度等因素的相关性难以代表因果关系,即不能解决内生性问题,同时也难以控制国家层面其他制度性因素的影响。从以中国为背景的研究来看,沈艺峰等(2004)根据法律和监管政策的颁布情况,对中国股票市场不同阶段的中小投资者法律保护程度进行了评分,但他们关注的是投资者法律保护的立法层面,而未关注其司法层面,也未考察投资者法律保护的影响因素。Firth et al. (2007)考察了政府控股和地方保护对中国企业之间的民事诉讼和判决的影响,但他们的研究未涉及投资者法律保护。陈志武(2003)、夏立军、方轶强(2005)注意到政府影响或地方保护与投资者法律保护的矛盾,但未对此进行大样本的实证研究,关于这一矛盾的经验证据依然非常缺乏。

本文利用最高人民法院 2002 年 1 月 15 日颁布《关于受理证券市场因虚假陈述引发的民事侵权纠纷案件有关问题的通知》(简称"1/15 通知")这一事件,以存在虚假陈述或有虚假陈述嫌疑的上市公司为样本,采用事件研究法,实证考察司法独立性对投资者保护法律实施的影响,以增进国际和国内"投资者法律保护与公司治理"领域的研究积累。选取"1/15 通知"这一事件是因为上市公司对其虚假陈述行为引起的投资者损失承担民事赔偿责任是投资者法律保护的重要内容,而"1/15 通知"的颁布首次为法院受理此类案件打开了大门。我们预期"1/15 通知"及与其相关的民事诉讼法律的实施将会导致本文的样本公司产生或有赔偿义务,进而导致这些公司的股价下跌。但是,当公司最终控制人为地方政府并且这一地方政府是公司虚假陈述案件管辖法院的本地同级政府时,法院的司法独立性可能受到影响,进而这类公司的股价下跌会更少。本文的实证检验结果支持这一预期。我们发现在"1/15 通知"颁布日前后几个交易日内,样本公司的市场反应显著为负;并且与司法相对独立组公司相比,司法相对不独立组公司的负向市场反应程度更小。这些结果表明,投资者倾向于认为"1/15 通知"及与其相关的民事诉讼法律能够得到一定程度的实施,但地方政府对当地法院的影响降低了这些投资者保护法律得到实施的可能性。

本文的主要贡献有以下几个方面。首先,本文基于中国的政治经济制度背景,考察了投资者保护法律得到实施的可能性以及司法独立性对这一可能性的影响,从法律实施的影响因素这一角度丰富和发展了国际上"法与金融"领域的文献。其次,本文的研究表明,在 La Porta et al.(1998,2008)提出的法律渊源因素以外,地方政府对当地法院的影响(可归类为"政治和司法制度因素")也是影响投资者保护法律实施的一个重要因素。再次,本文基于中国股票市场并采用事件研究法,在一定程度上减轻了以往跨国比较文献可能存在的内生性及遗漏变量问题,同时本文所发展的衡量司法独立性的方法也可能对相关研究具有一定参考价值。最后,本文所发现的司法独立性与投资者法律保护之间的矛盾,对如何改进和加强中国股票市场投资者法律保护的实践也有所启发。①

　　需要指出的是,由于采用事件研究法,本文的研究结论实际上是投资者整体对"1/15 通知"及与其相关的民事诉讼法律能否得到实施的看法,而并非这些投资者保护法律真正的实施情况。但本文的研究依然具有重要的理论和现实意义:其一,投资者保护法律要能在公司治理和保护投资者利益上发挥作用,其执行首先必须是可置信的(Pistor et al.,2000),若投资者不信任法律能够得到有效实施,其采用法律方式保护自身利益以及投资股票市场的积极性可能受到影响,进而股票市场的发展也会受到影响;其二,虽然单个投资者在面对"1/15 通知"时可能不够理性,但投资者整体更可能是理性的,换言之,市场反应能够在一定程度上代表"1/15 通知"及与其相关的民事诉讼法律能否得到实施;其三,鉴于直接检验投资者保护法律实施的困难性,本文至少为后续研究提供了市场反应角度的经验证据,并起到"抛砖引玉"的作用,引起更多的学者对中国股票市场投资者保护法律实施的关注和研究。

　　下文的安排是:第二部分介绍中国股票市场投资者法律保护的制度背景,对研究问题进行理论分析,并提出研究假说;第三部分介绍研究方法设计,包括对样本、数据和检验模型的说明以及变量描述性统计;第四部分给出实证分析结果和解释;最后一部分是研究结论和启示。

二、制度背景、理论分析和研究假说

(一)中国股票市场投资者法律保护简介

　　中国股票市场自 20 世纪 90 年代初设立以来,法制建设不断完善。沈艺峰等(2004)认为,以《中华人民共和国公司法》(简称"公司法")和《中华人民共和国证券法》(简称"证券法")的生效为界,我国中小投资者法律保护实践可以分为以下三个阶段:第一阶段是中小投资者法律保护的初级阶段(1994 年 7 月以前),第二阶段是中小投资者法律保护的发展阶段(1994 年 7 月至 1998 年 7 月),第三阶段是中小投资者法律保护的完善阶段(1999 年 7 月以后)。其中,《公司法》和《证券法》分别于 1994 年 7 月和 1999 年 7 月生效,这两部法律奠定了中国股票市场的法律框架。然而,在法制建设取得显著成绩的同时,投资者法律保护不力几乎也

---

① 　即使 Pistor and Xu(2005a、2005b)认为中国股票市场的行政治理安排在一定程度上代替了法律治理发挥了保护投资者的功能,他们也承认行政治理主要在股市发展的早期发挥作用,从中长期来讲,还是需要转向正式的法律治理。

是公认的事实。在股票市场发展过程中,虚假陈述、利润操纵、包装上市、大股东侵占、内幕交易等侵害中小股东利益的违法违规案件不断出现,典型的如琼民源、红光实业、东方锅炉、大庆联谊、蓝田股份、银广夏、科龙电器等。这说明虽然法律法规不少,但是未能有效执行。

2001 年 9 月 21 日,"银广夏"事件后,最高人民法院发布《关于涉证券民事赔偿案件暂不予受理的通知》,规定"内幕交易、欺诈、操纵市场等行为引起的民事赔偿案件,暂不予受理",其理由是,"受目前立法及司法条件的局限,尚不具备受理及审理这类案件的条件"。2002 年 1 月 15 日,在各方努力下,最高人民法院发布《关于受理证券市场因虚假陈述引发的民事侵权纠纷案件有关问题的通知》,其中规定,"人民法院对证券市场因虚假陈述引发的民事侵权赔偿纠纷案件,凡符合《中华人民共和国民事诉讼法》规定受理条件的,自本通知下发之日起予以受理"。这是我国证券法律实施的一大进步,也是中国股票市场有史以来首次明确要求法院受理虚假陈述民事赔偿案件的司法解释。这一通知为虚假陈述民事赔偿诉讼打开了大门,通知发布后,各地法院陆续开始受理此类案件。[①] 2003 年 1 月 9 日,最高人民法院发布《关于审理证券市场因虚假陈述引发的民事赔偿案件的若干规定》,在"1/15 通知"的基础上,对审理虚假陈述民事赔偿案件做出了更为详细的规定。本文关注的问题是,"1/15 通知"这一首次明确要求法院受理虚假陈述民事赔偿案件的司法解释,能够促使法院独立、有效地受理、审判和执行这类案件吗? 地方政府对司法独立性可能的干扰将对"1/15 通知"及与其相关的民事诉讼法律实施产生怎样的影响?[②]下文对此进行理论分析,并提出研究假说。

(二)司法独立性与投资者保护法律实施

中国自 1978 年以来的改革既包括经济体制上的改革,也包括政治体制上的改革。但是,相对于经济体制改革中整体渐进与局部推进相结合的劈波斩浪之势,政治体制改革力度不足、整体滞后,确为不争的事实(胡舒立,2007)。作为政治体制改革组成部分的司法体制改革,同样不容乐观。Lubman(1999)认为,中国

---

① 在 2002 年以前,曾有投资者对上市公司虚假陈述行为提起民事赔偿诉讼,例如 1998 年 12 月 4 日,上海股民姜顺珍一纸诉状将红光实业告上法庭,但 1999 年 4 月该案被上海浦东新区人民法院驳回,不予受理。此后,另有 11 名投资者继续起诉,也是屡次被法院驳回。直到 2002 年"1/15 通知"颁布后,各地法院才开始受理虚假陈述民事赔偿案件。据统计,从"1/15 通知"颁布到 2003 年年底的期间里,共有十余家上市公司的虚假陈述民事赔偿案件被法院受理。

② 本文将有关投资者保护的法律、法规、规章、司法解释、司法行政文件统称为"投资者保护法律",因此本文所研究的"投资者保护法律实施",是指"1/15 通知"及与其相关的《中华人民共和国民事诉讼法》有关条款的实施。

的法院系统犹如一只"笼中鸟"(bird in cage),倾向于随着政府工作重心的变化而将法律适用于特定的政策界限内。Potter(1999)和 MacNeil(2002)观察到中国的法院具有保护国家利益的传统,而缺乏判决私人诉讼的经验。Gong(2004)指出,中国的法院在运行中类似于政治系统中的一个行政单位,其权威来自国家而非法律,是否运用法律系统来解决争端以及运用到何种程度均取决于政府的决策。Clarke et al.(2006)认为,中国的法律系统总体上是政府实现对社会控制的一个工具,法律制度仍然是政府而不是公民或诉讼人导向的。最高人民法院前院长肖扬(2002)在 2002 年 12 月 9 日的一场演讲中则指出,中国现行司法制度存在三大问题:一是司法权力地方化,即人民法院的产生、法官任免、司法经费等都在同级地方政府控制之下,导致了司法权力的地方化;二是审判活动行政化,即长期以来,法院在一些重要环节上没有按照司法工作方式从事审判活动,反而借用了行政工作方式处理案件、管理审判工作,有的地方把法官当作行政官员管理,加剧了审判活动的行政化;三是法官职业大众化,相当一部分法官职业化程度不够。这些问题导致的结果是,中国的法院难以独立、有效地开展司法活动(贺卫方,2003)。[①]

　　从投资者法律保护来看,上述中国转型期的法治环境意味着,即使"1/15 通知"规定"人民法院对证券市场因虚假陈述引发的民事侵权赔偿纠纷案件,凡符合《中华人民共和国民事诉讼法》规定受理条件的,自本通知下发之日起予以受理",地方法院也不一定能够独立有效地受理、审判、执行这些案件。[②] 尤其是中国的分权式改革在充分调动起地方政府发展地方经济积极性的同时,也加剧了地方政府竞争全国性资源、保护其下属企业利益的动机(Qian and Weingast,1996;Cao et al.,1999;Poncet,2005;王永钦等,2007)。在虚假陈述民事赔偿案件的受理、审判和执行环节中,地方政府为了支持和保护其下属企业,防止"国有资产流失",可能利用其对当地同级法院的人事、财政、福利等控制权,干扰投资者保护法律的有效实施[③]。而"1/15 通知"规定虚假陈述民事赔偿案件的管辖采用"原告就被告

[①] 这与 La Porta et al.(2004)对全球 71 个国家司法独立性排名的结果也是一致的。在他们根据最高法院法官任期、行政诉讼判决最高级别法官任期、是否判例法三个方面衡量司法独立性的排名中,中国是司法独立性最低的几个国家之一。

[②] 根据活跃在虚假陈述民事赔偿诉讼一线的维权律师宣伟华的统计,自虚假陈述民事赔偿开闸以来的 20 例上市公司因虚假陈述而遭到投资者的起诉中,多个案件经历了"起诉不受理"、"受理不开庭"、"开庭不判决"或"判决不执行"的遭遇。

[③] 在我国股票市场上,一些地方政府为了实现其自身的社会性目标,往往帮助和纵容下属上市公司弄虚作假、违法违规,例如利用行政手段为不合格企业谋取融资资格、协助国有大股东通过关联交易转移上市公司资源、协助上市公司进行盈利操纵、出具虚假文件和证明等;一旦问题暴露,则利用自身的特殊地位干扰监管部门和司法部门的调查和处罚行为(刘鸿儒等,2003)。

原则",即"对凡含有上市公司在内的被告提起的民事诉讼,由上市公司所在直辖市、省会市、计划单列市或经济特区中级人民法院管辖",这也为地方政府干扰法律实施提供了便利。另一方面,当被告为政府或具有政治联系的当事人时,法院往往难以保持中立(La Porta et al.,2004)。换言之,当地方政府控制的上市公司因为虚假陈述被起诉时,这些公司可能会利用其政府背景对当地法院施加压力以影响诉讼结果。

因此,我们预期当公司最终控制人为地方政府并且这一地方政府是公司虚假陈述案件管辖法院的本地同级政府时,法院的司法独立性可能受到影响。我们将这类公司称为"司法相对不独立组",而将其他公司称为"司法相对独立组"。由于"1/15通知"及与其相关的民事诉讼法律的实施将会导致存在虚假陈述或有虚假陈述嫌疑的公司产生或有赔偿义务,进而导致这些公司股价下跌,因此这些公司中司法相对不独立的公司股价下跌应该更少。① 据此,我们提出如下研究假说。

研究假说:在存在虚假陈述或有虚假陈述嫌疑的上市公司中,司法相对不独立组公司比司法相对独立组公司在"1/15通知"颁布日前后期间的负向市场反应程度更小。

三、研究方法设计

(一) 样本选择和数据来源

1. 关于事件的选取

本文采用事件研究法对研究假说进行实证检验,而事件研究的基本要求是,要有一个相对来说突发性的重要事件,因此我们首先需要确定这一事件。根据上文的介绍,在"银广夏"事件后,最高人民法院分别于2001年9月21日、2002年1月15日、2003年1月9日发布了三份有关证券民事赔偿的文件。第一份文件明确规定"内幕交易、欺诈、操纵市场等行为引起的民事赔偿案件,暂不予受理",并且其理由是"受目前立法及司法条件的局限,尚不具备受理及审理这类案件的条件"。而在此之前,股票市场也从来没有受理证券民事诉讼的先例。1999年7月1日《证券法》生效后,曾有股民依据《证券法》对红光实业和亿安科技相关责

---

① 虽然上市公司遭受虚假陈述民事赔偿诉讼也可能促使其改进公司治理,避免将来出现类似情况,但这种公司治理的改进效应是一种长期效应,这种长期效应折现后对当前股价的影响应当比较小。换言之,在短期内,上市公司遭受诉讼的赔偿效应将超过其公司治理改进效应。因此,可以合理地认为,事件日附近的股价反应主要是由赔偿效应引起的。

任人提起民事诉讼,但法院将这些诉讼案一一驳回、不予受理(陈志武,2003)。因此,这份文件不大会改变投资者原有的"证券民事诉讼不予受理"预期。

第二份文件则大为不同,它规定"人民法院对证券市场因虚假陈述引发的民事侵权赔偿纠纷案件(简称'虚假陈述民事赔偿案件'),凡符合《中华人民共和国民事诉讼法》规定受理条件的,自本通知下发之日起予以受理"。这份文件是中国股票市场有史以来首次要求法院受理虚假陈述民事赔偿案件的规定,为虚假陈述民事赔偿诉讼打开了大门。文件中还规定了虚假陈述民事赔偿案件的定义、受理的前置条件、诉讼时效、诉讼方式、管辖法院等,具有可操作性。并且,虽然在第一份文件颁布后各方努力推动最高人民法院出台受理证券民事诉讼的司法解释,但第一份文件中"暂不予受理"的理由是"受目前立法和司法条件的局限",而这一局限在短期内应当难以改变,因此,投资者很难预期到最高人民法院短期内会颁布受理证券民事诉讼的规定,尤其是很难预期到第二份文件会在第一份文件颁布后不到四个月就颁布。而第三份文件仅是在第二份文件的基础上,对受理虚假陈述民事赔偿案件做出了更详细的规定,并未改变第二份文件的基本内容。根据以上分析,在三份文件中,第二份文件最可能改变投资者预期,因而最适合作为本文所要研究的事件。因此,本文将"1/15 通知"的颁布作为研究事件,并以其颁布日2002 年 1 月 15 日作为事件日。①

2. 样本公司的确定

由于"1/15 通知"规定"虚假陈述民事赔偿案件的诉讼时效为两年,从中国证监会及其派出机构对虚假陈述行为做出处罚决定之日起计算",因此投资者可以起诉的是那些因虚假陈述被中国证监会及其派出机构处罚且处罚日期在 2002 年1 月 15 日之前不足两年的公司。但这样的公司在"1/15 通知"颁布之时仅有 20家左右(我们将这类公司称为"存在虚假陈述的公司"),不足以构成实证检验的样本。为此,我们进一步补充那些明显有虚假陈述嫌疑的公司为样本。具体来说,我们将以下三类公司确定为有虚假陈述嫌疑:①因虚假陈述被沪深证券交易所公开谴责且谴责日期在 2002 年 1 月 15 日之前不足两年的公司,这类公司将来可能被证监会处罚,进而被投资者起诉;②不包含于第(1)类,但最近两个年度的财务报告(即 1999 或 2000 年度财务报告)被出具保留、否定或拒绝意见的公司,这类公司最近两个年度之一的财务报告被审计师认为存在较为严重的问题,因而存在

---

① 由于上市公司年报通常在下一年的 2 月份才开始披露,我们预期年报披露对事件日周围期间累计异常收益率计算的影响较小。

虚假陈述嫌疑；③不包含于第（1）类和第（2）类，但因虚假陈述被中国证监会及其派出机构处罚且处罚日期在 2002 年 1 月 15 日之后不足两年的公司，这类公司虽然在 2002 年 1 月 15 日之后被中国证监会及其派出机构处罚，但由于从调查到处罚通常需要两年左右时间，在 2002 年 1 月 15 日这类公司涉及被调查的信息可能已为投资者所知，进而可能会预期到后面的处罚结果。虽然在 2002 年 1 月 15 日投资者无法起诉嫌疑公司，但将来这些公司可能会被证监会处罚，进而被起诉。我们将上述三类嫌疑公司分别称为"虚假陈述嫌疑公司 A"、"虚假陈述嫌疑公司 B"、"虚假陈述嫌疑公司 C"。

根据以上界定存在虚假陈述以及虚假陈述嫌疑公司的标准，我们找到 141 家最终样本公司，其中存在虚假陈述和有虚假陈述嫌疑的公司分别为 19 家和 122 家。详细的样本选择和分布情况见表 1，各类公司的定义见表 1 下方的注释。如最高人民法院前院长肖扬（2002）所指出，在中国的司法体制下，人民法院的产生、法官任免、司法经费等都在同级地方政府控制之下，导致了司法权力的地方化。因此，当公司最终控制人为地方政府并且这一地方政府是公司虚假陈述案件管辖法院的本地同级政府时，法院的司法独立性可能受到影响。我们把这类公司界定为"司法相对不独立组"，把其他公司界定为"司法相对独立组"。根据"1/15 通知"的规定，各直辖市、省会市、计划单列市或经济特区中级人民法院为一审管辖法院；地域管辖采用原告就被告原则。这样，这些中级人民法院所在地的同级省会市、计划单列市或经济特区市政府控制的并且注册于其管辖范围内的公司，即为"司法相对不独立组"公司。① 由于直辖市中级人民法院没有对应的同级政府，我们将直辖市所属各级政府控制的公司归类为"司法相对独立组"公司。②

从表 1 可见，在 141 家样本公司中，存在虚假陈述的公司以及虚假陈述嫌疑公司 A、B、C 所占比例分别是 14%、31%、46%、9%，即样本公司主要由存在虚假陈述的公司和虚假陈述嫌疑公司 A、B、C 组成。此外，司法相对独立组和司法相对不独立组的公司分别为 112 家和 29 家，说明样本公司中司法相对独立的公司所占比重较大。在司法相对独立组中，存在虚假陈述的公司以及虚假陈述嫌疑公司 A、B、C 所占比例分别是 14%、31%、45%、10%；在司法相对不独立组中，存在

---

① 这里我们仅考虑一审法院的管辖，是因为一审法院的受理、判决和执行对投资者来说最为重要。

② 直辖市的法院在组织机构上具有特殊性。根据《中华人民共和国宪法》《中华人民共和国人民法院组织法》规定，直辖市的法院分为三级，分别是高级人民法院、中级人民法院和基层人民法院。但三级法院只对应两级政府，即高级人民法院对应直辖市政府，基层人民法院对应直辖市所属县、区政府，中级人民法院不依附于行政区划，而是划片设立。我们将在后文进行稳健性分析，以检验不同设定对研究结果的影响。

虚假陈述的公司以及虚假陈述嫌疑公司 A、B、C 所占比例分别是 10%、31%、52%、7%。可以看出,两组公司中各类虚假陈述或虚假陈述嫌疑公司的分布结构比较类似。总体上,样本分布未见异常。

表 1　样本选择和分布

样本组成情况	司法相对独立组		司法相对不独立组		合计	
	公司个数	比例	公司个数	比例	公司个数	比例
存在虚假陈述的公司	16	14%	3	10%	19	14%
虚假陈述嫌疑公司 A	35	31%	9	31%	44	31%
虚假陈述嫌疑公司 B	50	45%	15	52%	65	46%
虚假陈述嫌疑公司 C	11	10%	2	7%	13	9%
最终样本	112	100%	29	100%	141	100%

注:存在虚假陈述的公司 = 因虚假陈述被中国证监会及其派出机构处罚且处罚日期在 2002 年 1 月 15 日之前不足两年的公司。

　　虚假陈述嫌疑公司 A = 不包含于"存在虚假陈述的公司",同时因虚假陈述被沪深证券交易所公开谴责且谴责日期在 2002 年 1 月 15 日之前不足两年的公司。

　　虚假陈述嫌疑公司 B = 不包含丁"存在虚假陈述的公司"和"虚假陈述嫌疑公司 A",同时最近两个年度的财务报告(即 1999 或 2000 年度财务报告)被出具保留、否定或拒绝意见的公司。

　　虚假陈述嫌疑公司 C = 不包含于"存在虚假陈述的公司"、"虚假陈述嫌疑公司 A"和"虚假陈述嫌疑公司 B",同时因虚假陈述被中国证监会及其派出机构处罚且处罚日期在 2002 年 1 月 15 日之后不足两年的公司。

　　最终样本 = 存在虚假陈述的公司 + 虚假陈述嫌疑公司 A + 虚假陈述嫌疑公司 B + 虚假陈述嫌疑公司 C。

　　司法相对不独立组 = 公司最终控制人为地方政府并且这一地方政府是公司虚假陈述案件管辖法院的本地同级政府。

　　司法相对独立组 = 司法相对不独立组以外的公司。

　　3. 数据来源

　　本文使用的证监会处罚和交易所谴责数据、上市公司审计意见和财务数据、事件日前后期间的股票价格数据来自 CSMAR 中国股票市场研究数据库。我们对这些数据进行了抽样检查,并将其中的证监会处罚和交易所谴责数据与证监会和沪深交易所网站公布的相应数据进行了校对。参照夏立军、方轶强(2005)的做法,公司最终控制人类型数据根据上市公司 2001 年度报告中"股本变动及股东情况"逐一整理而得,上市公司年度报告来自中国证监会指定信息披露网站——巨潮资讯网。若公司最终控制人可确定为自然人、职工持股会、民营企业、村办集体企业、街道集体企业、乡镇一级的政府部门、乡镇集体企业或外资企业,则认定其为非政府控制。若最终控制人为县级或县级以上各级政府的有关政府机构,则认定其为相应级别的政府控制。对于部属院校控制的上市公司和地方政府教育部门所属院校控制的上市公司,分别认定其为中央政府控制和相应级别的地方政府控制。结合上市公司最终控制人类型和级别、公司详细注册地址以及中国直辖市、省会市、计划单列市和经济特区名单,我们可以判断出公司是否属于上文定义的"司法相对不独立组"。公司所在地区法律环境数据来自樊纲、王小鲁(2003)编制的 2000 年度中国各省、直辖市、自治区市场化相对进程指标的分指标"中介发育和法律制度环境"。

(二)检验模型和变量设定

根据上文的分析,我们采用以下模型来检验研究假说:

$$\text{Market Response} = \beta_0 + \beta_1 * \text{JudiDep} + \beta_2 * \text{LCourt} + \beta_3 * \text{LocalGov} +$$
$$\beta_4 * \text{CenGov} + \beta_5 * \text{LegIndex} + \beta_6 * \text{SUSP\_A} +$$
$$\beta_7 * \text{SUSP\_B} + \beta_8 * \text{SUSP\_C} + \beta_9 * \text{TOP1} +$$
$$\beta_{10} * \text{SIZE} + \beta_{11} * \text{LOSS} + \beta_{12} * \text{DR} + \sum_{i=1}^{5} + \varepsilon$$

其中,β_0 为截距,$\beta_1 \sim \beta_{12}$ 为系数,ε 为残差。模型中各变量的含义如下:

1. 因变量

Market Response 代表"1/15 通知"颁布前后的市场反应。为了增强研究结果的可靠性,我们分别采用三种方法来计算 Market Response:

(1)直接采用个股累计收益率,计算公式是 $\text{Market Response} = \prod_{t=-n}^{n}(1 + R_{it})$。其中,$R_{it}$ 为公司 i 在第 t 个交易日的股票收益率,$-n$ 和 n 分别表示事件日(2002 年 1 月 15 日)之前和之后的交易日天数。

(2)采用等权平均市场收益率调整后的个股累计异常收益率,计算公式是

Market Response $= \left(\prod_{t=-n}^{n}(1+R_{it})-1\right) - \left(\prod_{t=-n}^{n}(1+R_{emt})-1\right)$。其中，$R_{emt}$ 为第 t 个交易日深圳和上海 A 股市场综合计算的等权平均市场收益率，其他符号和方法(1)中的定义相同。

(3)采用总市值加权平均市场收益率调整后的个股累计异常收益率，计算公式是 Market Response $= \left(\prod_{t=-n}^{n}(1+R_{it})-1\right) - \left(\prod_{t=-n}^{n}(1+R_{vmt})-1\right)$。其中，$R_{vmt}$ 为第 t 个交易日深圳和上海 A 股市场综合计算的总市值加权平均市场收益率，其他符号和方法(1)中的定义相同。

为了表述方便，我们分别将方法(1)、(2)、(3)计算出的 Market Response 标记为 RCR($-n$，n)、ECAR($-n$，n)、VCAR($-n$，n)。我们将报告 n 为 1、2、5 天的情况，对应的($-n$，n)期间的交易日个数分别为 3、5、11。由于样本公司数量相对市场整体的上市公司数量较小[①]，虽然市场整体中已包含了样本公司，但我们预计上述方法(2)、(3)计算个股累计异常收益率的方法不会导致较大偏差。由于因变量是连续变量，检验模型采用 OLS 回归方法进行分析。

2.测试变量

JudiDep 是衡量司法独立性的哑变量，当公司 2001 年年末最终控制人为地方政府并且这一地方政府是公司虚假陈述案件管辖法院的本地同级政府时，该变量取值为 1(代表司法相对不独立)，否则为 0(代表司法相对独立)。更详细的界定参见上述"样本选择和数据来源"的"样本公司的确定"部分。如 Potter(1999)、MacNeil(2002)、陈志武(2003)、夏立军、方轶强(2005)、Firth et al.(2007)等以往研究所注意到的，中国的法院在司法活动中存在地方保护主义倾向和保护国有企业和国家利益的倾向。在 JudiDep 取值为 1 时，这两种倾向可能同时存在，并且作为公司最终控制人的地方政府有能力影响虚假陈述案件管辖法院的司法活动，因此法院的司法独立性容易受到影响。根据研究假说，这一变量应与因变量正相关。

3.控制变量

LCourt 代表公司 2001 年年末是否受本地法院管辖，若管辖法院与公司在同一地区，则 LCourt 取值为 1，否则为 0。这一变量用以控制法院的地方保护主义倾向对市场反应的影响。根据"1/15 通知"的规定，"各直辖市、省会市、计划单列

---

① 根据中国证监会的统计资料，在"1/15 通知"颁布日所在的 2002 年 1 月底附近，沪深两市已发行 A 股的上市公司总数超过 1140 家。

市或经济特区中级人民法院为一审管辖法院;地域管辖采用原告就被告原则",
"对凡含有上市公司在内的被告提起的民事诉讼,由上市公司所在直辖市、省会
市、计划单列市或经济特区中级人民法院管辖"。因此当公司注册于直辖市、省会
市、计划单列市或经济特区的行政管辖范围内时,若投资者对公司进行虚假陈述
民事赔偿起诉,则案件系由本地法院管辖,否则为外地法院管辖。例如,当公司注
册于浙江省宁波市这一计划单列市的行政管辖范围内时,管辖法院为宁波市中级
人民法院,此时对公司来说系本地法院管辖;而当公司注册于黑龙江省大庆市或
江苏省苏州市的行政管辖范围内时,因大庆市或苏州市并非直辖市、省会市、计划
单列市或经济特区,管辖法院分别应为黑龙江省省会哈尔滨市和江苏省省会南京
市的中级人民法院,此时对公司来说系外地法院管辖。

LocalGov 和 CenGov 分别代表公司 2001 年年末最终控制人为地方政府和
中央政府。若公司最终被地方政府控制,那么 LocalGov 取值为 1,否则为 0;若最
终被中央政府控制,那么 CenGov 取值为 1,否则为 0。我们加入这两个变量以控
制法院保护国有企业和国家利益的倾向对市场反应的影响。由于样本公司一共
包括非政府控制、地方政府控制和中央政府控制这三类,LocalGov 和 CenGov 的
回归系数分别代表其与非政府控制情况的比较。

LegIndex 代表公司所在省、自治区或直辖市整体的法律环境,其取值来自樊
纲、王小鲁(2003)编制的 2000 年度中国各省、直辖市、自治区市场化相对进程指
标的分指标"中介发育和法律制度环境"数据。[①] 由于在法律环境越好的地区,
"1/15 通知"及与其相关的民事诉讼法律更可能得到实施,预计这一变量与因变
量负相关。

SUSP_A、SUSP_B、SUSP_C 用来控制虚假陈述嫌疑公司的嫌疑类型对因变
量的影响。这些变量的取值方法如下:若公司属于"虚假陈述嫌疑公司 A",那么
SUSP_A 取值为 1,否则为 0;若公司属于"虚假陈述嫌疑公司 B",那么 SUSP_B
取值为 1,否则为 0;若公司属于"虚假陈述嫌疑公司 C",则 SUSP_C 取值为 1,否
则为 0。由于样本公司包括"存在虚假陈述的公司",以上这些变量的回归系数代
表着各类嫌疑公司相对"存在虚假陈述的公司"的情况,因此预计回归系数符号
为正。

TOP1 是年末第一大股东持股比例,用以控制股权集中度对市场反应的影

---

① 他们编制的各地区市场化相对进程指数及其分指数已被广泛用于研究中国各地区的制度环境,并显
　示出较好的解释力,如夏立军、方轶强(2005)、孙铮等(2005)、曾庆生、陈信元(2006)、方军雄(2006)、夏
　立军、陈信元(2007)、Wang et al.(2008)等。

响。SIZE 是公司 2001 年末总资产的自然对数值；LOSS 代表公司盈利状况，当公司 2001 年度净利润小于零时，LOSS 取值为 1，否则为 0；DR 是公司 2001 年末资产负债率，即负债与总资产的比率。由于规模小、风险大和财务状况差的公司在遇到坏消息时，股价下跌可能更为严重，因此在模型中纳入 SIZE、LOSS、DR 这三个控制变量。虽然"1/15 通知"颁布时上市公司 2001 年度报告基本都未披露，但因为 2001 年度已经结束，投资者应能预期到 2001 底的公司规模、是否亏损以及资产负债率情况，我们这里采用 2001 而不是 2000 年度指标。IND 是行业哑变量，样本公司一共涉及金融、公用事业、房地产、综合、工业、商业这六个行业，因此设置五个行业哑变量以控制行业因素对市场反应的影响。为简略起见，实证分析结果表中未报告这些行业变量的回归系数。

四、实证分析结果及解释

本文的实证分析分为三个部分：首先给出检验模型的变量描述性统计以及有关的均值 T 检验和中位数检验结果；接着报告司法相对独立组和司法相对不独立组在"1/15 通知"颁布前后市场反应的描述性图表；最后对司法独立性与"1/15 通知"颁布前后市场反应的关系进行多元回归分析。以下依次述之。

（一）变量描述性统计及均值、中位数差异检验

表 2 给出了检验模型的变量描述性统计、因变量的均值与零差异的 T 检验结果以及各变量均值和中位数在司法相对独立组和司法相对不独立组两组间的差异检验结果。

首先，从"全部样本公司"的因变量中可见，在"1/15 通知"颁布日前后各 1、2、5 个交易日的期间里，3 种方法衡量的市场反应与零差异的 T 检验结果显示，市场反应都显著为负。在自变量上，LCourt 的均值为 0.70，说明 70% 的样本公司由本地法院管辖；LocalGov 和 CenGov 的均值分别为 0.61 和 0.17，说明样本公司中由地方政府和中央政府控制的公司分别为 61% 和 17%；LOSS 的均值为 0.33，说明样本公司中有 33% 的公司 2001 年度亏损，这也意味着存在虚假陈述或有虚假陈述嫌疑的公司业绩较差。其次，从"司法相对独立组"的因变量可见，与零差异的 T 检验都显示，各变量均值显著为负。各因变量和自变量的均值与"全部样本公司"中的各因变量和自变量均值较为接近，这主要是由于司法相对独立组公

司占全部样本公司的比例较高。

　　最后,从"司法相对不独立组"可见,因变量与零差异的 T 检验显示,仅有未经市场收益调整的个股累计收益率以及"1/15 通知"颁布日前后各 5 个交易日的总市值加权平均市场收益调整后个股累计异常收益率显著小于 0。所有因变量的均值都大于"司法相对独立组"对应的因变量均值,并且两组因变量均值差异的 T 检验结果显示,除了"1/15 通知"颁布日前后各 5 个交易日的情况外,"司法相对不独立组"的因变量均值都显著大于"司法相对独立组"的因变量均值。除了"1/15通知"颁布日前后各 5 个交易日的市场收益调整后个股累计异常收益率,其他因变量的中位数都大于"司法相对独立组"对应的因变量中位数,并且两组因变量中位数差异检验显示,在"1/15 通知"颁布日前后各 2 个交易日的情况下,"司法相对不独立组"的因变量中位数均显著大于"司法相对独立组"的因变量中位数。这些结果与研究假说相符,即对司法相对不独立组的公司来说,"1/15 通知"及与其相关的民事诉讼法律得到实施的可能性更小。在自变量上,两组公司差别主要体现在 LCourt、LocalGov 和 CenGov 上,即与"司法相对独立组"中 63% 的公司由本地法院管辖、51% 和 21% 的公司分别由地方政府和中央政府控制不同,"司法相对不独立组"中所有公司均由本地法院管辖并由地方政府控制。

　　综上,表 2 显示,样本公司在"1/15 通知"颁布日前后各 1、2、5 个交易日的市场反应显著为负,并且与司法相对独立组公司相比,司法相对不独立组公司的负向市场反应程度更小。这些结果支持本文的研究假说。

表 2　变量描述性统计及均值、中位数差异检验结果

	全部样本公司					司法相对独立组					司法相对不独立组				
	均值	标准差	最小值	中位数	最大值	均值	标准差	最小值	中位数	最大值	均值	标准差	最小值	中位数	最大值
Panel A：因变量															
RCR(−1，1)	−0.06 ***	0.05	−0.08	−0.03	0.07	−0.06 ***	0.05	−0.18	−0.06	0.06	−0.04 #，***	0.05	−0.14	−0.04	0.07
ECAR(−1，1)	−0.01 ***	0.05	−0.03	0.02	0.12	−0.01 ***	0.05	−0.13	−0.01	0.11	0.01 ##	0.05	−0.09	0.00	0.12
VCAR(−1，1)	−0.02 ***	0.05	−0.04	0.01	0.11	−0.02 ***	0.05	−0.14	−0.02	0.10	0.00 ##	0.05	−0.10	−0.01	0.11
RCR(−2，2)	−0.14 ***	0.06	−0.18	−0.11	0.03	−0.14 ***	0.06	−0.29	−0.16	0.03	−0.12 #，***	0.06	−0.24	−0.13 ‖‖	0.00
ECAR(−2，2)	−0.02 ***	0.06	−0.05	0.02	0.15	−0.02 ***	0.06	−0.17	−0.03	0.15	0.00 ##	0.06	−0.11	−0.01 ‖‖‖	0.12
VCAR(−2，2)	−0.03 ***	0.06	−0.07	0.00	0.13	−0.04 ***	0.06	−0.19	−0.05	0.13	−0.02 #	0.06	−0.13	−0.03 ‖‖	0.10
RCR(−5，5)	−0.25 ***	0.11	−0.32	−0.19	−0.01	−0.26 ***	0.11	−0.52	−0.26	−0.01	−0.23 ***	0.11	−0.39	−0.25	−0.01
ECAR(−5，5)	−0.05 ***	0.11	−0.12	0.01	0.19	−0.06 ***	0.11	−0.31	−0.06	0.19	−0.03	0.11	−0.19	−0.07	0.19
VCAR(−5，5)	−0.09 ***	0.11	−0.16	−0.03	0.15	−0.10 ***	0.11	−0.35	−0.10	0.15	−0.07 ***	0.11	−0.22	−0.11	0.15
Panel B：控制变量															
LCourt	0.70	0.46	0	1	1	0.63	0.49	0	1	1	1 ###	0	1	1‖‖‖	1
LocalGov	0.61	0.49	0	1	1	0.51	0.50	0	1	1	1 ###	0	1	1‖‖‖	1
CenGov	0.17	0.38	0	0	1	0.21	0.41	0	0	1	0 ###	0	0	0‖‖‖	0
LegIndex	5.88	1.22	4.93	6.98	7.97	5.85	1.24	2.62	5.72	7.97	6.03	1.11	3.21	5.81	7.29

（续表）

	全部样本公司					司法相对独立组					司法相对不独立组				
	均值	标准差	最小值	中位数	最大值	均值	标准差	最小值	中位数	最大值	均值	标准差	最小值	中位数	最大值
SUSP_A	0.31	0.46	0	1	1	0.31	0.47	0	0	1	0.31	0.47	0	0	1
SUSP_B	0.46	0.50	0	1	1	0.45	0.50	0	0	1	0.52	0.51	0	1	1
SUSP_C	0.09	0.29	0	0	1	0.10	0.30	0	0	1	0.07	0.26	0	0	1
TOP1	0.40	0.17	0.28	0.52	0.82	0.39	0.17	0.02	0.39	0.82	0.42	0.19	0.13	0.41	0.74
SIZE	20.67	0.97	20.15	21.18	24.03	20.65	1.02	17.39	20.72	24.03	20.78	0.79	19.22	20.70	22.02
LOSS	0.33	0.47	0	0	1	0.30	0.46	0	0	1	0.41	0.50	0	0	1
DR	0.82	1.52	0.41	0.70	13.56	0.81	1.64	0.10	0.55	13.56	0.88	0.95	0.29	0.56	4.52

注：全部样本公司为141个，其中"司法相对独立组"和"司法相对不独立组"公司分别为112和29个。 *，** 和 *** 分别表示因变量均值与零差异 T 检验在0.10、0.05和0.01以下水平统计显著（双尾检验）。!、!! 和 !!! 分别表示"司法相对独立组"与"司法相对不独立组""均值差异 T 检验在0.10、0.05和0.01以下水平统计显著（双尾检验）。#、## 和 ### 分别表示"司法相对独立组"与"司法相对不独立组""中位数差异异检验在0.10、0.05和0.01以下水平统计显著（双尾检验）。

（二）"1/15 通知"颁布日前后市场反应的描述性图表分析

接下来,我们拉长事件窗口,对"1/15 通知"颁布前后各 30 个交易日的市场反应做描述性图表分析,以进一步比较司法相对不独立组与司法相对独立组公司市场反应的差异。图 1、图 2 和图 3 分别给出了采用未经市场收益调整的个股累计收益率、等权平均市场收益调整后个股累计异常收益率以及总市值加权平均市场收益调整后个股累计异常收益率这三种方法衡量市场反应的情况。图中样本公司数均为 141,其中"司法相对独立组"和"司法相对不独立组"样本公司数分别为 112 和 29。

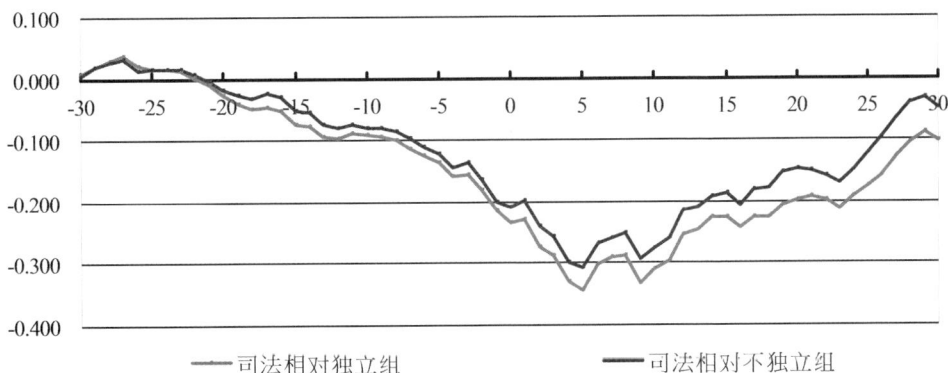

图 1　司法独立性与平均累计个股收益率

从图 1 可以看出,在"1/15 通知"颁布日前后各 30 个交易日的期间里,未经市场收益调整的个股累计收益率平均值呈现先下降后上升的趋势,说明市场对"1/15 通知"的颁布存在提前反应和过度反应的情况。在颁布日前后大约各 5 个交易日的期间里,未经市场收益调整的个股累计收益率平均值下降最为明显,并且无论在司法相对独立组还是司法相对不独立组中,都是在颁布日后 5 个交易日附近达到 30%以下的最低值,说明"1/15 通知"颁布日附近的市场反应较为明显。对比两组公司可见,在颁布日前后各 30 个交易日的期间里,司法相对不独立组公司的负向市场反应程度更小。不过,因为未扣除市场收益,这一市场反应不能很好地代表"1/15 通知"颁布的真实市场反应。

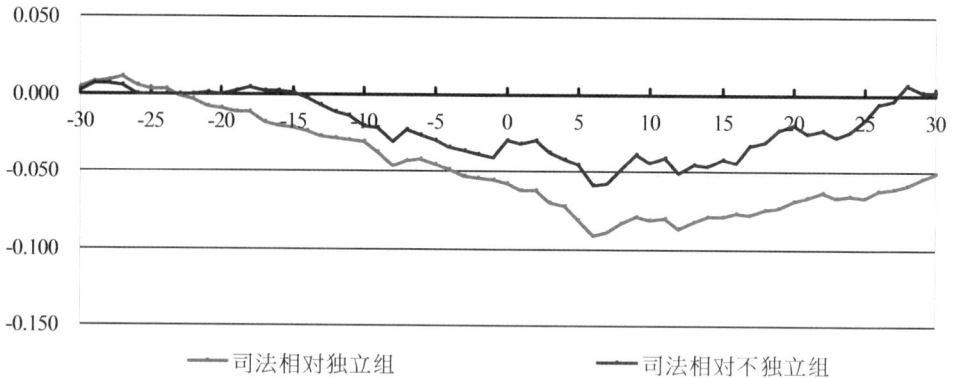

图 2　司法独立性与平均累计异常收益率（等权平均市场收益调整）

　　从图 2 可见，在"1/15 通知"颁布日前后各 30 个交易日的期间里，等权平均市场收益调整后个股累计异常收益率平均值同样呈现先下降后上升的趋势，并且与图 1 类似，颁布日前后各 5 个交易日的期间里市场反应较为明显。值得注意的是，司法相对独立组中，等权平均市场收益调整后个股累计异常收益率平均值的最低值在−9%附近，而司法相对不独立组中的最低值在−6%附近，并且在颁布日后第 30 个交易日，司法相对独立组的这一平均值大约为−5%，而司法相对不独立组的这一平均值大约为 0。这说明司法相对不独立组公司的负向市场反应程度更小，并且这种负向市场反应随着时间推移而消失。

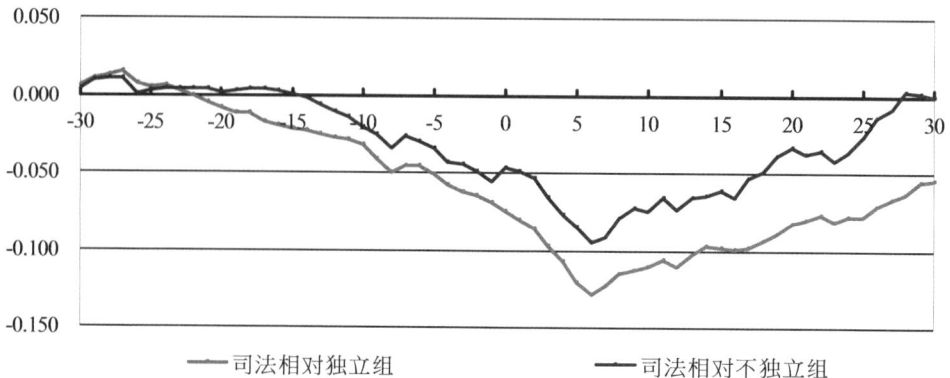

图 3　司法独立性与平均累计异常收益率（市值加权市场收益调整）

　　图 3 的结果和图 2 类似。所不同的是，图 3 中总市值加权平均市场收益调整后个股累计异常收益率的平均值低于图 2，并且司法相对独立组和司法相对不独

立组中这一平均值的最低值分别在－13%附近和－9%附近。这可能是因为图 3 采用总市值加权平均市场收益调整,而市值较大的公司在"1/15 通知"颁布日附近的股票收益率可能大于市值较小的公司。

总体上,图 1、图 2 和图 3 的结果显示,在"1/15 通知"颁布日前后期间,样本公司存在明显的负向市场反应,尤其是在颁布日前后各 5 个交易日的期间里。而司法相对不独立组公司的负向市场反应程度更小。这些结果进一步支持本文的研究假说。

(三)司法独立性与"1/15 通知"颁布日前后市场反应的多元回归分析

表 3、表 4 和表 5 分别给出了司法独立性与"1/15 通知"颁布日前后各 1、2、5 个交易日市场反应的最小二乘法多元回归分析。每个表中分别给出了控制和不控制 LCourt、LocalGov 和 CenGov 这三个变量的情况,以及采用未经市场收益调整的个股累计收益率、等权平均市场收益调整后个股累计异常收益率、总市值加权平均市场收益调整后个股累计异常收益率这三种方法衡量市场反应的情况。

从表 3 可见,在采用不同方法衡量市场反应时以及在控制或不控制 LCourt、LocalGov 和 CenGov 这三个变量时,JudiDep 的回归系数都在 0.024 左右,并且在 0.05 以下水平统计显著。这说明在控制了其他变量的影响后,司法相对不独立组公司比司法相对独立组公司的负向市场反应程度小 2.4%左右。这一结果支持本文的研究假说。LCourt、LocalGov 和 CenGov 的回归系数都不显著,说明投资者不认为法院的地方保护主义倾向或者保护国有企业和国家利益的倾向各自会损害"1/15 通知"及与其相关的民事诉讼法律的实施。其他控制变量的回归系数符号都和预期相符,例如 LegIndex 与因变量负相关,虽然不显著,但一定程度上说明在法律环境好的地区,"1/15 通知"及与其相关的民事诉讼法律更可能得到实施;SUSP_A、SUSP_B 和 SUSP_C 都和因变量正相关,说明虚假陈述嫌疑公司的赔偿可能性或赔偿规模小于存在虚假陈述的公司;TOP1 与因变量正相关,可能是因为大股东持股比例越高,其越有动机和能力阻止投资者保护法律的实施,或者是因为大股东持股比例越高,其帮助公司缓解虚假陈述民事诉讼问题的动机和能力越强;SIZE 与因变量正相关,而 LOSS 和 DR 与因变量负相关,说明在面临坏消息时,大规模公司的负向市场反应程度更小,而亏损公司和财务状况差的公司负向市场反应程度更大。

表 3 司法独立性与"1/15 通知"颁布日前后各 1 个交易日的市场反应

自变量及参数	预测符号	因变量					
		RCR(−1,1)	ECAR(−1,1)	VCAR(−1,1)	RCR(−1,1)	ECAR(−1,1)	VCAR(−1,1)
截距	?	−0.141	−0.112	−0.117	−0.146	−0.116	−0.122
		(1.49)	(1.18)	(1.24)	(1.50)	(1.19)	(1.25)
JudiDep	+	0.024 **	0.023 **	0.023 **	0.026 **	0.024 **	0.024 **
		(2.54)	(2.46)	(2.47)	(2.29)	(2.13)	(2.16)
LCourt	+				−0.005	−0.003	−0.004
					(0.46)	(0.34)	(0.36)
LocalGov	+				−0.002	−0.001	−0.001
					(0.17)	(0.06)	(0.08)
CenGov	+				−0.002	−0.002	−0.002
					(0.15)	(0.17)	(0.17)
LegIndex	−	−0.003	−0.003	−0.003	−0.003	−0.003	−0.003
		(0.97)	(1.00)	(1.00)	(0.77)	(0.79)	(0.79)
SUSP_A	+	0.014	0.014	0.014	0.014	0.014	0.014
		(1.11)	(1.11)	(1.10)	(1.12)	(1.11)	(1.11)
SUSP_B	+	0.014	0.014	0.014	0.015	0.015	0.015
		(1.19)	(1.20)	(1.20)	(1.22)	(1.19)	(1.20)
SUSP_C	+	0.027	0.031 *	0.030 *	0.028	0.032 *	0.031 *
		(1.63)	(1.89)	(1.86)	(1.66)	(1.89)	(1.86)
TOP1	+	0.035	0.034	0.034	0.037	0.035	0.036
		(1.51)	(1.44)	(1.45)	(1.52)	(1.44)	(1.45)
SIZE	+	0.003	0.004	0.003	0.003	0.004	0.004
		(0.59)	(0.77)	(0.74)	(0.62)	(0.78)	(0.76)
LOSS	−	−0.011	−0.009	−0.009	−0.011	−0.009	−0.009
		(1.22)	(1.01)	(1.04)	(1.19)	(0.99)	(1.02)
DR	−	−0.006 **	−0.006 **	−0.006 **	−0.006 **	−0.006 **	−0.006 **
		(2.24)	(2.22)	(2.23)	(2.15)	(2.15)	(2.16)
行业哑变量	?	控制	控制	控制	控制	控制	控制
样本数		141	141	141	141	141	141
模型 F 值		3.19	3.18	3.18	2.55	2.54	2.54
Adj-R^2		0.17	0.17	0.17	0.15	0.15	0.15

注:括号内为 T 值的绝对值,* 、** 和 *** 分别表示在 0.10、0.05 和 0.01 以下水平统计显著。

　　表 4 和表 5 的结果与表 3 非常类似。不同的是,表 4 和表 5 中 JudiDep 的回归系数更大,说明在"1/15 通知"颁布日前后各 2、5 个交易日的期间里,司法相对不独立组与司法相对独立组公司市场反应的差异更为明显。此外,表 4 和表 5 中部分控制变量上的结果也与表 3 稍有差别,但基本和预期相符。

　　综合表 3、表 4 和表 5 的结果可见,在"1/15 通知"颁布日前后各 1、2、5 个交易日的期间里,无论是采用未经市场收益调整的个股累计收益率还是市场收益调整后个股累计异常收益率衡量市场反应,司法相对不独立组公司的负向市场反应程度都显著小于司法相对独立组公司,并且两者差别达到 2% 至 5% 左右。这些结果支持本文的研究假说,说明法院司法的相对不独立降低了"1/15 通知"及与其相关的民事诉讼法律得到实施的可能性。

表 4　司法独立性与"1/15 通知"颁布日前后各 2 个交易日的市场反应

自变量及参数	预测符号	因变量					
		RCR(−2,2)	ECAR(−2,2)	VCAR(−2,2)	RCR(−2,2)	ECAR(−2,2)	VCAR(−2,2)
截距	?	−0.197	−0.099	−0.114	−0.215 *	−0.114	−0.129
		(1.63)	(0.81)	(0.94)	(1.73)	(0.91)	(1.04)
JudiDep	+	0.026 **	0.026 **	0.026 **	0.033 **	0.032 **	0.032 **
		(2.16)	(2.13)	(2.13)	(2.29)	(2.21)	(2.22)
LCourt	+				0.003	0.004	0.004
					(0.23)	(0.31)	(0.30)
LocalGov	+				−0.019	−0.018	−0.018
					(1.39)	(1.28)	(1.29)
CenGov	+				−0.008	−0.007	−0.007
					(0.43)	(0.37)	(0.38)
LegIndex	−	−0.005	−0.005	−0.005	−0.005	−0.006	−0.006
		(1.05)	(1.10)	(1.09)	(1.12)	(1.19)	(1.18)
SUSP_A	+	0.008	0.010	0.010	0.009	0.011	0.011
		(0.53)	(0.65)	(0.63)	(0.57)	(0.68)	(0.67)
SUSP_B	+	0.012	0.014	0.014	0.013	0.015	0.015
		(0.80)	(0.94)	(0.93)	(0.86)	(0.97)	(0.96)
SUSP_C	+	0.020	0.023	0.023	0.023	0.026	0.025
		(0.94)	(1.09)	(1.07)	(1.06)	(1.19)	(1.18)

（续表）

自变量及参数	预测符号	因变量					
		RCR(−2,2)	ECAR(−2,2)	VCAR(−2,2)	RCR(−2,2)	ECAR(−2,2)	VCAR(−2,2)
TOP1	+	0.046	0.046	0.046	0.055	0.053	0.053
		(1.54)	(1.52)	(1.52)	(1.75)	(1.70)	(1.70)
SIZE	+	0.002	0.003	0.003	0.003	0.004	0.004
		(0.33)	(0.51)	(0.49)	(0.52)	(0.68)	(0.66)
LOSS	−	−0.039***	−0.037***	−0.038***	−0.040***	−0.039***	−0.039***
		(3.47)	(3.34)	(3.36)	(3.57)	(3.43)	(3.45)
DR	−	−0.004	−0.003	−0.003	−0.004	−0.003	−0.003
		(0.99)	(0.91)	(0.92)	(0.99)	(0.92)	(0.93)
行业哑变量	?	控制	控制	控制	控制	控制	控制
样本数		141	141	141	141	141	141
模型 F 值		3.02	2.97	2.98	2.58	2.51	2.52
Adj-R^2		0.16	0.15	0.15	0.15	0.15	0.15

注:括号内为 T 值的绝对值,* 、** 和 *** 分别表示在 0.10、0.05 和 0.01 以下水平统计显著。

表 5　司法独立性与"1/15 通知"颁布日前后各 5 个交易日的市场反应

自变量及参数	预测符号	因变量					
		RCR(−5,5)	ECAR(−5,5)	VCAR(−5,5)	RCR(−5,5)	ECAR(−5,5)	VCAR(−5,5)
截距	?	−0.467**	−0.273	−0.313	−0.512**	−0.322	−0.361
		(2.31)	(1.35)	(1.54)	(2.49)	(1.56)	(1.75)
JudiDep	+	0.046**	0.044**	0.044**	0.054**	0.052**	0.052**
		(2.30)	(2.19)	(2.20)	(2.29)	(2.19)	(2.20)
LCourt	+				0.015	0.018	0.017
					(0.73)	(0.85)	(0.83)
LocalGov	+				−0.039	−0.042	−0.041
					(1.73)	(1.83)	(1.82)
CenGov	+				−0.027	−0.030	−0.030
					(0.90)	(0.98)	(0.97)
LegIndex	−	−0.009	−0.008	−0.008	−0.010	−0.010	−0.010
		(1.23)	(1.15)	(1.16)	(1.29)	(1.24)	(1.25)
SUSP_A	+	−0.012	−0.002	−0.003	−0.010	−0.001	−0.002

（续表）

自变量 及参数	预测 符号	因变量					
		RCR(−5,5)	ECAR(−5,5)	VCAR(−5,5)	RCR(−5,5)	ECAR(−5,5)	VCAR(−5,5)
		(0.43)	(0.09)	(0.13)	(0.39)	(0.04)	(0.08)
SUSP_B	+	−0.007	0.002	0.001	−0.008	0.001	−0.000
		(0.27)	(0.09)	(0.05)	(0.30)	(0.03)	(0.01)
SUSP_C	+	0.012	0.022	0.021	0.017	0.027	0.026
		(0.33)	(0.62)	(0.59)	(0.48)	(0.77)	(0.74)
TOP1	+	−0.009	0.001	−0.001	0.008	0.019	0.017
		(0.17)	(0.01)	(0.01)	(0.16)	(0.36)	(0.34)
SIZE	+	0.014	0.014	0.014	0.017	0.017	0.017
		(1.40)	(1.38)	(1.38)	(1.65)	(1.64)	(1.65)
LOSS	−	−0.113 ***	−0.124 ***	−0.122 ***	−0.118 ***	−0.129 ***	−0.127 ***
		(6.09)	(6.63)	(6.58)	(6.28)	(6.84)	(6.79)
DR	−	−0.005	−0.002	−0.002	−0.005	−0.003	−0.003
		(0.74)	(0.35)	(0.39)	(0.80)	(0.42)	(0.46)
行业哑变量	?	控制	控制	控制	控制	控制	控制
样本数		141	141	141	141	141	141
模型 F 值		5.22	5.63	5.59	4.49	4.87	4.84
Adj-R^2		0.28	0.30	0.30	0.29	0.31	0.30

注：括号内为 T 值的绝对值，*、** 和 *** 分别表示在 0.10、0.05 和 0.01 以下水平统计显著。

（四）稳健性分析

我们对表 3、表 4 和表 5 的结果进行了一系列稳健性分析，以考察研究结论的稳健性。在稳健性分析中，采用的是包含所有控制变量的检验模型。稳健性分析内容和结果汇总在表 6 中，但为了简洁起见，未报告各控制变量的结果。下面依次介绍稳健性分析结果。

（1）分别对存在虚假陈述和有虚假陈述嫌疑的公司进行检验。结果显示，对存在虚假陈述的公司单独回归时，JudiDep 都与因变量正相关且 T 值都超过 1.00。虽然大部分情况下在统计上不显著，但 JudiDep 都与因变量的正相关关系仍然存在，而结果不显著可能是因为样本量仅有 19 个，使得变量的估计结果有偏。在对虚假陈述嫌疑公司单独回归时，JudiDep 都与因变量正相关且都在 0.10 以下水平统计显著。

表 6　各稳健性分析中检测变量的回归结果

稳健性分析序号和内容	因变量								
	RCR(−1,1)	ECAR(−1,1)	VCAR(−1,1)	RCR(−2,2)	ECAR(−2,2)	VCAR(−2,2)	RCR(−5,5)	ECAR(−5,5)	VCAR(−5,5)
1　虚假陈述公司 (N=19)	0.050 (1.08)	0.047 (0.99)	0.048 (1.01)	0.149 (1.84)	0.137 (1.52)	0.139 (1.55)	0.203 * (1.96)	0.194 (1.64)	0.195 (1.68)
虚假陈述嫌疑公司 (N=117)	0.027 ** (2.32)	0.026 ** (2.16)	0.026 ** (2.18)	0.032 ** (2.16)	0.031 ** (2.12)	0.031 ** (2.13)	0.041 * (1.67)	0.044 * (1.80)	0.044 * (1.79)
2　配对样本调整收益 (N=136)	0.015 (0.95)	0.013 (0.83)	0.013 (0.85)	0.017 (0.81)	0.017 (0.81)	0.017 (0.82)	0.064 * (1.96)	0.067 ** (2.06)	0.067 ** (2.05)
3　剔除直辖市公司 (N=118)	0.031 ** (2.58)	0.028 ** (2.30)	0.028 ** (2.34)	0.038 ** (2.41)	0.037 ** (2.30)	0.037 ** (2.31)	0.058 ** (2.23)	0.059 ** (2.27)	0.059 ** (2.27)
4　上级政府控制变量 (N=141)	0.019 (1.37)	0.015 (1.10)	0.016 (1.14)	0.023 (1.32)	0.021 (1.20)	0.021 (1.21)	0.055 * (1.89)	0.055 * (1.90)	0.055 * (1.91)
下级政府控制变量 (N=141)	0.030 ** (2.49)	0.029 ** (2.47)	0.029 ** (2.47)	0.037 ** (2.43)	0.036 ** (2.37)	0.036 ** (2.38)	0.048 * (1.90)	0.046 * (1.81)	0.046 * (1.82)
5　JudiDep * LegIndex (N=141)	−0.016 * (1.73)	−0.015 (1.65)	−0.015 * (1.66)	−0.002 (0.17)	−0.002 (0.15)	−0.002 (0.15)	−0.017 (0.89)	−0.017 (0.90)	−0.017 (0.90)
6　事件前后交易日数 (N=141) 〔RCR(−10,10), ECAR(−10,10), VCAR(−10,10), RCR(−15,15), ECAR(−15,15), VCAR(−15,15), RCR(−30,30), ECAR(−30,30), VCAR(−30,30)〕	0.054 ** (2.46)	0.052 ** (2.42)	0.052 ** (2.41)	0.038 * (1.87)	0.034 * (1.67)	0.035 * (1.72)	0.056 ** (2.17)	0.052 ** (2.01)	0.053 ** (2.06)

注:N 为样本数,回归系数下方括号内为 T 值的绝对值。*、** 和 *** 分别表示在 0.10、0.05 和 0.01 以下水平统计显著。为了简洁,表中仅给出了检验模型中 JudiDep(稳健性分析 1、2、3、4、6)或 JudiDep * LegIndex(稳健性分析 5)上的回归分析结果,而未报告各控制变量上的结果。

附表：变量 Pearson 相关系数

	RCR(−1,1)	ECAR(−1,1)	VCAR(−1,1)	RCR(−2,2)	ECAR(−2,2)	VCAR(−2,2)	RCR(−5,5)	ECAR(−5,5)	VCAR(−5,5)
ECAR(−1,1)	0.994	1.000							
	0.000								
VCAR(−1,1)	0.995	1.000	1.000						
	0.000	0.000							
RCR(−2,2)	0.752	0.747	0.748	1.000					
	0.000	0.000	0.000						
ECAR(−2,2)	0.753	0.752	0.753	0.998	1.000				
	0.000	0.000	0.000	0.000					
VCAR(−2,2)	0.753	0.752	0.752	0.998	1.000	1.000			
	0.000	0.000	0.000	0.000	0.000				
RCR(−5,5)	0.490	0.495	0.494	0.757	0.758	0.758	1.000		
	0.000	0.000	0.000	0.000	0.000	0.000			
ECAR(−5,5)	0.489	0.490	0.490	0.765	0.766	0.766	0.988	1.000	
	0.000	0.000	0.000	0.000	0.000	0.000	0.000		
VCAR(−5,5)	0.490	0.491	0.491	0.765	0.766	0.766	0.990	1.000	1.000
	0.000	0.000	0.000	0.000	0.000	0.000	0.000	0.000	
JudiDep	0.181	0.176	0.177	0.136	0.137	0.137	0.104	0.091	0.093
	0.032	0.037	0.036	0.108	0.106	0.106	0.220	0.284	0.275
LCourt	−0.080	−0.072	−0.073	−0.025	−0.016	−0.017	0.012	0.022	0.021
	0.344	0.396	0.388	0.765	0.851	0.842	0.890	0.793	0.803

（续表）

	RCR(−1,1)	ECAR(−1,1)	VCAR(−1,1)	RCR(−2,2)	ECAR(−2,2)	VCAR(−2,2)	RCR(−5,5)	ECAR(−5,5)	VCAR(−5,5)
LocalGov	0.184	0.192	0.191	0.075	0.083	0.082	0.047	0.043	0.044
	0.029	0.022	0.023	0.377	0.328	0.333	0.582	0.610	0.606
CenGov	−0.091	−0.094	−0.094	−0.027	−0.026	−0.026	0.009	0.011	0.011
	0.283	0.266	0.268	0.752	0.764	0.764	0.916	0.894	0.895
LegIndex	−0.168	−0.172	−0.172	−0.170	−0.170	−0.170	−0.159	−0.146	−0.148
	0.046	0.042	0.042	0.044	0.044	0.044	0.060	0.083	0.080
SUSP_A	0.038	0.033	0.033	−0.012	−0.010	−0.010	−0.042	−0.034	−0.035
	0.655	0.700	0.695	0.886	0.904	0.903	0.622	0.694	0.684
SUSP_B	−0.030	−0.037	−0.036	0.022	0.024	0.024	0.018	0.032	0.030
	0.726	0.664	0.671	0.799	0.776	0.777	0.832	0.711	0.721
SUSP_C	0.104	0.133	0.129	0.043	0.051	0.050	0.034	0.033	0.033
	0.219	0.116	0.126	0.616	0.546	0.556	0.687	0.698	0.699
TOP1	0.226	0.220	0.221	0.210	0.210	0.210	0.088	0.102	0.101
	0.007	0.009	0.009	0.013	0.013	0.013	0.300	0.227	0.235
SIZE	0.197	0.204	0.203	0.162	0.173	0.172	0.245	0.248	0.248
	0.019	0.015	0.016	0.054	0.040	0.042	0.004	0.003	0.003
LOSS	−0.165	−0.151	−0.153	−0.333	−0.325	−0.326	−0.525	−0.549	−0.547
	0.050	0.075	0.071	0.000	0.000	0.000	0.000	0.000	0.000
DR	−0.288	−0.289	−0.289	−0.221	−0.219	−0.219	−0.262	−0.240	−0.242
	0.001	0.001	0.001	0.009	0.009	0.009	0.002	0.004	0.004

注：样本公司数为141。每个变量包括两行数值。上行为Pearson相关系数，下行为P值。

附表：变量 Pearson 相关系数（续）

	JudiDep	LCourt	LocalGov	CenGov	LegIndex	SUSP_A	SUSP_B	SUSP_C	TOP1	SIZE	LOSS
LCourt	0.331 0.000	1.000									
LocalGov	0.407 0.000	0.020 0.817	1.000								
CenGov	−0.231 0.006	0.130 0.125	−0.566 0.000	1.000							
LegIndex	0.060 0.479	0.321 0.000	−0.132 0.118	0.250 0.003	1.000						
SUSP_A	−0.002 0.982	−0.097 0.253	−0.058 0.497	0.143 0.091	0.045 0.593	1.000					
SUSP_B	0.057 0.499	0.260 0.002	0.098 0.248	−0.154 0.069	0.178 0.035	−0.623 0.000	1.000				
SUSP_C	−0.041 0.630	−0.060 0.476	0.054 0.526	−0.014 0.870	−0.230 0.006	−0.215 0.011	−0.295 0.000	1.000			
TOP1	0.051 0.552	0.019 0.825	0.191 0.023	0.084 0.325	−0.055 0.520	0.160 0.058	−0.085 0.317	−0.056 0.508	1.000		
SIZE	0.055 0.514	0.047 0.583	0.143 0.090	0.170 0.044	0.115 0.174	0.147 0.083	−0.039 0.650	−0.035 0.682	0.315 0.000	1.000	
LOSS	0.095 0.262	0.089 0.292	−0.064 0.452	−0.114 0.179	0.114 0.178	0.054 0.527	−0.097 0.251	0.092 0.278	−0.097 0.254	−0.219 0.009	1.000
DR	0.020 0.813	0.150 0.077	−0.063 0.455	−0.094 0.269	0.170 0.044	−0.092 0.278	0.115 0.173	−0.065 0.446	−0.173 0.040	−0.415 0.000	0.306 0.000

注：样本公司数为 141，每个变量包括两行值，上行为 Pearson 相关系数，下行为 P 值。

（2）找出和样本公司相同注册省份、相同行业并且规模最为接近的配对公司，采用这些配对公司在"1/15通知"颁布日前后的累计股票收益率调整后的样本公司累计异常股票收益率衡量市场反应。结果显示，在以事件日前后1或2个交易日的市场反应做因变量时，JudiDep与因变量正相关但不显著；在以事件日前后5个交易日的市场反应做因变量时，JudiDep与因变量显著正相关。这可能是因为投资者对样本公司和配对公司的差异有一个逐步识别的过程，也可能是因为配对公司在事件日附近发生的某些重要事项引起因变量计算的噪音。

（3）考虑直辖市中级人民法院的特殊性，将注册于上海、北京、天津、重庆的样本公司剔除。结果显示，JudiDep与因变量都显著正相关。

（4）在模型中增加一个控制变量，代表"公司最终控制人为地方政府并且这一地方政府是管辖法院的上级政府"或"公司最终控制人为地方政府并且这一地方政府是管辖法院的下级政府"的哑变量。未同时加入这两个变量是因为避免共线性问题。结果显示，在加入前一个控制变量时，JudiDep与部分因变量的正相关关系不显著，而在加入后一个控制变量时，其与所有因变量显著正相关。两种情况下的结果差异意味着管辖法院的下级政府相对管辖法院的上级政府来说更可能对司法独立性有一定负面影响。这可能与管辖法院通常和其下级政府在同一城市而可能受其影响有关。

（5）在检验模型中加入JudiDep与LegIndex的交叉项JudiDep * LegIndex，以检测地区法治环境的改善是否有助于减轻司法不独立对投资者保护法律实施的负面影响。如果能够减轻这一负面影响的话，JudiDep * LegIndex应当与因变量显著负相关。结果显示，JudiDep * LegIndex与因变量都负相关，但仅在事件日前后一个交易日的市场反应检验中在0.10附近统计显著。这说明，总体上，地区法治环境的改善仅能微弱地降低司法不独立对投资者保护法律实施的负面影响，增强样本公司的赔偿效应。

（6）对"1/15通知"颁布日前后各10、15、30个交易日的市场反应进行检验。结果显示，JudiDep与因变量都显著正相关。这说明研究结果受事件日附近时间窗口长短的选择影响较小。

综上，表6的结果显示，虽然在部分稳健性分析中，检测变量JudiDep的结果变弱甚至不显著，但在所有情况下JudiDep都与因变量正相关，并且在多数情况下JudiDep与因变量显著正相关。这说明本文的研究结论具有良好的稳健性。

五、研究结论和启示

　　近年来,大量文献强调了投资者法律保护对公司治理和金融市场发展的重要性,但少有研究考察投资者法律保护受什么因素影响。给定投资者法律保护是重要的,那么更进一步的问题是,哪些因素影响到一国的投资者法律保护程度? 本文利用 2002 年 1 月 15 日最高人民法院颁布《关于受理证券市场因虚假陈述引发的民事侵权纠纷案件有关问题的通知》(简称"1/15 通知")这一事件,以那些存在虚假陈述或有虚假陈述嫌疑的上市公司为样本,采用事件研究法,实证考察了司法独立性对投资者保护法律实施的影响。由于当公司最终控制人为地方政府并且这一地方政府是公司虚假陈述案件管辖法院的本地同级政府时,法院的司法独立性容易受到影响,我们据此将样本公司分为司法相对独立和相对不独立的两组公司。我们发现,在"1/15 通知"颁布日前后几个交易日内,样本公司的市场反应显著为负,这意味着投资者预期"1/15 通知"的颁布将导致这些公司产生或有赔偿义务;而与司法相对独立组公司相比,司法相对不独立组公司的负向市场反应程度更小。研究结果表明,投资者倾向于认为,"1/15 通知"及与其相关的民事诉讼法律能够得到一定程度的实施,但地方政府对当地法院的影响降低了这些投资者保护法律得到实施的可能性。

　　本义的研究结果不仅增进了国际和国内在"投资者法律保护与公司治理"研究领域的文献积累,同时也对如何加强和改进中国股票市场的投资者法律保护提供了启发。本文的理论启示是,在以往文献所强调的法律渊源因素以外,内生于政治和司法制度因素的司法独立性也是影响转型经济国家投资者法律保护的重要因素。本文的政策启示是,加强投资者法律保护,不仅需要关注立法层面,更需要关注司法层面,尤其是地方政府对当地法院的影响。从中国股票市场来看,未来需要应对的挑战是如何实现从行政治理向正式的法律治理的转型,解决"全国性股票市场却地方化司法"的问题。在司法体制短期内难以做出重大改革的情况下,有关决策部门或可考虑在全国范围内设立一些独立于地方政府的证券特别法庭以专门受理、审判和执行证券民事诉讼案件。

参考文献

陈志武.司法独立,判例法与股东权益保护[N].南方周末,2003-2-27.

樊纲,王小鲁.中国市场化指数——各地区市场化相对进程报告(2001 年)[M].北京:经济科学出版社,2003.

方军雄.市场化进程与资本配置效率的改善[J].经济研究,2006(05):50-61.

贺卫方.中国的法院改革与司法独立——一个参与者的观察与反思[EB/OL].(2003-12-22)[2008-10-8].http://news.sina.com.cn/c/2003-12-22/153332439365.shtml.

胡舒立.中共十七大之公众期待[N].财经,2007-10-15.

刘鸿儒,等.探索中国资本市场发展之路——理论创新推动制度创新[M].北京:中国金融出版社,2003.

沈艺峰,许年行,杨熠.我国中小投资者法律保护历史实践的实证检验[J].经济研究,2004(09):32-41.

孙铮,刘凤委,李增泉.市场化程度,政府干预与企业债务期限结构——来自我国上市公司的经验证据[J].经济研究,2005(05):52-63.

王永钦,张晏,章元,等.中国的大国发展道路——论分权式改革的得失[J].经济研究,2007(01):4-16.

夏立军,陈信元.市场化进程,国企改革策略与公司治理结构的内生决定.经济研究,2007(07):82-96.

夏立军,方轶强.政府控制,治理环境与公司价值——来自中国证券市场的经验证据[J].经济研究,2005(05):40-51.

肖扬.肖扬指出中国司法制度三大问题和法院改革八目标[N].中国青年报,2002-12-9.

宣伟华.为什么中国的证券民事赔偿总是美丽的昙花一现[EB/OL].(2006-11-8)[2008-10-8].http://xuanweihua.blog.sohu.com.

曾庆生,陈信元.国家控股,超额雇员与劳动力成本[J].经济研究,2006(5):74-86.

Ali A,Hwang L S. Country-specific factors related to financial reporting and the value relevance of accounting data[J]. Journal of accounting research,2000,38(1):1-21.

Cao Y,Qian Y,Weingast BR. From federalism,Chinese style to privatization,Chinese style[J]. Economics of transition,1999,7(1):103-131.

Choi J H,Wong T J. Auditors' governance functions and legal environments:an international investigation[J]. Contemporary accounting research,2007,24(1):13-46.

Claessens S,Djankov S,Fan J P H,et al. Disentangling the incentive and entrenchment effects of large shareholdings[J]. The journal of finance,2002,57(6):2741-2771.

Claessens S,Djankov S,Lang L H P. The separation of ownership and control in East Asian corporations[J]. Journal of financial economics,2000,58(1-2):81-112.

Clarke D C,Murrell P,Whiting S H. The role of law in China's economic development[M]//Rawski T,Brandt L. China's great economic transformation. Cambridge:Cambridge University Press,2008.

Defond M L，Hung M. Investor protection and corporate governance：evidence from worldwide CEO turnover[J]. Journal of accounting research，2004，42(2)：269-312.

DeFond M，Hung M，Trezevant R. Investor protection and the information content of annual earnings announcements：international evidence［J］. Journal of accounting and economics，2007，43(1)：37-67.

Firth M，Rui O M，Wu W F. The effects of political connections and state ownership on corporate litigation in China[J]. Journal of law and economics，2011，54(3)：573-607.

Gong T. Dependent judiciary and unaccountable judges：judicial corruption in contemporary China[J]. China review，2004：33-54.

Haw I M，Hu B B，Hwang L S，et al. Ultimate ownership，income management，and legal and extra-legal institutions[J]. Journal of accounting research，2004，42(2)：423-462.

Hung M. Accounting standards and value relevance of financial statements：an international analysis[J]. Journal of accounting and economics，2000，30(3)：401-420.

Kumar K，Rajan R，Zingales L. What determines firm size？［R］. CEPR discussion papers，1999.

La Porta R，Lopez-de-Silanes F，Shleifer A. Corporate ownership around the world[J]. The journal of finance，1999，54(2)：471-517.

La Porta R，Lopez-de-Silanes F，Shleifer A. The economic consequences of legal origins [J]. Journal of economic literature，2008，46(2)：285-332.

La Porta R，Lopez-de-Silanes F，Pop-Eleches C，et al. Judicial checks and balances[J]. Journal of political economy，2004，112(2)：445-470.

La Porta R，Lopez-de-Silanes F，Shleifer A，et al. Legal determinants of external finance[J]. The journal of finance，1997，52(3)：1131-1150.

La Porta R，Lopez-de-Silanes F，Shleifer A，et al. Law and finance[J]. Journal of political economy，1998，106(6)：1113-1155.

La Porta R，Lopez-de-Silanes F，Shleifer A，et al. Investor protection and corporate governance[J]. Journal of financial economics，2000a，58(1-2)：3-27.

La Porta R，Lopez-de-Silanes F，Shleifer A，et al. Agency problems and dividend policies around the world[J]. The journal of finance，2000b，55(1)：1-33.

La Porta R，Lopez-de-Silanes F，Shleifer A，et al. Investor protection and corporate valuation[J]. The journal of finance，2002，57(3)：1147-1170.

Leuz C，Nanda D，Wysocki P. Investor protection and earnings management：an international comparison[J]. Journal of financial economics，2003，69(3)：505-527.

Lubman S B. Bird in a cage：legal reform in China after Mao[M]. Redwood city：Stanford University Press，1999.

MacNeil I. Adaptation and convergence in corporate governance：the case of Chinese listed companies[J]. Journal of corporate law studies，2002，2(2)：289 - 344.

Nenova T. The value of corporate voting rights and control：a cross-country analysis[J]. Journal of financial economics，2003，68(3)：325 - 351.

Pistor K，Raiser M，Gelfer S. Law and finance in transition economies[J]. Economics of transition，2000，8(2)：325 - 368.

Pistor K，Xu C. Governing stock markets in transition economies：lessons from China [J]. American law and economics review，2005，7(1)：184 - 210.

Pistor K，Xu C. Governing emerging stock markets：legal vs administrative governance[J]. Corporate governance：an international review，2005，13(1)：5 - 10.

Poncet S. A fragmented China：measure and determinants of Chinese domestic market disintegration[J]. Review of international economics，2005，13(3)：409 - 430.

Potter P B. The Chinese legal system：continuing commitment to the primacy of state power[J]. The China quarterly，1999，159：673 - 683.

Qian Y Y，Weingast B R. China's transition to markets：market-preserving federalism，Chinese style[J]. The journal of policy reform，1996，1(2)：149 - 185.

Wang Q，Wong T J，Xia L J. State ownership, the institutional environment，and auditor choice：evidence from China[J]. Journal of accounting and economics，2008，46(1)：112 - 134.

Wurgler J. Financial markets and the allocation of capital [J]. Journal of financial economics，2000，58(1 - 2)：187 - 214.

Zingales L. The value of the voting right：a study of the Milan stock exchange experience [J]. The review of financial studies，1994，7(1)：125 - 148.

▶作者感谢国家自然科学基金(70772101)、国家社会科学基金(06BJY016)、教育部人文社会科学重点研究基地重大项目(05JJD630028)、上海高校选拔培养优秀青年教师科研专项基金及上海财经大学"211 工程"三期重点学科建设项目的资助;并感谢匿名审稿人、Charles J. P. Chen、Kevin Chen、Zhiwu Chen、Joseph Fan、T. J. Wong、陈超、陈冬华、陈钊、方军雄、洪剑峭、李远鹏、李增泉、刘峰、罗炜、吕长江、陆铭、聂辉华、伍利娜、吴联生、吴溪、徐浩萍、许年行、徐晓东、原红旗、张奇峰、张翼、周红以及《中国会计学刊》创刊会(2007)、北京大学会计研究论坛(2007)、复旦大学会计论坛(2008)、复旦大学中国经济研究中心"现代经济学系列讲座"(2009)参与学者的宝贵意见。文中的错误和不足由作者负责。

司法改革与股市发展
——中国股市能够无"法"而治吗?*

内容提要：好的股市促进创新、创业和经济发展，对于中国经济转型升级，好的股市尤其重要。好的股市离不开充分保护投资者权益的法律系统（立法、执法、司法）。中国股市在司法缺失的情况下，借助强有力的行政治理，取得惊人发展，但这种模式在股市发展到一定规模和阶段后不可持续，司法上位是建立好的股市的必然要求。近年来，中国股市司法制度建设取得显著进展，但仍有司法地方化等不少问题需要改进，司法的独立性和有效性有待加强。设立独立于行政区划的专门的证券法院可能是一个重要的改革方向。

关 键 词：司法改革；股市发展；司法独立性

自1990年A股市场正式设立以来，中国股市的发展取得了巨大成就，但依然面临许多深层问题亟待解决。其中，最重要的可能莫过于对投资者合法权益的有效保护。有效的投资者保护不仅关系到中国股市的进一步发展，牵涉到上亿投资者及其家庭的切身利益，同时也关系到中国经济的转型升级和长期发展。在过去的很多年里，中国股票市场的投资者保护主要依靠行政治理，司法机制尤其是民事诉讼机制对投资者的保护非常有限。这一模式在股市发展的早期适应了股市发展的需要，发挥了中国证券监管部门强行政治理能力的优势，但随着股市规模不断扩大，这一模式的缺陷也日益凸显。中国股市的治理未来不仅需要更好地发挥行政监管的功能，同时也特别需要加强司法机制对投资者权益的充分保护。

---

* 本文选自：夏立军：司法改革与股市发展——中国股市能够无"法"而治吗?《会计与经济研究》，2014年9月第5期，第3-9页(本期首篇)。本文是2014年5月上海交通大学中国企业发展研究院"深度思考"论坛演讲的简稿，该演讲被媒体大量报道，演讲和文章指出了中国资本市场上"全国性资本市场与地方化司法"的矛盾，提出了设立专门的证券法院以及废除民事诉讼前置条件等政策建议，这些政策建议已经陆续被中国资本市场其后的司法改革方案如中央深改委2018年决定设立的全国首家专门金融法院——上海金融法院等印证。

一、股市对于经济发展的重要性

早在 1911 年,Schumpeter(1911)就曾指出良好的银行系统对于识别和资助企业家创新活动的作用。但在后来很长一段时间内,金融系统尤其是股市在经济发展中的作用并未引起经济学家的重视。直到 20 世纪 90 年代,以加州大学伯克利分校罗斯·莱文(Ross Levine)教授为代表的金融学家才从理论和实证上论证了金融系统(包括银行和股市)对技术创新和经济发展的重要作用。莱文教授及其合作者的一系列研究发现,一个国家或地区的金融系统发展程度显著地影响了其经济发展,表现为金融系统发展越好的国家或地区,具有更高的长期经济增长率(Levine,1997;Levine and Zervos,1998;Beck et al.,2000)。

其实,这里的逻辑不难理解。技术创新需要资本支撑,而有效的金融系统可以帮助社会闲散的资本与技术高效地结合,从而促进企业和经济发展。然而,虽然银行和股市都是金融系统的重要组成,两者在促进技术创新的作用上却大不相同。技术创新本身具有高风险的特征,其成功与否面临很大的不确定性。从根本上讲,银行代表着债权融资,而债权人并不分享技术创新带来的高额回报,因而我们可以看到,很多创新企业在发展的早期,难以获得银行融资。但股市非常不同,它可以为企业提供股权融资,为股票投资者筛选创新企业和企业家,而股票投资者也能够分享技术创新带来的高额收益,同时通过投资组合承担投资风险。即使有些处于发展早期的小型技术创新企业依赖天使基金、私募基金获得风险投资,但最终这些风险投资也主要通过股市退出。股市在技术创新中相对银行的显著优势已经被 Brown et al.(2013)、Hsu et al.(2014)的实证研究所印证。

有趣的是,早在 1974 年出席联合国大会时,改革开放的总设计师邓小平就意识到股市的重要性。在《邓小平时代》一书中(傅高义,2013),我们可以看到如下描述:

> 星期天,邓小平在纽约的行程有一些空闲时间,手下人问他想做点儿什么,邓小平干脆地说:"去华尔街看看。"在邓小平看来,华尔街不但是美国资本主义的象征,而且是美国经济实力的象征。他具有一种寻找实力的真正来源并理解这种来源的本能。华尔街在星期天都关门歇业,邓小平还是让下属把他带到了那里,这样他至少可以对此地有一个印象。

而在1992年的南巡讲话中，邓小平又一次表明了他对股市的重视。在1992年，新生的中国股市还面临着"姓社姓资"的争议，邓小平一语定乾坤：证券、股市，这些东西究竟好不好，有没有危险，是不是资本主义独有的东西，社会主义能不能用？允许看，但要坚决地试。看对了，搞一两年对了，放开；错了，纠正，关了就是了。

很多的现实案例也足以看出股市的重要性。例如，世界五百强企业几乎都是上市公司，他们发行的股票都在某个和某些股票交易所上市交易。再如，我们今天耳熟能详的创新企业的代表苹果、微软、谷歌、脸书、英特尔、亚马逊、特斯拉等，都是美国纳斯达克上市公司，这些企业无一不是借助股票市场推动企业的创新和发展。中国创新企业的代表、互联网三巨头阿里巴巴、百度、腾讯则分别是美国纽交所、纳斯达克及香港联交所上市公司。目前，中国经济面临转型升级，一方面需要借助技术创新升级传统产业，同时需要大力发展新兴产业，而这都离不开一个高效的股票市场来评估、识别、资助和激励符合未来社会需求的各种创新和创业活动。因此，一个好的股市对中国经济转型升级尤其重要。

二、法律系统与股市发展：理论与证据

如果说股市对于技术创新和经济发展极其重要，那一定是说一个有效率的股市，一个好的股市的作用，而绝不是说任何股市都能发挥这样的作用。实际上，世界各国股市的发展千差万别，良莠不齐。这表明，要把股市发展好并不容易，甚至说非常困难。那么，好的股市从哪里来？

20世纪90年代末以来，世界各国公司治理和股市发展的差异及其背后的深层原因引起了经济和金融学家的关注，以哈佛大学安德烈·施莱弗（Andrei Shleifer）教授等为代表的学者对法律系统与股市发展的关系开展了一系列理论和实证分析（La Porta et al.，1997，1998）。他们的基本结论是，股市的发展（好的股市）离不开有效的公司治理，有效的公司治理取决于一国投资者法律保护程度，而一国投资者法律保护程度根源于法系的差异。具体而言，他们发现普通法系国家的投资者法律保护程度最高，德国和斯堪的纳维亚法系国家的投资者法律保护程度次之，而法国大陆法系国家的投资者法律保护程度最低，由此引起了这些不同法系国家公司治理和股市发展程度的上下之分。

这里的逻辑是，没有好的投资者法律保护，投资者的合法权益将很难保证。

久而久之,投资者意识到这一点,将会退出股市,从而造成股市发展不起来,而那些需要资金的技术创新和企业家则难以有效地获得资本。最终,技术、企业家的才能难以与资本有效地结合。

三、司法缺失与中国股市的发展

然而,中国股市似乎是"法与金融"理论的一个例外。长久以来,中国股市有全国人大的立法(《中华人民共和国公司法》《中华人民共和国证券法》),有中国证监会的执法。但在 2002 年以前,司法几乎未曾介入股市;而在 2002 年以后,司法介入股市的程度也非常有限。换言之,长久以来,司法系统基本上未在保护投资者权益上发挥作用。与此对照的是,在这样的制度环境中,中国股市竟然从无到有、从小到大,取得了巨大发展。截至 2012 年年底,中国股市的股票总市值已经达到 3.7 万亿美元,在全世界紧随美国和欧盟之后。那么,"法与金融"理论错了吗?实际上,中国股市的发展从本质上来讲并未违背"法与金融"的基本结论——好的股市离不开有效的投资者法律保护。

首先,"法与金融"的基本结论说的是一个长期的过程,中国股市虽然发展了二十余年,但相对于世界上很多国家的股市而言,发展时间还很短。其次,中国股市的规模虽然已经排名世界前列,但没有证据表明中国股市已经是一个好的股市,或是一个高效率的股市。第三,中国股市在过去多年里,在立法、执法上取得了很多进展(沈艺峰等,2004),同时证监会独特的审批、审核等管制性制度也在某种程度上弥补了司法的缺失,在一定程度上起到了保护投资者权益的作用(Pistor and Xu,2005)。第四,中国股市在中国经济高速发展的特定阶段发展起来,经济发展形成的大量社会储蓄为股市提供了巨额资金,中国庞大的人口基数又为股市提供了源源不断的新进场投资者。在这样的背景下,即使投资者保护落后,股市规模也可能快速扩张。

然而,随着股市规模进入世界前列,投资者人数过亿,仅仅依靠行政治理的方式必然难以支撑股市的继续发展,尤其是资源配置效率的提高。

首先,监管部门的人力、物力、能力、权限有限,同时监管部门本身的独立性也面临挑战。虽然证监会长期在其主页宣称"保护投资者利益是我们工作的重中之重",但信息欺诈、内幕交易、股价操纵、基金老鼠仓等问题屡见不鲜。行政执法的局限也被证监会主席肖钢 2013 年发表于《求是》的文章《监管执法:资本市场健康发展的基石》所印证。在文中,他提到:

> 行政执法普遍存在案件发现难、取证难、处罚难、执行难的问题……目前资本市场的法规规则超过 1 200 件，问责条款达到 200 多个，但其中无论是刑事责任还是行政、经济责任，没有启用过的条款超过 2/3……近年来证监会每年立案调查 110 件左右，能够顺利作出行政处罚的平均不超过 60 件；每年平均移送涉刑案件 30 多件，最终不了了之的超过一半。

其次，股市在投资者权益保护上的种种问题已经反映在股市的表现上。虽然美国是 2008 年金融危机的主要受害国，但美国的几大股票指数都已创出历史新高；相反，中国经济近年来虽然一直高速增长，但中国股票市场 2008 年大跌后直到现在表现低迷。

第三，监管和司法在投资者保护上的很大不同在于，监管的作用依赖监管部门有限的信息和人员，而司法对股市的监督可以调动起上亿投资者的参与，是对投资者权益的直接保护。只要设计好保护投资者权益的司法机制，上亿投资者出于自身的利益，将会自发地"监督"整个市场，而市场参与主体基于违规收益和风险的权衡，也会自发地约束自身的行为。

第四，如果不充分发挥司法在投资者权益保护中的作用，现有的投资者终会对中国股市失去信心，而新进场投资者也会逐渐枯竭。行政治理模式虽然适应中国股市早期的发展，却无法代替大规模股市中司法机制尤其是民事诉讼机制的作用。

四、中国股市司法：进展、问题及改革

自 2001 年银广夏财务造假案爆发以来，中国股市的司法制度建设取得了显著进展。银广夏案造成大量投资者损失惨重，却因此推动了虚假陈述民事赔偿机制的建立。但在银广夏案爆发后，2001 年 9 月 21 日，最高人民法院发布《关于涉证券民事赔偿案件暂不予受理的通知》，规定"暂不予受理证券民事赔偿案件"。2002 年 1 月 15 日，最高人民法院发布《关于受理证券市场因虚假陈述引发的民事侵权纠纷案件有关问题的通知》（以下简称为"1/15 通知"），规定证券市场因虚假陈述引发的民事侵权纠纷案件"自本通知下发之日起予以受理"。2003 年 1 月 9 日，最高人民法院发布《关于审理证券市场因虚假陈述引发的民事赔偿案件

的若干规定》(以下简称为"1/9 规定"),在"1/15 通知"的基础上,做出了更为详细的规定。2007 年 6 月 11 日,最高人民法院发布《关于审理涉及会计师事务所在审计业务活动中民事侵权赔偿案件的若干规定》。2012 年 5 月 22 日,最高人民法院、最高人民检察院公布了《关于办理内幕交易、泄露内幕信息刑事案件具体应用法律若干问题的解释》。可以看出,2002 年以来,投资者不再起诉无门。自 2002 年"1/15 通知"发布以来,已有 90 多家因虚假陈述被处罚或被制裁的上市公司被投资者告上法庭。然而,目前的司法机制在保护投资者权益上还存在着明显的问题。

首先,中国股市是全国性的(市场参与主体来自全国乃至全世界),股市立法和证监会的执法也是全国性的,但股市的司法却是地方化的。根据 2002 年"1/15 通知"和 2003 年"1/9 规定",虚假陈述民事赔偿案件的一审管辖法院有近 50 家,即被告所在地的省、直辖市、自治区人民政府所在的市、计划单列市和经济特区的中级人民法院。显而易见,这样的管辖法院无论是形式上还是实质上都难以体现独立性。难以想象,在目前法院的人、财、物都受制于同级地方政府的体制下,如果同级地方政府国资委控制的上市公司成为被告,当地的管辖法院能够完全保持独立、客观、公正。实际上,有研究证据显示,投资者也不相信这种情况下民事诉讼能够有效(陈信元等,2009)。这可能也是受害于虚假陈述的投资者参与起诉的积极性不高的重要原因。

其次,股市的牵涉面广、纠纷复杂、专业性极强,而分布于东、中、西各地区的近 50 家一审管辖法院的法官很难保持高水平的统一司法,司法专业性也很难发展起来。实际上,银广夏案爆发后,最高人民法院 2001 年发布通知"暂不予受理"证券民事赔偿案件的理由就是"受目前立法及司法条件的局限,尚不具备受理及审理这类案件的条件"。而在绿大地欺诈发行案中,昆明市官渡区人民法院 2011 年 12 月一审判决绿大地实际控制人何学葵有期徒刑 3 年,缓期 4 年。2012 年 1 月,昆明市人民检察院的《刑事抗诉书》认为,绿大地欺诈发行案一审判决有误,原审法院对欺诈发行股票罪部分量刑偏轻,且原审审级违法。2013 年 2 月,昆明市中级人民法院重新一审判决何学葵有期徒刑 10 年。2013 年 4 月,云南省高级人民法院终审裁定驳回何学葵对于一审刑事判决的上诉,维持原判。从这里可以看出前后判决结果的巨大差异,这种巨大差异如果不是源自当地司法独立性上的问题,那么应当和当地司法的专业性不够有关。因此,从提高司法专业性的角度考虑,一方面需要选择有限的少数几家目前司法水平较高的法院来管辖证券诉讼;另一方面,少数几家管辖法院通过经常性审理证券诉讼,也更容易提高专业水平,并且上级法院以及整个市场也更容易监督这些法院的行为。

再次,2002年"1/15通知"和2003年"1/9规定"都给证券民事诉讼设置了前置条件。投资者起诉的对象只能是中国证券会或其派出机构、财政部、其他行政机关以及有权作出行政处罚的机构作出虚假陈述行政处罚的上市公司或者因虚假陈述被人民法院认定有罪并做出刑事判决的上市公司。这种前置条件固然有很多的理由,但缺陷同样明显。在前置条件下,司法发挥作用的前提主要是行政执法的结果,但肖钢(2013)的文章表明,行政执法并非非常有效。一方面,证监会可能存在比较多的"误拒",很多的虚假陈述公司最终可能未被处罚,那么投资者便起诉无门;另一方面,如果证监会发生"误受",错误地做出了处罚,那么在前置条件下投资者的起诉使得公司可能很难在法院维护自身的正当权益。现实中,第一种情况可能居多。原本行政执法和司法机制是互相补充的两种机制,但前置条件的设立使得行政执法成为司法机制发挥作用的前提。未来随着司法独立性和专业性的提高,前置条件有必要放松乃至废除。

总体上,为了更好地发挥司法机制在股市上的作用,可能的改革方向有两个。一是在十八届三中全会审议通过的《中共中央关于全面深化改革若干重大问题的决定》的司法改革框架下,提高证券民事(刑事)诉讼管辖法院(检察院)的独立性和专业性。这一框架是:改革司法管理体制,推动省以下地方法院、检察院人财物统一管理,探索建立与行政区划适当分离的司法管辖制度,保证国家法律统一正确实施。二是尝试直接在少数地区如北京、上海、深圳设立几家专门的证券法院,管辖证券诉讼。第二个方向应当是更加直接和有效的股市司法改革方向,在提高股市司法独立性和专业性上具有显著优势,而第一个方向依赖于全国司法改革的进展,并且分布在各地区的大量管辖法院的司法专业性问题也难在短期内解决。

五、总结

好的股市大大促进创新、创业和经济发展,对于中国经济转型升级,好的股市尤其重要。要有好的股市,必须要有充分保护投资者权益的法律系统(立法、执法、司法)。中国股市在司法缺失的情况下,借助强有力的行政治理,取得惊人发展,但这种模式在股市发展到一定规模和阶段后不可持续,司法上位是建立好的股市的必然要求。近年来,中国股市司法制度建设取得显著进展,但仍有不少问题(如司法地方化等)需要改进,司法的独立性和有效性需要大力加强。其中,设立独立于行政区划的专门的证券法院可能是一个重要的改革方向。

参考文献

陈信元,李莫愁,芮萌,等.司法独立性与投资者保护法律实施——最高人民法院 1/15 通知的市场反应[J].经济学(季刊),2009(4):1-28.

傅高义.邓小平时代[M].北京:生活·读书·新知三联书店,2013.

沈艺峰,许年行,杨熠.我国中小投资者法律保护历史实践的实证检验[J].经济研究,2004(09):90-100.

肖钢.监管执法:资本市场健康发展的基石[J].求是,2013(15):5-9.

Beck T,Levine R,Loayza N. Finance and the sources of growth[J]. Journal of financial economics,2000,58(1-2):261-300.

Brown J R,Martinsson G,Petersen B C. Law,stock markets,and innovation[J]. The journal of finance,2013,68(4):1517-1549.

Hsu P H,Tian X,Xu Y. Financial development and innovation:cross-country evidence[J]. Journal of financial economics,2014,112(1):116-135.

La Porta R,Lopez-de-Silanes F,Shleifer A,et al. Legal determinants of external finance[J]. The journal of finance,1997,52(3):1131-1150.

Levine R. Financial development and economic growth:views and agenda[J]. Journal of Economic Literature,1997,35:688-726.

Levine R,Zervos S. Stock markets,banks,and economic growth[J]. American economic review,1998:537-558.

Pistor K,Xu C. Governing stock markets in transition economies:lessons from China[J]. American law and economics review,2005,7(1):184-210.

Porta R L,Lopez-de-Silanes F,Shleifer A,et al. Law and finance[J]. Journal of political economy,1998,106(6):1113-1155.

Schumpeter A. A theory of economic development[M]. Cambridge:Harvard University Press,1911.

让"两只手"形成合力[*]

内容提要：一个好的股市绝对不可能是完全自由的市场，需要政府之手加以监管；一个好的股市也绝对不可能依靠政府频繁的干预来运转。

在中国股市二十多年的历史中，2015 年 6 月爆发的股灾以及政府采取的救市行动可以说绝无仅有。股灾和救市行动还没有结束，但思考和厘清中国股市中政府与市场的关系不容等待。

一个好的股市绝对不可能是完全自由的市场，需要政府之手加以监管。股市是信息和资金高速流动的市场，其中可以被操纵的环节和漏洞太多。仅仅依靠市场自身的力量，无法形成一个好的市场。从各国股市发展历史和实践来看，将股市纳入法治和监管轨道已经没有争议。即使股市有了很好的法制规则，这些规则也要依靠监管部门去执行和落实。而规则法条不可能是完备无瑕的，股市发生各种"事故"也就不足为奇，因此监管部门的相机监管乃至干预市场也就非常重要。中国股市有大量的散户群体参与市场，因而更容易发生群体性的非理性行为，也更容易被各种市场操纵力量所利用。同时，中国的法院系统在股市治理中所能够发挥的作用还非常有限。中国股市的这些基本特点使得中国股市监管部门可能比成熟市场监管部门面临更大的挑战，因而更加需要积极地采取行动。从这次救灾来说，当股灾"事故"已经发生，意识到股灾对国家金融和经济全局的重大负面影响，采取果断的救市行动便是必要的。

一个好的股市也绝对不可能依靠政府频繁的干预来运转。中国股市自设立以来，监管部门乃至其他政府部门及官方媒体对股市的频繁干预一直没有停止过。从公司发行上市、增发重组、暂停上市到退市的整个过程，都长久地存在高度

---

* 本文选自：夏立军：让"两只手"形成合力——"股市危机的最大警示"圆桌讨论，《董事会》，2015 年 9 月。收录于《智汇安泰——交大安泰智库经管评论集》，文汇出版社，2016 年。

管制,用管制代替监管。虽然市场化一直是努力的方向,但是直到现在,大量事前的管制依旧代替了事后的监管。同时,股市无论是涨是跌,经常性地被官方媒体"引导"方向,似乎政府部门最清楚股市应该涨到哪里,又应该跌到哪里,甚至怎样涨跌是合理的。这种频繁的"引导"不仅可能扰乱市场本身的运行规律,还可能进一步使得大量散户被市场操纵力量利用。亚当·斯密早就警告,"在政府中掌权的人,容易自以为非常聪明……他似乎认为他能够像用手摆布一副棋盘中的各个棋子那样非常容易地摆布偌大一个社会中的各个成员;他以为:棋盘上的棋子除了手摆布时的作用之外,不存在别的行动原则;但是,在人类社会这个大棋盘上每个棋子都有它自己的行动原则,它完全不同于政府机关可能选用来指导它的那种行动原则"。从这次股灾而言,政府在紧急情况下采取的种种救市措施虽然是情理之中,然而某些措施与相关法律和契约精神相违背,救市措施对市场机制和理性预期的破坏等后遗症也将逐渐显露出来。

未来向何处去?中国股市现如今无论从参与人数、上市公司数量、成交额、市场总市值而言,放在全世界也已经是一个巨大规模的市场。这样一个巨大的市场,稍有不慎,便有可能对中国的金融系统乃至整个经济产生巨大的负面影响。这就要求监管部门需要有如履薄冰的精神,严密堵住股市各个环节的监管漏洞,谨防股市发生重大"事故"。然而,中国股市不仅规模巨大,散户众多,金融创新不断推进,同时法律责任薄弱,给各种无意的"事故"以及有意的市场操纵留下空间。要让这样的股市不出重大"事故",可以说中国股市监管部门面临巨大的挑战,这次股灾也是一次考验。

我们相信,在国家强力干预下,股灾终将过去。但是,股灾留下的教训是深刻的。展望未来,一方面需要继续培育和发挥市场本身的机能,引导投资者理性参与市场,让市场"看不见的手"充分发挥资源配置作用;同时,要对各种股市漏洞环节尤其是各种可能被操纵的环节查漏补缺,用法律责任和严厉监管堵住"事故"发生,让政府"看得见的手"真正到位而不越位。

IPO 制度改革亟待解放思想[*]

大国需要强大的资本市场,大国崛起需要强大的资本市场支撑。一个 IPO 受到严格限制,时不时因股市波动而暂停 IPO 的资本市场,难说强大。

我国 1993 年建立了全国统一的股票发行审核制度。大体而言,IPO 制度经历了两大阶段:1993 年至 2000 年实施的审批制,2001 年至今的核准制阶段。审批制具有明显的计划经济特征,在审批制下,先后实施了"额度管理"和"指标管理"的发行审核办法,由证监会根据下发各地区各部门的额度或指标对拟 IPO 企业进行实质性审核。自 2001 年开始,IPO 制度改为核准制,向市场化的方向迈进了一大步。在核准制下,IPO 发行审核更加依赖中介机构,由中介机构和证监会共同负责实质性审核。

IPO 制度作为资本市场的"入门关"制度,其好坏直接决定了资本市场资源配置功能的发挥。2018 年 2 月,全国人大常委会决定,2015 年授权国务院在实施股票发行注册制改革中调整适用《中华人民共和国证券法》有关规定的决定施行期限届满后,期限延长两年至 2020 年 2 月 29 日。这表明,中国资本市场 IPO 制度实行注册制的改革依然在路上。我国的 IPO 制度,有"大得"的同时有"大失"。

一、因地制宜之"得"

国际上,IPO 制度主要有注册制和核准制两种。中国资本市场在设立之初,并没有实行国际上通行的核准制或注册制。这不奇怪。我国资本市场诞生于中国从计划经济向市场经济转型的过程中。无论是计划经济的惯性,还是资本市场

---

* 本文选自:夏立军:IPO 制度改革亟待解放思想,《董事会》,2018 年 3 月。完整版本题为"中国资本市场 IPO 制度的演进与得失",收录于《智汇安泰——交大安泰智库经管评论集(第二辑)》,格致出版社、上海人民出版社,2018 年。本文在中央深改委于 2019 年 1 月做出设立科创板并设点注册制的决定之前一年,前瞻性地梳理了中国资本市场 IPO 制度的演进与得失,并呼吁解放思想、尽快实施注册制。

各方面的条件而言,在资本市场设立之初可能都不具备实行注册制或核准制的条件。例如,在资本市场设立之初,会计师事务所、券商、律师等中介机构没有发展起来,无法依赖中介机构进行 IPO 审核,而计划经济遗留下来的行政治理优势可以暂时起到替代市场筛选 IPO 企业的功能,从而让资本市场更快地起步。同时,从早期国家宏观经济管理的需要而言,需要对资本市场的融资规模进行调节和控制,因而审批制成为现实的选择,这应该说是"因地制宜"的选择。资本市场经历十年发展、改革开放二十年后,从审批制调整为核准制,朝着更加市场化的 IPO 制度迈进,是一种新的因地制宜。

　　因地制宜地实施审批制、核准制,是非常理性、实事求是的选择,总体上适应了我国资本市场和经济发展的需要。这一因地制宜的过程中,我国资本市场从无到有、从小到大,经过近三十年的发展,已经在规模上进入世界前列,取得巨大的成功。因地制宜的 IPO 制度,不仅引入了 3000 多家相对优秀的企业进入资本市场,也在筛选拟上市企业上起到了甄别筛选、优胜劣汰的功能,在很大程度上保护了投资者的利益。没有审批制和核准制下的严格筛选,上市公司可能难以像今天一样代表着中国经济中相对优秀和活跃的企业群体。

二、巨大代价之"失"

　　看到审批制、核准制历史意义的同时,应当意识到 IPO 制度改革止步不前的巨大代价。审批制和核准制的代价主要有三方面:一、"误拒"的代价;二、"误受"的代价;三、扭曲市场机能的代价。

　　从"误拒"而言,相比注册制,因为对 IPO 企业设立了严格的财务指标要求,审批制和核准制下的 IPO 速度大大下降,严重影响了大量企业通过资本市场发展壮大的可能性,限制了中国的投资者分享中国企业快速发展的红利。一些优秀的互联网企业比如百度、阿里巴巴、腾讯当初都不符合审批制和核准制下的 IPO 要求,只好赴海外上市。IPO 速度受到严重制约的情形下,巨大社会资本可以自由进出资本市场,由此造成股票估值长期虚高,同时造成了独特的"壳资源"价值,资源配置严重扭曲。因而,"误拒"的代价不仅体现为大大减少了中国企业和经济发展的空间,也体现为企业间资源配置效率的低下。

　　从"误受"而言,代价主要来自实质性审核的独立性和专业性难以保证。审批制和核准制下,谁能获得 IPO 资格,很大程度上取决于证监会的实质性审核。然而,在 IPO 速度受到限制、股票普遍估值过高的环境中,IPO 的"租金"巨大,获得

IPO 资格意味着廉价的融资机会和巨大的财富增值,进而造成 IPO 申请企业过度拥挤、一些企业的 IPO 动机不良。这样,证监会审核人员的独立性和专业性就面临巨大的挑战。证监会落马官员多来自发行审核相关部门,就是明证。此外,由于 IPO 带来巨大"租金",一些企业不惜铤而走险造假上市,而证监会的实质性审核难以万无一失,造假上市时有发生。

从"扭曲市场机能"而言,由于 IPO 制度的高度管制特征,加上退市制度的不畅通,造成股票供求关系严重扭曲。一些财务或信息披露严重造假、违规、基本面严重恶化的公司拥有很高的估值。有人统计,如果构建一个低市值 ST 公司的长期投资组合,竟然可以获取远超市场指数的超额收益。在这种环境中,无论企业的上市决策还是投资者的投资决策,普遍缺乏理性,概念包装和投机炒作盛行,进而使得市场的资源配置功能扭曲,几千万计的投资者耗费大量时间精力于可能并不给市场带来资源配置效率提升、价值创造的频繁交易活动之中。

三、需要的是解放思想

在 2018 年的全国两会上,政协委员张连起指出,当前证券发行上市存在诸多问题,比如:股票首次发行上市制度服务实体经济、服务新动能企业的能力不足;一批拥有核心技术的互联网公司赴海外上市;股票发行上市制度还不适应新技术、新产业、新业态、新模式的需要;发行上市"堰塞湖"现象依然存在。这些都是我国资本市场长期存在的顽疾,需要高度市场化的 IPO 注册制制度才能解决。如果不进一步解放思想、与时俱进地推行注册制,过去的因地制宜可能就意味着今天的"不思进取"。

在核准制实施了近二十年、资本市场发展了近三十年的今天,市场机能仍然无法在短期内健全,监管和司法也是如此。但如果屡屡以此为由,认为推进 IPO 制度的进一步市场化即实施注册制还未到时候、条件尚未成熟,可能就有点因噎废食了。大国需要强大的资本市场,大国崛起需要强大的资本市场支撑。一个 IPO 受到严格限制,时不时因股市波动而暂停 IPO 的资本市场,难说强大。更重要的是,市场机能的不健全本身在很大程度上内生于高度管制的 IPO 制度,它本身需要在进一步市场化的 IPO 制度下才能逐步健全,监管和司法也需要在进一步市场化的 IPO 制度倒逼下才能回归本位、不断完善。因而,从核准制到注册制的改革,需要的是解放思想。

2013 年,中共十八届三中全会提出推行股票发行注册制改革;2016 年以来,

IPO速度大幅加快,已经带有变相实施注册制的特征,但真正的注册制还需要正式的法律认定和配套的制度安排。在中国经济面临转型升级和增速放缓、我国资本市场已经发展近三十年、资本市场诸多顽疾长期无解的今天,资本市场发展需要进一步解放思想,尽快实施IPO注册制制度,进而倒逼证券监管转型、司法机制上位,充分释放中国企业利用资本市场发展壮大的潜能,激活市场自身的筛选、监督、自我约束和资源优化配置机能。

资本市场改革开放如何行稳致远?[*]

中国资本市场从无到有、从小到大,已有近三十年历史。如何理解近三十年来的成就和不足以及未来的方向,事关重大。在中国改革开放四十周年、中国资本市场发展将近三十年之际,本文在一个宏观的视野上,给出中国资本市场发展的逻辑、经验教训以及未来方向。

一、中国资本市场是如何发展起来的?

首先,中国资本市场是改革开放对资本市场的需求与供给共同作用的结果。从企业层面而言,1978 年开始的改革开放先是激活国有企业,经过近十年的国企改革,继续推进国企改革不仅需要银行系统的支撑,更需要资本市场提供融资和改革功能。同时,随着国企改革进展,一大批国有企业为资本市场的设立和发展提供了企业来源,而改革开放以来积累的社会资本则为资本市场提供了资本来源。此外,在邓小平等政治家的推动下,到 20 世纪 90 年代初期,设立资本市场的意识形态障碍得以破除,这为资本市场的设立创造了试错的条件。因此,与西方国家自发产生的资本市场不同,中国资本市场从一开始就服从和服务于国有企业改革和脱困的需要,并且由中央政府有意识地推动设立。

其次,中国资本市场设立时的初始条件和改革开放的战略目标决定了中国资本市场的基本制度框架和发展路径。在企业来源上,先是国有企业为主,进而发展到国有、民营齐头并进,资本市场同时服务于国企和民企发展;在资本来源上,

* 本文选自:夏立军:资本市场改革开放如何行稳致远? FT 中文网,2019 年 1 月 31 日。在中国改革开放四十周年、中国资本市场发展将近三十年之际,以及新任证监会主席易会满上任伊始,本文在一个宏观的视野上,给出中国资本市场发展的逻辑、经验教训以及未来方向,文中揭示的中国资本市场体制性问题以及提出的多项基础性制度改革方向已经陆续被中国证监会 2019 年以来提出的资本市场系统性改革方向所印证。本文亦收录于黄少卿、周伟民主编的《中国发展展望——重构中国经济的微观基础》(上海人民出版社,2019 年)一书中。

先是以境内中小投资者的资本为主,进而发展到引入境内外机构投资者资本,形成了个人投资者和机构投资者并存局面;在治理架构上,先是地方试验,再到成立中国证券监督管理委员会,建立了集中统一的垂直监管架构。

最后,中国改革开放带来的经济发展为资本市场提供了源源不断的企业和资金来源,而资本市场的发展进一步促进了中国企业和经济的发展。没有改革开放和经济发展带来的企业成长和社会资本增长,资本市场发展就是无源之水;反过来,资本市场的改革和发展,也促进了对有限的社会资源的优化配置,促进了企业成长和地方经济发展。二十多来,中国资本市场和中国上市公司、地方经济的快速发展,体现了两者的相辅相成。

二、中国资本市场发展的基本经验和教训

回顾中国资本市场发展历程,起码有两点重要的经验值得总结。一是中央权威和体制内协调力量的充分发挥。中国资本市场是一个从后发国家和前计划经济体中发展出来的新兴市场,计划经济遗留下来的行政协调和治理力量构成了中国资本市场发展的比较优势。无论是资本市场的设立,还是股票发行制度改革、股权分置改革、民事诉讼制度引入、资本市场对外开放以及资本市场异常波动的应对等重大事件,都可以从中看到这种强大的行政协调力量。资本市场未来的改革开放,依然需要充分发挥这种强大的中央权威和体制内的协调力量。

二是因地制宜的渐进式市场化、法治化、国际化改革取向。中国资本市场的改革开放固然有西方成熟市场上百年的历史经验和教训可以学习借鉴,然而它也面临自己独特的初始条件和政治经济约束,实践证明渐进式改革发展路径是一个非常有效的策略。例如,在资本市场设立初期,为了回避意识形态上对国有资产流失的担忧,设置了公开发行前股份不能上市流通的制度,后来到2005年条件成熟时再实施股权分置改革。再如,IPO制度从初始的审批制,演变到核准制,再到目前局部推行注册制改革,也体现了因地制宜的渐进式改革发展智慧。

二十多年的资本市场发展不仅有成功的经验,也留下了深刻的教训。这种教训主要是不完善的制度框架造成了资本市场的价格和激励扭曲,以致资本市场常常被诟病为"赌场""圈钱市""政策市"。长期存在的、高度管制的股票发行制度不仅制约了中国企业利用资本市场发展壮大的机会,也扭曲了股票供求关系和股票价格。大量的管制政策头痛医头、脚痛医脚,过多地与特定的会计指标挂钩,导致"数字游戏"盛行。资本市场立法、执法和司法上的缺陷,使得中小投资者保护难

以落实，扭曲了上市公司实际控制人和治理层的激励，也扭曲了资本市场其他参与方的激励。人造牛市的冲动和对高杠杆资金的失察则造成了资本市场的异常波动，给市场带来巨大代价。

三、中国资本市场的未来方向

过去二十多年的经验教训表明，中国资本市场未来发展强大的关键是解放思想，更大力度地实施改革开放，正确地处理好政府与市场的关系，把资本市场的价格和激励搞对。

首先，给定资本市场在中国经济转型和发展中的重要性，中国资本市场的改革开放有必要上升为国家战略。一个强大的资本市场才能造就一批批强大的中国企业。只有在国家战略层面上定位资本市场的改革开放，中国资本市场才能解放思想、更大力度地实施改革开放，也才能真正强大起来，为中国经济的持续发展发挥其应有作用。也只有上升到国家战略层面，才可能形成完善的资本市场制度基础设施，产生强大、超然、独立和专业的监管机构，实现从管制到监管的转型，为资本市场发展强大保驾护航。

其次，有必要系统性地反思中国资本市场在立法、执法和司法上的重大缺陷，实施大力度的系统性改革。长期以来，在立法上，对于财务欺诈、虚假信息披露等违法违规行为的法律责任惩戒力度严重不足；在执法上，大量违法违规案件最终不了了之；在司法上，投资者民事诉讼机制难以有效地发挥作用。这些立法、执法和司法上的重大缺陷，严重扭曲了上市公司实际控制人和治理层以及资本市场其他参与方的激励，制约了资本市场在资源优化配置和激励价值创造上的功能。近期，监管机构公布了 2018 年的行政处罚"成绩单"，处罚案件数量、罚没金额等均同比大幅度增长。令人担忧的是，被监管机构视为从严监管成效的这种大幅度的增长，到底是成绩，还是问题？为何违法违规屡禁不绝，甚至愈演愈烈？

再次，有必要建立更科学的资本市场局部实验和总结推广制度。中国资本市场在IPO、并购重组、退市、做空、T＋0、涨跌停、会计准则国际趋同与因地制宜的矛盾等方面，还存在大量的改革空间。资本市场未来的改革开放，定会面临大量疑难杂症。解决这些难题，既不能裹步不前，也不能冒失推进，这就需要更加科学地研究和探讨其中的利弊得失，采用更加科学的局部实验再总结推广的策略。监管机构有必要和学界合作，在一些利弊得失不太明确的改革开放问题上，引入更科学的局部实验设计，科学地识别各种改革方案的利弊，为资本市场改革开放提供科学的决策依据。

四、一些政策建议

当前,资本市场依然面临着 2015 年人造牛市和异常波动带来的巨大后遗症。大量的疯狂并购发生在当时泡沫形成的过程中,泡沫破裂后留下了股权质押、商誉减值等"地雷"。妥善处置这些问题的同时,需要加快资本市场制度基础设施建设。

其一,需要借助上海证券交易所设立科创板并试点注册制的契机,探索建立注册制下的股票发行和交易制度以及相应的法律责任制度。注册制是中国资本市场市场化改革的一个重大突破,也是中国资本市场基础性制度上的一次飞跃。在试点成熟后,有必要从局部推广到整个市场,彻底解决长期存在的资本市场价格和激励扭曲问题。

其二,需要系统地修订《证券法》,建立确保资本市场行政、民事和刑事责任合理界定并有效落实的治理体系,扭转市场参与各方尤其上市公司大股东和实际控制人法律责任松懈、违法违规行为屡禁不止的局面。除了继续发挥行政治理和体制内协调的优势,更需要发挥公、检、法尤其是投资者在资本市场治理中的作用。例如,需要完善投资者民事诉讼制度以及资本市场做空机制,激励投资者和相关机构识别、揭示和制约财务欺诈、虚假信息披露等违法违规行为的积极性。如何建立与资本市场发展需求相适应的公、检、法参与资本市场治理的制度安排,亦值得积极探索。

其三,资本市场的成熟离不开投资者自身的成熟,在试点注册制从而放松企业上市准入管制的同时,需要扩大资本市场对外开放,引入更多的全球机构投资者、更多的长期资金参与中国资本市场,同时加强中小投资者教育,弘扬理性投资和价值投资理念。

在中国改革开放刚刚迈过四十周年,中国资本市场发展也将近三十周年之际,期待着中国资本市场未来的改革开放能够行稳致远。